# Organizations in America

Arne L. Kalleberg
David Knoke
Peter V. Marsden
Joe L. Spaeth

# Organizations in America

## Analyzing Their Structures and Human Resource Practices

Based on the National Organizations Study

**SAGE Publications**
*International Educational and Professional Publisher*
Thousand Oaks   London   New Delhi

*For information address*:

SAGE Publications, Inc.
2455 Teller Road
Thousand Oaks, California 91320
E-mail: order@sagepub.com

SAGE Publications Ltd.
6 Bonhill Street
London EC2A 4PU
United Kingdom

SAGE Publications India Pvt. Ltd.
M-32 Market
Greater Kailash I
New Delhi 110 048 India

Printed in the United States of America

**Library of Congress Cataloging-in-Publication Data**

Main entry under title:

Organizations in America: Analyzing their structures and human
    resource practices / authors, Arne L. Kalleberg . . . [et al.].
        p.    cm.
    Includes bibliographical references (p. ) and index.
    ISBN 0-8039-5815-3 (cloth: acid-free paper).—ISBN
0-8039-5816-1 (pbk.: acid-free paper)
        1. Industrial organization—United States.    2. Personnel
    management—United States.    I. Kalleberg, Arne L.
    HD70.U5O73    1996
    338.7′0973—dc20                                                            96-4510

This book is printed on acid-free paper.

96  97  98  99  00  9  8  7  6  5  4  3  2  1

Sage Production Editor: Diana E. Axelsen
Sage Typesetter: Andrea D. Swanson

# Contents

# List of Tables

# List of Figures

# Preface

This book presents results from the National Organizations Study (NOS), a research project that has collected data on a representative sample of U.S. work establishments. The NOS surveyed a large number of diverse organizations about their structure, context, and personnel practices. The survey was conducted in 1991 as a multipurpose, multi-investigator project to produce a database suited to answering questions about social behavior in work organizations.

The idea for a NOS emerged from the directors of the National Science Foundation's (NSF) Sociology program (especially Joanne Miller and Mark Abrahamson), who encouraged initial steps toward developing more systematic databases to support knowledge about organizations. In 1986, the sociology program issued a call for proposals to conduct pilot projects on local organization populations to assess the feasibility of various sampling and measurement methods. Arne Kalleberg and Peter Marsden (together with Howard Aldrich) were funded to compare the representativeness, practicality, and costs of using five organizational sampling frames in one county of North Carolina (see Kalleberg et al. 1990). David Knoke (together with Paul Reynolds) collected data on organizational structures from multiple informants in a stratified sample of all formal organizations in the Minneapolis-St. Paul, Minnesota, area. The two other demonstration projects funded in 1987 were a multiplicity sample of Columbus, Ohio, establishments undertaken by William Form and his colleagues at the Ohio State University (see, e.g., Parcel et al. 1991), and a multiplicity survey of organizations in Los Angeles, Orange, and Ventura counties in California conducted by Lynne Zucker (1988).

In May 1988, the principal investigators of the pilot projects met in an ad hoc discussion group assembled by NSF to report their findings and discuss future steps toward developing organizational databases. Strong sentiment was expressed for the multiplicity or hypernetwork design used in the Ohio State project and previously by Spaeth (1985), McPherson (1982), Zucker (1988) and Bridges and Villemez (1994). Participants felt that this would be an economical method for generating a sample of work organizations representative of the U.S. labor force.

The 1991 General Social Survey (GSS) provided the opportunity to obtain such a nationally representative sample of U.S. work organizations. In 1991, the GSS topical module on "work organizations" collected, among other things, the names, addresses, and phone numbers of the places at which GSS respondents work. This information provided the basis for drawing a national multiplicity sample of work organizations (see Chapter 2). The combined NOS-GSS data became publicly available (from the Inter-University Consortium for Political and Social Research at the University of Michigan) in August, 1993 (see the Appendix to this book).

Many persons have helped collect, prepare, and analyze the data we discuss in this book. Diane P. O'Rourke of the University of Illinois Survey Research Laboratory directed the National Organizations Study field work and coauthored Chapter 2. Alisa Potter (University of Minnesota) prepared the final data file. Mark E. Van Buren (University of North Carolina) collected the auxiliary data on counties, helped organize the data files, and coauthored Chapters 10 and 11. Michael Wallace (Indiana University) graciously provided us with copies of his industry data.

Other persons gave us very helpful comments on earlier versions of individual chapters: Karen E. Campbell and Peter M. E. Hedström on Chapter 7; James Conley, Mamoru Ishikawa, Robert Althauser, and William Bridges on Chapter 8; David Levine and Donald Tomaskovic-Devey on Chapter 11; Eileen Appelbaum on Chapter 13; Barbara Reskin on Chapter 14; and April Brayfield, Catherine Hakim, Debra Minkoff, Barbara Reskin, Rachel Rosenfeld, and anonymous reviewers on the previously published version of Chapter 15. Elizabeth Gorman made useful suggestions on the late drafts of a number of the chapters. Finally, Mitch Allen read and commented on a previous version of the entire manuscript; his encouragement and suggestions were invaluable in our efforts to produce a coherent and, we hope, interesting manuscript.

Additional persons provided invaluable assistance in the preparation of various portions of the manuscript. Earlynn Gunter of the Department of Sociology at the University of North Carolina at Chapel Hill and Suzanne Washington of the Department of Sociology at Harvard University helped to organize and prepare the manuscript. Carolyn Marsden, Lincoln Quillian, and Joseph F. Swingle provided assistance with the graphics in Chapters 4 and 5. Cynthia Cook (a coauthor on Chapters 3, 4, and 15) assisted with the research for Chapters 5 and 7. Joseph F. Swingle provided research assistance, and Nancy Williamson assisted in data management, in the preparation of Chapter 7.

Financial support for the NOS was provided primarily by awards from the NSF sociology program: SES 89-11371 to Arne L. Kalleberg at the University of North Carolina at Chapel Hill, SES-89-11608 to David Knoke at the University of Minnesota, SES 89-11696 to Peter V. Marsden at Harvard University, and SES-89-08871 to Joe L. Spaeth and the Survey Research Laboratory at the University of Illinois. Additional funding to support the research was obtained from the Employment and Training Administration of the U.S. Department of Labor; these funds were specifically targeted toward data on organizations' job training programs. Preparation of Chapters 8, 9, and 12 was also supported by a grant-in-aid to Knoke from the University of Minnesota and a fellowship from the Center for Advanced Study in the Behavioral Sciences (supported by NSF grant SES 90-22192).

Most of the chapters in this volume are substantially revised versions of articles previously presented at conferences or published in journals. Previous versions of Chapters 1 through 4, 6, 7, 9, 11, and 12 were included in a Special Issue of *American Behavioral Scientist,* "Measuring Organizations: New Approaches," Volume 37, Number 4 (June, 1994). An earlier version of Chapter 2 was presented at the annual conference of the American Association for Public Opinion Research, St. Petersburg Beach, FL, May, 1992. Earlier versions of Chapters 7, 8, and 10 were presented at a conference sponsored by the Stanford Center for Organizations Research held in January, 1993. Part of Chapter 7 appeared in *Acta Sociologica* 37 (1994):287-301. A version of Chapter 8 was published previously in the *American Sociological Review* 59 (August 1994):537-36. Portions of Chapter 10 appeared in the *American Sociological Review* 61 (February, (1996):

47-66. An earlier version of Chapter 11 was presented at a meeting of the International Sociological Association's Research Committee #28, Duke University, August 9-11, 1993. Chapter 15 is adapted from an article published in *Work and Occupations* 20 (August, 1993):368-90.

# PART

# I

# The National
# Organizations Study

# 1

# Organizational Properties and Practices

ARNE L. KALLEBERG
DAVID KNOKE
PETER V. MARSDEN
JOE L. SPAETH

The radical transformation of the American economy continues at an accelerating pace into the 21st century. Every issue of the *Wall Street Journal, Fortune, Business Week,* and other chroniclers of economic and business activity brings new revelations about the worldwide turmoil engulfing markets, technologies, corporations, employees, communities, and governments. Driven by competition in the computer industry, IBM buys Lotus. Chase and Chemical banks merge, the Walt Disney Company takes over Cap Cities/ABC, and Westinghouse purchases CBS. Trends in spin-offs accompany the urge to merge: 1994 sees 27 spin-offs with a record value of over \$22 billion, numbers that are expected to be exceeded in 1995; while ITT—long regarded as the quintessential conglomerate organization—announces that it will split into three separate publicly traded companies (*Business Week* 1995, August 14). Microsoft reaches an agreement with the Justice Department that limits its domination over operating systems but leaves most of its other software untouched. The U.S. Treasury Department issues new regulations granting multinational companies more flexibility in pricing transactions between home and abroad—and probably heaves a sigh of relief that the Microsoft agreement did not go any farther. Wheeling Pittsburgh signs a joint venture with Ispat Mexicana to produce hot-rolled steel products.

Meanwhile, out on the street, customers, employees, patients, and clients observe other organizational changes in the course of doing their daily business. The Main Streets populated by independent retail establishments have been eclipsed to a significant degree by the Malls, with their large-scale "anchor" or "magnet" stores surrounded by much more specialized boutique stores (many of which are units of regional or national chains). Large "megastores"—warehouselike operations offering bulk purchases at low prices—have emerged to compete effectively with supermarkets. Franchised hotels and restaurants offer, indeed trade on, standardized accommodations and menus. Health care is less often delivered in an independent doctor's office than in a setting such as a multiphysician group practice or a clinic in a large hospital, or even a "Doc-in-a-box" facility offering immediate attention to walk-in patients. Irrespective of the site at which care is delivered, a third party—be it a health maintenance organization, a traditional insurer, or a government program—is generally involved in paying for it.

These examples are suggestive of some of the major changes that are occurring in product, labor, and capital markets, in ownership patterns, and in other aspects of the environments of organizations. Economically creative destruction, for which capitalism has always been praised and damned, took particularly strong root in the mid-1970s and reached a crescendo by the early 1990s. International competition intensified, making it imperative for companies to produce high-quality products and services. Rapid technological changes increased skill requirements of jobs. Accompanying these changes were demographic shifts in the composition of the labor force with the entry of greater numbers of women, immigrants, and minorities.

Employers attempted to respond to these changes by reengineering their work structures and human resource management practices to become "lean-and-mean" competitors that had greater flexibility in their production processes and in their relations with their employees (Piore and Sabel 1984; Lawler 1992; Useem 1993a; Harrison 1994). Blue-chip companies such as IBM, General Motors, and Kodak downsized or abandoned key elements of their elaborate human resource systems such as long-term commitments to employees through internal labor market arrangements. Campaigns to decentralize organizations often froze hiring, cut salaries and benefits, terminated career trajectories, increased workloads, heightened stress, and undermined morale. White-collar employees, especially middle managers, were hit as severely as blue-collar workers: perhaps a million middle managers lost their jobs during the 1980s as companies sought to "trim the fat" by flattening managerial hierarchies. For example, Hyatt Hotels Corporation reduced costs by eliminating more than 1,000 of its 7,000 managers (*Business Week* 1995, August 14). Other corporate executives saw externalizing production as the fastest way to reduce labor costs (Parker 1994). Large numbers of workers found employment as part of the growing nonpermanent, contingent workforce (part-time, temporary, and subcontracted from outside firms) (Belous 1989; Abraham 1990; see also Chapter 13, this volume). By 1994 Manpower, Inc., had supplanted the shrinking General Motors as the largest U.S. employer. The use of contingent workers is not limited to clerical workers, but embraces such high-skill occupations as engineering, computer programming, and drafting.

The employees who survived the stress and insecurity of workforce reductions in the "cost conscious 1990s" shouldered even greater burdens, ranging from pay cuts to heightened workloads. The new employment arrangements yielded organizational configurations more favorable to shareholder interests, especially large institutional investors, while pushing greater costs and risks onto employees (Useem 1993a). These contracts were more consistent with short-term, narrow indicators of economic performance and motivated organizations to seek to reduce their labor costs by lowering wages and, especially, reducing fringe benefits. Earnings stagnated throughout the 1980s, while inequality increased (Levy 1987): In 1979, a recent male college graduate earned about 30% more than his high school counterpart; by 1993, the gap had widened to 70% (*Business Week* 1995, February 27). Accompanying the growth in earnings inequality was a widening gap in fringe benefits such as health care coverage: By 1992,

75% of college graduates had health care coverage, compared to 54% for high school drop-outs (*Business Week* 1995, February 21).

Increasing inequality in earnings, fringe benefits, and other job rewards can be traced in part to the growing polarization of the workforce inside many companies: Regular employees enjoy greater opportunities for autonomy, skill acquisition, and high earnings and fringe benefits at the same time that temporary and other contingent workers are constrained to work in low-skilled jobs that receive marginal market wages and few benefits. The greater concentration of women and minorities in the organizations most vulnerable to market fluctuations exposes these groups to greater job insecurity. These examples of corporate restructuring and organizational transformation can be understood in part as efforts of companies to remain financially viable by altering their traditional employment practices (Doeringer et al. 1991; Mirvis 1993; Blair 1993; Cappelli 1996).

The flux in employment practices and organizational structures of the early 1990s presents organizational researchers with prime opportunities for developing and testing ideas about the changing structure of work organizations and the nature of employment relations. Many of the recent social forces that drive the continual restructuring of work organizations have centered on human resources: Managers, government officials, and social science researchers have come to recognize the importance of human capital for competitive advantage (Pfeffer 1994) and the nation's future economic growth (Reich 1992). "Strategic human resource management" has replaced "personnel management" (Kochan and McKersie 1992) and is now a central feature of organizational forms alongside technology and administrative systems (Staber and Aldrich 1988). The difference in these labels reflects systemic—not piecemeal—changes in objectives, strategies, policies, and practices for managing people. Kochan and Useem (1992) bluntly underscore the necessity for advanced industrial economies to excel in the development and full utilization of their human resources to be competitive and thereby preserve the standards of living their citizens have come to expect. This sentiment echoes former Labor Secretary Ray Marshall's (1986) prescription for raising American productivity, which emphasized more effective use of physical and human resources as the most important source of productivity improvements (see also Dertouzos, Lester, and Solow 1989).

A valid portrait of how widespread these transformations are—and where they are happening—should be based on representative data covering the full range of work organizations. Unfortunately, such data are conspicuously scarce, as sociologist John Freeman (1986) pointed out nearly a decade ago. Taking stock of the empirical foundations of organizational research, he lamented the lack of careful studies based on large samples, drawn from theoretically meaningful populations, noting that the literature instead is still based on small convenience samples. His conclusions were consistent with an earlier analysis of more than 700 articles in 10 journals from 1965 to 1979, which revealed that only 13% were based on simple or stratified random samples (Drabek, Braito, Cook, Powell, and Rogers 1982; also Zucker 1988). Although attentiveness to such matters has risen in recent years, the vast majority of organizational research studies are still based on designs that cannot yield broadly generalizable findings.

The data collected by the National Organizations Study (NOS) that we describe and analyze in this book help to fill this vacuum. The NOS consists of information obtained from a nationally representative sample of organizations. As we will demonstrate in subsequent chapters, the NOS data are useful for analyzing the structures and human resource practices of U.S. organizations and for studying how these arrangements may be affected by some of the recent changes we noted above.

In this introductory chapter, we situate the NOS in broader theoretical and methodological contexts. We first provide an overview of social science thinking about organizational structures and human resource practices and describe how the NOS data can be used to address some of these structural theories of organizations. We then compare various research designs that have been used to collect organizational data, and argue that an unrestricted diverse organizational design such as the NOS offers major advantages for studying the issues we have discussed. We finally provide an overview of the content of the NOS project and preview the other chapters in this book.

## Organizational Structures and Human Resource Practices

Organizational research is a multiple-paradigm social science. A wide variety of perspectives and frameworks guide the selection of research problems, levels of analysis, and data collection strategies. We focus, in this book, on theories of organizations' relations to their employees or, as they have come to be known in recent years, their "human resources." Theories of the organization of human resources have changed over the past half century, as the result of both the changing realities of how organizations relate to their employees and the changing currents in social science thinking. In this section, we review briefly some of the major structural approaches to studying organizations and human resource management over the past half century and suggest how the NOS data can be useful in testing hypotheses derived from these structural perspectives.

**Structural Approaches to Organizations:**
**The 1945 to Early 1970s Period**

In the United States, the years from 1945 to the early 1970s were characterized by rising productivity and dominance in the world economy. Bluestone and Harrison (1982) refer to this era as the Pax Americana. Economic prosperity coupled with growing markets in mass production industries produced a period of relative stability and prosperity for U.S. work organizations and the American economy in general. Stability and growth, in turn, fueled the development of large, bureaucratic organizations in the United States.

The employment relations of this period mirrored the bureaucratic structures of these organizations. Employers sought to reduce the costs and uncertainties implicit in casual, short-term, open-market labor relations by erecting internalized systems of mutual obligations between them and their employees. To secure long-term supplies of skilled workers, the larger corporations offered job security, complex pay schedules, extensive internal labor markets, promotion opportunities, and elaborate training programs (Edwards 1979; Osterman 1984). During these less competitive times, even medium-size corporations could pay their production employees high wages and generous benefits, offer lifelong job security to middle managers and professionals, negotiate union contracts with core production and service workers, and maintain career ladders that both developed workers' skills and protected them from the vagaries of the business cycle. Institutional forces propagated this employment contract as labor unions and governmental regulators pressured companies to adopt standardized employment practices (Baron, Dobbin, and Jennings 1986; Kochan, Katz, and McKersie 1986). Business associations, professional societies, and academic consultants touted "best practice" personnel systems, often modeled after the Japanese lifetime company employment contract (Wyatt Company 1993).

A structural approach to organizational analysis became prominent in the early 1960s and continued throughout this period. Structural theories of organizations fell in a middle range between micro and macro levels of analysis: Structural analysts sought to understand the structural features that characterize organizations as a whole (e.g., division of labor and specialization or authority hierarchies) and their subunits (internal labor markets or work groups) (see Scott 1992). Studies focused on the interrelations among organizational structures (e.g., Hall 1963; Blau and Schoenherr 1971) and how organizational structures were affected by extraorganizational contingencies related to size, technology, and other aspects of the organization's environment (Pfeffer 1982). Structural analysts tended to conceptualize organizations as rational and goal-directed systems (highlighting their goal specificity and formalization—e.g., Weber's theory of bureaucracy), rather than as natural systems (with complex goals and informal structures).

Structural theories underscored the importance of issues related to the design of organizational incentive and control systems, which were assumed to be crucial to the attainment of organizations' goals. The postwar era saw the solution to many of the crises of control in the corporation in the development of "bureaucratic control" systems that redefined the way that work was directed, evaluated, and rewarded (Edwards 1979). A key element in this strategy was, as we suggested above, the firm internal labor market, by which workers' commitment to the organization was obtained via promises of career advancement and job security. Elaborate job ladders further encouraged company-provided training as a key element in firm internal labor markets, assisting employees in advancing to positions of greater skill and responsibility (Althauser and Kalleberg 1981; Knoke 1996). Unions supported the idea of firm internal labor markets so long as it incorporated the seniority principle underlying worker solidarity (see Chapters 5 and 9).

The NOS data are useful for these kinds of structural analyses. This data set contains a rich set of indicators of internal administrative, managerial, and workforce arrangements. These measures are suitable for testing hypotheses about how these structures are related to each other and to various environmental contingencies. Survey informants responded to numerous questions about the internal division of labor, governance and control, resource acquisition and allocation, labor recruitment and composition, and material incentives offered by the organization. The survey generated numerous indicators of organizational size and formal structures, and so the NOS is particularly well suited to the task of spelling out "clearly what is meant by distinctive structural arrangements" (Scott 1992, p. 8). Covariations among these measures can be used to examine hypotheses about how formal organizational structures vary with size, industry, environmental contingencies, and other factors (e.g., Blau and Schoenherr 1971; Hickson, Hinings, Lee, Schneck, and Pennings 1971; Child 1972). Chapters 4 and 5 pursue such questions using the NOS, exploring relationships between organizational structures and environments in this diverse population.

### Organizations and Stratification:
### The Mid-1970s to 1990s Period

Starting in the mid-1970s and continuing through the 1990s, the economic stability, dominance, and growth of the U.S. economy came to an end as upheavals in the world economy brought the Pax Americana to a close. Increased international competition, combined with industrial restructuring and declining productivity growth, caused the U.S. share of the world economy to plunge dramatically, from 39.9% of total gross domestic product in 1965 to 28.5% in 1988 (World Bank 1990, p. 183). From the largest creditor nation, the United States became the largest debtor. Manufacturing profit rates were halved (Grayson and O'Dell 1988, pp. 8-10), as America's technological advantages in older industries such as textiles, steel, automobiles, consumer electronics, and shipbuilding drastically eroded. Moreover, U.S. superiority in new industries such as aerospace, computers, robotics, and biotechnology came under increasing challenge from Europe, Japan, and the newly industrializing East Asian countries. A wave of *deindustrialization* involving U.S. plant closings and disinvestment in domestic manufacturing facilities crested in the 1980s (Bluestone and Harrison 1982).

A changing labor force complicated attempts by U.S. employers to redevelop a competitive economy. The long-term trend away from agriculture and heavy industry toward service industries, together with the addition of increasingly high-technology components to many new jobs, called for greater cognitive skill levels—reading, verbal communication, basic mathematics, and computer literacy—and higher performance standards than were demanded of workers in earlier eras. Flexible technologies and continuous production innovations compelled firms to develop workforces capable of keeping pace.

Accompanying these industry and job shifts were continuing changes in labor force entrants, particularly involving youths, women, immigrants, and minorities. Because of labor shortages among young workers—especially 16 to 24 year olds—companies had difficulty in making good matches between new workers and new jobs (Flamholtz, Randle, and Sackmann 1987; Narisetti 1995). Women no longer offered an untapped pool for plugging the gaps in entry-level positions in that the huge inflow of women into the labor force abated in the 1980s (Hill and O'Neill 1992). These demographic trends forced U.S. firms to initiate major human resource policy adjustments to accommodate new workers who brought diverse cultural understandings, family responsibilities, work motivations, and skill levels into the workplace.

These changes in the economy and labor force altered the employment relationship based on firm internal labor markets that had grown during the post-World War II period. The emerging employment understanding involved a more casual relationship between employers and employees in which external labor markets assumed much greater importance and emphasis was less on commitment to a particular employer and more on a worker's "employability" with other companies. Workers were encouraged or obliged to take on more of the risks involved in doing business and to develop their own skills and careers (Heckscher 1995; Cappelli 1996). Premiums were placed on continuous training and development of general skills in that rapid changes could make workers' skills grow obsolete quickly.

As a consequence of these changes in organizations, in their workforces, and in the employment relations between them, examining the linkages between organizations and the wider stratification system became more essential. Organizational social scientists as well as managers gained a greater appreciation that an organization's relations with its employees depend heavily on the nature of labor markets and other features of the organization's environment. "Closed system" approaches that focused on the internal structures of organizations increasingly came to be seen as inadequate for understanding the changes taking place in employment relations and their implications for the productivity and performance of organizations and the careers and commitments of individuals. Rather, it became clearer that understanding these changes required an "open system" approach that investigated how organizations interact with other organizations (such as subcontractors) and related institutions such as labor markets.

The organizational theories that developed in the 1970s and 1980s reflected this emphasis on social context as a basis for understanding organizations and employment relations. Out of "contingency" theories emphasizing adaptation by organizations to the levels of uncertainty in product technologies and markets (e.g., Lawrence and Lorsch 1967) grew a variety of sophisticated perspectives stressing different environmental conditions. Ecological theories (Hannan and Freeman 1989) stressed the density of competition among forms as a basis for answering the question, Why are there so many kinds of organizations?, arguing that organizational change was more often a result of replacement of old by new organizations than of adaptation at the level of particular organizations.

Institutional theories (Meyer and Rowan 1977; DiMaggio and Powell 1983) emphasized an organization's need to acquire legitimacy for its activity patterns. Such theories assigned a significant role to general societal understandings about employment relations and to those specific elements of an organization's setting that have the power to grant or withhold judgments of legitimacy—including governmental regulatory agencies, associations of peer organizations, and professional societies.

Institutional economists entered organizational debates with view-points such as that embodied in *transaction cost economics* (Williamson 1981, 1985). This held that efficient organizational arrangements were to be seen as contingent on certain properties of transactions between an organization and its environment; this perspective suggests, for example, that an organization should retain long-term "regular" employees to per-form complex and uncertain tasks, while turning to shorter-term "market" arrangements for the performance of routine work.

The *new structuralist* paradigm in stratification research (e.g., Baron and Bielby 1980; Berg 1981; Kalleberg and Berg 1987; Farkas and England 1988) has been particularly fruitful in highlighting the interplay between organizations and the broader stratification system. A key tenet of this perspective is that organizations are central components of the stratification system and are the sites where outcomes such as earnings inequality and career mobility are generated. The new structuralists go beyond attempting to understand organizations qua organizations by posing questions about the relationship of organizations to their employees and to labor markets.

The NOS data are very useful for addressing the kinds of issues raised by the new structuralist perspective, as we illustrate by our analyses in Chapter 7 through Chapter 15. There we examine prominent questions on the new structuralist research agenda such as how organizations recruit and select workers and how they train workers once they are hired. We also analyze important stratification outcomes of the employment relation such as earnings differences and inequalities in fringe benefits, as well as contingent employment, sex segregation, and organizational commitment. The NOS data are also well suited to testing implications of some of the organizational theories we have mentioned (see, for example, Chapters 4 and 5 on organizational structures and elements of the employment relation). As a cross-sectional survey, however, the NOS is not an effective vehicle for examining the dynamic propositions included in organizational ecology, for example.

## Organizational Research Designs

The research design used by the NOS offers major advantages for studying the kinds of issues we have discussed. In this section, to situate the NOS in the context of other organizational research, we highlight the predominant strategies used by organizational researchers and illustrate them with classic studies and recent exemplars. We discuss the strengths and drawbacks of these alternatives and conclude that a design calling for a large sample from a diverse organizational population offers unique opportunities for studying the kinds of empirical questions discussed previously. We stress the value of representativeness and other advantages that our preferred design provides.

### The Single-Case Study

Probably the original, and still most prevalent, type of organization research is conducted on a single organization by a single investigator or a small team. The classic Hawthorne studies of scientific management practices, which, nonetheless, led to insights about the importance of group structures and norms in work organizations, were conducted in the 1920s and 1930s at a Western Electric plant outside Chicago (Roethlisberger and Dickson 1939). A research site for this type of study may be selected because the researcher has special access, because of geographic convenience, or because the organization exhibits unusual characteristics that excite analytic curiosity. The substantive research interest in a single-case study usually focuses either on discovering the recurrent patterns of action that comprise the organization's internal structures or on understanding the phenomenological significance of the observed social relationships to the individual participants (see Burawoy 1979; Smith 1990; Barnett and Miner 1992; Burt 1992; Ibarra 1992).

The most serious limitation of the single-case research design is its inability to support generalizations that go beyond that particular organization. Few theorists are willing to assume that all organizations are fundamentally alike and consequently, that one research site is as good as another for making observations. Researchers have no way to determine the extent to which the observed structures and processes found in such studies are typical or unusual. Case studies are, however, unsurpassed as a fruitful source of suggestive hypotheses.

## Multiple-Case Studies

One possible way to guard against the idiosyncrasies of the single organization study is to replicate the project at other sites. The locations may be purposively selected to maximize contrasts of some theoretically major dimension; for example, concern with effects of labor organization would lead to a design comparing union and nonunion shops. Cross-national studies of workplaces often explicitly anticipate that the cultures or the institutional environments in which they are embedded generate divergent production practices (Dore 1973). Alternatively, the cases may be chosen with an expectation that equivalent results will lend credence to a researcher's claim that a common dynamic underlies each organization. For example, Barley (1990) concluded that roles and social networks similarly mediated the structural effects of introducing new imaging technologies in the radiology departments of two hospitals.

Multiple-case studies permit comparisons and, therefore, some tentative conclusions about the importance or unimportance of fundamental organizational factors. Usually, however, they involve small numbers of cases and thus are unable to control simultaneously for numerous possible confounding influences. An enormous investment of investigator time is necessary for data collection and analysis in a multiple in-depth case study design, and even a team of collaborators can seldom cope with more than a handful of sites.

## Single-Type Organization Surveys

Probably the most common research design used to compare appreciable numbers of organizations focuses on a single "type" of organization, assembling data via either survey methods or from archival sources. A researcher first designates some criteria for distinguishing eligible from ineligible organizations. The criteria usually lead to inclusion of organizations in some conventionally understood industry category such as banks, hospitals, airline companies, farms, police departments, or automobile plants. Sometimes lists maintained by industry-level associations are available that enumerate all organizations satisfying the selection criteria (e.g., the American Association of University Professors' directory of universities and colleges). But, at other times, the project investigators must painstakingly assemble their own sampling frame from various sources (e.g., combining listings in a community's telephone white pages with those in a restaurant association's membership roster to find all food establishments). Original data in single-type studies may be gathered from managers or employees using structured personal or telephone interviews or self-administered questionnaires. By measuring organizational structures and processes in a standardized fashion, a survey allows meaningful comparisons across organizations. With data on the organization, its departments and divisions, and its employees, complex multilevel relationships may be examined, as in Lincoln and Kalleberg's (1990) study of organizational commitment and job satisfaction among 8,302 workers in 52 U.S. and 46 Japanese manufacturing plants.

A major strength of the single-type organization survey is that researchers using it can estimate covariations among organizational properties of interest while controlling statistically for the effects of confounding factors. Numerous factors are held constant by confining the study to a specific type of organization, making it possible to develop, for example, objective performance measures (see, e.g., Kelley's, 1994, study of machining organizations). This research design is, however, unable to support generalizations that go beyond the specific organizational type. Consequently, findings about the advantages of "lean production" technologies in Japanese automobile factories relative to American and European plants (Womack, Jones, and Roos 1990) may have little to say about such structures in the steel and textile industries, let alone such radically different settings as banks, hospitals, and retail stores. When researchers specialize in a particular type of organization, they tend to "develop different theories for different kinds of organizations" (Freeman 1986, p. 299). To avoid tendencies toward such fragmentation, survey designs that include broader organizational populations are needed.

**Restricted Diverse Organization Surveys**

In contrast to the single-type survey, a diverse organizational survey seeks in principle to represent a broader range of organizational types. (The distinction between *single-type* and *restricted diverse* studies is of course a matter of degree: Studies of seven manufacturing industries such as Lincoln and Kalleberg's, 1990, exhibit more breadth than an investigation that focuses on only one of these industries.) In practice, certain restrictions nonetheless are imposed. The most common restrictions involve either geographic locale, organization size, or both. For example, the organizations in the classic Aston studies of technology and structure (Pugh, Hickson, and Hinings 1968) covered a broad range of products and purposes, but they were limited to units having at least 250 employees in Birmingham, England (they also mixed together independent organizations and branches or subsidiaries of larger firms). Gordon and Thal-Larsen's (1969) sample of 309 establishments came from all industry sectors (for-profit, nonprofit, and government), but they were located in the San Francisco Bay Area and had 100 or more employees (see Cohen and Pfeffer 1986). And Osterman's (1994a) national survey of 875 establishments was restricted to those with 50 or more employees, thus eliminating the large majority of all workplaces (see Chapters 2 and 3 in this volume). He drew his sample from the Dun and Bradstreet establishment file, which mainly includes those organizations that seek credit ratings.

Surveys with size restrictions tend to truncate the full range of variation on many other variables of substantive interest. For example, small organizations tend to be less formalized and departmentalized, but more centralized, than larger organizations (see Chapter 4). If small workplaces are eliminated from a diverse organization survey, descriptive statistics misstate the prevalence of those structures for the entire organizational population, and statistical leverage for estimating relationships among them is reduced. When researchers concentrate their analyses on restricted diverse samples with a size threshold for inclusion, they run the risk of constructing theories applicable only to large organizations. Particularly seductive are analyses that examine the *Fortune* 500 companies (e.g., Davis and Stout 1992). Although *Fortune* 500 companies account for substantial portions of the total U.S. workforce and economic activity, they are far from the whole story; smaller organizations need to be considered as well.

**Unrestricted Diverse Organization Surveys**

The National Organizations Study illustrates the organizational research design with the broadest scope in that it studies a diverse population of organizations and places no limits on type, geography (within the United States), size, or any other dimension. Surveys using this design permit investigators to observe the full range of variation in structures and processes in the U.S. economy. If several hundred units of analysis are selected, sufficient numbers of cases become available to permit detailed comparisons across contexts and conditions. For example, suppose researchers want to know whether the relationship between internal labor market structures and job training programs differs in union and nonunion firms; in small, medium, and large establishments; in agricultural, manufacturing, and service sectors; or across organizations with varying levels of centralization (Knoke and Kalleberg 1994). An assessment of the scope of their covariation could readily be undertaken by dividing the firms or establishments in an unrestricted diverse survey into appropriate subsets. If organizational structures and processes exhibit truly universal properties, then patterns should remain basically unchanged regardless of the settings observed. But, if context makes a real difference, then empirical analyses should reveal significant interaction effects. If, as may reasonably be surmised, many relationships are likely to differ in systematic ways, organizational analysis will benefit if data are available that permit, and even compel, examination of such differences. On discovering them, it will then be necessary to construct new theories that explain the differences in observed covariation.

Despite the great intellectual promise inherent in the unrestricted diverse organization survey design, none were attempted on a national basis in the United States prior to the National Organizations Study. The only examples of unrestricted organizational studies were in local areas, such as Bridges and Villemez's (1994) study of hiring practices and other aspects of employment relations in an economically diversified standard metropolitan statistical area (SMSA). One reason for the paucity of such studies is that comprehensive and reliable lists of the universe of work places are difficult to obtain in the United States—unlike Sweden and Norway, for example (see Kalleberg, Marsden, Aldrich, and Cassell 1990). Fortunately, a practical alternative is available that makes effective use of the well-understood technology for drawing a representative national sample of individuals (see Chapter 2).

The unrestricted diverse organizational survey could be used to examine even more issues bearing on organizations and employment relations if the design were to be generalized further to incorporate a longitudinal dimension. The NOS was a one-time, cross-sectional study conducted in the early 1990s. Expanding on this design by conducting additional cross section surveys (with new diverse samples) at 2- to 5-year time intervals would allow the tracking of aggregate trends; by instead returning to the same set of organizations surveyed in the first "wave," important questions about organizational transformation, change, and persistence could be answered confidently.

## Content of the National Organizations Study

The NOS is unusual among organization studies because of the large number of work establishments it surveyed and because of the wide variety of these establishments. Combined with its probability sampling plan, these features mean that the NOS rates well on representativeness and the capacity to support generalizations. Additionally, the NOS gathers data on multiple levels of the work establishment, the larger organizational setting (if any) of which it is a part, and the work experiences of an employee within it. Consequently, it is suited to studying a broad scope of issues involving organizations and work relations; analysts can conduct a concerted inquiry into many of the organizational human resource responses to economic and social changes that less extensive designs cannot examine satisfactorily. As noted, adding a longitudinal component to the NOS would enable researchers to trace trends in organizational social indicators such as the amounts of training that work organizations provide their workers, or the methods they use to find and select employees. The research procedures used in the NOS may be fruitfully applied to many substantive topics; as such, they hold the potential to deepen considerably analysts' understanding of organizations.

The issues bearing on work organizations and their employees investigated in the NOS are of considerable importance to social scientists as well as to managers and public policymakers. The NOS interview focused on four basic kinds of human resource practices and policies: (a) recruitment and staffing, (b) job training, (c) promotion opportunities, and (d) incentives such as earnings and fringe benefits. The topics studied were influenced by the research design, which provided better opportunities for studying some questions as opposed to others.

In addition to these substantive foci, the NOS also collected data on a set of structural features that have been frequently used to describe organizations. These variables—which include organizational complexity, formalization, and decision centralization, among others—should be measured in any large study of work organizations in that they are of interest to organizational researchers with a variety of diverse theoretical orientations. These items are also important for describing and explaining phenomena related to organizations' human resource policies and practices. In addition to organizational structures, such variables include the establishment's legal form; its workforce demography (size and gender-race-age composition); its principal product or service; its auspices (for-profit, nonprofit, or public sector); and performance indicators. Also included as important "background" indicators are aspects of the establishment's environmental situation: (a) whether it is part of a multiestablishment organization, (b) the labor market and competitiveness problems the organization anticipates, (c) the complexity and uncertainty of the organization's environment, and (d) the organization's relations with other institutions.

## Chapters in This Book

Chapter 2 describes the NOS sample and how data were collected. It summarizes the study's data collection procedures, research design, sampling plan, and response patterns. In this chapter, we also assess the representativeness of the NOS with regard to industry and occupational distributions in the United States found in other statistical sources.

Chapter 3 presents a descriptive overview of the establishments included in the NOS. It presents summary statistics on survey items and composite scales that describe the composition and settings of these workplaces. It reviews the organizations' auspices, industry settings, workforce composition, and environmental settings. The NOS includes a quite diverse set of establishments, most of which provide services rather than produce goods. The public, nonprofit, and private, for-profit sectors are well represented. A sizable fraction of the workplaces form parts of larger organizations. There are considerable differences between establishments in the minority and female composition of their workforces.

The second part of the book (Chapters 4, 5, and 6) focuses on organizational structures. Chapter 4 reports data on organizational correlates of systems of coordination and control used by the NOS establishments. It introduces the survey items and scales used to measure coordination and control structures, including structural differentiation, formalization, decentralization, and the presence of internal labor markets. It shows that, for the diverse set of establishments in the NOS, measures of coordination and control techniques—including structural complexity, formalization, decentralization—are related to one another in theoretically anticipated ways.

Chapter 5 discusses two key elements of formalization in employment relations: (a) firm internal labor markets, an important structure that emerged to shape the way organizations recruit, train, and reward their employees and (b) formalized dispute resolution procedures that offer "due process" to employees. Firm internal labor markets play a central role in our analyses of various human resource issues in subsequent chapters. Together with lawlike dispute resolution procedures providing for the legitimate handling of workplace grievances, such internal labor markets help to constitute the inclusive "corporatist" organizations (Lincoln and Kalleberg 1990) of the Pax Americana era. The end of Chapter 5 identifies five common profiles of coordination-control strategies. Two of these are variations on "simple structure" found predominantly in small, independent firms. The other three are varieties of bureaucracy seen in small branch establishments and in large nonunionized and in large unionized establishments.

Chapter 6 extends the structural theme toward the 1990s, using clustering techniques to identify the organizations in the NOS data that conform best to the emerging imagery of a "high performance" work organization. The idea of a "transformed" or high-performance work system has attracted considerable attention in the United States as an alternative to traditional, mass production forms of work organization. Chapter 6 also examines the relationships between indicators of high performance work organizations, on the one hand, and measures of organizational performance, on the other.

Chapters 7 through 12 consider four basic aspects of organizations' human resource practices and policies. Chapter 7 examines the hiring process, a key interface between workers and organizations. From the individual's standpoint, hiring decisions are central elements of careers, as individuals searching for employment must gain access to the channels through which job information is disseminated. From the organization's side, they are ways to acquire needed human resources. Organizations seeking employees must reach the pools of potential workers having relevant skills and qualifications. Chapter 7 examines establishment-level correlates of staffing practices, including both the recruitment of candidates and the selection of employees from applicant pools; this design overcomes a major limitation of much research on staffing, which has focused primarily on the supply-side or worker's-side of job search processes.

Chapters 8 and 9 examine patterns of job training among U.S. work organizations. Corporate training efforts are becoming increasingly important as organizations' involvements in training and employee development are growing. Chapter 8 documents the greater use of formal training programs by large establishments than by small ones and then considers various explanations of why larger organizations provide more training. Chapter 9 looks at the effects of internal labor markets and unions on occupational training. In particular, it investigates whether blue-collar occupations receive as much company training as white-collar occupations.

Chapters 10, 11, and 12 address human resource issues related to compensation. Chapter 10 examines how employees' earnings levels depend on characteristics of their work organizations. In that work organizations are central to stratification systems in industrial societies, studying the sources of organizational differences in employees' earnings is important for understanding structural variations in economic rewards. Chapter 11 examines why earnings dispersion is greater in some organizations than in others in the NOS and then tries to identify some of the main organizational correlates of earnings inequality. Our measures of the distribution of earnings within organizations are based on information collected on different occupations within the establishment. We test three sets of determinants of organizational earnings inequality: (a) the organization's structure, (b) its context, (c) and the composition of its labor force.

Chapter 12 describes the extent to which employers provide various types of fringe benefits. Together with rising competitive pressures, the growing diversity of the labor force has greatly complicated managers' efforts to match types of incentives to the needs and wants of their employees. Organizational differences in fringe benefits reveal much about the nature of compensation and employment relations; they also inform debate about timely policy issues such as the provision of health care and child care. We examine three types of fringe benefits: (a) personal benefits such as medical, dental, and life insurance, pensions, disability, and drug or alcohol abuse treatment; (b) familial benefits such as maternity leave, sick leave, elderly care, child care, and job training programs; and (c) participant benefits such as cash bonuses and profit sharing. Our analyses assess how organizational capacity, employee demand, and environmental factors are associated with more comprehensive employee benefit programs.

The last part of the book—Chapters 13, 14, and 15—examines three emerging issues associated with the changing nature of employment relations and organizations' workforces. Chapter 13 describes U.S. work organizations' use of three major types of contingent employment relations: part-time employees, temporary workers, and subcontracting. These three employment arrangements are becoming increasingly common, as organizations seek to achieve greater flexibility in their human resource practices. Chapter 13 also analyzes some of the environmental, organizational, occupational, and labor force variables associated with these three contingent relations.

Chapter 14 looks at patterns of organizational gender segregation. The NOS data contain the first estimates of this that are based on a national sample of organizations. The NOS provides estimates of gender segregation for three distinct samples of occupations. Chapter 14 highlights consequences of gender segregation for gender wage and career inequality, and then it examines how the degree of gender segregation in workplaces is related to measures of organizational structure, market competition, and demography.

Chapter 15 focuses on male-female differences in organizational commitment, using the 1991 General Social Survey that was used to draw the NOS sample (see Chapter 2). These data reveal a small but significant tendency for employed men to display higher organizational commitment than employed women do. We consider two kinds of explanations for this gender difference in commitment: (a) *job* models highlighting gender differences in job attributes such as autonomy or rewards and (b) *gender* models that stress socialization, family ties, and differential labor market opportunities. After statistical adjustments for work positions and family roles, the gender difference in commitment vanishes; if anything, the data suggest that women may be slightly more committed to the organizations that employ them than are men.

Chapter 16 summarizes the major findings from the 1991 NOS and suggests some alternative research designs and project topics that future national surveys of diverse organizations might consider.

# 2

# Design of the National Organizations Study

JOE L. SPAETH

DIANE P. O'ROURKE

This chapter reports on the procedures used to draw a sample of and collect data on a national probability sample of work establishments for the National Organizations Study (NOS). This sample was generated by asking respondents to the General Social Survey (GSS) to give the names, addresses, and telephone numbers of the establishments that employed them and their spouses. In principle, this procedure yielded a probability sample of all work establishments in the United States, with the probability of selection being proportionate to size (number of employees). Probability proportionate to size (PPS) samples are statistically optimal for populations, such as organizations, in which the elements vary widely in size (Kish 1965, 1966; Sudman 1976).

Using a questionnaire that asked about the characteristics, practices, and policies of these establishments, the NOS is based on telephone interviews conducted with personnel officials by the Survey Research Laboratory (SRL) of the University of Illinois. These interviews, which averaged 42 minutes in length, helped establish a nationally representative database on work establishments that has been supplemented by aggregate data on the counties in which the establishments were housed and the industries in which they operated.

The sampling design is a straightforward one capable of providing an up-to-date sample of all types, sizes, and ages of work establishments. Executing the study, on the other hand, is a complicated, multistage process that provides ample opportunities for failing to implement the design. We first discuss the sampling design, then the outcomes involved in the transmission of information from the GSS to SRL, and then the outcomes of SRL's attempts to collect data on establishments. Next we compare distributions of key variables between the NOS database and the GSS, between the NOS and the Current Population Survey (CPS), and between the GSS and the CPS. These comparisons establish that the NOS succeeded in obtaining a representative sample of establishments. In Appendix 2.1 we give recommendations for improving the execution of the sampling design and the data collection.

## Sampling Design

In the past, a basic problem in generating a sample of establishments or organizations has been the absence of a complete sampling frame. Most lists of organizations are incomplete (Kalleberg et al. 1990). They may be limited to organizations of one or a few types, and they often omit or underrepresent certain organizations, especially small or new ones. A procedure for producing a probability sample of all types, sizes, and ages of establishments (and the larger organizations that contain them) is simple but moderately expensive. Respondents to a standard survey of a human population are asked to identify the establishments where they work by name, address, and telephone number. The establishments nominated by this method are drawn with probability proportionate to size. All units containing the survey respondent, from the smallest work unit to the largest, most encompassing organization, are drawn PPS. Such a survey-based sample is as current as the time of each survey interview, a notable advantage given the time lag that may be required for an organization to enter published or even machine-readable directories (Kalleberg et al. 1990).

This sampling method works because each potential respondent represents the establishment where he or she is employed. The more employees an establishment has, the more likely it is to be sampled. If the method for sampling persons gives each individual an equal chance of selection, the probability that an establishment will fall into the sample of organizations is proportionate to the number of its employees. This method has also been used in the study of voluntary associations (McPherson 1982, 1983; McPherson and Smith-Lovin 1982).

In organizational research, this method is known as *hypernetwork sampling* (McPherson 1982). In statistics, it is a special case of multiplicity sampling (Sudman, Sirken, and Cowan 1988). In this sampling method, survey respondents are asked to nominate people known to them who have a rare characteristic, such as having a specific disease or being a Vietnam veteran. The nominators must be in a specific, countable relationship to the nominees. Relatives are often used as nominators because the number of relatives (parents or siblings, for example) can be counted. The probability that a nominee will fall into a sample is proportionate to the number of nominators in the population. This number is known as the *multiplicity*. In a survey-based sampling design for establishments, an establishment's multiplicity is its total number of employees.

The design aspect of sampling establishments is thus rather simple. Realizing the design in practice, however, is another matter. The next section discusses some of the issues involved.

## Implementing a PPS Sampling Design

The GSS is a nearly annual survey of the adult U.S. population that has been conducted since 1972 by the National Opinion Research Center (NORC); it is funded primarily by the Sociology Program of the National Science Foundation (see Davis and Smith 1992). The GSS measures a variety of social and political attitudes, together with ample background and sociodemographic data on respondents; a primary GSS objective is to monitor trends in important social indicators.

Since the mid-1980s, the GSS has included topical modules focusing on active areas of social science. In 1991, the GSS module dealt with work organizations. A subcommittee of the GSS Board of Overseers consulted widely with specialists in the discipline as it constructed the questions in this module, which gathered information on the job search methods, organizational commitment, promotion experiences, perceptions of work roles and work organizations, supervisory experiences, and work experiences of respondents.

The work organizations module in the 1991 GSS also asked respondents to give the names, addresses, and telephone numbers of the establishments where they and their spouses worked. This information, along with answers to questions on respondents' and spouses' occupation and industry, was transmitted to the University of Illinois Survey Research Laboratory. SRL interviewers attempted to conduct telephone interviews with informants at each of the establishments nominated by the GSS respondents. Thus, there were two stages in the collection of data on establishments: (a) collecting nominations of establishments, done face-to-face by NORC interviewers and (b) interviewing establishment informants, done by telephone by SRL interviewers.

### Collecting and Transmitting Nominations

As noted previously, respondents were asked for the names, addresses, and telephone numbers of their establishments and those of their spouses. Owing to the possible complexity of persons' relationships to the establishment for which they work, three sets of questions were used: (a) a straightforward set asking for the name, address, and telephone number of the "one place" where they worked; (b) a set asking for the place where respondents or spouses would "find out where you will be working"; and (c) a set asking if they "have any kind of base of operations at all." Photocopies of the GSS questionnaire pages containing this information, plus data on respondents' and spouses' occupations and industries (but *not* respondents' names), were transmitted from NORC to SRL.

Of the 1,517 GSS respondents, 912 were working, as were 519 of their spouses, for a total of 1,431. A total of 1,427 nominations were transmitted from NORC to SRL; of these, 909 were respondents and 518 were spouses.[1] Tables 2.1 through 2.3 show the distributions of answers to questions requesting the name, address, and telephone number of employers, according to whether the data pertained to respondents or spouses.

As Table 2.1 shows, 86% of the respondents (who were always the nominators) were able to supply the establishment name, 3% did not know

**Table 2.1** Information on Establishment Name, by Target of Nomination (in percentages)

| | | Target of Nomination | |
|---|---|---|---|
| *Response* | *Total* | *Respondent* | *Spouse* |
| Supplied | 85.6 | 87.5 | 82.4 |
| Refused | 10.9 | 9.5 | 13.3 |
| Don't know or incomplete | 3.5 | 3.1 | 4.2 |
| Total | 100.0 | 100.1 | 99.0 |
| *N* | 1,427 | 909 | 518 |

NOTE: $\chi^2$ (2 *df*) = 6.78. *p* < .05.

**Table 2.2** Information on Establishment Address, by Target of Nomination (in percentages)

| | | Target of Nomination | |
|---|---|---|---|
| *Response* | *Total* | *Respondent* | *Spouse* |
| Supplied | 76.6 | 80.6 | 69.5 |
| Refused | 11.6 | 10.3 | 13.9 |
| Don't know or incomplete | 11.8 | 9.0 | 16.6 |
| Total | 100.0 | 99.9 | 100.0 |
| *N* | 1,427 | 909 | 518 |

NOTE: $\chi^2$ (2 *df*) = 25.05, *p* < .001.

the name or did not answer, and 11% refused to provide this information. Although differences between respondents and spouses were significant at the .05 level, they were not large. Respondents were 5% more likely to provide an establishment name for their employers than for those of their spouses.[2]

Table 2.2 shows that 77% of respondents gave a street address for employers when asked, while 12% did not know the address or gave incomplete information, and an additional 12% refused. Respondents were substantially better able to provide a street address for their own employers than for the employers of their spouses. The 11% difference was significant at better than the .001 level. Much of this difference arose because respondents did not know work addresses for their spouses. In most of these cases, respondents were able to supply a place name but not a street address.

Finally, 73% of the respondents provided a telephone number for an employer, 15% did not know the telephone number or did not answer the request, and 12% refused to provide it (see Table 2.3). Again, the difference

**Table 2.3** Information on Establishment Telephone Number, by Target of Nomination (in percentages)

| | | Target of Nomination | |
| Response | Total | Respondent | Spouse |
| --- | --- | --- | --- |
| Supplied | 73.1 | 77.0 | 66.2 |
| Refused | 12.1 | 10.8 | 14.3 |
| Don't know or inadequate | 14.9 | 12.2 | 19.5 |
| Total | 100.1 | 100.0 | 100.0 |
| N | 1,427 | 909 | 518 |

NOTE: $\chi^2$ (2 df) = 20.41, p < .001.

in the availability of a phone number between employers of respondents and spouses was 11%, significant beyond the .001 level. The largest difference continued to be in knowledge of the telephone number, not in refusing to provide it. Respondents were more likely to refuse to answer about their spouses than themselves on all three items, but these differences were not large, about 4%.

For the question on establishment address, a response was coded inadequate if a street address was missing. In many cases, however, a place name was given, and it was often possible to obtain a telephone number through directory assistance. In general, inadequate information was a real but relatively minor problem. Ultimately, the refusal problem was twice as serious as the inadequate information problem. Furthermore, respondents who refused to answer one of the identifying questions were very likely to refuse the other two. Nearly 90% of those who refused to answer one item about the employer refused to answer all three. Refusals are thus a serious problem.

As might be expected, the ultimate outcome of the nomination attempts was a function of the completeness of the data collected by NORC interviewers. If a telephone number was available, nominations were usable over 99% of the time.[3] Information on establishment names and addresses yielded usable nominations 83% of the time, whereas one or the other piece of information produced usable nominations 63% of the time. Not surprisingly, if none of the three pieces of information was present, usable nominations were very rare.[4]

As Tables 2.1 through 2.3 indicate, respondents provided more complete data on themselves than on their spouses. With differences in completeness of data taken into account, differences in usability of nominations between employers of respondents and those of spouses were rather small.

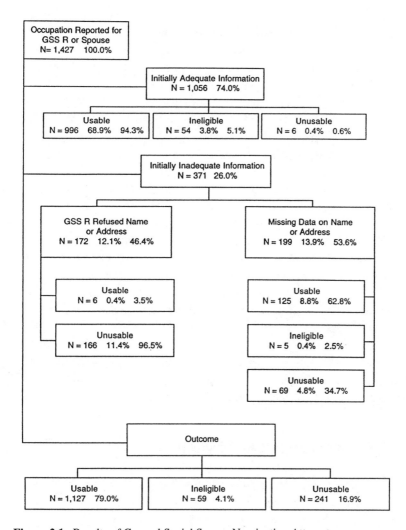

**Figure 2.1.** Results of General Social Survey Nomination Attempts

The stages and ultimate outcomes involved in collecting nominations and transmitting them to SRL are diagramed in Figure 2.1. Each box in the figure represents a stage in the processes, beginning with the GSS attempts to collect usable nominations from respondents and continuing through SRL's attempts to convert the unusable nominations. Figure 2.1 refers to the ultimate outcome of GSS and SRL nomination attempts, not to the nominations as transmitted by the GSS.

The first box shows that the GSS produced establishment nominations for 1,427 respondents and spouses. Of these 1,056, or 74.0% were initially adequate: the nominating information was sufficient to begin interviewing immediately. The numbers in the next set of three boxes are the number of cases, the percentage of the total of 1,427, and the percentage of the 1,056 providing initially usable information. Among the latter, 94.3% produced usable interview attempts, 5.1% were ineligible, and only 0.6% turned out ultimately to be unusable.

There were two kinds of ineligible cases, both of which refer to organizations for which there was identifying information. The first kind were organizations that went out of business or for which identifying information was erroneous. The second were mainly military establishments; we did not attempt to interview informants for such establishments in that the informants might have been placed in jeopardy had they answered.

Of the 1,427 nominations, 26.0% provided initially inadequate information. Of these, nearly half (46.4%) were GSS refusals, and of the refusals, virtually all remained unusable. Of the 53.6% that lacked information on name or address, about two thirds were usable and one third remained unusable.

Ultimately, therefore, 79% of the nominations led to interview attempts, 4% were ineligible, and 17% were unusable. Given the available information and procedures, incomplete information was not a major problem, but the refusals appeared to be quite intractable.

## Collecting Data From Establishments

The results of an earlier study (Spaeth 1985, 1989) strongly suggested that the SRL data collection effort would be intensive and time consuming. The study design allowed for many more contacts than would be attempted in a standard population sample. Especially well-qualified interviewers were recruited and paid at a higher than normal level. The interviewers received 3 days of training on the design of the study, its content, and how to persuade reluctant respondents to cooperate.

Data collection began on April 18, 1991, after the training period, and continued through November 29. It took a median of 2 contact attempts to reach an eventual respondent, with a range of 1 to 29. Five contact attempts (median) were required to complete an interview; the range was between 1 and 33. In all, the median interview involved 6 contacts; the maximum number of contacts was 58.[5] Most interviews were completed in one session, but 18% required two and 8% three or more. Because extensive factual data were required, a number of interviews were done with more than one respondent, 17% with two or more. The length of the interviews ranged from 10 to over 100 minutes, with a median of 42. Clearly, our expectation that data collection would require considerable time and effort was amply borne out.

The outcomes of the 1,127 possible interview attempts are shown in Figure 2.2. As the figure indicates, there were two contingencies, one major and one minor, in this process. The major contingency occurred when a potential informant, designated as "the head of the personnel department or the person responsible for hiring," asked to receive a questionnaire by mail, even though the study design called for a telephone interview. This was usually because an informant refused to be interviewed by telephone, although some simply wanted to be able to examine the questionnaire before answering it. Self-administered questionnaires, differing as little as possible from the interview version, were mailed to these people. Mailed questionnaires were followed up by telephone reminders and by subsequent mailings.

The minor contingency was the existence of more than one nominator for a given establishment; such cases are labeled *duplicate employers* in Figure 2.2. Some of these duplicates were the result of the GSS multistage area probability sampling design, for which the smallest area was a single block. In one instance, eight people worked for the same employer. Some duplicates were cases in which spouses worked for (or were) the same employer. To avoid unnecessary respondent burden, informants for such establishments were interviewed only once.[6] Data from this interview were transferred to the records pertaining to the other nominators.

There were three possible outcomes for each case: (a) The potential informant(s) could refuse to be interviewed or fail to return a self-administered questionnaire; (b) the data collection attempt could still be pending after a period as long as 7.5 months; or (c) a completed questionnaire could have been collected, by telephone or mail.

Turning to the right-hand side of Figure 2.2, we see that SRL attempted to collect data on 1,067 separate establishments. Of these establishments, 59.4% were finalized by telephone—52.6% were completed, 1.7% were pending at the close of the field period, and 5.1% refused to be interviewed. Questionnaires were sent by mail to 40.7% of the establishments. Of these, 29.3% returned completed questionnaires, 44.2% refused, and 26.5% were still pending at the close of the field period.

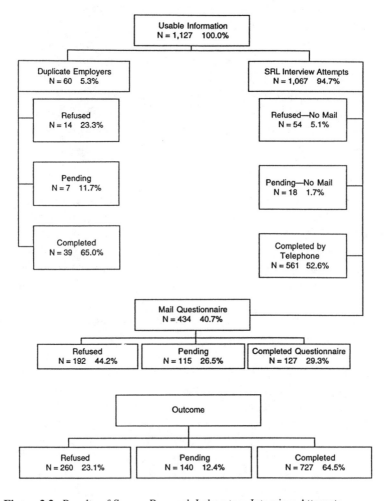

**Figure 2.2.** Results of Survey Research Laboratory Interview Attempts

There are several ways to view the 29% completion rate for mailed questionnaires. As the overall response rate to a survey, it is not good; but as a supplement to the telephone interviewing, it was well worth the effort. Telephone interviewing collected data from 52.6% of the establishments. The 127 questionnaires returned by mail raised that to 64.5%. Had we limited our efforts to telephone interviewing, there would have been as many nonrespondents as respondents, which is a poor completion rate for a survey. Adding the mailed cases makes for a response rate that is respectable by the standards of organizational research, though low for most surveys. The cases for duplicate employers produced an additional 39 completions, 14 refusals, and 7 pendings.

The bottom of Figure 2.2 shows the distribution of the combined outcomes: 64.5% completions, 23.1% refusals, and 12.4% pending. Of the data collection attempts with separate establishments, 83% of the refusals were in response to the mailed questionnaire, as were 89% of the pendings. In response to extensive, repeated follow-up telephone calls, those who refused and those who did not return a questionnaire tended to be apologetic. People in both groups most often said that they did not have the time. Both the 29% completion rate and the reactions of nonrespondents indicate that there is substantial room for improvement in returns to the mailed questionnaire. Appendix 2.1 suggests some approaches for increasing the response rate for mailed questionnaires.

## The Representativeness of the NOS Sample

The 727 cases that provided complete data on establishments are 50.9% of the original 1,427. Although even this percentage is respectable in organizational research, it raises a question of the representativeness of the NOS sample. We examine this by studying the distributions of certain key variables in comparison with distributions of the populations on which they are based. Appendix 2.1 addresses the related question of how the overall response rate can be improved.

Key variables available for this analysis are occupation, industry, and establishment size. For the first two variables, two comparison populations exist. First, the NOS is a sample of the population of employed GSS respondents and spouses. Second, both the NOS and the GSS are samples of the U.S. labor force. Comparison data on the labor force can be obtained from reports of the Current Population Survey prepared by the Bureau of Labor Statistics. Three comparisons are possible: CPS-GSS, CPS-NOS, and GSS-NOS.

One way of framing the research issue statistically is to ask whether the NOS can be considered representative of the same population as the GSS and whether either or both of these samples can be considered representative of the U.S. labor force, data on which are provided by the CPS. Data on the GSS and the NOS come from the same source—respondents to the GSS reporting on themselves or their spouses. CPS respondents

**Table 2.4**  Distribution of Industry, by Source (in percentages)

| | Source | | |
| | National Organizations Study | General Social Survey | Current Population Survey[a] |
| Industry | | | |
|---|---|---|---|
| Agriculture | 2.2 | 2.2 | 2.4 |
| Mining-construction | 5.9 | 7.1 | 6.5 |
| Durable manufacturing | 11.1 | 10.8 | 10.2 |
| Nondurable manufacturing | 5.8 | 6.8 | 7.4 |
| Transportation | 8.8 | 7.8 | 7.0 |
| Wholesale trade | 2.2 | 3.3 | 4.0 |
| Retail trade | 14.2 | 14.4 | 16.6 |
| Finance, insurance, real estate | 5.7 | 6.3 | 6.8 |
| Professional services | 25.7 | 23.3 | 22.5 |
| Other services | 10.2 | 10.8 | 11.7 |
| Public administration | 8.1 | 7.2 | 4.8 |
| Total | 99.9 | 100.0 | 99.9 |
| N | 724 | 1,426 | 230,789 |

NOTE: NOS versus GSS: $\chi^2$ (10 $df$) = 9.8, NS; index of dissimilarity = 4.8%; GSS versus CPS: $\chi^2$ (10 $df$) = 28.2, $p < .01$; index of dissimilarity = 5.1%; NOS versus CPS: $\chi^2$ (10 $df$) = 38.5, $p < .001$; index of dissimilarity = 7.5%.
a. February and March, 1991; $N$ is weighted.

provide the CPS data. Some part of the differences between GSS-NOS and CPS could stem from different questions that were asked and from different staffs coding the answers into standard occupation and industry categories.[7] Another difference is that CPS data are presented for all employed adults in a sampled household, whereas GSS-NOS data pertain to respondents and spouses but not other employed adults.

Table 2.4 compares the distribution of industry in the three samples, including tests of significance of the differences between them. Chi-square is the test statistic, but it is a test for goodness of fit, not the usual contingency table chi-square.[8] In our comparisons, the GSS and CPS are treated as criteria against which to test the NOS distribution, and the CPS serves as a criterion for the GSS. In addition to chi-square, values for the index of dissimilarity are presented. For goodness-of-fit tests, this index reports the percentage of cases that would need to change categories for the observed distribution in a sample to match exactly the criterion distribution.

As Table 2.4 shows, the three industry distributions are quite similar. The difference between the NOS and the GSS is not statistically significant, and the index of dissimilarity is 4.8%, indicating that only 4.8% of the NOS cases would have to change categories for the NOS percentage distribution

**Table 2.5**  Distribution of Occupation, by Source (in percentages)

|  | *Source* | | |
|---|---|---|---|
| *Occupation* | *National Organizations Study* | *General Social Survey* | *Current Population Survey*[a] |
| Executives | 12.0 | 13.6 | 12.9 |
| Professional specialty | 18.6 | 16.9 | 14.0 |
| Technicians | 3.2 | 3.5 | 3.3 |
| Sales | 11.2 | 11.2 | 12.0 |
| Administrative support | 15.4 | 14.8 | 15.9 |
| Service | 12.0 | 12.0 | 13.6 |
| Precision production | 11.7 | 12.3 | 11.3 |
| Operators | 7.0 | 7.0 | 6.5 |
| Transportation | 3.4 | 3.5 | 4.2 |
| Handlers | 3.6 | 3.1 | 3.8 |
| Farmers | 1.8 | 2.0 | 2.5 |
| Total | 99.9 | 99.9 | 100.0 |
| *N* | 725 | 1,420 | 230,792 |

NOTE: NOS versus GSS: $\chi^2$ (10 *df*) = 4.04, NS; index of dissimilarity = 2.9%; GSS versus CPS: $\chi^2$ (10 *df*) = 19.4, $p < .05$; index of dissimilarity = 5.3%; NOS versus CPS: $\chi^2$ (10 *df*) = 16.5, NS; index of dissimilarity = 5.6%.
a. February and March 1991; $N$ is weighted.

across industries to match exactly the GSS percentage distribution. Thus, even though the NOS sample contains only half of the cases that were sought, its industry distribution is virtually the same as that of the population from which it was drawn.

Although the GSS-CPS comparison is significant at the .01 level, the two distributions are quite similar, as the small index of dissimilarity (5.1%) indicates. With the CPS as criterion, the NOS distribution is even more discrepant, but not substantially so (index of dissimilarity = 7.5%). Some of the differences between the CPS and NOS-GSS may be traceable to differences between federal and private surveys. Whereas the response rate to the CPS is well over 90%, the response rate for the GSS is about 75%. Among the variables related to survey nonresponse are sex, age, race, education, and location of residence. Males, the young, blacks, the less educated, and residents of central cities tend to be less cooperative. These biases could account for some of the discrepancy between the CPS and the GSS, and therefore some of the discrepancy between the NOS and the CPS.

The distributions for occupation are even closer to each other than those for industry (see Table 2.5). Both comparisons involving the NOS are not significant. The NOS-GSS index of dissimilarity is 2.9% and the

**Table 2.6**  Distribution of Establishment Size, by Source (in percentages)

| | Source | |
| | National | General |
| Number of Employees | Organizations Study | Social Survey |
| --- | --- | --- |
| 1 to 9 | 23.8 | 26.3 |
| 10 to 49 | 26.7 | 26.0 |
| 50 to 99 | 13.2 | 12.4 |
| 100 to 499 | 19.4 | 19.6 |
| 500 to 999 | 5.9 | 5.0 |
| 1,000 to 1,999 | 3.4 | 3.3 |
| 2,000 and over | 7.6 | 7.4 |
| Total | 99.9 | 99.9 |
| N | 724 | 1,426 |

NOTE: NOS versus GSS: $\chi^2$ (6 $df$) = 3.2, NS; index of dissimilarity = 2.7%.

NOS-CPS index is 5.6%. The GSS-CPS comparison is significant at the .05 level, but the index of dissimilarity for that comparison is only 5.3%. With regard to an establishment's number of employees (Table 2.6), available data permit only the GSS-NOS comparison. The differences between the two distributions are small and not statistically significant.

We may therefore conclude that, at least with regard to industry, occupation, and number of employees, the NOS sample is in fact reasonably representative of the labor force that it was designed to represent.

## The Flexibility of a Survey-Based Design

The premise of this section is that it would be desirable to have a national database on organizations available to the organizations research community. This data set could consist of a core of structural variables that pertain to all organizations plus modules that address specific research interests. The sample of organizations included should be a probability sample and not a convenience sample as is common in organizations research (see Drabek et al. 1982).

The probability proportionate to size design discussed in this chapter is appropriate for creating such a database. It represents all types, ages, and sizes of work organizations.

A word about the size issue is appropriate here. As Table 2.6 showed, this design yields a substantial number of small organizations, despite the fact that it is PPS. Some organizations researchers seem to have little interest in investigating small organizations as separate research subjects. Many use size, however, as a variable in analyses of organization structures and outcomes. With the exception of the NOS, few, if any, samples of organizations contain the full distribution of organizational size. Either by accident or design, they underrepresent the smallest organizations. Truncated distributions underestimate relationships. A national database that represented small organizations would provide more accurate estimates of size effects. Because relatively small amounts of data would be needed for such organizations, the additional cost would be minimal, especially since much of the data could be collected in individual interviews with the self-employed (see Appendix 2.1).

Other organizations researchers maintain that small organizations are major sources of employment. A PPS sample would yield a relatively large, representative sample of small organizations. Reynolds (1994) is actively pursuing a study of organizational start-ups that would be based on a PPS sample drawn using a survey of the general population.

It would also be desirable for an organizations database to be a continuing panel study. The opportunity to study births, deaths, mergers, takeovers, and other outcomes is strong justification for this position. In addition, of course, trends and changes in structural characteristics and other remeasured core items could be investigated.

Of the several possible designs that could be used, one will be mentioned here as an example. A Year 1 survey of individuals would produce a sample of organizations on which data would be collected in Year 1. In Year 2, longitudinal data on these organizations would be collected. In Year 3, a new sample of individuals would be surveyed, thus producing a new sample of organizations. Both samples of organizations would be recontacted in Year 4. This is an ambitious design, only one of the many designs that could be used.

Variations on the basic design would permit many other elements of flexibility. For example, it would be possible to have multiple informants within each establishment. More than one establishment could be included, for those organizations that have more than one establishment. The database could be supplemented with archival and other data on the larger organization, as was done with county-level and industry data in the NOS. Multiple levels within establishments or organizations could be represented, as was done in an Illinois study by Spaeth (1989). That design is a good one for investigating inequality within organizations.

The basic sample could be supplemented with samples of additional organizations. For any given year, the *Fortune* 1,000 companies are a universe. If it were desirable to include more of these than appear in the basic sample, a supplemental sample of them could be added. The resulting sample would still be a probability one, as would that of any organizational type for which there was an available universe. In addition, part or all of the basic sample could be used as a comparison group against which results obtained with convenience samples could be evaluated.

Thus, the PPS sampling design used for the NOS not only offers a statistically valid way of representing all types, ages, and sizes of work organizations, but it also provides a flexible basis for extensions and supplements that would be desirable for constructing organizational databases.

## Conclusion

This chapter has shown that it is feasible to collect data on a national probability sample of work establishments. The response rate to the NOS survey of organizational informants was 64.5%, which is respectable by organizational research standards. The vast majority of respondents to the survey (GSS) of individuals provided information adequate to identify the establishments where they and their spouses worked. Distributions of key variables—industry, occupation, and number of employees—were comparable to those of the GSS, from which the sample of establishments was drawn, and to the CPS.

Nevertheless, our experience in carrying out this survey pointed to several areas where there was room for improvement and indicated how those improvements could be brought about. These are discussed in the appendix to this chapter. The survey of individuals and the data collection from organizations should be done by the same survey organization. Several coordination problems would be reduced or eliminated by doing so. The survey of individuals should be carried out by telephone. This would substantially improve the nominating information by allowing the use of a small, highly selected, highly trained, and closely supervised interviewing staff. In particular, it is likely that a refusal problem as serious as that encountered by the GSS face-to-face interviewers would be avoided. Finally, the response rate of organizational informants could be improved by paying those who were reluctant to cooperate.

As noted in the previous section, the procedures discussed in this chapter provide a statistically valid sample of all types, ages, and sizes of work organizations. They can be flexibly adapted: Many variations and extensions of the basic design can be envisioned, appropriate for different research needs. The remaining chapters in this book illustrate the variety of research topics that can be investigated using this flexible sampling method, as implemented for the NOS.

## Notes

1. The discrepancy of 4 cases probably arose because NORC necessarily transmitted "dirty" data to SRL but released clean data to the social science community.

2. It should be noted that several establishments had no name.

3. A usable nomination was one that permitted contact with the establishment, resulting in an SRL interview attempt or the discovery that an establishment was ineligible.

4. Most of the 34 cases for which names, addresses, and telephone numbers were missing were transmitted without the questionnaire pages containing that information. The two cases that produced usable nominations presumably represented establishments in the military and were therefore ineligible.

5. We spoke to a few persons several times, not with 58 different people.

6. There was one exception to this procedure. Several series of questions pertained to the occupation held by the GSS respondent or spouse. Informants were asked these series for all distinct occupations given by GSS nominators.

7. The GSS industry question, "What kind of place do you work for?" was embedded in a series of questions on occupation. The CPS question, "What kind of business or industry is this? *(For example, TV and radio mfg., retail shoe store, State Labor Dept., farm)*" (italics in original; U.S. Bureau of the Census 1976), was embedded in a series of questions that asked for the name of the employer and occupation.

8. A goodness-of-fit test compares the distribution observed in a sample with the distribution of a criterion that can be theoretically based or based on a population (Bohrnstedt and Knoke 1988, pp. 124-6). Degrees of freedom are computed as one less than the number of categories in the marginal distribution, not as the product of the number of rows minus one times the number of columns minus one. In our case, we use the criterion distributions from CPS and GSS to estimate proportions for assessing the goodness of fit of the NOS; similarly, expected proportions for assessing the goodness of fit of the GSS are based on the CPS criterion.

# APPENDIX 2.1

## Improving Data Collection Procedures

Although data collection for the NOS was quite successful by the standards of organizations research, there is ample room for improvement. The experience of implementing the PPS design reported in Chapter 2 provides a basis for proposing changes in the procedures used for collecting nominations and those used for actually collecting data from sampled organizations.

For purposes of this discussion, we are assuming that the basic two-stage design used for the NOS would be followed—collecting data on randomly sampled individuals and nominations of employers from them to generate a sample for gathering data on organizations.

The new steps recommended can be summarized as follows: Collect data on individuals by telephone, use the same agency to collect data on individuals and establishments, screen for employed persons, collect nominations of employers for respondents only, and interview the self-employed regarding their establishments as part of the household survey. The one major step advocated for collecting data from establishments is to pay nonrespondents to answer self-administered questionnaires.

### Collect Data on Individuals by Telephone

Collecting data by telephone costs substantially less than collecting the same data face-to-face. This is largely because interviewers need not travel to and from each assignment and need not be paid to do so. If a telephone attempt is unsuccessful, it is easy to try another one. Another advantage of a random-digit-dialing telephone design would be a reduction in the number of duplicate nominations of establishments. One NORC primary sampling unit produced eight persons who worked for the same employer. This was a result of the clustering associated with a multistage area probability sample. A sampling design for a telephone survey would not have this degree of clustering.

In addition, telephone interviews are conducted from a central location by a relatively small number of interviewers. The multistage area probability sampling design of the GSS required approximately 165 interviewers to collect data from respondents in about 1,500 households. A national telephone survey of the same size would use about 20 interviewers. Together with the smaller number of interviewers, the central location for telephone interviewing has several advantages. Training can be much more concentrated and intense. Monitoring of an interview can take place during that interview, and correction of interviewing problems will be virtually instantaneous. At times the supervisor can be called on to provide support for the interviewer. Incomplete or ambiguous information can be corrected immediately. Identification and replacement of ineffective interviewers can be faster and more effective.

Conducting a study using a small number of interviewers can make substantial contributions to data quality, especially by reducing refusals to questions asking for information about employers. As Table 2.3 showed, the refusal rate to the question on telephone number was 12%. Of the 165 NORC interviewers, 68 conducted five or more GSS interviews. Of these, 38 had no refusals on the items about employers. Adequate selection of interviewers is therefore likely to reduce substantially the number of refusals to answer the nominating questions.

Furthermore, the identity of the interviewer is a far stronger predictor of such refusals than are characteristics of the respondent. Appendix Table 2.1 shows the correlations between selected variables and refusal to answer at least one (usually all three) of the nominating questions. The table, which is presented in descending order of correlations, contains several groups of variables. The first is the identity of the interviewer. Each GSS interviewer was assigned her own identification number, and this is the variable presented. All interviewers who had conducted five or more interviews were treated separately; those who had conducted four or fewer were combined into one group. The second variable is refusing to answer the GSS question on family income, which is one of the more sensitive questions in the GSS. The next group of questions pertains to respondents' reports of their attitudes toward or experiences at their jobs. The last group contains a mixture of items of which some (e.g., sex, race, education, occupation, and income) are related to refusing to be interviewed. They are, however, basically unrelated to refusing to answer the nominating questions. In addition, the table indicates what kind of correlation was computed for each variable.

As Appendix Table 2.1 shows, the strongest correlate of refusing to provide nominating information was the identity of the interviewer, with an adjusted correlation of .34.[1] Refusing to answer the family income question was also strongly related to refusing to provide nominating information, with a value of .26. Income refusals are also strongly related to interviewer identity. All of the other correlations pertain to various characteristics of respondents. Although several are statistically significant, all are less than .1. None of the usual correlates of refusing to be interviewed—education, income, race, occupation, gender, and age—is statistically associated with refusal to nominate employers.[2]

Thus, the identity of interviewers was an important determinant of refusing to provide nominating information, whereas characteristics of

**TABLE 2.1A**  Correlations Between Refusing to Provide Information Identifying
Establishments and Selected Variables

| Variable | Correlation | Value |
|---|---|---|
| Interviewer identity | $\eta$ | .341*** (adjusted) |
| Refused family income question | $\Phi$ | .260*** |
| First job with organization | $\Phi$ | .097*** |
| Management-worker relations are not "bad" | $\Phi$ | .082** |
| Feel little loyalty (*strongly agree*) | $\Phi$ | .078** |
| People notice when I do my job well (*agree*) | $\Phi$ | .071** |
| Self-employed | $\Phi$ | .059* |
| Education (stages) | $\eta$ | .059 |
| Family income | $r$ | .058 |
| Management cares only about profits (*strongly agree-strongly disagree*) | $\eta$ | .051 |
| R or spouse belongs to union | $\Phi$ | .041 |
| Race (black) | $\Phi$ | .041 |
| I have a lot to say about my job (*strongly agree-strongly disagree*) | $\eta$ | .035 |
| Occupational prestige | $r$ | .033 |
| Gender (female) | $\Phi$ | .031 |
| Age | $r$ | .030 |
| R or spouse has no supervisor | $\Phi$ | .029 |
| R or spouse is supervisor | $\Phi$ | .008 |
| Ever unemployed in last 10 years | $\Phi$ | .008 |

*$p < .05$; **$p < .01$; ***$p < .001$.

respondents were not. Thirty-eight GSS interviewers had no refusals to these questions. If the survey of individuals were to be done by telephone, about half this number of interviewers would be required. It seems likely that the refusal to provide nominating information would be a minor problem with a well-conducted telephone interview. It is possible that the seemingly intractable problem presented by this kind of refusal would be solved by doing the survey of individuals by telephone.

## Use the Same Agency to Collect Data on Individuals and Establishments

A major advantage of having the same agency collect the data from individuals and from establishments would be better coordination between the stages of collecting nominations and surveying establishments. At times, the liaison between NORC and SRL involved considerable delays, both in transmitting nominating data in the first place and in clarifying ambiguities in that information as they arose. Because of confidentiality issues, it was not possible for NORC to identify GSS respondents to SRL, and it was, therefore, not possible to recontact nominators to resolve problems of inadequate information. A single agency would not have had this problem.

Furthermore, in a national face-to-face study, there are lags between the time of the interview, the time that the questionnaire arrives in the central office, and the time that it takes for the central office to communicate with the interviewer in the field. None of these possible time lags need occur with telephone interviewing. Interviewers or supervisors can take action to correct problems as they arise.

## Screen for Employed Persons

Screening for employed persons would contribute to the efficiency of field procedures. Nearly 40% of the GSS respondents were not employed. Although many of these had employed spouses, a design that collected a nomination from every respondent would have been more productive. The work organizations module of the 1991 GSS pertained to respondents but not spouses. The individual data for spouses that could be matched to NOS data on spouses' employers, therefore, were not complete. Finally, the magnitude of the screening task itself is not great; most sampled households have at least one employed person.

## Collect Nominations on Respondents Only

Some of the reasons for collecting nominations on respondents only have just been mentioned. Parallel data on organizations and individuals would be complete. In addition, because respondents are somewhat better informants on themselves than on their spouses (as shown in Tables 2.1 through 2.3), there would be some increase in the efficiency of data collection. There would also be some decrease in the incidence of duplicate employers.

## Interview the Self-Employed Regarding Their Establishments as Part of the Survey of Individuals

Self-employed persons are likely to be about 15% of a survey of the labor force. As Appendix Table 2.1 showed, they were slightly more likely than other respondents to refuse to provide nominating information. If the minimal organizational data required of such people were collected during the individual interview, the situation would be transformed from one in which a request for a new interview carries with it the opportunity to refuse to one in which organization questions flow naturally from the individual ones. The data collection problem would then be one of break-offs rather than refusals. Break-offs are rare in survey interviewing. This step, then, could help to raise the establishment-level response rate.

### Improving Establishment Data Collection

As Figure 2.2 showed, 41% of the establishment data collection attempts were conducted by mail with self-administered questionnaires. Of these, 71% were refusals or still pending at the end of the field period despite extensive follow-up efforts. Following up on these informants required considerable time, effort, and money. Whether they ultimately refused or did not respond, most of these persons were apologetic about their failure to return a questionnaire. This implies that it would be useful to attempt to motivate them to respond.

An obvious device in these circumstances is to offer to pay for a completed questionnaire. Doing so could have several advantages. It would increase the return of completed questionnaires, and even a modest increase would make the overall completion rate more respectable. It would probably substantially shorten the data collection period, which would make the organization data more current. And, as long as this incentive was offered only to those who seemed reluctant to return mailed questionnaires, it would not be costly.

## Notes

1. Because the correlation ratio ($\eta$) produces a coefficient that is equivalent to that produced by a dummy variable regression, this coefficient is adjusted by the 68 degrees of freedom that would have been required for such a regression. The unadjusted value was .42.

2. One major correlate of refusing to be interviewed was omitted from this data set—location of residence. Central city residents are more likely to refuse to be interviewed than are persons living elsewhere; however, it was possible to estimate the relationship between refusing the family income question and residential location for all GSS respondents. It was not statistically significant.

# 3

# American Organizations and Their Environments

*A Descriptive Overview*

PETER V. MARSDEN
CYNTHIA R. COOK
DAVID KNOKE

This chapter gives a general description of the establishments included in the National Organizations Study, concentrating on variables that describe the composition and settings of these workplaces. The beginning of the chapter demonstrates that the organizations included in the NOS reflect the concentration of the U.S. economy in service-producing activities and industries. Next, we review demographic features—both distributions within establishments and establishment-level demographic variables—and examine some gross indicators of occupational composition. The closing part of the chapter discusses some indicators and scales that tap features of the

technical and institutional settings in which the NOS establishments operate. Many of the succeeding chapters in this book make use of the variables
and multiple-item indices that we review here.

The multiplicity design of the NOS sample, reviewed in the preceding
chapter, permits a researcher to examine the data using two alternative
perspectives. If the NOS sample is not weighted, statistics will describe the
typical work settings to which employees in the U.S. labor force are
exposed; each worker is given an equal weight. Because the General Social
Survey that served as the sampling frame for the NOS selected eligible
*individuals* with equal probability, establishments that employ many people have proportionately higher chances of being included in the NOS.
Consequently, descriptive statistics for the unweighted sample, such as the
mean number of departments or the average percentage of women employees, will reflect this skew toward larger establishments and will be descriptive of employment settings experienced by the labor force. In contrast, if
observations in the NOS sample are weighted inversely proportional to the
number of employees in an establishment, statistics will represent the
population of U.S. establishments, as if each *establishment* has an equal
probability of inclusion. When the sample is weighted, smaller organizations become more numerous. Hence, statistics for the weighted sample
describe attributes of the typical establishment. If a measure is moderately
to highly correlated with organizational size (as measured by the number
of employees), then weighted and unweighted statistics will take markedly
different values.

For the descriptive purposes of this chapter, we often report percentages and measures of central tendency and variation in both weighted and
unweighted form.[1] We shall see that weighting the sample so that it reflects
the typical establishment rather than the experience of the typical employee
often makes a dramatic difference in descriptive statistics (see, for example, Table 3.1), which in turn indicates that there are substantial differences
between large and small organizations for many of the measures examined.

## Activity, Auspices, and Industry

We begin by examining the sectoral distributions of the 688 distinct
NOS establishments. We classified the auspices under which they operate
into the conventional three sectors: (a) public, (b) nonprofit, and (c) private,
for-profit. The weighted and unweighted sector distributions are displayed

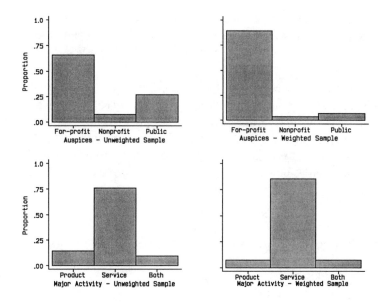

**Figure 3.1.** Auspices and Major Activity

in the upper part of Figure 3.1. Private-sector establishments constitute 66% of the unweighted sample; since such establishments tend to be smaller than public (27% of the unweighted sample) or nonprofit units (7%), use of the multiplicity sampling weights—which give greater weight to smaller organizations—leads us to estimate that nearly 90% of U.S. workplaces are private, profit-oriented ones.

We asked informants for each establishment whether the work done there was concerned primarily with producing a product or delivering a service. The unweighted figures illustrate the numerical dominance of service-providing units: More than three quarters of the sampled organizations provide services, an additional 9% volunteered that they produce both products and services, and only 14% are working exclusively on products (see also the graphs in the lower part of Figure 3.1). In that the latter establishments tend to be larger, the service-sector majority appears even greater when the observations are weighted inversely proportional to the number of employees.

The product-producing organizations are concentrated in the private sector; unweighted figures show that 98% of the product-producing establishments are private, for-profit, as are nearly 90% of the workplaces that produce both products and services. Slightly more than half of the service-sector establishments have private auspices; virtually all the public-sector and nonprofit workplaces produce services, either exclusively or together with products.

Service-sector concentration is also clear from the informant reports of the main product or service produced. Establishments in manufacturing industries make up 17% of the unweighted sample but constitute just 7% after weights are applied. Extractive industries (mining, forestry) and agriculture together account for less than 3% of the establishments. The broad bulk of NOS workplaces are in service industries, including the following:

> Construction (15% of the weighted sample)
> Infrastructural activities such as transportation, communications, and utilities
> (5%)
> Trade (14%)
> Professional services (19%)
> Finance, insurance and real estate (10%)
> Other services, including personal services (25%)
> Public administration (4%)

## Demography and Occupational Composition

Two types of demographic considerations apply to the study of organizations. First, "global" demographic indicators describe the establishment as a whole; here, we examine measures of size or scale and establishment age. Second, "compositional" variables reflect the division of personnel into different sociodemographic and occupational categories. Below, we present data on the gender and minority composition of the workforces in the NOS establishments (see Chapter 14 for a much more detailed discussion of gender composition). As well, we look at within-workplace occupational distributions, distinguishing between "core" employees and managerial/administrative workers.

### Establishment Size and Age

Kimberly (1976) wrote an insightful essay on the measurement of the size of organizations. He observed that size can be measured in different

**Table 3.1**  Weighted and Unweighted Establishment Size Distributions (full-time employees; $N = 688$)

| Establishment Size | Percentages | |
| --- | --- | --- |
| | Unweighted | Weighted |
| 1-9 | 25.6 | 87.5 |
| 10-49 | 23.4 | 8.4 |
| 50-99 | 12.8 | 1.3 |
| 100-499 | 18.3 | 0.8 |
| 500-999 | 6.1 | 0.1 |
| 1,000-1,999 | 5.8 | 0.0 |
| 2,000+ | 8.2 | 2.0 |
| Total | 100.2[a] | 100.1[a] |

a. Totals differ from 100.0% due to rounding.

ways, that these different measures need not be closely associated, and that the appropriate way to measure size depends on the purpose of a given study.

NOS informants provided data on three indicators of size: (a) the number of full-time employees, (b) the number of part-time employees, and (c) the approximate total annual operating budget. Unweighted means show that the typical U.S. employee works in an establishment with 599 full-time workers ($SD = 2395$) and 72 part-time workers ($SD = 406$); the respective median numbers are 50 full-time and 2 part-time employees. The mean annual operating budget is $75 million; the median, $3 million.

The differences between the means and medians show that all three of these size indicators have quite substantial positive skews, as is typical for organizational size distributions (see Table 3.1 for a demonstration of this point for full-time employees). Most units are relatively small, and the means reflect the influence of the few very large establishments in the sample. This skew is usually reduced by using a natural log transformation of the size measures in analyses. The three log-transformed size indicators are substantially but imperfectly associated with one another; using the unweighted data, the correlation between full-time employees and budget is 0.88, whereas the (log) size of the part-time workforce is correlated with both of the other measures at a level of 0.46. Since many of the substantive concerns of later chapters have to do with practices and policies for managing personnel, a measure based on the number of employees is usually taken as the indicator of size.

When the sample is weighted to reflect the size of a typical establishment rather than the experience of a typical worker, the size distributions change

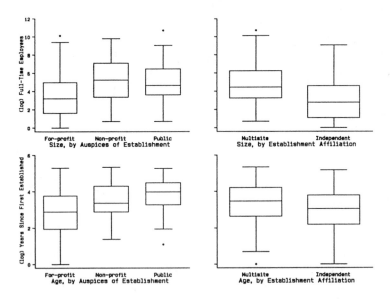

**Figure 3.2.** Boxplots of Size and Age Distributions (Unweighted NOS Sample)

markedly (contrast the columns in Table 3.1). The typical establishment is very small, with about seven full-time workers and just over one part-time employee, and an annual budget of $1.6 million.

The "boxplots" in the upper left of Figure 3.2 show that public and nonprofit establishments tend to be larger than for-profit ones. The line in the middle of the box in each plot indicates the median value of the size distribution for the unweighted NOS sample; so, for example, 50% of the for-profit workplaces have a log number of full-time employees that exceeds 3.2, or a number of full-time employees greater than exp(3.2) = 25. The box in each plot encloses the middle 50% of the establishments in a given category; in the for-profit sector, the box encloses values between 1.6 and 5 log employees (or about 5 and 150 full-time employees). Consequently, 25% of for-profit establishments are smaller than size 5, and 25% have more than 150 full-time workers.[2] We thus observe, even in the unweighted data, the preponderance of small establishments highlighted by Granovetter (1984). Similar plots for the weighted data set would accentuate the concentration of small workplaces within the size distribution (see Table 3.1).

Nonprofit establishments are much larger than for-profit ones. People employed by nonprofit establishments work in places that have a median log number of full-time employees equal to 5.25, or a median full-time size of about exp(5.25) = 190. Thus, the median nonprofit establishment has more full-time personnel than do 75% of for-profit workplaces. Public sector establishments, with a median of 105 full-time workers, are somewhat smaller than nonprofit workplaces, but appreciably larger than for-profit concerns.

Some establishments are subunits—branches or subsidiaries—of larger, multisite organizations. In the unweighted NOS sample, more than half (55%) of the establishments are affiliated with a larger organization in some fashion. Of these, over a third (36.8%) are schools, campuses, and governmental units within multiorganizational complexes. More than half (55.4%) are wholly owned subsidiaries or branch facilities. About 6% of the affiliated establishments are locally owned franchise units.

Establishments that are part of a larger organization tend to be bigger themselves, as shown by the pair of boxplots at the upper right of Figure 3.2. Independent workplaces are mainly small; half of those in the unweighted sample have 15 or fewer full-time personnel (that is, a log number of full-time employees smaller than 2.75). More than five times as many people (85) are employed on a full-time basis in the median establishment that is part of a larger organization. Because of the skew in the size distribution (see Table 3.1), the *mean* affiliated establishment in the unweighted NOS has a full-time contingent numbering 852.

The larger organizations that include these establishments are very large indeed. In the unweighted sample, they have a median size of 3,750 full-time and part-time employees and a mean of nearly 40,000!

We measured organizational age by asking informants to give the year in which their organization was "first established" and subtracting the response from 1991, the year in which the survey was conducted.[3] In the unweighted data set, the establishments surveyed range in age from 1 to 205 years, with a mean of 39 and a standard deviation of 38; the distribution is skewed, however, including many more younger establishments than older ones. Younger organizations tend to be smaller; mean establishment age is 20 (*SD* = 32) when multiplicity weights are used.

The boxplots in the bottom half of Figure 3.2 display age differences (on a logarithmic scale) by sector and by whether an establishment is affiliated with a larger organization. Public-sector establishments tend to be the oldest. They have a median age of over 53 (that is, exp[3.98]) in the unweighted NOS sample, and less than 25% of them are younger than 25 (=exp[3.2]). Nonprofit workplaces are younger, with a median age since first establishment of nearly 30 (=exp [3.37]) years. Fewer than half of the for-profit workplaces have been operating for as long as 20 years. In the bottom right of Figure 3.2, we observe that establishments that are affiliated with larger organizations tend to be older than independent workplaces.

### Occupational Composition of Workforce

Many of the substantive topics investigated in the NOS concern policies and practices that may differ substantially from one occupation to another within a workplace. For this reason, it was necessary to repeat many sequences of questions for different occupations. Informants were asked about a "core" occupation—the occupation that NOS respondents considered to be most directly involved with producing the establishment's main good or service. Respondents were first asked, "What is the product produced or service provided here?" They were then asked, "What is the job title for the employees who are most directly involved with [the product or service described]?" If there was more than one such occupation, the core occupation was defined as the one with most employees.

The sequence of questions leading to the identification of core occupations identified a position that is central to the workflow of the establishment. We illustrate this for workplaces in selected categories of the 1980 Standard Industrial Classification (SIC; Davis and Smith 1994, pp. 901-907). The largest number of establishments in any single SIC category was found in elementary and secondary schools (SIC 842), of which the NOS sampled 64. In 58 (91%) of these, the core occupation was coded as a teacher (counselors, records clerks, bus drivers, and child care workers were among the exceptions). Likewise, some group of teachers was designated as the core occupation in 12 of the 14 colleges and universities (SIC 850) in the NOS, whereas nurses or orderlies/nursing aides were the core occupation in all but one out of 30 hospitals (SIC 831; the one exception was a social worker).

There was more variety in the definition of the core occupation in other industries, but the range of occupations identified appears quite reasonable. The core occupations in eating and drinking places (SIC 641), of which the NOS sampled 22, were spread across cashiers (U.S. Census occupation code 276), waiters and waitresses (code 435), cooks (code 436), food counter and fountain workers (code 438) and miscellaneous food preparation occupations (code 444), among others. In the 35 establishments in the construction (SIC 60) industry, the core occupation is usually from one of the skilled trades, but in six cases it is an engineer, and in five establishments it is a manager or administrator. In heterogeneous industrial groupings, the distribution of core occupations is sometimes highly diverse; there are 10 different core occupations among the 11 NOS establishments in business services (SIC 742), for example.

The NOS informants were also queried about the occupation of the General Social Survey (GSS) respondent who had nominated the respondent for the NOS (see Chapter 2); these were also coded using U.S. Census occupational categories and NORC prestige scores.[4] To obtain some data on supervisory work, informants were also asked for information about "managers and other administrators"; no specific job title, however, was identified for the managerial occupations.

In some establishments, there was overlap among the core, GSS, and managerial occupations. Slightly fewer than half (314, or 46%) of NOS informants reported about three distinct occupations. For nearly the same number (43%) of the establishments, two of the three occupations were distinct. In 11% of the cases, the NOS obtained data about only one occupation.

We obtained some basic data on the numbers of employees in these different occupations. We focus here on the core and managerial ones for purposes of describing the occupational composition of establishments. Full-time and part-time core employees constitute about 52% ($SD = 40\%$) of the workforce of the typical establishment (unweighted) in the NOS. The (unweighted) mean percentage of managers or administrators in an establishment is 21%, with a standard deviation of 26%; this is positively skewed by a number of small establishments with high proportions of managers, so the median managerial percentage is 11%.

### Demographic Composition of Workforce

NOS informants were also asked to estimate the percentages of women and whites among the employees in their workplaces. These compositional questions were repeated for certain subcategories of employees.

Unweighted sample figures indicate that in the median establishment, women constitute half of the full-time workers with whom a typical employee works. There is considerable variation (the standard deviation is 32% around a mean percentage women of 49%). According to NOS informants, women constitute an even larger fraction (75% in the median

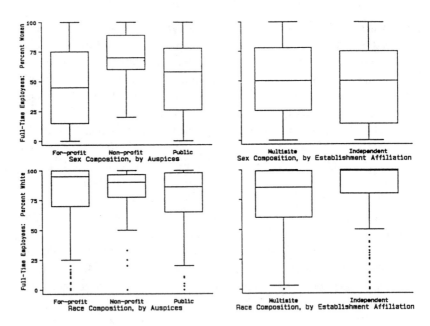

**Figure 3.3.** Boxplots of Sex and Racial Composition (Unweighted NOS Sample)

establishment) of part-time employees. The estimated percentages of women are slightly lower for the weighted sample.

As shown by the boxplots in Figure 3.3, the percentages of women among full-time employees are higher than the overall median in the public sector (58%) and, especially, in the nonprofit sector (70%). In the private sector, women constitute, on average, 45% of the full-time employees. Larger percentages of women are found among the full-time workforces of service-producing establishments (in which the median workplace has 57% women) than in establishments making only products (a median of 32.5% women). There is little difference in sex composition between independent establishments and those that are within larger organizations (Figure 3.3).

According to our informants, women fill a median of 30% and a mean of 37% of the full-time and part-time managerial or administrative positions in a typical establishment and 45% of the core occupational roles. Both of these percentages are less than the overall percentages of women among full-time and part-time employees, so many women evidently are in positions other than core and managerial ones. Thus the NOS data reflect previously documented tendencies (e.g., Reskin and Roos 1990) for men and women to be concentrated in different occupations within a workplace (see Chapter 14 for a more detailed consideration of gender segregation in NOS establishments).

Less extensive data were obtained on the racial composition of these establishments. The unweighted data indicate that full-time employees are 90% white in the median establishment in which a typical employee works, and more than a third (34%) of the unweighted sample establishments have *only* whites among their full-time workers. Because there are also a few establishments that are exclusively nonwhite (2% of the sample), the mean percentage white is 80% ($SD = 26\%$). Among part-time employees the mean percentage of whites is not appreciably smaller, 78% ($SD = 30\%$, median = 92%). When the data are weighted to reflect the distribution of establishments rather than employee settings, the mean percentages of whites are higher, 88% among full-time and 87% among part-time employees; hence, nonwhites tend to be concentrated within larger workplaces. We did not ask informants for occupation-specific estimates of the percentage of whites.

Sectoral differences in majority/minority composition are less extensive than gender differences, as shown in the lower left of Figure 3.3. (The circles at the bottom of each boxplot highlight "outlier" establishments with very low percentages of whites; see Note 2.) The median percentage of whites in the public sector (86%) is only slightly less than that in the nonprofit (90%) and private sectors (95%). There are somewhat more whites (a median of 93%) in the workforces of service-producing establishments than in those that are exclusively product oriented (82%). Nonwhite composition is appreciably higher in establishments that are affiliated with larger organizations; here, the median percentage of whites is 85. In typically smaller independent workplaces, the median workplace is composed almost entirely (99%) of white employees.

## Environmental Settings

The dominant movement in organizational analysis during the past two or three decades has been from theoretical models concerned with the internal structure and dynamics of organizations toward those that emphasize features of the contexts or environments in which organizations are situated (Aldrich and Marsden 1988; Scott 1992). Environments, in turn, may be conceived and measured in a wide variety of ways; a conceptual distinction between technical and institutional aspects (Scott 1983) has proved important and useful in recent theorizing and helps to organize a number of more specific measures. In this section, we review some of the NOS indicators and scales that are available to measure features of the environments of the sampled establishments.

### Technical Aspects

Technical aspects of environments include variables that refer to Dill's (1958) notion of the "task environment": the set of actors directly relevant to workflows involved in the attainment of an organization's purposes. These flows involve the acquisition of supplies and personnel, as well as the disposition of products or output. In addition, actors to which a focal organization is not directly connected, such as competitors, constitute important features of a task environment.

Many different features of task environments can be measured. A very coarse indicator of environmental setting is the industry in which an establishment is active—that is, its product or service market. Various industry-level contextual variables coded from U.S. Census sources (at the 2-digit SIC level) are included in the NOS database.

Some such industry-level indicators are interpretable as measures of environmental "munificence" (Staw and Szwajkowski 1975). Indices of asset concentration are one example; they reflect the degree to which the industry setting is dominated by large firms. The median (unweighted) NOS workplace operates in an industry in which just over 40% of the assets are owned by firms having more than $250 million in assets. Wealth is much more evenly distributed in other industries—more than 5% of NOS establishments face environments in which such large firms own 25% or less of the assets. At the other extreme, 5% of the unweighted sample establishments are in settings where large-asset firms control 93% or more of industry assets; there, competition is principally among very large concerns.

Published data on the geographic areas in which establishments lie were also coded and appended to the NOS survey data. Among these is an indicator of the unemployment rate in the civilian labor force (available for year 1986), which can be used to measure the looseness or tightness of the local labor market. The median unemployment rate in the areas containing a NOS establishment was 6.7%. About 25% of the establishments confronted relatively tight labor markets, with unemployment rates of 5% or less, but the local unemployment rate was above 10% for more than 10% of the establishments.

The geographic scope of the product/service market is another pertinent aspect of an establishment's environmental setting. For profit-oriented establishments in the NOS, unweighted figures indicate that nearly 55% of employees work in places for which the "main market area" lies within a city, county, or metropolitan area. Only about a fifth of these establishments have markets of national scope, and less than 5% serve a market beyond the United States. Orientation toward local markets is even more pronounced in the weighted figures for profit-oriented establishments, and for the "main areas served" by nonprofit and government organizations.

Theorists have given special attention to the extent to which an organization is dependent on, rather than autonomous from, the actors in its surroundings, and to the level of uncertainty that environmental elements pose. There are several facets, in turn, of both dependence and uncertainty (Aldrich 1979, Chapter 5; Scott 1992, pp. 134-5).

The NOS included several survey questions in an effort to tap aspects of dependence and uncertainty. One set of items asked about the informant's views as to whether certain issues would be "problems" for the establishment during the short-term (3-year) future. Descriptive statistics for these items appear in Table 3.2.

The problems listed in Table 3.2 are environmental ones, broadly conceived. Several refer to issues involving the relation of the establishment to its labor market: recruitment and retention of qualified workers, maintaining competitiveness in compensation/benefits, and relations with organized labor. Other items refer, instead, to competitiveness in the development and production of new products and services. Environments in which these issues are problematic are more challenging, and we infer that establishments with many perceived problems are subject to both greater uncertainty and increased dependence.

We see from the unweighted figures in Table 3.2 that labor market problems and product problems are regarded as "major" or "minor" by the informants in about half of the establishments sampled. Government regulation and the improvement of employee compensation are especially common challenges—about two thirds of employees work in places where these are expected to be problematic. Only about a third of the informants for the unweighted sample of workplaces expects that relations with unions will be troublesome.

**Table 3.2** Perceived Problems Items[a]

| | Percentage of Establishments Claiming Item Is a Major or Minor Problem | | |
| | Unweighted | Weighted | N |
|---|---|---|---|
| Hiring enough qualified workers | 58.4 | 31.2 | 654 |
| Retaining qualified employees | 50.8 | 25.3 | 650 |
| Improving compensation/benefits | 64.8 | 39.4 | 633 |
| Improving product/service quality | 49.8 | 31.6 | 665 |
| Developing new products/services | 50.4 | 32.6 | 611 |
| Increasing productivity | 56.1 | 37.1 | 658 |
| Relations with unions | 34.1 | 11.2 | 593 |
| Government regulations | 66.1 | 41.6 | 664 |
| Perceived problems scale[b] | | | |
|   Mean | 1.69 | 1.38 | 659 |
|   Standard deviation | 0.48 | 0.39 | |
|   Median | 1.63 | 1.25 | |
|   Interquartile range | 0.75 | 0.63 | |
|   Cronbach's $\alpha$ | 0.84 | | |
| Employee problems scale[c] | | | |
|   Mean | 1.74 | 1.41 | 659 |
|   Standard deviation | 0.58 | 0.52 | |
|   Median | 1.67 | 1.00 | |
|   Interquartile range | 0.67 | 1.00 | |
|   Cronbach's $\alpha$ | 0.74 | | |
| Product problems scale[d] | | | |
|   Mean | 1.63 | 1.37 | 672 |
|   Standard deviation | 0.60 | 0.48 | |
|   Median | 1.67 | 1.00 | |
|   Interquartile range | 1.00 | 0.67 | |
|   Cronbach's $\alpha$ | 0.87 | | |

a. The survey question asked was, Over the next *3 years,* how big a problem will each of the following be for (establishment)? What about . . .? "Don't know" responses are excluded from percentage reported.
b. Mean of all eight variables; coded as follows: "major problem" (3), "minor problem" (2), "not a problem" (1). For construction of the scale, values for "don't know" responses were imputed if the respondent answered five or more of the other items.
c. Mean of the first three items; see note b.
d. Mean of the fourth, fifth and sixth items; see note b.

Establishments encountering one type of problem tend to encounter others as well: A scale based on all of the items in Table 3.2 has high reliability ($\alpha = 0.84$).[5] We constructed subscales reflecting the extent to which labor markets ($\alpha = 0.74$) and product/service markets ($\alpha = 0.87$) were seen as problematic.

We also asked informants to assess the competitiveness of their product/service markets directly: They rated the level of competition in the establishment's main market or service area from "none" to "a great deal." More than half of the informants (unweighted) say that they face a "great deal" of competition; in general, perceived competition is greater among establishments facing markets of national or international scope. For-profit informants say that their domains are more competitive than those in nonprofit and public establishments.

To measure aspects of environmental uncertainty and complexity, the NOS asked informants to respond to several items adapted from scales used in Knoke's (1990) study of collective action associations. Table 3.3 reports the items and the scales built from them.

Large percentages of the informants agree that their establishments face complex and uncertain environments, in that cooperation with other organizations is required (83% of the unweighted sample), necessary techniques and skills are subject to rapid change (66%), and long-range planning is difficult (55%). The political environment is viewed as favorable by only about a third of the sample, and a similar fraction notes that its interorganizational relations are marked by conflict. In contrast to many of the other items (and scales) reviewed in this chapter, the items measuring complexity and uncertainty differ little between the unweighted and weighted samples.

We built one scale based on all seven items in Table 3.3 and two subscales focusing on aspects of complexity and uncertainty. Unlike the remaining indexes presented here, these scales have relatively low and problematic reliability. The reliability estimates in this heterogeneous sample of organizations are appreciably smaller than those for Knoke's associations.

### Institutional Aspects

Since the publication of Meyer and Rowan's (1977) classic essay, organizational sociology has given renewed attention to the social and cultural interdependence of organizations (e.g., Meyer and Scott 1983; Powell and DiMaggio 1991). The central insight of this "institutional" perspective is that organizational environments are more than sources of information and pools of resources that can facilitate or impede the attainment of goals. Both resource acquisition and goal attainment require that an organization's activity patterns be viewed as legitimate, and those institutional actors that can convey or withhold legitimacy are essential features of environments. Such actors are not necessarily involved in

**Table 3.3**  Complexity/Uncertainty Items[a]

| Item | Percentage of Establishments Agreeing With Item | | |
| | Unweighted | Weighted | N |
|---|---|---|---|
| Techniques, skills, and information changing rapidly | 66.4 | 49.7 | 685 |
| Must cooperate with other organizations | 83.2 | 60.2 | 684 |
| Relations with other organizations conflictual | 37.8 | 23.6 | 675 |
| Establishment takes few risks | 71.6 | 78.2 | 666 |
| Establishment reacts to outside pressures | 26.7 | 25.3 | 667 |
| Long-range planning difficult | 55.0 | 54.5 | 676 |
| Political climate is favorable | 37.8 | 32.8 | 633 |
| Environmental scale[b] | | | |
| Mean | 0.53 | 0.62 | 681 |
| Standard deviation | 0.21 | 0.22 | |
| Median | 0.57 | 0.57 | |
| Interquartile range | 0.29 | 0.43 | |
| Cronbach's $\alpha$ | 0.41 | | |
| Complexity scale[c] | | | |
| Mean | 0.46 | 0.61 | 681 |
| Standard deviation | 0.27 | 0.27 | |
| Median | 0.50 | 0.50 | |
| Interquartile range | 0.50 | 0.25 | |
| Cronbach's $\alpha$ | 0.42 | | |
| Uncertainty scale[d] | | | |
| Mean | 0.59 | 0.60 | 681 |
| Standard deviation | 0.36 | 0.38 | |
| Median | 0.50 | 0.50 | |
| Interquartile range | 0.50 | 0.50 | |
| Cronbach's $\alpha$ | 0.33 | | |

a. The survey questions asked were dichotomous agree/disagree items. Exact item wordings differ slightly from those given above.
b. Mean of all seven variables; the "few risks" item was reverse-coded. For construction of the scale, values for "don't know" responses were imputed using logistic regression, if the respondent answered four or more of the other environmental items.
c. Mean of the first four items; see note b.
d. Mean of the fifth and sixth items; see note b.

workflows, but they are sources of definite coercive or normative constraints on organizational behavior (DiMaggio and Powell 1983).

Many organizational measures that we have already discussed may be interpreted in institutional terms; for example, size is one indicator of visibility and thus of the likelihood that an organization will be noticed by institutional actors. Likewise, organizations in the public sector are thought

**Table 3.4** Institutionalization Items[a]

| Item | Percentage | | N |
| | Unweighted | Weighted | |
|---|---|---|---|
| Subject to periodic review by an outside accreditation/ licensing organization | 57.0 | 34.3 | 681 |
| Belongs to association of like organizations | 69.3 | 43.5 | 680 |
| Pays very much attention to the practices of other organizations | 38.0 | 21.0 | 681 |
| Regulated very much or almost completely by government agencies | 49.3 | 24.6 | 678 |
| Institutionalization scale[b] | | | |
| Mean | 3.47 | 2.62 | 683 |
| Standard deviation | 1.08 | 1.11 | |
| Median | 3.75 | 2.50 | |
| Interquartile range | 1.75 | 2.00 | |
| Cronbach's α | 0.56 | | |

a. The specific survey questions asked were, Is (establishment) subject to a periodic review by an outside accreditation or licensing organization? Does (establishment) belong to an association of organizations like it? In evaluating (establishment's) performance, to what extent do you pay attention to the practices of other organizations like (establishment)? How much are (establishment's) operations regulated by government agencies? "Don't know" responses are excluded from percentages reported.
b. The institutionalization scale is made up of four questions asking about outside pressures. All items were recoded to a 1 to 5 scale prior to computing the scale score, with high scores indicating the presence of more institutional pressure. Values for missing responses were imputed if the respondent answered the other three items.

to be subject to special pressures to conform to wider societal understandings (Dobbin, Edelman, Meyer, Scott, and Swidler 1988), whereas those that are parts of larger interorganizational entities may have centrally developed structures, procedures, and policies imposed on them. The indicators reviewed in this section were included in the NOS to measure the extent to which an establishment's context includes external institutional actors having the potential to shape its internal organizational policies and practices.

*Institutionalization Scale*

The items included in Table 3.4 measure the presence of external organizations that can convey institutional pressures via the processes identified by DiMaggio and Powell (1983). Nearly half of the organizations in the unweighted sample say that they are highly regulated by governmental agencies and thus open to coercive pressure. A larger percentage (57%) of the informants say that their establishments are subject to periodic review or accreditation by external bodies and thus, potentially, to normative influences of professional bodies. The other items in Table 3.4 ask about membership in an association of similar organizations and about the level of attention given to the practices of similar organizations; these items measure openings for "mimetic" processes.

To some extent, establishments subject to one sort of institutional pressure also are subject to others; the four-item institutionalization scale has a moderate reliability coefficient ($\alpha = 0.56$). The level of institutional pressure is lower for the weighted sample, indicating that smaller organizations are less subject to it.

The level of institutionalization differs substantially across establishments. Larger establishments are subject to more extensive institutional pressure; the correlation between the logarithm of the number of full-time employees and institutionalization is 0.38 in the unweighted NOS sample. Likewise, older organizations are somewhat more subject to external institutional influence; the correlation of institutionalization with the logarithm of establishment age is 0.22. The mean level of institutionalization is lower, at 3.15, for establishments that make products rather than provide services, 3.53. It is also lower among independent establishments than in those that are affiliated with larger organizations (see the upper right bar chart in Figure 3.4).

Figure 3.4 also displays a bar chart in the upper left indicating that public and nonprofit organizations are more subject to the sources of regulation and external influence that constitute the institutionalization scale. Mean levels of institutionalization are 3.53 among nonprofit organizations, 3.44 in public-sector workplaces, and 3.15 among for-profit concerns in the unweighted NOS sample.

*Unionization*

Unions are external agents that have been and remain highly relevant to the development of personnel practices in U.S. organizations (Kochan, Katz, and McKersie 1986). They may be seen both as elements of the technical environment, setting terms of exchange in the labor market, and as institutional elements forming and conveying norms about appropriate activities. No specific NOS survey item asked informants to estimate the degree to which the workforces of their establishments were organized by

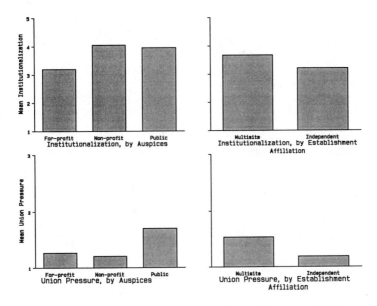

**Figure 3.4.** Institutionalization and Union Pressure (Unweighted NOS Sample)

trade unions. Several items that did appear in the survey, however, are indicative of the presence of organized labor, and these were combined into the "union pressure" scale presented in Table 3.5.

We inferred the presence of a union when informants told us that formal training was offered by virtue of provisions in union contracts, when union negotiations were said to be an important criterion in the determination of earnings of core or GSS employees, or when it was anticipated that union relations would be a problem for the establishment over the short (3-year) term. These indicators are well correlated with one another, so the scale has an estimated reliability ($\alpha$) of 0.82.

We examined the associations of the union pressure scale with two other variables having to do with unions that appear in the NOS data set. The measure has a correlation of 0.36 with the percentage unionized in the 2-digit SIC industry in which the establishment was coded. Also, it correlates at 0.62 with the GSS respondent's self-report of union membership; by contrast, the industry-level union penetration measure is correlated at only 0.28 with the self-report. Consequently, though it is an indirect measure, the union pressure scale would appear to do well in reflecting the presence of unions at the establishment level.

**Table 3.5**  Union Pressures Items[a]

| | Percentage | | |
|---|---|---|---|
| *Item* | *Unweighted* | *Weighted* | *N* |
| Formal training offered | | | |
| because of union contracts | 14.7 | 7.7 | 490 |
| Union negotiations somewhat/ | | | |
| very important for determining | | | |
| earnings of cores | 26.7 | 3.4 | 679 |
| Union negotiations somewhat/ | | | |
| very important for determining | | | |
| earnings of GSSs | 22.4 | 2.4 | 643 |
| Union relations perceived to be | | | |
| a major or minor problem | | | |
| over next 3 years | 34.1 | 11.2 | 593 |
| Union pressures scale[b] | | | |
| Mean | 1.38 | 1.06 | 683 |
| Standard deviation | 0.58 | 0.23 | |
| Median | 1.00 | 1.00 | |
| Interquartile range | 0.75 | 0.00 | |
| Cronbach's $\alpha$ | 0.82 | | |

a. The specific survey questions asked were, Is any of the formal training offered because of union contracts? How important are each of the following for determining the earnings of (COREs) here? What about union negotiations? How important are each of the following for determining the earnings of (GSSs) here? What about union negotiations? Over the next *3 years*, how big a problem will each of the following be for (establishment)? What about relations with unions? "Don't know" responses are excluded from percentages reported.
b. The union pressures scale is made up of four questions asking how unions affect the establishment. For construction of the scale, missing values were imputed if the respondent answered two or three of the other union pressures items.

The union pressure scale differs across establishments in predictable ways, lending confidence to the use of this scale as a proxy for the presence of unions in the environment of an establishment. Larger and older organizations tend to have higher scores on the scale; the respective correlations of union pressure with the logarithms of establishment size (full-time employees) and age are 0.4 and 0.2. Workplaces that produce products have higher mean levels of union pressure (1.51) than do those oriented to services (1.35). Independent establishments are surrounded by appreciably less union pressure (mean of 1.19) than are those affiliated with larger organizations (1.53); see the lower right chart in Figure 3.4.

The lower left bar chart in Figure 3.4 illustrates sectoral differences in union pressure. The levels in the for-profit and nonprofit sectors are rather similar; their respective means are 1.26 and 1.21. Public-sector establishments have substantially higher scores on the union pressure scale, with a mean level of 1.70. This result reflects the greater comparative success of public-sector unions in organizing employees during recent years (see Kochan et al. 1986, p. 39).

*Branches and Subsidiaries*

The unit of analysis in the NOS is the work establishment. As we have observed, some establishments are stand-alone, whereas others are part of larger, multiestablishment firms, and this distinction is an important aspect of an establishment's context. Those that are part of larger organizational entities are likely to be constrained by centrally set policies on many matters, and this can be understood as institutional pressure from the standpoint of the establishment. As noted in the course of our discussion of size, 55% of the establishments in the unweighted NOS sample are part of some larger organization. In that these establishments tend to be substantially larger than independent workplaces, the corresponding figure for the weighted sample is 20%.

## Conclusion

This chapter has surveyed the composition and environmental settings of the work establishments in the NOS. These workplaces are quite diverse in size, age, sociodemographic composition, and external context. As is to be expected from a random sample of U.S. workplaces in the 1990s, most of them provide services rather than produce goods. The public, nonprofit, and private, for-profit sectors are well represented. A sizable fraction of the establishments are tied to larger organizations. There are notable differences in composition and environmental conditions between organizations differing in their major activities, auspices, size, age, and affiliation with a larger entity.

These establishments also differ considerably in their human resource policies and practices—such as recruitment, compensation, and training. Succeeding chapters examine such differences using many of the items, measures, and indices reviewed here.

## Notes

1. For a discussion of the question of whether sample weights should be used when estimating regression models for analytical purposes, see Winship and Radbill (1994).

2. The "whiskers" at each end of the box each extend 1.5 times the length of the box, or to the maximum/minimum value in the (log) size distribution, if that is less than 1.5 box lengths away. A circle beyond the whisker highlights an establishment with an extreme ("outlying") value in the distribution. For more about boxplots, see Knoke and Bohrnstedt (1994, pp. 69-72).

3. Informants for multiestablishment organizations were reminded that we were interested in the date of first establishment at any location.

4. The identity of the GSS respondent was never revealed to NOS informants. Indeed, because the NOS and the GSS were conducted by different survey organizations, NOS interviewers did not even know the identity of the GSS respondent.

5. For this and other scales, some missing data were imputed from other scale items using linear regression or logit regression. On imputation methods, see Little and Rubin (1987). The conditions under which imputed values were used are indicated in notes to Tables 3.2 through 3.5.

# II

# Organizational Structures

# 4

# Bureaucratic Structures for Coordination and Control

PETER V. MARSDEN
CYNTHIA R. COOK
ARNE L. KALLEBERG

Two central problems that work organizations face are those of ensuring that employee actions are directed toward organizational goals—*control*—and of integrating the goal-directed efforts of multiple members—*coordination*. Organizations approach those problems in a variety of ways, but efforts to achieve coordination and control through structural arrangements are particularly common.[1]

Organizational research perennially seeks to understand variations in the internal structure of organizations. This effort takes numerous theoretical forms: macrosociological observations about social conditions associated with the rise and diffusion of organizations in contemporary society (e.g., Stinchcombe 1965); contingency propositions about technical and environmental conditions associated with "mechanistic" rather than "organic" structures (e.g., Mintzberg 1979); and more recent theoretical work that sees structures as those that survive processes of ecological competition (Hannan and Freeman 1989) or as reflections of taken-for-granted societal understandings (Meyer and Rowan 1977; Powell and DiMaggio 1991).

This chapter examines the organizational structures of establishments in the National Organizations Study, drawing on theoretical formulations advanced over the past 3 decades. We begin by studying variations in formal structure and administrative arrangements, using models of structure that were developed in the 1960s and 1970s. These view organizational structure as a set of devices for coordinating work and take structural variations to be the result of efforts to minimize coordination costs. Another tradition of organizational analysis (e.g., Edwards 1979) sees structures less as coordination devices than as a sometimes unobtrusive means of exerting control over employees. Our statistical results can certainly be interpreted using this alternative framework.[2]

The empirical documentation undergirding these structural models remains among the strongest in the literature on organizations. Most of it is based, however, on samples that are much less diverse than the NOS—studies that often include only a single type of organization, such as public employment agencies. The statistical results in this chapter provide estimates for these models using our large and representative sample of establishments. They also move beyond the internal factors emphasized in this research tradition and examine structural differences using several contextual and environmental indicators suggested by extant theory.

The principal postulate of the models in this chapter is that organizations use structural arrangements to achieve coordination and control over activities. We study the formal administrative design of establishments—including vertical and horizontal differentiation, formalization, and the allocation of responsibilities for decision making. We begin by introducing arguments about how these coordination-control structures should vary with organization size and one another.

## Coordination and Control
## Through Administrative Design

Coordination and control problems increase with the size of an organization, and thus a great deal of research attention in the 1960s and 1970s was devoted to examining the relations between the size and structure of organizations. This work conceived of organizational structure as a set of devices for the efficient coordination of diverse actions, placing special emphasis on the differing capacities of complexity, differentiation, and formalization to manage large volumes of activity. These structural features were viewed as both complements to and substitutes for one another—and particularly as alternatives to direct managerial supervision (the "administrative component" or "administrative intensity" of an organization).

In what Scott (1992, p. 260) terms a "remarkable series of propositions," Blau (1970, 1972) discussed the way in which organizational structures would vary with organization size. Blau focused on how size and complexity (structural differentiation) affect the volume of managerial or supervisory work. He contended that larger organizations would be apt to specialize and subdivide work to realize economies of scale. On the one hand, such differentiation would permit relative reductions in supervisory activity, in that tasks would tend to be homogeneous within specialized subunits and managerial spans of control could grow. At the same time, increased differentiation would require the use of additional managerial resources to coordinate increasingly interdependent subunits. Between-unit relationships could be smoothed either by creating additional vertical ranks or by creating horizontal liaison devices such as the integrating managers described by Lawrence and Lorsch (1967). Hence, Blau argued that growth would increase differentiation and thereby, alter the administrative component in two conflicting ways—decreasing it by virtue of within-unit efficiencies, but increasing it by creating a need for more extensive between-unit coordination.

Blau, his associates, and others working at the same time (e.g., Pugh, Hickson, Hinings, and Turner 1968; Pugh et al. 1969; Blau and Schoenherr 1971; Meyer 1972; Child 1973; Mansfield 1973) elaborated these and related ideas. Organization size, an indicator of the magnitude of the tasks to be coordinated, was usually the dominant contingency thought to necessitate structural differences. Beyond differentiation—the development both of specialized departments and of taller hierarchies—alternatives to direct supervision studied were the allocation of decision-making responsibilities to different levels in the organization and the formalization of behavior through rules and written documents.

In Figure 4.1, we present a summary of this work adapted from Daft (1986, p. 185). (Simple correlations estimated from the NOS data set are given beside the arrows in the figure.) At the left are arrows representing

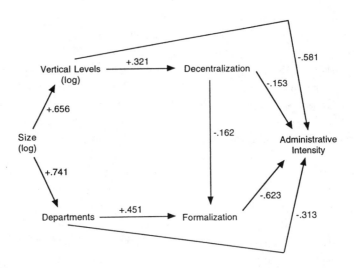

**Figure 4.1.** Relations Between Coordination and Control Structures
NOTE: Zero-order correlations appear beside arrows.

Blau's propositions about the impact of size on the division of labor (departments) and the height (vertical levels) of an organization. Increased height is associated with decentralization of decision making. Such delegation of authority allows actions to be adjusted to local conditions by workers at the decision point and also prevents decision overload at upper levels of the hierarchy. In this view, the upper levels are principally concerned with conflict resolution, interunit coordination, and strategic planning as distinct from operations.

Size and structural complexity also operate through the device of formalization. As noted by Scott (1992, p. 22), formalization via the creation of written rules and procedures is one of the essential ways in which organizations differ from other collectivities. In contemporary society, codification of organizational routines can legitimate the exercise of authority, serving to delimit the arbitrary exercise of power by superiors in an association. Additionally, formalization through the creation of routines and standard operating procedures serves to channel and limit the actions of subordinates, thus reducing the need for direct supervision. Increased horizontal complexity (departmentalization) is managed in part through this device; rules and routinized procedures permit specialized departments to work with one another in predictable ways. Moreover, formalization often accompanies increased decentralization—"rules define boundaries so that decisions can be made at a lower level without a loss of control" (Daft 1986, p. 179).

The arrows at the right of Figure 4.1 represent hypotheses about the substitutability of structural devices. The general notion is that organizations begin as relatively simple structures in which activities are coordinated via direct supervision, with managers issuing personal directives to operatives. With growth come vertical and horizontal complexity, decentralization and formalization—all of which should reduce the relative amounts of direct managerial work by structuring the activities of lower participants. In accord with such claims, the arrows leading to administrative intensity are accompanied by the negative correlations between our measures of these concepts (described in the next section) estimated from the unweighted NOS data set.

The organizational theory that leads to Figure 4.1 developed from a largely managerial perspective emphasizing imperatives of coordinating activities. Alternatively, Figure 4.1 may be interpreted as a depiction of managerial efforts to maintain and extend control over employees (Edwards 1979; Salaman 1980). In this understanding, specialization and departmentalization, for example, increase predictability by narrowing the set of activities in which employees can potentially engage. Formalization is seen as an indirect means of maintaining control that operates by establishing premises for decision making. With such premises firmly in place, owners or managers take few risks when they delegate the authority to make decisions.

## Measuring Coordination and Control Structures

Direct supervision of employees by managers is the most basic mechanism of hierarchical coordination (Mintzberg 1983). The NOS indicator of the extent to which this is used is the proportion of managers among employees (unweighted mean = .21; median = .11; $SD = .26$).

### Structural Differentiation

*Vertical Levels*

NOS informants were asked about the number of vertical levels separating the highest and lowest positions at their establishment. The

**Table 4.1** Departmentalization Items[a]

|  | Percentage of Establishments Having Department for Function | | |
|---|---|---|---|
| Function | Unweighted | Weighted | N |
| Finance | 37.3 | 6.3 | 679 |
| Personnel/labor relations | 34.6 | 2.4 | 679 |
| Accounting | 31.8 | 5.6 | 679 |
| Health and safety | 23.3 | 1.5 | 679 |
| Public relations | 23.0 | 1.9 | 679 |
| Research and development | 16.9 | 1.4 | 682 |
| Long-range planning | 15.5 | 2.6 | 676 |
| Marketing or sales | 10.8 | 1.8 | 648 |
| Departmentalization scale[b] | | | |
|   Mean | 0.26 | 0.03 | 679 |
|   Standard deviation | 0.31 | 0.12 | |
|   Median | 0.13 | 0.00 | |
|   Interquartile range | 0.50 | 0.00 | |
|   Cronbach's $\alpha$ | 0.86 | | |

a. The specific survey question asked was, Is there a separate department or section responsible for (function)? "Don't know" responses are excluded from percentages reported.
b. The departmentalization scale is the proportion of the eight departments present in an establishment. For construction of the scale, values for "don't know" responses were imputed using logistic regression, if the respondent answered five or more of the other departmentalization items.

(unweighted) median number of levels is 5; there is substantial positive skew in this measure, so the mean is just over 7, with a standard deviation of nearly 10. Because of this, we use a natural logarithmic transformation of the levels measure in our analyses below. Due to the tendency for more levels to be present in larger establishments, the typical establishment has fewer vertical levels than the establishment in which a typical employee works.

*Departmentalization*

Table 4.1 reports the items used to construct a scale measuring horizontal complexity. NOS informants were asked to say whether there were separate "departments or sections" responsible for each of eight functions;[3] an establishment's scale score is the proportion of the eight for which separate subunits exist.[4] The unweighted percentages in Table 4.1 show that finance, accounting, and personnel-labor relations are most likely to be in separate subunits; marketing-sales, long-range planning, and research and development are less apt to have their own distinct departments.

**Table 4.2** Formalization Items[a]

| Document | Percentage of Establishments Having Document | | |
| | Unweighted | Weighted | N |
| --- | --- | --- | --- |
| Rules and procedures manual | 80.0 | 38.3 | 684 |
| Documents on fringe benefits | 77.6 | 28.5 | 688 |
| Written job descriptions | 74.1 | 26.6 | 688 |
| Documents on safety and hygiene | 73.9 | 29.8 | 686 |
| Written performance records | 70.0 | 22.0 | 687 |
| Documents on hiring/firing procedures | 67.3 | 17.3 | 688 |
| Documents on personnel evaluation | 66.6 | 17.1 | 688 |
| Formalization scale[b] | | | |
| Mean | 0.73 | 0.26 | 688 |
| Standard deviation | 0.35 | 0.34 | |
| Median | 0.86 | 0.00 | |
| Interquartile range | 0.43 | 0.43 | |
| Cronbach's $\alpha$ | 0.90 | | |

a. The specific survey question asked was, Do each of the following documents exist at (establishment name)? What about . . . In addition to the seven documents listed here, respondents were also asked about the presence of employment contracts. "Don't know" responses are excluded from percentages reported.
b. The formalization scale gives the proportion of the seven documents present in an establishment. For construction of the scale, values for "don't know" responses were imputed from responses to the other formalization items using logistic regression.

The overall level of departmentalization is low: Unweighted statistics show that a typical employee works in an establishment that has separate units for about two of the eight functions; median departmentalization is just over one out of eight. Those establishments departmentalizing one function, however, are quite likely to departmentalize others; the estimated reliability (Cronbach's $\alpha$) of the 8-item departmentalization scale is 0.86. There are very large differences in departmentalization between large and small establishments, as shown by the difference between the weighted and unweighted scale distributions.

*Formalization*

The NOS measured formalization by asking informants to indicate whether their establishments have written documentation for several types of personnel-related processes, including hiring and firing, personnel evaluation, and fringe benefits. Table 4.2 lists the seven documents used to construct a formalization scale.[5]

Most employees work in establishments that have substantial written documentation for personnel matters; the unweighted percentages range from 80% for a rules and procedures manual to 66% for documents on personnel evaluation procedures. The variables indicating the presence or absence of the different documents are strongly correlated with one another, as indicated by the high (.90) estimated scale reliability. In the unweighted data set, many (62%) of the sampled establishments have six or seven of the documents, but an appreciable number (11%) have none of them. The weighted distribution exhibits a similar clustering of values. As the descriptive statistics in Table 4.2 make clear, however, the overall level of formalization in the average establishment is much lower than that to which the average worker is exposed, and the modal value in the weighted scale distribution is 0.

*Decentralization*

The NOS followed prior organizational researchers such as the Aston group (Pugh et al. 1968; Pugh et al. 1969) and Lincoln and Kalleberg (1990, Chapter 7) in measuring decentralization by asking establishment informants about the level at which certain decisions are made. The decentralization items are listed in Table 4.3 together with descriptive statistics on the decentralization scale.

Informants were asked about the actual level at which a given decision was made, not the level to which it is formally assigned. Responses distinguished three levels: the establishment "head," someone at a lower level, and (for establishments that are part of multisite firms) someone at a different location.

Table 4.3 indicates that lower-level employees are most often involved in decisions such as performance evaluation, scheduling, and overtime. Employees lower than the establishment head are less often involved in setting wage levels, deciding the number of personnel to be employed, or determining when subcontractors or temporary workers will be used.

The decentralization scale is quite reliable, with an estimated reliability ($\alpha$) of 0.91. The (unweighted) median level of decentralization is 3.5, a score that indicates some below-head-level participation in decisions in an establishment. When the data are weighted to better represent the preponderance of small establishments, the median level is 3, indicating that decisions tend to be made by the establishment head instead of by subordinates.

We note that NOS informants were asked about decisions involving matters of personnel policy. High scores on the decentralization scale do not necessarily indicate that operational decisions have, or have not, been delegated to lower-level employees. Indeed, we suspect that centralization

**Table 4.3** Decentralization Items[a]

| | Percentage of Establishments Where Final Decision About Issue Involves Someone Below Establishment Head | | |
|---|---|---|---|
| *Issue* | *Unweighted* | *Weighted* | *N* |
| Performance evaluation | 58.5 | 12.7 | 655 |
| Scheduling/overtime | 57.2 | 17.0 | 663 |
| Which employees to hire | 47.1 | 8.7 | 664 |
| Promotions | 40.8 | 7.2 | 645 |
| Use of subcontractors/temporaries | 37.6 | 9.1 | 623 |
| Discharges/layoffs | 34.3 | 7.5 | 653 |
| Wage/salary levels | 17.0 | 2.8 | 663 |
| Number of employees | 13.4 | 3.3 | 665 |
| Decentralization scale [b] | | | |
|   Mean | 3.46 | 2.94 | 679 |
|   Standard deviation | .96 | .65 | |
|   Median | 3.50 | 3.00 | |
|   Interquartile range | 1.25 | 0.00 | |
|   Cronbach's $\alpha$ | .91 | | |

a. The specific survey question asked was, We are interested in who is responsible for making different kinds of decisions in your workplace. I am going to read a list of decision areas, and ask you to tell me who *actually* makes the final decision in each area. Is it the head of (establishment), someone below that, [or someone at (larger organization, if establishment is part of a larger organization)]? "Don't know" or "does not apply" responses are excluded from percentages reported.
b. The departmentalization scale is the mean level at which the eight decisions were made in the establishment. Scores were assigned to responses as follows: *someone at larger organization* (1), *establishment head and someone at larger organization* (2), *establishment head* (3), *establishment head and someone below* (4), *someone below establishment head* (5). For construction of the scale, values for "don't know" and "does not apply" responses were regression-imputed, if the respondent answered four or more of the other decentralization items.

of personnel decisions and operational ones may differ in important ways. Although there are some contemporary trends toward increasing the operational autonomy of employees, the development of "modern personnel procedures" (Jacoby 1985; Baron, Dobbin, and Jennings 1986; Bridges and Villemez 1994) involves the movement of some matters of personnel policy from within the purview of lower-level supervisory staff to central, formalized personnel and labor relations units.

## Size, Differentiation, and Organizational Structure

We begin our analysis by examining how the coordination/control structures just described differ across organizations that vary in size. Figure 4.2

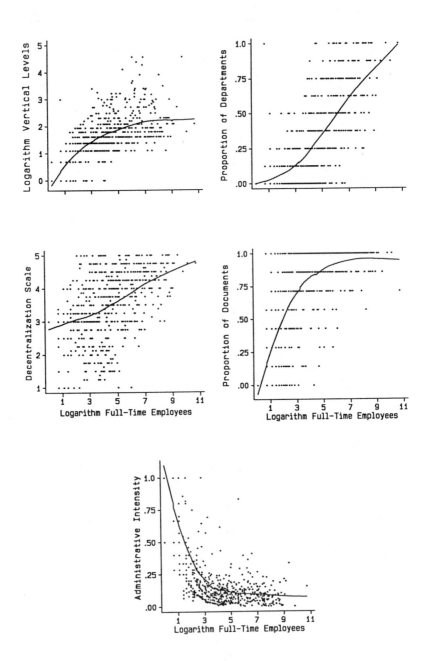

**Figure 4.2.** Establishment Size and Coordination and Control Measures

displays the nonlinear bivariate relationships between the number of full-time employees in an establishment (natural log) and the structural measures in Figure 4.1. Running through the scatterplots in Figure 4.2 are nonparametric regression lines estimated via the lowess technique described in Härdle (1990).

Vertical differentiation rises rapidly as small organizations grow larger. Levels, however, are added at a decelerating rate. Once there are eight [=exp(2.08)] supervisory levels, a point reached for establishments with roughly 1,000 [=exp(6.9)] full-time employees, increases in size have little further effect. Increases in departmentalization also accompany growth, but the relationship is closer to (log-)linear.

Similarly, decentralization rises more or less smoothly with size. In small (1 to 10 employees) establishments, the head (score 3 on the decentralization scale) controls decisions, but the typical decision is shared by the head and subordinates (score 4) in workplaces with 1,000 employees. There is even more delegation of decision responsibilities to lower levels in establishments with over 1,000 full-time employees.

As with vertical levels, formalization rises rapidly with size, at a decelerating rate. Very small workplaces have few of the documents the NOS asked about, but a typical establishment of 10 employees has more than half of them. The rate of increase in formalization falls off quickly beyond a level of 150 [=exp(5.01)] full-time workers—at which size establishments have an average of six out of the seven documents that constitute the formalization scale.

As the literature summarized in Figure 4.1 predicts, there is a strong negative relationship between size and administrative intensity. The decrease in the managerial ratio is particularly steep at lower levels of size; the decline in administrative intensity is much gentler among establishments having more than 10 employees.

We concluded our examination of the propositions summarized in Figure 4.1 by estimating linear regression equations for vertical and horizontal complexity, decentralization, formalization, and administrative intensity, using establishment size and other structural measures as predictors. The results for this "internal" structural model appear in Table 4.4; we included linear and quadratic terms for establishment size to take into account the nonlinearities seen in Figure 4.2. Of particular interest is the degree to which intervening structural factors interpret the associations between size and variables at the right in Table 4.4, especially administrative intensity.

**Table 4.4**  Relationships Between Size and Structural Variables (regression coefficients)

| | | | Dependent Variable | | |
|---|---|---|---|---|---|
| | | | Decentral- | | Administrative |
| Predictor | Log Levels | Departments | ization | Formalization | Intensity |
| Log size (linear) | .571** | .034** | .089** | .263** | −.220** |
| Log size (quadratic) | −.038** | .008** | — | −.020** | .017** |
| Log levels | | | −.008 | .041* | −.040** |
| Departments | | | 1.182** | .097 | .169** |
| Decentralization | | | | −.49** | .015 |
| Formalization | | | | | −.061* |
| Constant | .060 | −.036 | 2.766** | .190** | .760** |
| $R^2$ | .491 | .568 | .296 | .505 | .596 |
| N | 644 | 676 | 617 | 617 | 592 |

$**p < .01; *p < .05.$

The coefficients displayed in Table 4.4 confirm, by and large, the hypotheses depicted in Figure 4.1. Size and other structural measures account for around half or more of the variance of each structural device (except decentralization, for which $R^2$ is just under .30).

The measures that intervene between size and administrative intensity in Figure 4.1 interpret some, but by no means all, of the effects of size. The latter remain highly significant, and they correspond to the curves shown in Figure 4.2: Growth increases levels and formalization at a decreasing rate and reduces administrative intensity at a declining rate. There is a slight acceleration in the rate at which departmentalization rises with size, evidently attributable to the slow increases in departmentalization in the lower ranges of size (see Figure 4.2). Decentralization increases linearly with size; the effects of size are largely mediated by the two indicators of complexity.[6]

Turning to predictors other than size, we observe that decentralization is strongly influenced by departmentalization (standardized β = 0.379); delegation of decision-making responsibility grows more common when separate subunits exist. Formalization is higher in establishments with many vertical levels than it is in "shorter" workplaces; it is also substantially lower—contrary to the prediction implied by Figure 4.1—when there is substantial decentralization. This unexpected result may arise in that the items in the decentralization scale refer to personnel-related decisions rather than operational issues (see Table 4.3).

Administrative intensity is lower in establishments with many levels of authority than in those with few levels, and the negative coefficient for formalization in the final column of Table 4.4 confirms that standard operating procedures are substituted for direct supervision. Hence, structural devices do appear to yield managerial economies. Among establishments similar in size, vertical complexity, formalization, and decentralization, however, higher departmentalization is associated with a higher managerial ratio. This is as Blau's (1970, 1972) theory of differentiation predicts: It reflects the more extensive between-unit coordination requirements of a horizontally specialized organization. Note also that departmentalization has indirect *negative* effects on the administrative ratio by virtue of its positive influences on decentralization and formalization, as Blau's observations about increased efficiency suggest. The effects through decentralization are themselves mediated by formalization, for decentralization per se has no significant link to the administrative ratio. Again, we think that the content of the items in the decentralization scale may account for this anomaly.

Although the results in Table 4.4 do not lead us to conclude that size is the *only* factor driving the development of organizational structures (cf. Meyer 1972), they do highlight its importance. Small and large establishments have quite distinct structural arrangements. As Scott (1992, p. 258) points out, size may be understood in a number of different ways; it can be seen as a structural property of an organization, as an element of the organization-environment interface, or as a contextual indicator of the level of demand for an organization's activities. We next consider other environmental correlates of the coordination-control structures examined in this section.

## Contextual Factors and Organizational Structure

With the discovery of variety in the structure of organizations (Burns and Stalker 1961; Woodward 1965; Lawrence and Lorsch 1967) came efforts to dimensionalize and explain such diversity. The principal contrast drawn was between "mechanistic" or "bureaucratic" structures and "organic" ones.

"Contingency theory" suggested that differences in structure were largely attributable to the level of uncertainty and complexity that an organization faced. Uncertainty could be a result of technological requirements or limitations, or a product of conditions in the technical/task environment. According to contingency theory, mechanistic structures—with tall hierarchies, numerous departments, limited decentralization, and many rules and procedures—

would be found under stable and well-understood conditions, in situations requiring the efficient execution of repetitive tasks. More flexible, organic forms—with less structural complexity, fewer rules, and extensive decentralization—would be found in the presence of substantial uncertainty, in conditions involving innovation or adjustment to changing circumstances. Consequently, researchers seeking to explain coordination strategies looked beyond organizational boundaries.

More recent developments in institutional theory (Meyer and Rowan 1977; Meyer and Scott 1983; Powell and DiMaggio 1991) point instead to nontechnical elements in the environment as influences shaping structure. Structural arrangements are adopted, in this understanding, because of their widespread social acceptance rather than any demonstrated effectiveness or efficiency. By adopting institutionalized structures, organizations conform to normative prescriptions about appropriate ways to organize and acquire the key resource of legitimacy within their environments—thereby rendering themselves less subject to external scrutiny.

We drew on both contingency theory and institutional theory in selecting a set of variables that describes the environmental settings of NOS establishments (see Chapter 3, this volume, for details on most of these measures). It proved difficult to measure technology at the establishment level.[7] We do distinguish between organizations that make products, provide services, or do both. Making products involves the management of employees with different skill levels and the coordination of sometimes-complex supplier chains. Mechanistic structures may lend themselves to such tasks. The provision of services, on the other hand, requires some contact between the customer and the service provider, which makes some aspects of organic structure likely, especially decentralization. As measures of technical elements of an establishment's environment, we included the environmental problems and complexity scales (see Tables 3.2 and 3.3) and an item measuring the geographic scope of the establishment's market area.

We used several measures to capture potential institutional sources of structural forms. Among these are the auspices—public, nonprofit, or private—under which an establishment operates, whether the establishment is subject to extensive government regulation, the level of union pressure it faces, and whether it is an independent establishment or a part of a larger, multisite organization. All of these variables are indicative of the presence of powerful actors having the capacity to mandate, or at least to advocate strongly, the adoption of structural forms. Arguments of this sort seem most applicable to formalization.

In addition to these environmental covariates, we also included the age of the establishment, to examine Mintzberg's (1979) proposition that organizations become more bureaucratized as they grow older. The results of regression analyses involving these variables are reported in Table 4.5. We first regress each of the five dependent variables from Table 4.4 on the environmental indicators by themselves, and then watch how these coefficients change when size and other "internal" structural measures are added.

As shown by the columns labeled 1 in Table 4.5, the 11 environmental variables account for between a quarter (for levels and administrative intensity) and two fifths (for formalization) of the variance in the structural measures. Establishments with broad market areas and those scoring high on the environmental complexity scale display greater structural complexity (more departments and levels), decentralization, and formalization. Older organizations are structurally more elaborate and formalized than younger ones; they also appear to be more decentralized, with somewhat lower managerial ratios.

Among the institutional factors, there are notable differences between public, nonprofit, and for-profit establishments. Personnel related decisions in public establishments tend to be highly centralized, whereas those in nonprofit workplaces tend to be made at lower levels than in the private, for-profit sector. As institutional theory anticipates, public and nonprofit establishments are more formalized than for-profit concerns, as are establishments that are subject to extensive regulation.

Workplaces that are subunits of multisite firms differ from independent establishments in several predictable ways. Their decision-making structures are much more centralized, and more procedures are formalized. Establishments in multisite organizations have taller hierarchies and lower managerial proportions than independent establishments in otherwise similar environmental circumstances.

Many, but by no means all, of these associations between contextual and structural features vanish when size and the other predictors used in Table 4.4 are added, as shown in the columns of Table 4.5 labeled 2. The differences in formalization and decentralization in public, nonprofit, and for-profit concerns remain significant, net of size and complexity; likewise, the differences between branches or subsidiaries and independent establishments persist. Contextual variables have their most notable net effects on formalization and decentralization; variations in structural complexity (both horizontal and vertical) and in administrative intensity can be traced, in a proximate sense, to size and other measures of coordination/control. Together, the contextual and

**Table 4.5** Contextual Features and Coordination and Control Measures (regression coefficients)

| Predictor | Log Levels (1) | Log Levels (2) | Departments (1) | Departments (2) | Decentralization (1) | Decentralization (2) | Formalization (1) | Formalization (2) | Administrative Intensity (1) | Administrative Intensity (2) |
|---|---|---|---|---|---|---|---|---|---|---|
| Log size (linear) | | .526** | | .047** | | .182** | | .202** | | -.223** |
| Log size (quadratic) | | -.033** | | .006** | | — | | -.017** | | .017** |
| Log levels | | | | | | .090* | | .029 | | -.039** |
| Departments | | | | | | .661** | | .071 | | .160** |
| Decentralization | | | | | | | | .033* | | .011 |
| Formalization | | | | | | | | | | -.063* |
| Service | -.059 | .107 | -.007 | .058* | -.015 | .091 | -.012 | .021 | .004 | -.018 |
| Service and product | -.030 | .069 | .010 | .051 | .127 | .192 | -.015 | .013 | .041 | -.044 |
| Market scope | .104** | -.002 | .072** | .022** | .238** | .092** | .026** | -.004 | -.014 | .009 |
| Log age | .133** | .022 | .073** | .024** | .184** | .031 | .032** | -.005 | -.032** | .002 |
| Problems | .014 | -.094 | .000 | -.033 | .060 | .029 | .091** | .045* | -.070** | -.021 |
| Complexity | .280* | .015 | .124** | .024 | .375** | .034 | .129** | .047 | -.098** | -.025 |
| Public | .068 | -.044 | .002 | -.051* | -.329** | -.421** | .090** | .073** | -.064* | -.022 |
| Nonprofit | .169 | -.107 | .257** | .111** | .495** | .054 | .163** | .081* | -.055 | -.009 |
| Government regulated | .071* | .014 | .009 | -.003 | .005 | -.040 | .035** | .017 | -.012 | .014* |
| Union pressure | .193** | .038 | .060** | -.019 | .076 | -.120* | .032 | -.002 | -.039* | -.005 |
| Multisite organization | .257** | .077 | .038 | -.016 | -.614** | -.752** | .245** | .196** | -.079** | .019 |
| Constant | .053 | .021 | -.378** | -.143 | 2.155** | 2.687** | .022 | -.157 | .652** | .768** |
| $R^2$ | .243 | .478 | .317 | .605 | .324 | .540 | .416 | .593 | .247 | .616 |
| N | 597 | 595 | 615 | 614 | 612 | 583 | 622 | 583 | 598 | 565 |

*$p < .05$; **$p < .01$.

structural predictor variables account for fractions of the variance approaching or exceeding .5 for all five structural measures.

## Conclusion

Propositions drawn from organizational theory about the relationships of size and measures of organizational structure were largely confirmed for the diverse set of establishments in the NOS. Measures of coordination and control techniques—including structural complexity, formalization, decentralization, and administrative intensity—are related to one another in ways that are theoretically anticipated, under the assumption that organizational structures are used to realize coordination economies.[8] In addition, there are quite strong differences in structure between large and small organizations, which persist even after statistical adjustments for effects of contextual features.

We found appreciable differences in formalization and decentralization between public-sector (formalized and centralized), nonprofit (formalized and *de*centralized), and private for-profit establishments (less formalized, moderately decentralized) net of size and complexity. Establishments within multisite organizations also display higher levels of formalization and (especially) centralization than do comparable independent workplaces. These findings substantiate theoretical accounts that emphasize external, institutional sources of structural forms.

Our focus in this chapter has been on bureaucratic control structures identified by classical organization theory and its more contemporary "open-system rational" variants (Scott 1992). Other organization theory suggests that coordination and control problems can be managed with structural devices that focus on the employment relation, including internal labor markets and pay-for-performance compensation strategies. In the next two chapters, we draw on the NOS data to investigate the use of these and related human resource practices (which may either supplant or supplement those studied in this chapter) by American organizations.

## Notes

1. One alternative approach that has received increased attention of late is normatively or culturally based; see Deal and Kennedy (1982) or Barker (1993).

2. See Baron, Dobbin, and Jennings (1986) on the difficulties involved in distinguishing empirically between efficiency and control explanations.

3. Additionally, NOS informants were asked whether there was one employee who had a "main responsibility" for covering each of the eight functions. In measuring departmentalization, however, we are concerned solely with the existence of separate departments or sections.

4. For this and other scales, some missing data were imputed from other scale items using linear regression or logit regression. On imputation methods, see Little and Rubin (1987). The conditions under which imputed values were used are indicated in footnotes to Tables 4.1 through 4.3.

5. As noted in Table 4.2, informants were also asked about the existence of employment contracts. The presence of these is only moderately correlated with the presence of the other documents, and the estimated reliability of the formalization scale is lower if this item is included.

6. When a quadratic term in (log) size was added to the equation for decentralization in Table 4.4, its coefficient was insignificant ($t = 0.76$). The bivariate coefficient for the regression of decentralization on the linear term in size is 0.209 ($t = 13.9$).

7. We are persuaded by Scott's (1992, p. 241) view that it is hazardous to measure technology at the organizational level due to heterogeneity in technology that penetrates to departmental, subunit, and even work process levels of an organization.

8. By showing that most results predicted by received theory are replicated using the measures of structure used in the NOS, our findings serve to construct-validate those measures.

# 5

# Formalizing the Employment Relation

## *Internal Labor Markets and Dispute Resolution Procedures*

ARNE L. KALLEBERG
PETER V. MARSDEN
DAVID KNOKE
JOE L. SPAETH

Among the most important changes in the structure of the work setting during the 20th century have been developments in the manner in which employees and employers are related to one another. Sometimes described as the "legalization of the workplace" (Sutton, Dobin, Meyer, and Scott 1994) or the development of "modern personnel administration" (Baron, Dobbin, and Jennings 1986; Bridges and Villemez 1994), these changes involved increased formality in several facets of the employee-employer linkage. An increasingly bureaucratized employment relation has replaced the personalized, arbitrary "drive system" of control described by Jacoby (1985). The study of these changes at the level of the organization or work establishment is a key item on the research agenda of the "new structuralism" that seeks to integrate the study of organizations, labor markets, and social stratification (see Baron and Bielby 1980; Baron 1984; Bridges and Villemez 1994).

In this chapter, we draw on the NOS to examine two important aspects of formalization in employment relations: (a) firm internal labor markets and (b) formal dispute resolution procedures. Firm internal labor markets (FILMs) are central features of employment relations in modern industrial societies. FILMs are integral to theories of stratification within organizations and human resource management because they are contexts wherein many skills are acquired, mobility and career advancement take place, and higher earnings are often attained. "Good jobs at good wages" are located in FILMs. In that they offer important positive incentives—particularly employment security, the prospect of rising income, and seniority-related fringe benefits—FILMs create strong ties between workers and employers.

The availability of formal channels through which workplace disputes can be aired and resolved is a key element of workplace "legalization" (Edelman 1990; Sutton et al. 1994). By providing for due process in the handling of grievances, formal dispute resolution procedures limit the capricious use of authority on the part of supervisors and managers. They create enhanced legitimacy within the workplace and confer organizational citizenship on employees. The heightened mobility opportunities provided by FILMS and the increased legitimacy flowing from formal dispute procedures are two key dimensions of "corporatist organization" identified by Lincoln and Kalleberg (1990, pp. 13-16).

We begin by discussing briefly how we conceptualize and measure these important organizational structures in the National Organizations Study. FILMs, in particular, are a pivotal structure with respect to many topics elsewhere in this book, and we highlight those relationships. We describe the indicators that we use to measure the presence of FILMs and dispute resolution procedures, and then show how these measures are associated with some of the other main indicators of organizational structures and environments in the NOS.

At the end of the chapter, we illustrate an alternative to the variable-centered study of coordination and control structures pursued here and in

Chapter 4. In place of separate consideration of the various ways in which workplaces and the employment relation are structured, we examine them jointly, isolating five configurations of coordination/control strategies. We demonstrate that these five structural profiles are common in different kinds of establishments: Size, the presence of trade unions, and embeddedness within a larger organizational setting are especially important conditioning factors.

## Defining FILMs

A firm internal labor market (FILM) can be defined as "an administrative unit, such as a manufacturing plant, within which the pricing and allocation of labor is [sic] governed by a set of administrative rules and procedures" (Doeringer and Piore 1971, pp. 1-2). FILMs are "any cluster of jobs, regardless of occupational titles or employing organizations, that have three basic structural features: (a) a job ladder, with (b) entry only at the bottom and (c) movement up this ladder, which is associated with a progressive development of knowledge and skill" (Althauser and Kalleberg 1981, p. 130).

A common theme in this definition of FILMs is access to "job ladders" that provide opportunities for within-firm career advancement. This usually means that newly hired employees are concentrated in certain lower-level "port-of-entry" positions, whereas higher-level jobs are filled predominantly or exclusively through internal promotion. Conceptual analyses and reviews of empirical research on FILMs can be found in Althauser (1989); Baron, Dobbin, and Jennings (1986); Osterman (1984); and White and Althauser (1984).

Althauser and Kalleberg's (1981) definition underscores the centrality of mobility opportunities, along with skill acquisition and development, to the idea of FILMs. Mobility chances are especially important, and our measure of FILMs (see the following) is principally based on mobility indicators. The concept of FILMs, however, is multidimensional. Two other major dimensions of FILMs include the existence of (a) formal, and probably written, rules regulating entry into job ladders (see Baron, Davis-Blake, and Bielby 1986; Osterman 1984) and (b) job competition, where people compete for jobs only with those inside the FILM and where wages and other rewards are attached to positions rather than to individuals (Thurow 1975).

## FILMs and Human Resource
## Practices and Policies

FILMs are important to our inquiry because they help to shape the various human resource policies that we study in this book. Here, we briefly suggest how FILMs are related to each of the topics that we consider in other chapters.

### FILMs Are Structures of Control and Coordination

Managers incorporate FILMs into the design of employment relations to gain better control over their workforces and to coordinate organizational activities (see Chapter 4). Edwards' (1979) influential historical analysis of the evolution of worker control identified FILMs as the major element of a "bureaucratic control" strategy. In this understanding, firms obtained workers' compliance by tying their future interests to the continued success of the firm and by using incentives such as career advancement and promotion opportunities to elicit employee loyalty and attachment to the organization (e.g., Lincoln and Kalleberg 1990).

### FILMs Influence Hiring Practices

FILMs affect an organization's recruitment and hiring practices. Organizations are more likely to spend much time and resources searching for qualified persons to work in FILMs,[1] in that they expect such employees to be with the organization for a long time. Within an establishment, FILMs should lead to more formalized procedures for promotion and transfer.[2] Moreover, a primary function of a FILM is to allocate the available workers (including applicants) into a set of open firm positions (jobs). Managers assume that this sorting process will eventually result in a maximally efficient match between workers' skills and the firm's production requirements (Granovetter 1981). A FILM restricts the number and type of workers who are eligible to enter the vacancies in an organization, generally giving priority to employees previously hired at or promoted from lower levels in a job ladder.

### FILMs Are Structural Contexts for Training

Much company training occurs within FILMs (see Chapters 8 and 9), which creates an incentive structure that encourages experienced workers to pass on their skills to new workers (Thurow 1975; Williamson 1981). Training and skill transfer in organizations are often hampered because older workers fear that by training new workers, they will reduce their own relative value to the firm and thereby increase their risk of being laid off (or at least reduce their bargaining position). FILMs help to counteract these fears by instituting a more or less formal practice of protecting and rewarding experienced employees via job security, wage raises, and promotions. This reasoning suggests that firm-specific skills should tend to develop in FILMs and vice versa: FILMs should emerge primarily in organizations that depend more on firm-specific training. To the extent that skills are firm-specific, the firm invests considerable resources in training new workers. This makes it important for the firm to reduce quits, particularly when it is costly to replace workers.

### FILMs and High-Performance Work Organizations

FILMs are closely related to several characteristics of "high performance" work organizations (see Chapter 6): They provide contexts that facilitate informal exchange of skills and other types of job training and worker development (see Chapters 8 and 9); they influence wage schedules and differentials within the organization (see also Chapters 10 and 11); and they facilitate the employment security enjoyed by workers who are insulated from competition with persons in the external market. Our analysis in Chapter 6 also reveals that organizations with FILMs perform better with regard to product development and innovation, attracting and retaining employees (which suggests the importance of FILMs for skill development and incentives), and financial performance (for profit-making organizations). On the other hand, FILMs appear to be unrelated to the quality of employee relations, which partly reflects the tendency of FILMs to create competition among employees who seek career advancement within the organization (Edwards 1979).

### FILMs and Organizational Earnings Inequality

Chapter 11 shows that organizations with FILMs have higher degrees of inequality within occupations, but less dispersion between occupations. A theoretical explanation for this result is that FILMs help to create and legitimate inequality within occupations or job clusters by stratifying individuals vertically via a hierarchy of positions with increasing levels of pay. At the same time, FILMs help to reduce wage differentials between one occupation and another. As part of a bureaucratic control strategy, FILMs tend to promote meritocracy by standardizing wage structures across different job clusters; consequently, employees at the same level in different occupations are more likely to receive similar wages when FILMs are present.

Organizations with FILMs also pay higher *levels* of earnings (Chapter 10). Other than size, FILMs are the organizational characteristic that is most strongly related to earnings. This is consistent with most previous research in the United States, which has also found that FILM incumbents generally receive higher earnings than employees who are not in FILMs (see also Kalleberg and Marsden 1995, for evidence based on a Norwegian sample). An institutional explanation for this positive association is that high wages reflect a strategy used by firms to establish a favorable position in the labor market. It may also be the case that this positive relationship is largely spurious: Organizations with FILMs may face less competition in product markets, for example, and therefore be able to garner higher profits, some of which can be shared with employees.

### FILMs Enhance Fringe Benefits

Kalleberg and Van Buren (1996, Table 2) also found that there was a positive correlation between FILMs and fringe benefits. This correlation may be because organizations with FILMs have, and seek to maintain, long-term relations with their employees.[3]

### FILMs and Contingent Work

FILMs are associated with relatively long-term, stable employment relations. Such relations are the flip side of contingent work arrangements, which we examine in Chapter 13. FILMs are related to contingent employment relations in the sense that the ability of organizations to employ part-time, temporary, and other types of contingent workers may depend on the presence of a core of highly committed, fairly permanent workers (such as those found in FILMs) who provide continuity and stability for the organization. Kalleberg's (1994) analysis of the NOS data supports this argument, as he finds that there is a positive correlation between the presence of FILMs and the use of subcontractors in "flexible firms."

### FILMs and Organizational Gender Segregation

FILMs are a principal channel by which intraorganizational mobility occurs, and that men are more likely than women to be in FILMs is an important reason why women experience less career advancement than men. Chapter 14 looks at the relationship between gender segregation and one important aspect of FILMs: promotion opportunities associated with occupations. We find that occupations composed mainly of men provide the greatest opportunities for promotion.

### FILMs and Organizational Commitment

FILMs have important incentive effects in that they make it individually rational to exhibit certain attitudes and behaviors that permit an individual to maximize expected lifetime earnings and other job rewards. Among these are to work harder, to stay with the firm, to share his or her skills with less experienced workers, to experience mobility within an organization or to expect promotion in the future, and to refrain from participating in collective action with other workers. All these factors have been hypothesized to affect workers' levels of organizational commitment—that is, loyalty, attachment, and effort (Burawoy 1979; Edwards 1979; Lincoln and Kalleberg 1990). Kalleberg and Mastekaasa's (1994) analysis of the NOS and 1991 GSS data shows that FILMs are related on a bivariate level to many of the variables associated with organizational commitment, though there is little overall relationship between FILMs and commitment once other correlates of commitment are controlled. They report a similar result for a Norwegian data set. Chapter 15 presents relevant findings based on the 1991 GSS data.

## Measuring FILMs and Dispute Resolution Procedures

We base our measure of FILMs on managers' reports of how much mobility (both potential and actual) there was in several occupations (including managerial ones) in their establishments. Directly measuring FILMs from data supplied by organizational informants is an advance over the indirect indicators of FILMs used by most previous studies.

Table 5.1 presents the items we used to construct a FILM scale from the NOS data. The scale includes items measuring whether vacancies tend to be

**Table 5.1** Internal Labor Market Items in FILMs Scale[a]

|  | Percentage | | |
| Item | Unweighted | Weighted | N |
| --- | --- | --- | --- |
| Vacancies filled with current employees: | | | |
| Core occupations | 57.5 | 12.8 | 678 |
| General Social Survey (GSS) occupations | 55.1 | 12.1 | 657 |
| Managerial/administrative occupations | 72.3 | 16.7 | 664 |
| Multiple grades/levels within occupation: | | | |
| Core occupations | 51.6 | 15.1 | 674 |
| GSS occupations | 41.7 | 14.1 | 654 |
| Managerial/administrative occupations | 66.1 | 12.7 | 666 |
| Promotion occurs often or very often from: | | | |
| Core occupations | 30.8 | 6.9 | 672 |
| GSS occupations | 26.3 | 6.3 | 654 |
| Firm-internal labor market scale[b] | | | |
| Mean | 2.55 | 1.39 | 678 |
| Standard deviation | 0.91 | 0.72 | |
| Median | 2.75 | 1.00 | |
| Interquartile range | 1.25 | 0.38 | |
| Cronbach's α | 0.84 | | |

a. Three specific survey questions were asked. "Yes" or "No" answers were requested from: [vacancies] "Do you sometimes fill (occupation) vacancies with people already employed at (establishment)?" and [grades] "Are there different levels of (occupation)?" The third type of question asked, [frequency] "Is it possible for a (occupation) to be promoted to a level above (occupation)? How often does this happen?" Answers ranged from *not at all* to *very often.* "Don't know" and "does not apply" responses are excluded from percentages reported.
b. The firm-internal labor market scale is the mean score for an establishment on the eight items listed in this table. All items were recoded to a 1 to 4 scale prior to computing the scale score, with high scores indicating presence of internal labor markets; values for missing responses were imputed if the respondent answered six or more of the other items.

filled with current employees, whether there exist multiple levels or grades within occupations (which provide for promotion opportunities), and the frequency of actual promotion out of particular occupations. These items were repeated for core, GSS, and managerial/administrative occupations.[4] The 8-item FILM scale has a relatively high estimated reliability ($\alpha = 0.84$).

We see from the unweighted percentages in Table 5.1 that half or more of the sampled establishments have multiple grades within both core and managerial/administrative occupations, and that more than half of them tend to fill vacancies with current employees in all three occupations studied—especially in the managerial/administrative ranks. Promotion occurs "often" or "very often" from core and GSS occupations only in a quarter to a third of the establishments, however.

This approach to measuring FILMs corresponds to that used by Pfeffer and Cohen (1984), whose empirical indicators of FILMs were also based on mobility patterns within the organization: whether most employees with 5 years or more of service had been promoted at least once and whether the organization filled almost all jobs from within. We reiterate that this organizational indicator of FILMs assesses only the probability of internal job mobility—a central dimension of FILMs, but not the only one—within the establishment. Moreover, our establishment-level measure does not tell us whether a particular employee is within a FILM. Thus, our measure does not capture that these structures exist for some groups of employees but not others (Baron, Davis-Blake, and Bielby 1986; Althauser 1989).

## Due Process in the Workplace

Those examining the bureaucratization or legalization of employment relations (e.g., Sutton et al. 1994; Bridges and Villemez 1994) approach this phenomenon from multiple perspectives. The common theme of these is the impersonalization of the relationship between employers and employees, especially the provision of protection for employees against particularistic treatment by employers.

Similar to internal labor markets, structures ensuring due process have been measured in a variety of ways by different authors. Sutton et al. (1994) consider disciplinary hearings and grievance procedures for nonunion employees. Bridges and Villemez (1994) study grievance procedures and the provision of notice and/or severance pay in the event of employee firing. Dobbin et al. (1988) examine grievance procedures and the presence of affirmative action offices and plans.

Grievance procedures are common to all of these studies, and the sole indicator of due process obtained in the NOS measures this feature. The informant for each establishment was asked to say whether there are "formal procedures for resolving disputes between employees and their supervisors or coworkers." Of 675 establishments providing responses, 68% indicated that such procedures are present, for the unweighted NOS sample. So about two thirds of the U.S. workforce in 1991 had access to such procedures. In that, as we shall see, the presence of dispute resolution procedures is appreciably associated with establishment size, the percentage is lower in the weighted sample; we estimate that formal dispute resolution procedures are present in only about 18% of U.S. work establishments.

## Correlates of FILMs

A vast amount of scholarship has been devoted to understanding the conditions under which FILMs are most apt to appear (see Althauser and Kalleberg, 1981, and Althauser, 1989, for reviews). Considerations both within and outside organizations have been introduced. One perspective sees FILMs as adaptations by employers to such problems as skill scarcity or the need to control workers. By paying above-market "efficiency wages" and offering security and good promotion opportunities, firms make the acquisition of employer-specific skills less risky for workers; organizations are thereby better able to attract and retain employees with scarce abilities (Williamson 1981). Clearly, this is costly, so such strategies are available only to those firms having the resources to afford them.

On the other hand, Marxist scholars depict the linkage of jobs into elaborate promotion chains as a control strategy created by capitalists to fragment the workforce, thwart labor union organizing drives, and foster worker compliance with management directives to extract surplus labor value for the corporation (Burawoy 1979, pp. 95-108; Edwards 1979, pp. 130-162). By enticing employees to seek highly stratified job placements that are differentially graded in pay and status, the company induces individual striving for upward mobility at the expense of working-class solidarity.

Still another view holds that FILMs are a product of external, institutional influences rather than organizational strategy. Baron, Dobbin, and Jennings (1986), for example, point to government pressure toward the adoption of various bureaucratic personnel practices, including internal promotion and transfer systems, as well as seniority provisions; this emerged in the course of promoting labor peace to avoid disruptions in production during World War II. Trade union presence (or its threat) can also be an impetus toward the creation of FILMs, either as a means of ensuring a stable union-management relationship or as part of an alternative nonunion employment system (Kochan, Katz, and McKersie 1986). The professional affiliations of personnel or labor relations managers are an additional institutional consideration that has been brought to bear on the explanation of FILMs: By creating bureaucratized employment relations to be administered centrally, such managers enhanced their standing within firms (Jacoby 1985; Baron, Dobbins, and Jennings 1986).

A final set of factors relevant to FILMs includes structural conditions such as complexity and formalization within a workplace or firm. Opportunities to create promotion ladders are clearly greater when the structure of an organization includes many ranks. Likewise, within-firm career progression can occur more frequently if there are other units in a multisite organization that can offer prospects for upward mobility. We also expect that FILMs, which formalize promotion procedures, will be more common when an organization has formalized its procedures for doing other things (see Baron, Davis-Blake, and Bielby 1986).

We will not attempt here to examine these hypotheses about the determinants of FILMs exhaustively. Testing many of them requires historical data on the origins and evolution of these structures. Our aims in this chapter are more modest: We will present some correlation and regression analyses that show how FILMs are associated with some of the main measures of organizational structures and environments that we discuss elsewhere in this book. These analyses, for our large and representative database, complement longitudinal studies based on more specialized samples (e.g., Dobbin et al. 1993).

Figures 5.1 through 5.3 and the first column of Table 5.2 show how our measure of FILMs is related to industry, size, and other key correlates measured by the NOS. FILMs are most likely to be found in manufacturing industries and in public administration. They are also comparatively common in professional services, transportation, and establishments in finance, insurance, or real estate. FILMs are least likely to be found in establishments working in agriculture-mining, construction, or business and personal services (see Figure 5.1). The measures available to us do not capture technology with any precision; however, bivariate results in the first column of Table 5.2 do indicate that FILMs are more common in establishments that produce products rather than services, and especially within those that produce both products and services.

Establishment size differences in FILMs account in part for these industry differences. The scatterplot in Figure 5.2 shows that the presence of FILMs is strongly related to establishment size; FILMs are more likely to be found in larger establishments (Villemez and Bridges 1988; Brown and Medoff 1989; Van Buren 1992; Bridges and Villemez 1994; Kalleberg and Van Buren 1996). This relationship is nonlinear but monotonic, with

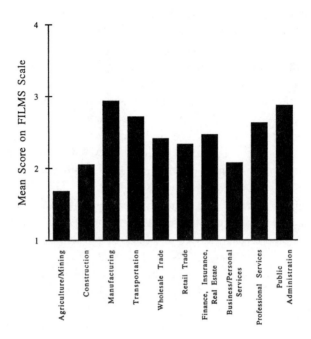

**Figure 5.1.** FILMs Scale, by Major Industry

a drop-off in the rate at which FILMs increase with size among the very largest organizations. We also observed the size-FILMs link in Table 5.1: The tendency of FILMs to be found in larger establishments was reflected in the marked differences between the weighted and unweighted percentages and FILM scale scores.

The upper left bar chart in Figure 5.3 shows that FILMs are most likely to be found in public and nonprofit organizations (see also the first column of Table 5.2). Organizations in the private sector are least likely to have FILMs, reflecting perhaps the greater competitive pressures on organizations in this sector to be "lean and mean" by reducing their dependence on fixed-cost, full-time permanent workers, as well as reflecting the fact that establishments in this sector tend to be smaller than those in the public and private nonprofit sectors (see Chapter 3).

The upper right graph in Figure 5.3 shows that FILMs are more likely to be found in unionized organizations (see also the first column of Table 5.2). This reflects in part the tendency of unions to organize large establishments. It is also partly due to the success that unions have had in

**Table 5.2** Correlates of Presence of Firm Internal Labor Markets (regression coefficients)

| Predictor | Bivariate Coefficients | Contextual Variables | Structural Variables | Structural and Contextual Variables |
|---|---|---|---|---|
| | | *Predictors Included* | | |
| Log size (linear)[a] | 0.649** | | 0.328** | 0.352** |
| Log size (quadratic)[a] | −0.042** | | −0.017** | −0.020** |
| Log levels | 0.646** | | 0.131** | 0.118** |
| Departments | 1.424** | | 0.046 | 0.085 |
| Decentralization | 0.217** | | −0.066* | −0.032 |
| Formalization | 1.734** | | 0.738** | 0.609** |
| Service | −0.325** | −0.134 | | 0.051 |
| Service and product | 0.225 | 0.126 | | 0.303** |
| Market scope | 0.160** | 0.111** | | −0.008 |
| Log age | 0.273** | 0.141** | | 0.024 |
| Employee problems | 0.401** | 0.134* | | 0.038 |
| Complexity | 1.053** | 0.427** | | 0.138 |
| Public | 0.445** | 0.068 | | −0.128 |
| Nonprofit | 0.268* | 0.127 | | −0.175 |
| Institutionalization | 0.268** | 0.113** | | −0.026 |
| Union pressure | 0.498** | 0.152** | | −0.020 |
| Multisite organization | 0.845** | 0.534** | | 0.233** |
| Constant | (varies) | 0.513** | 1.059** | 0.779** |
| $R^2$ | (varies) | 0.376 | 0.550 | 0.599 |
| $N$ | (varies) | 616 | 611 | 579 |

a. Bivariate equation for size includes both linear and quadratic terms.
*$p < .05$; **$p < .01$.

creating differentiated jobs that are distributed to workers on the basis of seniority (see Elbaum 1984; Jacoby 1984; Kochan et al. 1986).

Organizations that are subject to greater institutional pressures are more likely to have FILMs. The results for union pressure are one indication. We also observe that FILMs are, on average, better developed in establishments that are part of larger organizations than in independent workplaces (bottom left of Figure 5.3) and that those with high scores on the institutionalization scale are more apt to have FILMs (lower right of Figure 5.3). All of these findings are consistent with the arguments that attribute the emergence of FILMs to external influences rather than to internal organizational strategies.

Bivariate associations (see the first column of Table 5.2) also reveal that extensive promotion opportunities are more common in establishments

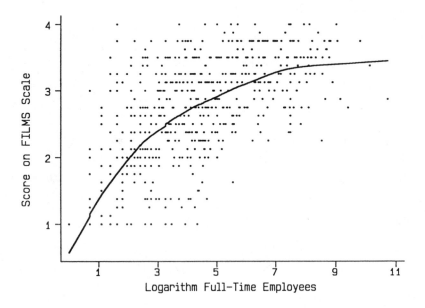

**Figure 5.2.** FILMs Scale, by Establishment Size

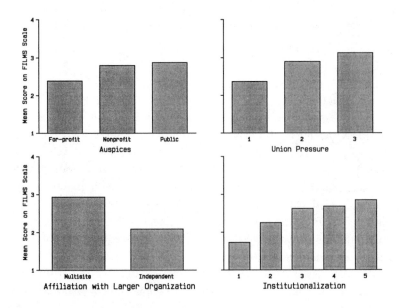

**Figure 5.3.** Bivariate Differences in FILMs

having wider market areas, in older establishments, and in establishments that anticipate problems in attracting or retaining qualified employees. FILMs appear to be more common in complex environments than in simple ones.

## Multivariate Analysis

The predictors of FILMs discussed previously are intertwined with one another, of course; in particular, most of them are closely linked to establishment size. For this reason it is important to examine the correlates of FILMs in a multivariate context. We did this using regression models that contain sets of structural and contextual variables that are related to the arguments about FILMs discussed earlier. Explanations related to size, structural complexity, and formality are represented using structural indicators introduced in Chapters 3 and 4. Measures relevant to institutional accounts include the variables used in the plots in Figure 5.3. We also introduced a number of other environmental variables discussed in Chapter 3 as predictors of FILMs.

The multiple regression results reported in the second and third columns of Table 5.2 include, respectively, the sets of contextual and structural variables used in the analysis of coordination and control structures in Chapter 4. All predictors are included in the equation reported in the final column.

Considering contextual indicators first (column 2), we observe tendencies for FILMs to be more common in establishments that have wider market scope; that are older; that anticipate more problems in attracting, retaining, and compensating qualified employees; and that are confronted with greater environmental complexity. The results for the employee problems scale lend some plausibility to accounts that see FILMs as solutions to incentive problems.

Continuing, we observe that (net of other contextual predictors) FILMs are more common in more institutionalized settings, in workplaces that are unionized, and in those that are affiliated with larger organizations. After adjustments for the other contextual variables, the sectoral differences between public, nonprofit, and for-profit establishments displayed in Figure 5.3 become statistically insignificant.

Column 3 of Table 5.2 includes size together with indicators of organization structure from Chapter 4. In keeping with the pattern shown in Figure 5.2, the estimates for size indicate that FILMS rise with the number of full-time employees, but at a declining rate. Taller organizations are more apt to have FILMS, which is consistent with the claim that structurally, such organizations yield more opportunities to construct promotion ladders. And workplaces that have formalized the personnel practices studied in Chapter 4 (Table 4.2) are more likely, net of size and other structural features, to have the multiple grades, internal promotion practices, and promotion rates that constitute our FILMs scale. Interestingly, column 3 shows that FILMs are less common in establishments having considerable decentralization—that is, personnel decisions made by employees beneath the level of the establishment head. This finding is consistent with accounts that ascribe a central role to personnel professionals in the creation of FILMs.[5]

When all predictors are considered, in the rightmost column of Table 5.2, we observe that several bivariate and partial coefficients vanish statistically. Net of all other structural and environmental considerations, we find that FILMs are more common in large, tall, and formalized organizations. They are also significantly better developed in establishments that are affiliated with larger organizations and in those that produce both products and services. These results suggest that, in a proximate sense, structural features of establishments are very important considerations in the explanation of FILMs.[6] Taken together, the factors introduced in Table 5.2 account for nearly three fifths of the variation in the FILM scale within the NOS sample.

## Correlates of Dispute Resolution Procedures

Theoretical accounts of the sources of grievance procedures and other aspects of due process in organizations have been offered by Dobbin et al. (1988), Edelman (1990), Sutton et al. (1994), and Bridges and Villemez (1994), among others. As in the case of FILMs, some of these emphasize technical factors, seeing the formality of dispute resolution procedures as an instance of a more general process of formalization that accompanies increased scale and complexity. Others see such procedures as the result of collective action on behalf of employees through unionization, or as employer actions designed to forestall unionization. Institutional accounts argue that lawlike methods for resolving workplace disputes are a reflection of developing societal understandings about employee rights within the workplace (see especially Sutton et al. 1994).

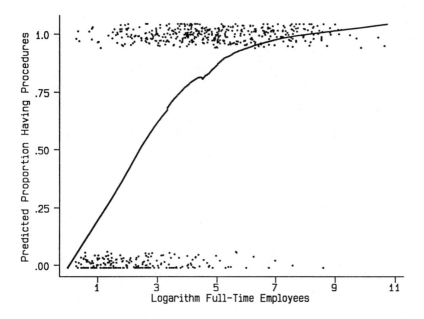

**Figure 5.4.** Grievance Procedures, by Establishment Size

In general terms, correlates of the presence of formal dispute resolution procedures in the NOS appear to be remarkably similar to those of FILMs. Figures 5.4 and 5.5 illustrate this. Figure 5.4 shows that such procedures are rare in small establishments.[7] The predicted probability of finding them is above 0.5, however, in workplaces that have 20 (=exp[3]) full-time employees, and more than 0.75 in workplaces larger than size 148 (=exp[5]). In larger establishments, the probability of finding formal procedures for disputes verges on certainty.

The patterns in the barcharts of Figure 5.5 are highly reminiscent of those seen in Figure 5.3. As with FILMs, dispute resolution procedures are more often found in public and nonprofit establishments than in for-profit ones, in establishments that are unionized, in those affiliated with larger organizations, and in workplaces that have high values on the institutionalization scale. The bivariate regression coefficients in the first column of Table 5.3 illustrate these patterns as well; they also show that dispute resolution formality tends to be found in vertically and horizontally complex establishments and in formalized and older ones.

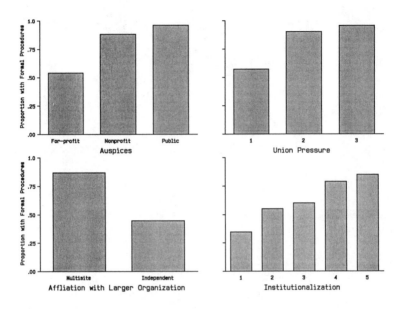

**Figure 5.5.** Bivariate Differences in Grievance Procedures

## Multivariate Analysis

We used logistic regression to examine further the correlates of formal procedures for disputes while controlling for other predictors. All structural variables and a subset of the contextual variables used to study FILMs were included in these analyses. As in Table 5.2, we first entered the contextual (column 2) and structural (column 3) correlates separately. Then we considered all correlates simultaneously in the equation reported in the final column.

Findings from the analysis involving contextual variables only (column 2) are parallel to those reported on a bivariate level (Figure 5.5 and the first column of Table 5.3). In the third column of Table 5.3, we see that after adjusting for other structural variables, the log-odds that an establishment has formal procedures rises linearly with log establishment size; the evident curvilinearity in Figure 5.4 does not appear. The formalization scale (Table 4.2) is very strongly related to dispute resolution procedures, as accounts based on scale and formalization would anticipate. Consistent with the parallel result for FILMs, establishments with decentralized decision-making structures for personnel matters (Table 4.3) are notably less likely to have grievance procedures, net of other structural features.

**Table 5.3.** Correlates of Presence of Formal Procedures for Resolving Disputes (logistic regression coefficients)

| Predictor | Bivariate Coefficients | Predictors Included Contextual Variables | Structural Variables | Structural and Contextual Variables |
|---|---|---|---|---|
| Log size (linear)[a] | 1.320** | | 0.653** | 0.641** |
| Log size (quadratic)[a] | −0.068* | | __[b] | __[b] |
| Log levels | 1.558** | | 0.147 | −0.067 |
| Departments | 3.263** | | −0.850 | −1.682* |
| Decentralization | 0.143 | | −0.647** | −0.270 |
| Formalization | 5.228** | | 3.675** | 3.144** |
| Log age | 0.625** | 0.283** | | 0.014 |
| Public | 2.932** | 2.295** | | 2.428** |
| Nonprofit | 1.329** | 1.669** | | 1.653** |
| Institutionalization | 0.644** | 0.290** | | −0.174 |
| Union pressure | 2.625** | 1.846** | | 1.169** |
| Multisite organization | 2.094** | 1.706** | | 0.784** |
| Constant | (varies) | −4.518** | −2.032** | −4.051** |
| Log likelihood | (varies) | −250.47 | −215.80 | −177.92 |
| N | (varies) | 640 | 612 | 592 |

a. The bivariate equation for size includes both linear and quadratic terms.
b. The quadratic term was removed from the equation due to insignificance.
$*p < .05; **p < .01$.

In contrast to the results for the FILMs scale, we see that most of these findings hold up when contextual and structural variables are used simultaneously to predict dispute resolution procedures. Among the structural variables having significant coefficients are size and formalization; there is also a somewhat curious tendency, net of other predictors, for dispute resolution procedures to be less common in horizontally complex workplaces.

Table 5.2 showed that few contextual factors, other than affiliation with a larger organization, had net effects on the FILMs scale. The results for dispute resolution procedures are quite different in this regard. Even after statistical adjustments for size and formalization, the presence of dispute resolution procedures differs by auspices: Public organizations are most likely to have them, followed by nonprofit and for-profit establishments. This is consistent with the argument (Dobbin et al. 1988) that organizations with exposure to the public sphere are especially apt to conform to emergent standards of citizenship. Similarly, net of all other predictors, dispute resolution procedures are more often found in establishments surrounded by unions; this finding lends support to accounts stressing worker collective action (or its threat) as a stimulus for the creation of due-process structures.

The rightmost column of Table 5.3 also shows that formal methods for handling disputes are more often found, as were FILMs, in establishments that are part of a larger organization than in independent concerns. This can be interpreted as an external effect of centralized personnel policy. The results of our multivariate analysis of dispute resolution procedures, then, highlight the part played by factors external to the establishment (auspices, unions, and headquarters units) to a much greater degree than did those pertaining to FILMs.

## Control Clusters and Profiles

The propositions examined in this and the previous chapter have treated the different structural devices and elements of employment relations in establishments separately. The implicit presumption is that they are always complementary or alternative to one another. In this section, we summarize the empirical examination of the coordination and control strategies of NOS establishments presented here and in Chapter 4 by looking instead for particular profiles or combinations that co-occur frequently. A given pair of structural features may appear together in one of these configurations, but not in others. The combination of decentralization and formalization represents a quite different form of structure than does either of these features taken by itself, for example.

We began by selecting eight structural indicators. These include coordination and control structures studied in Chapter 4—departmentalization, vertical levels, decentralization, formalization, and administrative intensity—together with the FILMs scale and two other indicators that describe aspects of the employment relation—the presence or absence of employment contracts and of formal procedures for resolving workplace disputes.[8] Detailed written employment contracts may signal a stable relationship between an employer and a labor union. We gave these eight variables equal weight in our analysis by converting them to standardized ($z$) scores. The profiles of $z$-scores were then studied using cluster analysis. We used Ward's method (Kaufman and Rousseeuw 1990, pp. 230-234) to place the 582 establishments with valid scores on all eight variables into five disjoint clusters. Figure 5.6 displays the results.

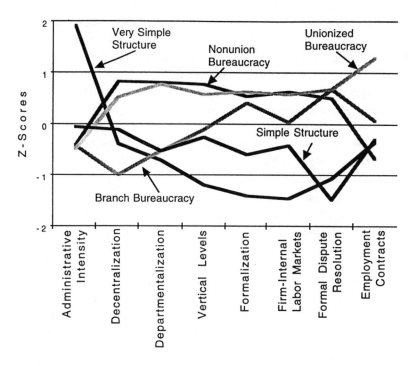

**Figure 5.6.** Five Coordination and Control Profiles

The five configurations identified can be loosely grouped into two variations on "simple structure" and three versions of "bureaucracy." The first configuration, which we label the *very simple structure,* is distinguished by its extremely high administrative ratio and the relative absence of other structural features. Decisions tend to be in the hands of the establishment head, there is little vertical or horizontal elaboration, and neither administrative procedures nor the employment relation are highly formalized. This minimal-overhead configuration is suggestive of a small, free-standing organization, similar to the office of an independent professional or a small shop.

The configuration called the *simple structure* in Figure 5.6 has below-average scores on all eight indicators in the profiles clustered; its features resemble those given for the simple structure described by Mintzberg (1979). The level of administrative intensity here is smaller than that in the *very simple* configuration, though larger than in the three bureaucratic forms. The simple structure has correspondingly higher levels of structural complexity, decentralization, and formalization, but establishments in this group *never* provide access to formal dispute resolution procedures for their employees. This is reminiscent of what Edwards (1979, p. 52) calls "hierarchical control"—a coordination/control pattern relying on close supervision and direct, unsupplemented managerial authority. Local restaurants or small construction concerns are plausible examples of organizations that might fall in this cluster.

Turning now to the bureaucratic configurations, we note first that two of them—the *unionized bureaucracy* and *nonunion bureaucracy*—have similar scores on all indicators except the last, employment contracts. These coordination/control patterns involve comparatively low concentrations of managers and high scores on decentralization and both vertical and horizontal differentiation. Formalization is extensive for administrative procedures, promotion, and dispute resolution alike. The unionized pattern is highly likely to include employment contracts; this item is least often found at establishments in the nonunion cluster. We suspect that the employment contracts item proxies other differences between unionized and nonunion industrial relations patterns. Especially suggestive is that the nonunion pattern combines the highest level of decentralization in any of the five configurations with elaborated internal labor markets and due process in dispute resolution. These are held by Kochan et al. (1986, Chapter 3) to be key features of the nonunion employment model that has grown more prominent since 1960. Examples of establishments to be found in this cluster would include factories and large offices (in the for-profit sector) and schools, colleges, and hospitals (in the public and nonprofit sectors).

We have labeled the last of our five clusters the *branch bureaucracy*. It combines the formalization and low administrative intensity found in the two bureaucratic forms just discussed with minimal departmentalization, a comparatively short hierarchy, and very high centralization. Indeed, the average (unstandardized) score of branch bureaucracies on our decentralization scale is 2.53; this value indicates that someone above the establishment head—at another location—is involved in most of the decisions that make up that scale. This pattern would seem to be characteristic of the satellite establishments of multisite organizations, or retail or restaurant franchises.

Like the Aston researchers (Pugh et al. 1969), who also developed a taxonomy of organizational structures by examining profiles of structural

**Table 5.4**  Contextual Differences Between Establishments Using Different Coordination and Control Profiles

| Contextual Feature | Coordination and Control Cluster | | | | |
|---|---|---|---|---|---|
| | (1) Very Simple Structure | (2) Simple Structure | (3) Nonunion Bureaucracy | (4) Unionized Bureaucracy | (5) Branch Bureaucracy |
| Mean number full-time employees | 7.70 | 26.10 | 1357.62 | 1285.93 | 65.00 |
| Mean age | 24.03 | 24.96 | 49.36 | 50.71 | 39.60 |
| Mean scope of market | 2.29 | 2.64 | 3.51 | 3.15 | 2.25 |
| Proportion | | | | | |
| For-profit | 0.89 | 0.93 | 0.62 | 0.46 | 0.47 |
| Nonprofit | 0.05 | 0.04 | 0.13 | 0.11 | 0.05 |
| Public | 0.06 | 0.04 | 0.25 | 0.43 | 0.47 |
| Products | 0.08 | 0.11 | 0.29 | 0.18 | 0.05 |
| Services | 0.86 | 0.79 | 0.61 | 0.70 | 0.87 |
| Both | 0.06 | 0.11 | 0.10 | 0.12 | 0.09 |
| Multisite organization | 0.17 | 0.32 | 0.63 | 0.64 | 0.81 |
| Mean union pressures | 1.03 | 1.08 | 1.41 | 1.80 | 1.50 |
| N | 63 | 114 | 142 | 111 | 152 |

indicators, our analysis points to the existence of multiple forms. The Aston group identified seven structural types, six of which they labeled as different forms of bureaucracy (the seventh was called the "implicitly structured organization"). These types were based on variables related to formalization ("structuring of activities"), centralization ("concentration of authority"), and administrative intensity ("line control of workflow"). The most common type found in the Aston study, the "workflow bureaucracy," is similar to our union and nonunion variants—it scores high on structuring of activities, but low on concentration of authority and line control of workflow. It is difficult to draw precise comparisons between our coordination/control types and those found in the Aston study because of the different structural indicators included in the two studies; moreover, the Aston study included only organizations having more than 250 employees (Pugh et al. 1968, p. 67), so it was necessarily unable to identify configurations that pertain to small workplaces.

The data in Table 5.4 further characterize the five coordination/control configurations found for the NOS. This table presents descriptive statistics on size, age, market scope, auspices, product or service mix, affiliation with a larger (multisite) organization, and union pressure for the five types of establishments. Differences between groups here are notable because the variables included in Table 5.4—unlike those appearing in Figure 5.6—were not used in constructing the clusters.

The differences shown in Table 5.4 are broadly congruent with the descriptions of the five coordination/control types given above. Very simple structures are quite small and comparatively young. Their markets tend to be located within a city or metropolitan area, and they concentrate on service production in the private sector. Few very simple structures are subunits of larger organizations, and they seem little affected by the presence or prospect of unions. Simple structures have similar features, though they tend to be somewhat larger than very simple ones.

The nonunion and unionized bureaucracies are found in larger work-places, averaging over 1,000 full-time employees. Establishments of both types are, on average, about 50 years old. The nonunion form is the most likely of the five to be concerned with the production of products; the unionized form includes nearly as many public-sector establishments as it does for-profit ones. The mean market scope of organizations of these types is statewide to regional. Establishments clustered in the unionized type have the highest average score on the union pressures scale, but informants of establishments in the nonunion cluster also indicated that organized labor was an appreciable feature of their contexts. For each of these types, over three fifths of the establishments are part of multisite organizations.

As its label suggests, however, branch bureaucracy establishments are the most likely of the five types to be subunits of larger complexes. Nearly half of the establishments in this cluster are in the public sector. Their market areas tend to be local, and they concentrate on service provision. Though they employ more workers than do the two variants on simple structure, their mean full-time employment level (65 workers) is about 5% as large as that of nonunion or unionized bureaucracies.

## Conclusion

This chapter has drawn on the National Organizations Study in analyzing two ways in which employee-employer relations have grown more formalized: the development of internal labor markets with strong promotion prospects and of formal dispute resolution procedures. These elements of the employment relation tend to be found in similar types of organizations. Both are more common in large and otherwise formalized establishments, in the public and nonprofit sectors, in unionized workplaces, and in units affiliated with larger organizational complexes. External considerations and pressures are of special relevance to the development of dispute resolution structures.

By creating the prospect of a career within an organization and heightening the degree of legitimacy within the workplace, devices of employment bureaucracy like FILMs and dispute resolution procedures foster long-term and close ties between employees and employers. As such, they may be seen as elements of the coordination/control structures of establishments. At the end of this chapter, we summarized the analyses of coordination and control presented in Chapters 4 and 5. We identified five distinct configurations of coordination/control strategies, which involve both the administrative design of the establishment and the structure of its relationship to employees. Two of the five are variations on simple structure used predominantly by small, independent firms. The other three are varieties of bureaucracy found in large nonunionized, large unionized, and smaller branch or subsidiary establishments.

The structural questions studied in Chapter 4 involved coordination and control devices that animated organizational researchers in the 1970s and 1980s. In this chapter, we have focused on the features of employment relations that have drawn attention in the 1980s and early 1990s. The discussion proceeds in Chapter 6 with a study of features of "high-performance" work organizations that have been emerging in the 1990s. Later in the book, Chapter 13 examines the phenomenon of contingent employment, one that may reverse the trend toward closer employer-employee linkages on which our discussion in this chapter has centered.

## Notes

1. Bivariate correlations indicate, for example, that NOS establishments with FILMs are somewhat more likely to use employment agencies in recruiting applicants and to use tests in selecting new employees. They tend to interview more applicants, for longer periods of time, before offering a position to an applicant. See Chapter 7, especially Table 7.6.

2. Bivariate NOS correlations indicate that establishments having FILMs are more likely to post internal vacancies.

3. In the NOS, we find bivariate correlations above 0.4 between the FILMs scale and the availability of the following fringe benefits: medical insurance, dental benefits, life insurance, sick leave, maternity or paternity leave, pension plans, drug and alcohol abuse programs, and long-term disability insurance.

4. Informants were not asked about the frequency of promotion from managerial-administrative occupations.

5. Note, however, that the measure of departmentalization does not have a significant influence on FILMs in Table 5.2. Nor does a dummy variable indicating the presence of a separate personnel-labor relations department (results not shown).

6. Of course, the findings can be interpreted in more than one way. For example, size is to some degree a measure of visibility and thus susceptibility to institutional pressure, whereas formalization may be one channel through which institutional and union pressures encourage the formation of internal labor markets.

7. Similar to Figure 5.2, Figure 5.4 includes a nonparametric regression line. Because the dependent variable here has only two values, the points in the scatterplot have been randomly "jittered" around the values 0 and 1, to provide a better graphical sense of the density of observations at different values of (log) establishment size. This adjustment in the presentation of data does not, however, play a part in determining the position of the regression line.

8. The item on employment contracts was part of the sequence of NOS questions used to measure formalization. It was not part of the formalization scale because its inclusion reduced scale reliability.

# 6

# Human Resource Management and Organizational Performance

ARNE L. KALLEBERG

JAMES W. MOODY

The traditional model of human resource management systems in the United States, which was based on bureaucratic control mechanisms and designed for mass production, has come under attack in recent years. Pressures deriving from intensified foreign competition, rapid technological change, greater needs for innovation, and workers' demands for empowered jobs have led some American organizations to search for alternatives to this traditional model. Theorists have developed the idea of a "transformed" or "high-performance" work system in the United States that represents a composite of several models that are alternatives to mass production (Bailey 1992; Kochan and Useem 1992; Lawler 1992; Osterman 1994a; Appelbaum and Batt 1994).

Different labels have been used to contrast the ideal "old" and "new" forms of human resource management (HRM) systems (see Bailey 1992). These labels include *mass* versus *flexible production* (Piore and Sabel 1984); *industrial* versus *salaried* (Osterman 1988); *old competition* versus *new competition* (Best 1990); *conflict* versus *commitment* (Walton 1985); *cost reduction* versus *commitment maximizing* (Arthur 1992); and *high performance work organizations* versus *mass production-low wage organizations* (Commission on the Skills of the American Workforce 1990). These labels point to four basic features that are believed to characterize high performing work organizations: (a) decentralized decision making, (b) teamwork and flexible deployment of workers, (c) human resource practices emphasizing training and performance-based compensation, and (d) consultative labor-management relations (see Table 6.1).

Despite the importance and timeliness of this topic, few empirical studies of the effects of high performance human resource policies and practices on organizational performance are based on representative samples of diverse work organizations.[1] The few extant national-level surveys of the diffusion of various work reform and employee involvement practices generally do not examine the relationship between human resource management practices and organizational performance (see Appelbaum and Batt 1994; Bailey 1992).[2] Some evidence on this issue comes from case studies and from nonrepresentative surveys (i.e., convenience samples, or mail surveys in which transformed organizations are more likely to respond) conducted by membership organizations, consulting firms, and other private industry sources. These nonrepresentative surveys and case studies, however, vary in quality, leading Appelbaum and Batt (1994, p. 58) to conclude that our understanding of what has taken place in American workplaces still is poor—despite the widespread interest in work reorganization—and that careful studies of this need to be done.

The NOS data enable us to take a look, albeit a very incomplete one, at the extent to which U.S. work organizations' human resource management practices display features of a high performance work organization system (HPO). In this chapter, we examine the relationships between the HPO characteristics that were measured in the NOS, on the one hand, and organizational performance, on the other. We first summarize a portion of the vast and growing literature on HPOs and identify some of the key

**Table 6.1**   Common Features of High Performance Work Organizations

---

Management Methods
  Organization structure
    (*Decentralization*[a])
  Use of flexible technologies
  Quality consciousness
Work Organization
  Teamwork
  Flexible deployment of workers
  Small distance between managers and workers
Human Resource Practices
  Substantial worker education and training
    (*Did organization provide any formal job training in past two years; effectiveness*
      *of training*[a])
    (*Firm internal labor markets*[a])
  Compensation strategies (Gainsharing)
    (*Cash or stock bonuses for performance or merit; profit-sharing or stock option*
      *programs*[a])
  Commitment to employment security
    (*Firm internal labor markets*[a])
Industrial Relations
  Consultative labor-management relations

---

a. Measures available in the National Organizations Study.

human resource management policies and practices that are commonly associated with this organizational form. We then discuss the measures of these characteristics and examine how they cluster to form discrete groups of organizations in the NOS. We next relate these HPO features to measures of organizational performance to test hypotheses about whether organizations that have features commonly associated with HPOs actually perform better than other organizations.

## Characteristics of High Performing Organizations in the United States

Writers disagree about some of the specific characteristics of HPOs, though most would agree on four basic dimensions that constitute elements of a model of a "high performance work organization." These four components of HPOs are summarized in Table 6.1, which we have adapted from Appelbaum and Batt (1994, Table 4.1).

First, HPO *management methods* are characterized by a concern with quality and employee participation. Quality consciousness often takes the form of practices such as Total Quality Management, quality circles, or quality improvement teams. HPOs also tend to use flexible technologies that allow them to produce custom products for specific market niches (Piore and Sabel 1984). Moreover, HPOs emphasize employee involvement and participation in decision making. HPOs empower employees to make decisions in that they believe that employees are closer to the customer than highly placed managers and are thus better able to identify and solve problems in the production process. Managers in HPOs assume that by decentralizing decision making and involving workers more in the running of the business, they will be able to improve product quality, reduce costs, increase communication, enhance morale, and reduce conflict.

Second, HPOs have distinctive forms of *work organization*. Most striking here is the reliance on teams, often self-directed teams, to carry out product tasks (Osterman 1994a). The "team-based" production model of HPOs relies on the frontline workforce as the main source of competitive advantage and continuous improvement (see Appelbaum and Batt 1994). Team production helps to reduce the company's dependence on detailed job descriptions and encourages job rotation and the deployment of employees to various tasks in the organization. Working in teams also creates a sense of shared purpose and common effort, values that HPOs rely on to obtain the maximum discretionary effort from their employees (Bailey 1992).

Third, HPOs have adopted *human resource practices* that are consistent with, and supportive of, the focus on quality, employee participation, and teamwork. HPOs invest considerable resources in training their workers to perform a variety of tasks within the organization and to adapt to the changes that will inevitably occur in a dynamic economy. HPOs also gear compensation to group rather than individual performance—for example, by implementing profit sharing or gainsharing programs. They seek to reward performance by compensation schemes based on knowledge and skills and also seek to induce worker effort and commitment by providing employment security, at least to their core workers.

Finally, HPOs are characterized by *industrial relations* systems that emphasize consultation rather than confrontation. Status differences between managers and workers are reduced in most HPOs, so as to facilitate labor-management cooperation. In addition, joint labor-management committees designed to solve particular problems (such as training or health and safety) are fairly common.

The NOS data set was not designed explicitly to measure HPOs, and it contains better measures of some of these components than others. Fairly good measures are available of compensation and training strategies. By contrast, we have only indirect measures of an organization's flexibility in the deployment of workers and no measures of the use of teams and consultative structures such as quality circles and employee-involvement programs. Thus, we do not have measures that would enable us to replicate Osterman's (1994a) definition of HPOs. He classifies plants as "transformed" based on four characteristics (two indicators of teams, as well as job rotation and the presence of a total quality management program). We do, however, have information on some of the human resource management practices that Osterman identifies as supporting the adoption of workplace transformation, such as gainsharing and extensive training.

## HPO Concepts Measured in the NOS

In this section, we describe the primary measures of HPOs that are available in the NOS. These HPO measures are identified in Table 6.1.

1. *Decentralization:* This is an indicator of the degree to which employees are able to participate in making various kinds of decisions (e.g., hiring, evaluating performance, scheduling—see Chapter 3). These, however, are mainly personnel decisions not operational ones. Consequently, the decisions on which our decentralization scale is primarily based constitute only a portion of those implicated in the notion of worker participation, which refers to a wide range of practices, including soliciting workers' suggestions, forming self-managing teams with almost total control of production, and helping to make decisions at plant and company levels (Cotton, Vollrath, Froggatt, Lengnick-Hall, and Jennings 1988; Lawler 1992).

2. *Job training:* Appelbaum and Batt (1994, p. 85) note that the best-practice firms invest heavily in training; they estimate that the amount of resources devoted to training by HPOs is at least 5% of payroll and sometimes 15% or more in self-directed team-based systems. Job training in HPOs facilitates flexible deployment of employees among job tasks. Moreover, job rotation has been used as an indicator of whether a plant is transformed (Osterman 1994a; see also Berger et al. 1989). Our measure

**Table 6.2** Correlation Matrix for High Performance Work Organizations (HPO) Measures

|                    | FILMs       | Training | Performance-Based Compensation | Decentral- ization |
|--------------------|-------------|----------|--------------------------------|--------------------|
| FILMs              | 1.00        | —        | —                              | —                  |
| Training           | 0.479       | 1.00     | —                              | —                  |
| Performance-based compensation | 0.214 | 0.178 | 1.00                      | —                  |
| Decentralization   | 0.211       | 0.167    | 0.202                          | 1.00               |
| Mean               | −0.053      | 1.8      | 1.74                           | 3.45               |
| Standard deviation | 2.55        | 1.22     | 0.433                          | 0.964              |
| Range              | −3.6 to 5.1 | 0 to 3   | 0 to 3                         | 1 to 5             |

NOTE: All correlations are significant at the .0001 level.

(*training*) is the manager's evaluation of the effectiveness of the organization's employee training (0 = *no training provided,* 3 = *highly effective*).

3. *Performance-based compensation:* Many writers identify gainsharing or profit sharing as a key characteristic of HPOs. This form of compensation is used as a strategic variable to improve firm competitiveness (Shuster and Zingheim 1992) in that this incentive ties the interests of workers more closely to that of the organization and enhances effort and performance. (See Freund and Epstein 1984, for empirical evidence on the incidence of gainsharing plans in the United States.) Our measure (*compens*) is a 5-item index including whether the organization offers profit sharing or stock option programs, cash or stock bonuses for performance or merit, and the importance of job performance for determining the earnings of the core occupation, the GSS respondents' or spouses' occupation, and managers.

4. *Firm internal labor markets.* FILMs are closely related to several characteristics of HPOs (see Chapter 5). They provide contexts that facilitate informal exchange of skills and other types of job training and worker development, they are associated with wage schedules and differentials within the organization (see Footnote 6), and they are indicators of employment security enjoyed by workers who are insulated from competition with persons in the external market. Table 6.2 presents descriptive statistics on our measures of HPO characteristics, and the correlations between them.

## Are There Distinct Clusters of HPO Characteristics?

HPO characteristics should be examined simultaneously rather than separately. Such a configurational approach is consistent with the idea of a system of work structures. Whereas many companies may have adopted one or another aspect of an HPO (e.g., Dulworth et al. 1990 found that 70% of 476 large companies had installed the most common form of participation—quality circles), relatively few companies have implemented work systems that require high integration with the organization's primary systems and processes (e.g., Dulworth, Landen, & Usilaner 1990 found that only 10% were high involvement, having three or more systems, with more than 40% of workers covered by each).

Levine and Tyson (1990) (see also Levine 1990) argue for a system approach, claiming that the benefits of participation on performance are contingent on four features of a firm's human resource practices and industrial relations systems: (a) whether the gains from improvements in productivity are shared with the workers (gainsharing), (b) whether the workers have employment security, (c) whether the firm has adopted measures to build group cohesiveness, (d) and whether there are guaranteed individual rights for employees. Similarly, Bailey (1992) argues that participation requires complete commitment to be effective. Thus, it is necessary for researchers to characterize the nature of the organization, not rely simply on information about whether firms use a particular technique.

Bailey (1992) and Appelbaum and Batt (1994) summarize the small number of studies that have sought to (a) classify groups of organizations using clustering techniques or indexes of transformed human resource policies and (b) examine whether adopting a cluster of organizational changes makes a difference. Studies emphasizing the interactions and complementarities among various human resource practices, however, are relatively scarce. Their paucity reflects the difficulties in gathering extensive organizational level data on performance, as well as human resource and industrial relations practices. So far, this has been possible with only a few data sets (e.g., Cutcher-Gershenfeld 1991; Arthur 1992).

Figure 6.1 presents the results of our configurational analysis of the four main HPO characteristics described in Table 6.2.[3] Applying clustering methods to these four characteristics revealed three major clusters.[4] *HPOs* are the organizations in the NOS that most closely correspond to the model

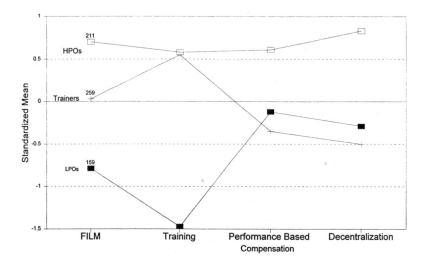

**Figure 6.1.** Three Human Resource Management Profiles

of high performing organizations: These establishments score highest on all four characteristics (FILMs, training, benefits, and decentralization). *Trainers* also have high scores on training but lower scores on the other three dimensions. Low performance work organizations (*LPOs*) have the lowest scores on FILMs and training but slightly higher scores than trainers on benefits and decentralization.

## Correlates of HPOs, LPOs, and Trainers

Table 6.3 shows how the characteristics of the three groups of organizations (looking at the individual variables and the clusters identified in Figure 6.1) are associated with central aspects of organizational differentiation identified in the NOS: size (the number of employees in the establishment and whether the establishment is an independent company or part of a larger firm); industry (whether the organization is in a manufacturing or service industry, based on the census classification); union pressure (see Chapter 3); and organization type (whether the organization is profit seeking, a government agency, a public or a private nonprofit organization).

Compared to other NOS organizations, HPOs are larger and more likely to be in manufacturing industries (see also Lawler, Ledford, and

**Table 6.3** Correlates of High Performance Work Organizations Measures and Clusters

| | FILMs | Training | Performance-Based Compensation | Decentralization | High Performance Work Organizations | Low Performance Work Organizations | Trainers |
|---|---|---|---|---|---|---|---|
| Size (logged) | 0.614*** | 0.469*** | 0.138*** | 0.423*** | 5.55 | 2.76 | 4.41 |
| Independent company | -0.436*** | -0.320*** | -0.089* | 0.264*** | 38.4% | 72.3% | 28.2% |
| Union pressure | 0.295*** | 0.244*** | -0.159*** | -0.015 | 1.42 | 1.11 | 1.55 |
| Manufacturing (census) | 0.164*** | 0.062 | 0.092* | 0.254*** | 29.3% | 10.1% | 11.2% |
| Service (census) | -0.109** | -0.030 | -0.009 | 0.079* | 61.1% | 71.7% | 70.3% |
| Profit | -0.254*** | -0.231*** | 0.172*** | 0.109** | 66.3% | 84.9% | 50.1% |
| Nonprofit public | 0.134*** | 0.091* | -0.239*** | -0.121*** | 9.9% | 5.7% | 22.8% |
| Nonprofit private | 0.051 | 0.077* | 0.089* | 0.146*** | 12.3% | 4.4% | 6.2% |
| Government | 0.180*** | 0.172*** | -0.063 | -0.142*** | 11.4% | 5.0% | 20.9% |
| Product | 0.114** | 0.066 | 0.053 | 0.197*** | 24.6% | 6.9% | 10.8% |
| Service | -0.125** | -0.014 | -0.090* | -0.206*** | 64.5% | 80.5% | 82.6% |
| Both, product and service | 0.046 | -0.058 | 0.068 | 0.063 | 10.9% | 13.2% | 6.6% |

a. Cell entries are percentage of the cluster with the attribute for all dummy variables, means for all others.
*$p < .05$; **$p < .01$; ***$p < .001$.

Mohrman 1989, p. 59). The relationship between union pressure and HPOs is more complex: Unionization is positively associated with FILMs and training and negatively correlated with gainsharing and performance-linked rewards. These results for unions are similar to Eaton and Voos' (1992) findings: Using the GAO data, they found that nonunion firms were more likely to use profit sharing, but unionized firms made relatively greater use of reforms that directly influence the nature and organization of the work.

## Measuring Organizational Performance

To test hypotheses regarding HPOs, we also need measures of an organization's performance. The performance measures used by researchers do not often represent the variety of goals and functions that organizations pursue. Appelbaum and Batt (1994, p. 145), after reviewing studies of HPOs, conclude with the hope that future research will compare the performance of transformed and untransformed plants using outcome measures that assess the impact on *all* stakeholders—including shareholders, suppliers, customers, unions, managers, and frontline employees.

The NOS contains measures of the plant manager's subjective assessment of the organization's performance relative to other, comparable organizations on a wide range of dimensions. We adopted this "subjective benchmarking" approach to measuring performance because we wanted comparative indicators that were applicable to all organizations, from manufacturing plants to schools. Our measures are thus implicitly industry normed in that the manager presumably chose other organizations in the same line of activity in which to compare his or her organization's performance.

Our performance indicators are based on responses to the following question:

How would you compare [*Your Organization's*] performance over the past 3 years to that of other organizations that do the same kind of work?" (*Much better, somewhat better, about the same, worse*) What about . . .

1. Quality of new products, services, or programs
2. Development of new products, services, or programs
3. Ability to attract essential employees
4. Ability to retain essential employees

5. Satisfaction of customers or clients
6. Relations between management and other employees
7. Relations between employees in general
8. Marketing
9. Growth in sales
10. Profitability
11. Market share

Figure 6.2 presents descriptive information on the distribution of responses to each of these performance variables (the horizontal axis indicates the response category, ranging from 1 [worse] to 4 [much better]).

These distributions indicate that a majority of plant managers in the United States feel that their organizations perform better on the various dimensions than those to which they compared themselves. Responses to these performance questions reflect both actual performance and aspiration levels; it is performance relative to aspiration that defines the organization's perceptions of success and failure in that organizations set goals and aspiration levels and compare their actual performance to their goals. This interpretation is consistent with Kalleberg and Marsden's (1994) argument regarding individuals' assessments of their performance: Organizations, as with individuals, are likely to have a target level of performance (aspiration level) to which they compare their actual performance.

Do organizations that perform well on one dimension also perform better than average on others? Table 6.4 presents correlations of the performance measures. The performance indicators are positively correlated, though some are more strongly related than others. Based on the patterns of covariation between these items, we constructed five performance scales: *Products* (composed of items measuring product quality and product development), *employees* (attract and retain essential employees), *customer satisfaction* (single item), *relations* (labor-management relations and employee relations), and (for profit-seeking organizations) *market factors* (composed of items measuring marketing, growth in sales, profitability, and market share).[5]

## HPOs and Organizational Performance: Results

Do HPO organizations actually perform better than other NOS organizations? An initial answer to this question is provided in Table 6.5, which

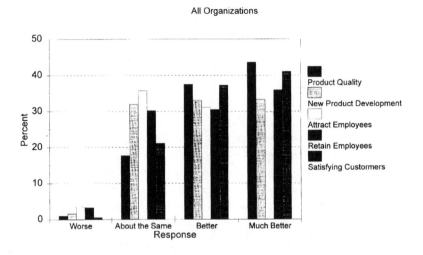

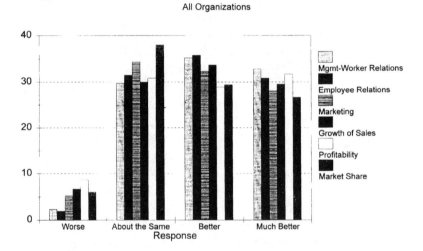

**Figure 6.2.** Performance Measures

presents correlations between our four HPO variables, on the one hand, and the five performance indicators, on the other. Table 6.5 indicates that HRM practices and policies associated with HPOs are associated with better performance on some, but not all dimensions.

Organizations with FILMs perform better with regard to product development and innovation, attracting and retaining employees, and (for

**Table 6.4** Correlations Between Performance Variables

| | Product Quality | Product Development | Attract | Retain | Customer Satisfaction | Labor Management | Employee Relations | Marketing | Sales Growth | Profits | Market Share |
|---|---|---|---|---|---|---|---|---|---|---|---|
| **Products** | | | | | | | | | | | |
| Quality of products and services | 1.00 | — | — | — | — | — | — | — | — | — | — |
| Development of new products and services | 0.538 | 1.00 | — | — | — | — | — | — | — | — | — |
| **Employees** | | | | | | | | | | | |
| Ability to attract essential employees | 0.422 | 0.453 | 1.00 | — | — | — | — | — | — | — | — |
| Ability to retain essential employees | 0.471 | 0.375 | 0.691 | 1.00 | — | — | — | — | — | — | — |
| Customer satisfaction | 0.553 | 0.423 | 0.454 | 0.516 | 1.00 | — | — | — | — | — | — |
| **Relations** | | | | | | | | | | | |
| Management and employees | 0.434 | 0.352 | 0.431 | 0.499 | 0.535 | 1.00 | — | — | — | — | — |
| Employees in general | 0.438 | 0.362 | 0.426 | 0.490 | 0.535 | 0.823 | 1.00 | — | — | — | — |
| **Market factors** | | | | | | | | | | | |
| Marketing | 0.349 | 0.434 | 0.322 | 0.250 | 0.331 | 0.296 | 0.338 | 1.00 | — | — | — |
| Growth in sales | 0.427 | 0.474 | 0.397 | 0.339 | 0.356 | 0.320 | 0.327 | 0.534 | 1.00 | — | — |
| Profitability | 0.355 | 0.433 | 0.369 | 0.325 | 0.317 | 0.302 | 0.363 | 0.477 | 0.722 | 1.00 | — |
| Market share | 0.388 | 0.392 | 0.417 | 0.345 | 0.340 | 0.331 | 0.395 | 0.498 | 0.668 | 0.679 | 1.00 |
| Mean | 3.25 | 2.983 | 2.873 | 2.990 | 3.191 | 2.998 | 2.969 | 2.830 | 2.859 | 2.833 | 2.769 |
| Standard deviation | 0.777 | 0.857 | 0.885 | 0.898 | 0.784 | 0.849 | 0.839 | 0.909 | 0.930 | 0.978 | 0.913 |

NOTE: All cells are significant at the .0001 level. $N$s range from 578 to 604 for product quality to employee relations, 401 to 412 for marketing to market share.

Table 6.5  Correlations of High Performance Work Organizations Measures With Performance Scales

|  | Products | Relations | Employees | Market Factors | Customer Satisfaction |
|---|---|---|---|---|---|
| FILMs | 0.106** | −0.053 | 0.083* | 0.208*** | −0.064 |
| Training | 0.181*** | 0.097** | 0.149*** | 0.221*** | −0.007 |
| Performance-based compensation | 0.135*** | 0.133** | 0.145*** | 0.230*** | 0.103** |
| Decentralization | 0.076 | −0.015 | 0.088* | 0.011 | 0.024 |

$*p < .05; **p < .01; ***p < .001.$

profit-making organizations) financial performance. On the other hand, FILMs appear to be unrelated to customer satisfaction and employee relations. The former results suggest the importance of FILMs for skill development and incentives. The result for employee relations may reflect in part the tendency of FILMs to create competition between employees who seek career advancement within the organization (Edwards 1979).

Training appears to enhance all dimensions of performance except customer satisfaction, whereas benefits (gainsharing, profit sharing, and having compensation tied to performance) are positively related to all types of performance. By contrast, decentralization is weakly related to performance; it is significantly (and positively) related only to employee relations.[6]

Figure 6.3 shows the means of the various types of performance for each of the three clusters of organizations. These results provide additional support for the hypothesis that HPO organizations perform better than others: HPO organizations score highest on all dimensions of performance except customer satisfaction, where they are second to LPO organizations. LPO organizations score lowest on four dimensions, though they score highest on customer satisfaction. Recall that LPO organizations were relatively small establishments (see Table 6.3) providing little training and few FILMs, but having relatively high (compared to trainer organizations) benefits and decentralization (see Figure 6.1). One might hypothesize that LPO organizations are composed of professionals (such as law firms) that require relatively little within-organization training and have limited opportunities for advancement yet are rewarded based on performance and are able to participate extensively in decision making.

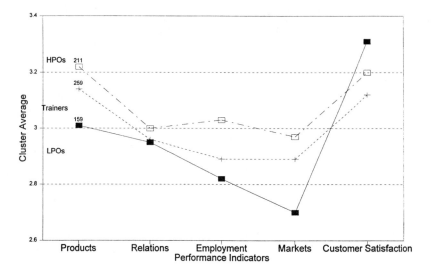

**Figure 6.3.** Human Resource Management Clusters and Performance Measures

## Conclusion

Our results are generally consistent with the view that some human resource policies and practices often identified with high performance organizations do, in fact, enhance organizational performance. In particular, organizations that offer profit sharing or stock option programs and bonuses for performance and merit and that link earnings to performance, appear to perform better on all five dimensions. Organizations that invest more in training their employees perform better on all dimensions except customer satisfaction. Organizations with FILMs perform better than those without internal job ladders with regard to the quality and development of their products and services, attracting and retaining essential employees, and market performance. Decentralization enhanced only one dimension of performance: attracting and retaining valued employees.

Our analysis showed that there is a tendency for some of these characteristics of HPOs to cluster together in organizations. In this sense, some of these NOS organizations may be said to constitute a high-performing organization "system." The results of our cluster analysis thus support the arguments made by writers (e.g., Levine and Tyson 1990; Bailey 1992) who maintain that it is not enough for organizations to adopt one or another of the characteristics typically identified with transformed organizations. Rather, the features of HPOs are interrelated and mutually reinforcing: For example, allowing workers to make decisions is more effective when they can benefit from those decisions by sharing in the gains and profits that result from the success of those decisions. As a consequence, performance gains accrue mainly to those organizations that have transformed themselves broadly by adopting a number of the characteristics listed in Table 6.1.

An advantage of the NOS data is that they enabled us to examine the relationships between these human resource management policies and organizational performance for a nationally representative sample of U.S. work organizations, not just a particular sector such as manufacturing or services. Hence, we have evidence, albeit tentative, that these characteristics of HPOs enhance performance for a diverse group of organizations.

We recognize that our analysis of the relationship between human resource management and organizational performance was limited in several ways. It would have been good to have had objective measures of performance, for example. It is not clear, however, whether it is possible to develop objective measures of performance that are comparable across a diverse sample of organizations. This suggests the need to study the determinants of performance within particular industry sectors, where objective and precise measures of performance could be developed (see, e.g., Kelley 1994).

A more severe limitation of our analysis was the lack of information in the NOS on relevant aspects of HPOs, such as teams and other structures that promote employee involvement and empowerment (see Osterman 1994a). Further tests of the idea of high performing work organizations await more detailed measures of the extent and type of teams (e.g., whether they are self-directed or autonomous), degree of quality consciousness, cross-training, extent of flexibility in the deployment of workers, and the other concepts described in Table 6.1.

## Notes

1. Organizational performance is not the only objective of work participation and reform; these practices have had a strong normative and ideological content for many decades (e.g., Bailey 1992). Gandz (1990) points out that employee involvement was practiced from

humanitarian motives in the 1950s and 1960s. In 1990s, it is done primarily for business reasons.

2. The most widely cited studies are a 1982 survey of New York stock exchange members with more than 100 employees (Freund and Epstein 1984); a 1987 survey by the General Accounting Office of *Fortune* 1000 companies (Dulworth, Landen, and Usilaner 1990; Eaton and Voos 1992; Lawler, Ledford, and Mohrman 1989); a 1990 follow-up to that survey (Lawler, Mohrman, and Ledford 1992); and Osterman's (1994a) national study of workplace practices.

3. According to a *confirmatory factor analysis* of these four variables, a 1-factor solution has a goodness of fit (GFI) statistic of .99 and an adjusted GFI of .94.

4. We first standardized the variables to a mean of 0 and a standard deviation of 1. We then used the *Ward's minimum variance clustering algorithm* in the SAS 6.08 statistical package. The clustering process produced a cluster tree with three distinct branches.

5. In a confirmatory factor analysis of the performance items, we tested two models because a subset of the performance questions was asked only of for-profit organizations: a 5-factor model for profit-only organizations and a 4-factor model for all organizations (i.e., with the market factor removed). The profit model had a GFI statistic of .96, with an adjusted GFI of .93. The 4-factor model had a GFI of .99 with an Adjusted GFI of .97. We also tested both models with an *incremental fit statistic* (Bollen 1989, p. 269). We compared these factor structures to a 1-factor model (incremental GFI = .878 for Profits, .949 for all organizations) and a 2-factor model (with product quality, product development, and customer satisfaction loading on one factor; attract, retain, labor-management relations, and employee relations on the second factor). The incremental GFI for profits against the 2-factor model was .703, the incremental GFI for all organizations was .933.

6. Another aspect of compensation that is often linked to the concept of high-performance organizations is the extent of *wage dispersion* (see Chapter 11 for an expanded discussion of earnings inequality in the NOS organizations). A great deal of wage dispersion is thought to foster competition, whereas narrow dispersion should favor cooperation and build group cohesiveness (Appelbaum and Batt 1994, p. 81). To examine whether within-organization earnings inequality affects performance, we computed a measure of dispersion: the difference between the average earnings of managers and the average earnings of GSS and core occupations. We found that greater wage dispersion was negatively and significantly related to two dimensions of performance: employee relations and customer satisfaction.

# III

# Organizations' Human Resource Practices

# 7

# The Staffing Process
*Recruitment and Selection Methods*

PETER V. MARSDEN

This chapter presents findings from the National Organizations Study on methods used by employers to locate, screen, and select new employees. It documents some major patterns in methods used to recruit from the external labor market and in the extensiveness and intensity of searches. It also reports on organizational and occupational differences in the use of reference checks and four kinds of tests (for intelligence or personality, ability, physical condition, and drug or alcohol use).

Recruitment and selection methods are two distinct elements of staffing practices. Together, they constitute an important interface between employers and employees in labor markets. From the organizational standpoint, staffing practices are the means through which the essential resource of human activity is acquired. Effective staffing practices are a component of effective organizational performance (Olian and Rynes 1984; Herman

1994). As with other organizational properties, staffing practices are shaped by the goals, structure, and environmental setting of an organization.

Organizational staffing practices are the other side of employment-seeking activities by potential workers (Marsden and Campbell 1990). A good deal has been written about the information-seeking efforts of different types of workers (e.g., Corcoran, Datcher, and Duncan 1980; Campbell and Rosenfeld 1985). Such work often examines the way in which search methods vary with the socioeconomic or personal characteristics of job-seekers. To be successful, however, a job seeker must gain access to the channels that employers use to disseminate information, and then pass through the filters that establishments use to select new employees within a set of applicants.

This implies attention to the employer's side of the interface, to which less research has been devoted. The next section of this chapter situates recruitment and selection methods in the hiring process. The NOS data on recruitment and selection practices are then introduced. Because staffing practices may vary within as well as between employers, their study requires a multilevel approach. This chapter examines ideas about how the use of different staffing methods varies with organizational properties such as size and auspices, as well as with occupational features including prestige and gender composition. Analyses reported at the end of the chapter reveal variations at both the organizational and the occupational levels in the use of particular recruitment and selection methods. They also show differences in the extensiveness and intensity of the staffing efforts undertaken for different occupations by different establishments.

## Stages of the Staffing Process

The staffing process consists of two essential phases: (a) recruitment or *extensive search* and (b) selection or *intensive search* (Rees 1966; Barron and Bishop 1985). Herman (1994) distinguishes several activities in the selection stage: screening, testing, interviewing, and reference checking. The process ends with the negotiation of agreements between organizations and employees; this may, of course, involve very little if terms of employment are collectively bargained.

### Recruitment Methods

Recruitment practices publicize the availability of openings to qualified applicants and assemble modest information about a pool of eligible persons. Common recruitment practices include the use of formal channels, such as advertisements and employment agencies, as well as informal ones, such as referrals from coworkers or business and professional colleagues.

Recruitment practices differ in several important ways, among them formality, subtlety, and cost (see Marsden and Campbell 1990). Formality has been a major dimension studied in the sociological job search literature; there, much attention has been given to the question of how social resources, notably informal network channels, facilitate access to information about available jobs (see, e.g., Lin 1990). From the standpoint of employers, the use of interpersonal links is thought to have several advantages. Such ties can convey more subtle information than "broadcast" methods such as advertisements or signs. It is claimed that hiring via informal referrals results in a better fit between employee and employer by providing a trustworthy and realistic description of a job to a prospective employee. Referrals may also result in a higher quality stream of applicants, if the person making a referral is selective about whom she or he passes information to, thus serving to screen or vouch for the person referred. Informal referrals are, in addition, inexpensive modes of recruitment.

Informal recruitment practices also have notable drawbacks. Current employees and others who distribute information about openings through interpersonal channels will tend to pass it along to socially similar persons, Granovetter's (1973) "weak ties" argument notwithstanding. Organizations that recruit informally thus will be unlikely to reach heterogeneous applicant pools. This is generally disadvantageous to the degree that employers miss opportunities to attract qualified personnel, and particularly troublesome in environments that are sensitive to the employer's efforts to comply with equal employment opportunity regulations (Herman 1994). Moreover, the size of the applicant pools that can be recruited through purely informal techniques is limited; such approaches are not well suited to recruiting over a broad geographic region.

Formal recruitment practices include both broad-based methods of distributing information via advertisements and signs and the interposing of intermediary organizations (employment agencies or placement services) between job seeker and employer. These methods involve at least nominal costs to the employer; some of them—such as advertisements or signs—require considerable screening activities, in that they can generate large, rather undifferentiated pools of applicants. Other methods (executive recruiters, for example) incorporate many screening activities; they are correspondingly more expensive. Formal methods have the advantage of being accessible—in principle—to all potential employees, and guides to personnel practices (e.g., Ivancevich and Glueck 1983; Herman 1994) almost invariably recommend that employers make use of such methods.

Finally, employers may choose not to undertake any special efforts to locate new workers. Job seekers can and do make unsolicited approaches to prospective employers in person, by mail, or by telephone. As with formal methods, this approach is open to all job seekers, at least all who know about an employer; as with informal ones it does not involve any well-specified process for disseminating information about vacancies.

## Selection Methods

In the selection stage of staffing, employers undertake *intensive* search, learning more about prospective employees. At a minimum, most selection efforts include a screening interview. This may be quite brief, perhaps simply involving the distribution of forms for applicants to fill out. Virtually all establishments in the NOS indicated that they interview prospective employees in the course of hiring. Applicants may then be further screened on the basis of applications or work histories, and winnowed still further on the basis of longer and deeper interviews.

Here, we direct particular attention to the use of relatively formal selection procedures: testing and solicitation of letters of reference. The tests studied include general examinations of intelligence or personality and temperament, more specific tests of mental or physical skills, and two types of physical tests—for health and substance abuse. Herman (1994) claims that tests are "the most useful screening device in predicting an employee's success on the job" (p. 93). Using tests costs both time and money, however, and is subject to various legal restrictions that seek to guarantee employee privacy and prevent discrimination in employment on the basis of sex, race, or age.

Employers can select informally by inquiring about the validity of the credentials that applicants present through contacts with former employers or current employees who have referred the applicants to them. Reference checking often proceeds formally, however, through requests for letters of reference or through the use of intermediary agencies that specialize in such services. Similar to the use of tests, reference checking in the United States is increasingly subject to legal regulations (see Herman 1994, Chapter 8).

Differences between organizations in resources and structure should influence the likelihood that they make use of these formal approaches to selection. In addition, occupational variations in selection methods are to be expected: For example, skills or performance tests are more applicable to some positions than others, and drug or alcohol tests are more defensible for safety-sensitive jobs than for jobs in general (Herman 1994).

## Measures of Staffing Methods

The following analyses focus on four distinct elements of staffing, two for each stage. For recruitment, we examine the methods used to disseminate information about vacancies. As well, we look at measures of the extensiveness of an establishment's search for a particular type of employee. Indicators studied at the selection stage include reports about reference checking and use of tests, as well as a measure of intensity—the amount of time devoted by an establishment to interviewing a prospective employee.

All of these measures are obtained at the occupational level—that is, separately for the core, GSS, and managerial or administrative occupations discussed in the course of the NOS interview (see Chapter 3). The staffing questions were asked only when an establishment's informant said that it had hired new employees in a particular occupation from outside the organization within the past 2 years.[1] This limitation helped to encourage accurate recall and ensured that information on recruitment methods was reasonably timely. It has the effect, however, of removing many small establishments, which hire infrequently, from the analyses reported in the following.

### Measuring Recruitment Methods

The NOS measured recruitment methods with a sequence of questions that asked the informant for the establishment to give the information sources typically used in locating potential new employees. The sequence was worded as follows:

How often do you use each of the following methods to find ["cores"/ GSSs/managers or administrators]? What about

1. Newspaper advertisements?
2. Signs posted outside the building?

**Table 7.1** Marginal Distributions for Recruitment Methods

| | Percentage of Establishments Using Method Frequently[a] | | | | | |
|---|---|---|---|---|---|---|
| Occupation | Newspaper Ads | Signs Posted | Employee Referrals | Professional Referrals | Employment Agencies | Unsolicited Inquiries |
| Core | | | | | | |
| Unweighted | 40.8 | 13.1 | 36.7 | 20.7 | 18.9 | 33.0 |
| Weighted | 36.1 | 14.6 | 36.7 | 23.3 | 12.7 | 23.7 |
| N | 468 | 467 | 469 | 469 | 470 | 469 |
| GSS | | | | | | |
| Unweighted | 48.0 | 7.7 | 28.6 | 19.9 | 17.3 | 35.7 |
| Weighted | 34.4 | 3.7 | 21.0 | 30.3 | 15.0 | 15.9 |
| N | 196 | 196 | 196 | 196 | 196 | 196 |
| Managerial | | | | | | |
| Unweighted | 50.2 | 10.1 | 22.2 | 27.1 | 17.2 | 22.0 |
| Weighted | 32.2 | 7.1 | 26.2 | 29.8 | 20.3 | 18.9 |
| N | 269 | 267 | 266 | 266 | 267 | 268 |

a. Ns provide the case bases for percentages. Questions about recruitment were asked only when a given type of employee had been hired from outside within the preceding 2 years.

    3. Referrals from current employees?
    4. Referrals from business or professional contacts?
    5. Employment agencies or placement services?
    6. Unsolicited inquiries by telephone, mail, or in person?

The informant was asked to say whether the establishment used each method "frequently, "sometimes," or "never."

Methods 1 and 2 (ads and signs) represent relatively indiscriminate formal information channels accessible to all. Method 5 (agencies) involves an organizational intermediary between the prospective employee and the hiring establishment. Methods 3 and 4 (employee and business or professional referrals) cover informal information channels, whereas method 6 is the organizational analog of direct applications by job seekers.

Table 7.1 presents data, by occupation, on the recruitment practices said to be used frequently. In general, newspaper advertisements and employee referrals are the most used methods; employment agencies and signs are substantially less common. There is some interesting occupational variation: Employee referrals and unsolicited inquiries are more often used for locating core and GSS employees than for finding managers and administrators. The latter are more commonly located through professional referrals than are other employees.

There are comparatively few differences between the weighted and unweighted figures in Table 7.1. For core and GSS employees, the percentage of workplaces that rely on unsolicited inquiries is smaller in the weighted NOS sample, suggesting that larger establishments are more apt to recruit this way. The unweighted percentages for use of newspaper advertisements in recruiting are somewhat higher than the weighted ones, indicating that this too may be more common among larger concerns.

### Measuring Selection Methods

To measure the information sources used in an establishment to choose new employees from applicant pools, the NOS used the following questions:

When you are selecting new employees for [core/GSS/managerial] positions, do you require

1. Intelligence tests or other psychological tests?
2. Skills or proficiency tests?
3. Letters of reference?
4. A physical examination?
5. Drug or alcohol tests?

As for recruitment methods, this sequence of questions was repeated for the core, GSS, and managerial occupations in an establishment whenever these were distinct.

Table 7.2 reports on the frequency with which employers say that they use the five selection methods in the process of hiring. Letters of reference are the most widely used method. The unweighted results show that references are required by three fifths or more of the workplaces in the NOS, for each of the three occupations; more than 75% of the establishments in the sample require letters of reference for managerial and administrative workers. When the data are weighted to take into account the overrepresentation of large establishments in the NOS sample, these percentages decline slightly.

Physical examinations are part of the hiring process in more than 40% of NOS establishments, whereas tests for drug or alcohol use are to be found in roughly 30% of them. These percentages decline substantially when the data are weighted, suggesting appreciable differences between large and small establishments in the use of these methods.

**Table 7.2** Marginal Distributions for Selection Methods

| Occupation | Percentage of Establishments Using Method[a] | | | | |
| | Intelligence Tests | Skills Tests | Physical Exams | Drug/Alcohol Tests | Letters of Reference |
|---|---|---|---|---|---|
| Core | | | | | |
|   Unweighted | 11.6 | 39.7 | 45.0 | 31.7 | 63.6 |
|   Weighted | 7.4 | 31.2 | 30.0 | 19.8 | 54.7 |
|   N | 473 | 471 | 473 | 473 | 473 |
| GSS | | | | | |
|   Unweighted | 9.6 | 36.5 | 40.9 | 28.3 | 59.6 |
|   Weighted | 10.1 | 25.5 | 9.0 | 4.8 | 61.0 |
|   N | 198 | 197 | 198 | 198 | 198 |
| Managerial | | | | | |
|   Unweighted | 13.3 | 21.9 | 43.0 | 34.8 | 75.9 |
|   Weighted | 9.1 | 13.0 | 19.9 | 15.3 | 71.3 |
|   N | 270 | 270 | 270 | 270 | 270 |

a. Ns provide the case bases for percentages. Questions about selection were asked only when a given type of employee had been hired from outside within the preceding 2 years.

Tests of skills or proficiency are used in hiring core and GSS employees by between 35% and 40% of the NOS establishments. Skills tests are only about half as common for managerial and administrative occupations. Again, differences between the weighted and unweighted figures suggest that larger establishments are more apt to use skills tests than are small ones.

Only about a tenth of the establishments in the unweighted NOS sample report that they require prospective employees to take intelligence or personality tests. Herman (1994) notes that some states forbid the use of psychological tests. Moreover, court decisions require that employers be able to show that tests used for selection are valid—that is, that test results predict job performance. The low frequency with which general intelligence and personality tests are used, by comparison with more targeted skills tests, is understandable in this light.

### The Extensiveness and Intensity of Staffing Processes

Barron and Bishop (1985; see also Barron, Bishop, and Dunkelberg 1985) introduced indicators of the costs that employers incur in the course of hiring new employees. These measure the volume of work undertaken by an establishment before a new employee is hired. Some pertain to the recruitment stage; others, to the phase of selection.

**Table 7.3**  Measures of Extensiveness and Intensity of Searches[a]

| Occupation | Mean Number Applications | Mean Number Interviews | Mean Interview Length (minutes) |
|---|---|---|---|
| Core | | | |
| Unweighted | 35.01 | 7.50 | 77.21 |
| Weighted | 22.76 | 5.69 | 72.21 |
| *N* | 405 | 436 | 456 |
| GSS | | | |
| Unweighted | 31.02 | 9.18 | 76.57 |
| Weighted | 12.87 | 6.60 | 52.74 |
| *N* | 175 | 183 | 187 |
| Managerial | | | |
| Unweighted | 26.47 | 7.58 | 169.65 |
| Weighted | 18.04 | 5.68 | 112.09 |
| *N* | 245 | 253 | 252 |

a. *N*s provide the case bases for means. Questions on applications and interviews were asked only when a given type of employee had been hired from outside within the preceding 2 years. Excludes cases in which an informant could not estimate number of applications, interviews, or interview length.

The NOS included several occupation-specific measures of extensive and intensive search related to those used by Barron and Bishop. These are examined here as a supplement to the discussion of the specific channels and tests used in the hiring process. Informants were asked to estimate the number of applications typically considered for a core, GSS, or managerial opening; the usual number of applicants interviewed prior to an offer for a given type of position; and the length of a typical interview for a particular type of job.

Table 7.3 reports weighted and unweighted means for these three measures for each of the three occupations covered in the NOS interview. The number of applications is the clearest indicator of the extensiveness of a search. In the unweighted NOS sample, the number of applications for a vacancy is smallest (at 26.5) for managerial and administrative occupations and ranges upward to 35 for core workers.

The number of interviews prior to an offer can be viewed as a measure of both the extensiveness and the intensity of a search. For core and managerial positions, about 7.5 applicants are interviewed prior to an offer being made.

Interview length, however, is an indicator of search intensity. It measures the amount of effort devoted to the selection stage of staffing. Mean interview length (reported here in minutes) is somewhat over 1 hour (77 minutes) for the core and GSS occupations and verges on 3 hours (170 minutes) for managerial and administrative employees.[2]

All three of the measures in Table 7.3 have smaller mean values in the weighted NOS sample than in the unweighted one. This is an indication that the extensiveness and intensity of selection processes is lower in smaller establishments, a result consistent with what Barron and Bishop (1985) report.

## Organizational and Occupational Differences in Staffing Practices

This section discusses reasons that organizational, environmental, and occupational factors should be associated with differences in the use of different methods for recruitment and selection of employees, and differences in the extensiveness and intensity of those efforts. It then presents evidence from the NOS that bears on the hypotheses presented.

### Organizational Differences

A substantial body of recent organizational research has examined the factors associated with the development of formalized, "modern" personnel practices in U.S. organizations (e.g., Baron, Dobbin, and Jennings 1986). Such practices include, among others, the development of specialized personnel or labor relations units to replace the decentralized administration of hiring, promotion, wage setting, discipline, and firing by foremen or production supervisors (Jacoby 1985); job descriptions and wage classification systems (Baron, Jennings, and Dobbin 1988); performance evaluation systems and job ladders (Dobbin et al. 1993; Chapter 5, this volume); and provisions for due process in the resolution of grievances (Dobbin et al. 1988; Edelman 1990; Chapter 5). Several studies (Baron, Davis-Blake, and Bielby 1986; Baron et al. 1988; Dobbin et al. 1993; Cohen and Pfeffer 1986) also examine employment testing.[3] In this section, I draw on ideas from these studies to formulate expectations about the organizational features associated with the use of formal methods of recruitment and selection by NOS establishments.

The clearest "technical" case for the use of formal methods would predict that formal staffing techniques will be found in larger organizations. This rests on the claim that routinized hiring procedures are an efficient way in which to cope with the larger volume of hiring to be expected in larger organizations, a rationale parallel to that used to explain why formalization in general increases with organization size (e.g., Daft 1986; Chapter 4).

Larger organizations are also more likely than small ones to have the resources required to implement costly staffing techniques. Barron and Bishop (1985) argue that hiring errors impose greater costs in larger firms, and reason that such firms will therefore exercise greater care in the selection of new workers.

A distinct "institutional" argument leads to the same prediction about size differences (Dobbin et al. 1993). Larger establishments are more visible to regulators, and consequently, large concerns should be apt to adopt formal procedures because such methods demonstrate a concern for fairness in the treatment of applicants rather than because they help an employer to realize efficiencies. In addition, some employment-related laws mandating the use of particular hiring methods provide exemptions for smaller employers.

There are good reasons to expect that structural features of organizations will also be associated with the use of particular selection methods. As formal selection devices, tests and reference checks should be more common in organizations that have formalized their approaches to accomplishing other tasks (Baron, Davis-Blake, and Bielby 1986). Moreover, the proper and legal use of tests requires that those responsible for personnel selection be familiar with a body of knowledge about test validity and proper administration (e.g., Schmidt, Borman, and Associates 1993; Herman 1994). Such knowledge will be more common in organizations that have created specialized departments to administer personnel or labor relations and in those that have hired personnel professionals to operate these departments.

Cohen and Pfeffer (1986) offer a political argument that also leads to the expectation that formalized staffing methods will be more common in organizations with personnel departments. They reason that personnel professionals preserve and enhance their standing within an organization through familiarity with an arcane body of knowledge about hiring and promotion (see also Jacoby 1985; Baron, Dobbin, and Jennings 1986).

Many aspects of environmental context are arguably associated with staffing techniques (Olian and Rynes 1984). Here, we confine the discussion to three environmental features: (a) whether trade unions are present in the workplace, (b) whether the establishment is part of a larger, multisite organization, and (c) whether the establishment is in the private or public sector.

Differences in personnel practices between unionized and nonunion workplaces have been stressed by a number of those cited above (e.g., Jacoby 1985; Baron, Dobbin, and Jennings 1986; Dobbin et al. 1988). Cohen and Pfeffer (1986), for example, suggest that unions have an interest in the development of formalized hiring procedures, because such procedures can prevent employers from excluding employees with prounion attitudes. In their analyses of data for a sample of large (over 100 employees) establishments in the San Francisco Bay area, however, they find that unionization is associated with less extensive use of employment testing.

Independent establishments are expected to be less likely to make use of formalized approaches to staffing than are those that are part of multisite organizational complexes. The basis for this claim is similar to that introduced above for organizational size; for reasons of efficiency and visibility, multisite organizations may adopt common hiring policies, including regulations that govern the use of tests and reference checks. Cohen and Pfeffer (1986) found that testing was indeed less common in independent establishments, but the difference vanished after they controlled for unionization, presence of a personnel department, and internal labor market practices (primarily promotion from within).

Finally, differences in the use of staffing methods between organizations operating under public and private auspices are to be anticipated. As observed in Chapter 5, institutional arguments (e.g., Dobbin et al. 1988) hold that exposure to the public sphere places organizations under special pressure to conform to evolving norms about legitimate employment practices. The precise nature of public-private differences to be expected is not fully clear, however, because there are numerous normative considerations that sometimes lead in different directions. "Public trust" organizations are expected to demonstrate a high level of fairness in their employment practices, and as such, they seem apt to use formal methods. One would expect them to be averse to the use of informal referrals, especially as a sole recruitment technique.

Selection techniques such as drug tests, however, can come into conflict with norms against the invasion of privacy. Thus, we might expect that public sector organizations are especially unlikely to use these methods; a further cross-pressure, however, is that many public sector positions in transportation and public safety are security sensitive, which would suggest that the use of drug and alcohol tests will be higher there.

**Occupational Factors**

The ideas about occupational differences in staffing methods to be examined here rest on a cost-benefit logic. Extensive recruitment efforts and intensive personnel selection practices are costly, so it stands to reason that they will be adopted when there are sufficient benefits to good decisions or sufficient risks associated with bad ones.

On the benefit side are investment considerations. More intensive staffing procedures should be used when hiring employees who will enter internal labor markets (Chapter 5, this volume). Employers will expect such employees to have long tenure in the organization, and will anticipate that they will be eligible for promotion to higher ranks where they may exercise authority. Hence, there is greater reason to avoid hiring errors by using exacting selection methods. Once employees are on such job ladders, moreover, due process guarantees may make it difficult to discharge them. This also leads to the expectation that staffing decisions for positions in FILMs will be made more carefully (Barron and Bishop 1985).

For similar reasons, it would be expected that substantial selection effort will be devoted to hiring employees who are to receive additional training within the organization (Barron and Bishop 1985). Cohen and Pfeffer (1986) report that establishments providing training are indeed more likely to make extensive use of tests. In their analysis of an employer survey, Barron and Bishop (1985) show that hiring costs—that is, the extensiveness and intensity of searching—were higher for employers providing either general or specific training.

Risk considerations exist when individual actions have the potential of seriously reducing organizational performance or exposing the establishment to legal liability (Jacobs 1981). Examples include occupations that involve the operation of machinery or the potential misuse of weapons. It is to be anticipated that employers will be especially careful in choosing employees for positions of this kind.

**Measures of Explanatory Variables**

Several organization- and occupation-level measures described in previous chapters will be used to examine the hypotheses just outlined. At the organizational level are measures of establishment size (natural logarithm), presence of a personnel department, extent of firm internal labor markets (FILMs), inclusion in a multisite organization, presence of unions, and public sector status.

Occupational data are less extensive in the NOS. Provision of formal training was not measured separately for the three occupations studied, so it is included as an organization-level variable. Similarly, the FILMs scale at the organizational level is used both as a measure of the general level of formalization within the establishment and as an indication that hiring decisions may lead to long-term attachments between the individual and the workplace.

Two occupational measures include (a) a measure of occupational prestige or social standing (Nakao and Treas 1994) and (b) the NOS informant's estimate of the percentage of women among employees in each of the three occupations.[4] The occupational prestige variable is indicative of the "general goodness" (Goldthorpe and Hope 1974) of an occupation. To the extent that high-prestige occupations have greater responsibility, risk considerations would be higher for them, and staffing effort on the establishment's part presumptively greater. In the absence of other occupational data, the percentage of women in an occupation is likely a proxy for characteristics associated with "female" jobs, such as lack of authority, low pay, less opportunity for training, and limited chances of advancement (Reskin 1993; Chapter 14, this volume). According to the logic outlined previously, we would expect less intensive approaches to recruitment and selection for such jobs.

### Multilevel Analysis

The previous discussion argued that both organizational and occupational characteristics affect the staffing process for jobs. The following analysis takes a multilevel approach, which permits the two types of factors to be taken into account simultaneously.

The unit of analysis here is the occupation. Separate records are created for the core, GSS, and managerial occupations (if all three were observed) in each establishment. This permits us to introduce variables that measure occupational heterogeneity together with organization-level indicators. The observations are clustered: The NOS design nests up to three observations on occupations within each establishment. The analytic techniques used here adjust for this by including "establishment effects" that account for the homogeneity of staffing methods used to fill the different positions within a particular establishment.

The appropriate statistical techniques are elementary multilevel models (Bryk and Raudenbush 1992; Longford 1993). For the six recruitment indicators and the three indicators of staffing extensiveness and intensity, these analytic methods are similar to ordinary regression analysis:

$$y_{ij} = \sum b_k x_{kij} + u_j + e_{ij,}$$

where $y_{ij}$ is a dependent variable for the $i^{th}$ occupation in the $j^{th}$ establishment, $x_{kij}$ is the $k^{th}$ explanatory variable for the $i^{th}$ occupation in the $j^{th}$ establishment, $b_k$ is a regression parameter for the $k^{th}$ explanatory variable and $e_{ij}$ is a random error term referring to within-establishment variation across occupations. Usually one of the $\{x_{kij}\}$ is a constant term.

The model used here differs from conventional regression analysis by virtue of its inclusion of the term $u_j$, an establishment-level "random effect" that captures between-organization differences in the probability of using a given staffing method that are not associated with the establishment-level covariates. It is assumed that the $\{u_j\}$ are normally distributed within the population of establishments. Multilevel analysis estimates the variance of the $\{u_j\}$; it does not seek to estimate the random effects themselves. Inclusion of the random effects provides an indication of establishment-level homogeneity in staffing procedures, in that the random effect $u_j$ refers to all occupational observations in a given establishment. As such, it serves to adjust statistically for the clustering of observations on occupations within establishments.

Because the five indicators of selection methods are dichotomous, the appropriate model to use for analyzing them is the multilevel logistic regression model (Paterson 1991). It is specified as follows:

$$y_{ij} = \exp(\sum b_k x_{kij} + u_j)/(1 + \exp(\sum b_k x_{kij} + u_j)) + e_{ij,}$$

where $y_{ij}$ is a dichotomous indicator of whether a given selection method was used for the $i^{th}$ occupation in the $j^{th}$ establishment, and the random occupation-level error term $e_{ij}$ is assumed to follow a binomial distribution.

Estimates for multilevel models of the staffing indicators in Tables 7.1 to 7.3 are reported in Tables 7.4 to 7.6. These results were obtained using the iterative generalized least-squares algorithm implemented in the computer program ML3 (Prosser, Rasbach, and Goldstein 1991).

**Table 7.4** Correlates of Recruitment Methods (multilevel regression coefficients)

| Explanatory Variable | Newspaper Ads | Signs Posted | Employee Referrals | Professional Referrals | Employment Agencies | Unsolicited Applications |
|---|---|---|---|---|---|---|
| Establishment size (log) | 0.030 | -0.009 | 0.008 | -0.001 | 0.064* | 0.038# |
| Personnel department | 0.118 | -0.063 | 0.017 | 0.013 | -0.035 | 0.034 |
| Firm internal labor markets | -0.032 | -0.033 | 0.044 | 0.018 | 0.076 | 0.069 |
| Formal training | 0.172# | -0.037 | 0.117 | 0.129# | -0.014 | 0.091 |
| Union pressure | 0.022 | 0.129** | 0.114* | 0.051 | 0.003 | -0.009 |
| Multisite organization | -0.167* | 0.085 | -0.042 | -0.129* | 0.037 | -0.081 |
| Public sector | -0.027 | 0.255** | -0.216** | -0.089 | -0.100 | 0.039 |
| Occupational prestige | 0.0047* | -0.0078** | -0.0015 | 0.0076** | -0.0022 | -0.0002 |
| Managerial occupation | 0.100* | -0.094** | -0.243** | 0.144** | -0.004 | -0.174** |
| Percentage women in occupation | 0.0015* | 0.0005 | 0.0009 | -0.0004 | -0.0009 | 0.0016* |
| (constant) | 1.687** | 1.539** | 1.914** | 1.505** | 1.291** | 1.637** |
| Establishment variance | 0.339** | 0.258** | 0.132** | 0.165** | 0.322** | 0.227** |
| Occupational variance | 0.312** | 0.144** | 0.274** | 0.244** | 0.242** | 0.260** |
| N | 870 | 867 | 869 | 868 | 870 | 870 |

#$p < .10$; *$p < .05$; **$p < .01$.

## Recruitment Methods

Table 7.4 includes estimates of the effects of organizational and occupational correlates on the six recruitment methods measured in the NOS.[5] At the organizational level, differences were found by establishment size, by the presence of unions, affiliation with a larger organization, and between the public and private sectors.

Net of the other variables considered here, larger establishments are more apt to make use of employment agencies to recruit new employees. There is also a suggestion in the results that larger organizations are more likely to rely on unsolicited approaches by potential workers.[6] Establishments that are unionized are significantly more likely to recruit via signs and employee referrals.

Public sector workplaces are substantially more likely than those in the private sector to locate new workers using signs. As expected, however, they are significantly less apt to rely on employee referrals. Establishments that are part of multisite organizations tend to avoid the use of newspapers and professional referrals. There are no significant differences in recruitment methods that involve the presence of a personnel department or the

FILMs scale. The provision of formal training is marginally associated with recruiting through newspapers and professional referrals.

Occupational variables too are associated with the recruitment techniques on which establishments rely. Applicants for high-prestige jobs are more often sought through advertisements and professional referrals than are lower-prestige prospects; high-prestige recruiting also makes less frequent use of signs. Recruiting for managerial and administrative work is especially likely to involve frequent use of advertisements and professional referrals; it less often involves referrals by coworkers, the posting of signs, or reliance on unsolicited approaches to the employer than do the search processes for other kinds of workers (see also Table 7.1).

There are also two significant differences in recruiting related to occupational gender composition. Recruiting for positions in which women are concentrated tends to rely on advertisements and unsolicited inquiries to a greater degree than that for occupations that are predominantly male.

Through the inclusion of a variance component for establishment effects, multilevel analysis takes account of the clustering of observations within particular workplaces. The unexplained variance in recruitment method use is partitioned into between-establishment and within-establishment components at the bottom of Table 7.4. The between-establishment component of variance is substantial and significant for all six recruitment methods. In fact, the establishment-level variance is larger than the estimated residual variance among occupations within establishments for three comparatively formal recruitment methods—advertisements, signs, and employment agencies. The proportion of the unexplained variance that is at the establishment level ranges between 0.32 (coworker referrals) and 0.64 (signs).

There is much to be learned about the sources of these establishment-level commonalities. They do reinforce a point made by Cohen and Pfeffer (1986) about hiring standards: Establishments tend to develop characteristic methods of recruiting that are used to attract workers to a variety of different jobs. Hence, this aspect of staffing appears to be, in part, an organizational phenomenon.[7]

### Selection Methods

The results presented in Table 7.5 pertain to the use of the four types of tests and letters of reference in the selection stage of staffing. Controlling for the other variables considered here, establishment size per se is linked

**Table 7.5** Correlates of Selection Methods (multilevel logistic regression coefficients)

| Explanatory Variable | Intelligence Tests | Skills Tests | Physical Exams | Drug/Alcohol Tests | Letters of Reference |
|---|---|---|---|---|---|
| Establishment size | | | | | |
| (log) | −0.039 | 0.025 | 0.286** | 0.270** | −0.004 |
| Personnel | | | | | |
| department | −0.014 | 0.117 | 0.365 | 0.589# | −0.209 |
| Firm internal | | | | | |
| labor markets | 0.505* | −0.025 | −0.158 | 0.248 | −0.133 |
| Formal training | 0.566 | 0.524# | 0.635* | 1.093** | 0.143 |
| Union pressure | 0.129 | 0.452** | 0.768** | 0.370# | −0.017 |
| Multisite | | | | | |
| organization | 0.172 | −0.022 | 0.625** | 0.597* | −0.341 |
| Public sector | 0.534# | 0.337 | 0.029 | −1.077** | 0.354 |
| Occupational | | | | | |
| prestige | −0.0012 | −0.0032 | 0.0004 | −0.0122 | 0.0435** |
| Managerial | | | | | |
| occupation | 0.179 | −0.915** | −0.363* | −0.339# | 0.719** |
| Percentage women | | | | | |
| in occupation | −0.0049 | −0.0017 | 0.0031 | −0.0177** | 0.0072** |
| (constant) | −4.079** | −1.527** | −3.268** | −3.368** | −1.191** |
| Establishment | | | | | |
| variance | 1.572** | 0.999** | 1.655** | 2.016** | 1.292** |
| N | 876 | 874 | 876 | 876 | 876 |

$\#p < .10$; $*p < .05$; $**p < .01$.

only to the use of physical examinations and drug and alcohol tests. The presence of a personnel department has no net relationship to any of the five selection methods, and the presence of FILMs is linked only to the use of intelligence or personality tests.

Among the environmental variables included in the multilevel analysis, the presence of unions is generally positively linked to the use of the four types of tests, significantly so to skills tests, physical examinations, and tests for substance abuse. This is consistent with the Cohen and Pfeffer (1986) suggestion that unions prefer impersonal hiring standards, though it does not accord with their empirical results. The result, significant at the .10 level, indicating that unionized establishments are more apt to make use of drug tests is notable because collective bargaining agreements often provide protections for unionized workers. Herman (1994, p. 99), however, notes that such protections have greater force for current employees than they have for applicants.

The odds of using physical examinations or drug and alcohol tests are about 1.82 [=exp(0.60)] times higher in establishments that are branches or subsidiaries of larger organizations than in comparable independent establishments. Public sector establishments are dramatically less likely to use tests for substance abuse, perhaps reflecting their sensitivity to norms of privacy. The odds of drug and alcohol tests in public-auspice workplaces are estimated to be only a third [=exp(−1.08)] the size of those in otherwise comparable private-sector establishments.

Turning to occupational variables, first note that the provision of training—measured at the establishment level in the NOS—is positively associated with all four types of tests, significantly so with skills, drug and alcohol tests, and physical examinations. This is consistent with Cohen and Pfeffer's (1986) findings for the San Francisco Bay area establishments and with the aforementioned hypothesis about training.

The odds of requiring references rise by about 4% with each occupational prestige point. Hiring for managerial and administrative occupations is unlikely to involve intensive testing, particularly for skills, by comparison with core and GSS positions with similar properties in comparable establishments. The odds that an employer requires letters of reference, though, are more than twice as great [exp(0.719) = 2.05] for managerial and administrative occupations as they are for the core or GSS occupations.

Two selection methods, drug and alcohol tests and reference letters, are significantly associated with the within-establishment percentage of women in an occupation. Drug tests are much less common in a highly female occupation; letters of reference are somewhat more common. It seems unlikely that these findings are results of gender composition per se. Instead, they probably reflect the effects of unmeasured establishment or occupational characteristics that are associated with the percentage of women. For example, many safety-sensitive jobs in which preemployment drug testing is permissible (or even obligatory), such as those in police work or the operation of heavy equipment, may be predominantly male.

For all five selection methods, the estimated variance component for the establishment-level random effects $\{u_j\}$ is substantial and statistically significant.[8] This again indicates that, despite the interoccupational variation just discussed, there are substantial tendencies for organizations to make use of favored selection practices when hiring employees for any occupation. This establishment-level homogeneity is net of similarities to be anticipated on the basis of the explanatory variables introduced in

**Table 7.6**  Correlates of Search Extensiveness and Intensity (multilevel regression coefficients)

| Explanatory Variable | (log) Number of Applications | (log) Number of Interviews | (log) Length of Interview (minutes) |
|---|---|---|---|
| Establishment size (log) | 0.079# | 0.012 | 0.078** |
| Personnel department | 0.066 | 0.031 | 0.118 |
| Firm internal labor markets | 0.240** | 0.120* | –0.008 |
| Formal training | 0.006 | 0.000 | 0.160# |
| Union pressure | 0.016 | 0.098# | –0.117* |
| Multisite organization | –0.282* | –0.108# | –0.032 |
| Public sector | 0.226# | 0.193** | –0.177* |
| Occupational prestige | –0.0088** | –0.0025 | 0.024** |
| Managerial occupation | –0.188* | –0.066 | 0.798** |
| Percentage women in occupation | –0.0012 | –0.0011 | –0.0025** |
| (constant) | 1.940** | 1.306** | 2.548** |
| Establishment variance | 0.619** | 0.167** | 0.256** |
| Occupational variance | 0.860** | 0.383** | 0.329** |
| N | 787 | 830 | 843 |

$\#p < .10; *p < .05; **p < .01.$

Table 7.5, and further supports Cohen and Pfeffer's (1986) claim that staffing practices are an establishment-level phenomenon.

*Staffing Extensiveness and Intensity*

Table 7.6 presents evidence from the NOS about correlates of the indicators of staffing effort and costs.[9] As Barron and Bishop (1985) anticipated and documented with their data from an employer survey, larger establishments search both more extensively by receiving more applications for positions (a result significant at the .10 level) and more intensively by interviewing applicants for longer periods of time. The NOS data do not permit a judgment as to whether this is a matter of risk aversity to possible hiring errors, the availability of greater resources for staffing, visibility and the consequent wish to project an image of fairness in staffing practices, or some combination of these factors.

Establishments that have well-developed firm internal labor markets expend more effort in the course of searches; they tend to receive more applications for positions—perhaps because of the comparative attractiveness of positions in FILMs—and also interview more applicants before making offers. This result is understandable in light of the long-term affiliations between employees and employers that are normative within FILMs. Unionized establishments have significantly shorter interview periods; the data suggest, at the .10 level, however, that more interviews are conducted prior to offers when a union is present.

Public sector workplaces tend to receive more applications and conduct more interviews than those in the private sector, a finding consistent with the proposition that pressures toward fair hiring procedures are especially strong in this sector. Typical interviews in public sector workplaces tend to be about 17% [exp(−0.177) = 0.83] shorter than those in for-profit or private nonprofit concerns. Establishments affiliated with a larger organization receive appreciably fewer applications than independent workplaces, and there are no evident differences in the extensiveness or intensity of staffing practices associated with the presence of a personnel department. Indeed, the presence of a personnel department is not associated, net of the other indicators considered, with any of the staffing indicators in Table 7.4 to Table 7.6. The presence of formal training is marginally (.10) associated with longer interview times.

There are several substantial associations between hiring costs and the occupational indicators in Table 7.6. Searches are significantly less extensive for higher-prestige and managerial occupations. Applicants for such positions are interviewed for significantly longer periods of time, however; for example, with each additional occupational prestige point, interviews grow about 2.5% longer. After taking other predictors into account, managerial and administrative interviews are more than double [exp(.798) = 2.22] the length of those for core or GSS positions (see also Table 7.3).

The percentage of women in an occupation is not associated with differences in the number of applications received or interviews conducted. Interviews are significantly shorter in highly female occupations, though. This is as one would expect if sex composition is serving as a proxy for low-responsibility, routine work (see Chapter 14, this volume). According to the reasoning outlined earlier, fewer resources should be devoted to filling such positions.

The establishment-level variance component is significantly larger than its standard error for all three indicators of the extensiveness and intensity of staffing activities. This again indicates that there are important organization-specific commonalities in these hiring practices that apply across the occupations within an establishment. Establishment-level variation constitutes about 30% to 40% of the total unexplained variation in the measures of extensiveness and intensity.

## Conclusion

American establishments use a variety of formal and informal methods for publicizing the availability of job opportunities to potential workers. Newspaper advertisements and referrals from employees are used most frequently. Reliance on signs and employment agencies is less common. Letters of reference are the most common formal approach used to screen and select applicants for employment. A substantial minority of workplaces requires physical examinations and skill or proficiency tests; an appreciable number use tests for drug and alcohol use. Very few, however, draw on intelligence tests or similar general psychological batteries.

Large and small establishments have different ways of securing a workforce. Large workplaces are more apt to recruit via employment agencies, to expend more resources on hiring by searching through more applicants and interviewing candidates for longer periods of time, and to use tests more often. Organizations with firm internal labor markets appear to devote greater effort to hiring by reviewing more applications and conducting more interviews prior to offering a position to an applicant.

Organizations display strong proclivities to rely on the same approaches to recruitment and selection for different types of employees. There are, however, some notable occupationally related variations in approaches to hiring. Professional referrals and newspaper advertisements are among the channels that tend to be activated for high-prestige employees. They are especially common for locating managerial workers; reference checking is substantially more common, and testing somewhat less likely, for such employees. Interviews last appreciably longer for high-prestige and managerial work.

Occupations differing in sex composition tend to be filled in different ways. Applicants for typically female positions tend to be recruited through newspaper advertisements or unsolicited approaches. The selection stage is generally less intense for occupations that are predominantly female: Interviewing is comparatively brief, and testing (particularly for drug and alcohol use) is less common.

Many of the findings above are consistent with claims that staffing methods are chosen by organizations on the basis of the resources available and the anticipated risks and benefits associated with hiring decisions. Findings involving establishment size, FILMs, occupational prestige, and the provision of training are especially conducive to such an interpretation.

These interpretations are not, however, unambiguous. Alternative accounts can be rendered for most findings. Some findings here seem clearly to be most interpretable as results of institutional pressure. Among these is the association of labor union presence with the use of formal, impersonal selection methods. Likewise, the findings that public sector organizations are less likely to recruit via informal referrals, more apt to expend substantial effort in the review of applications and the interviewing of applicants, and much less likely to give drug or alcohol tests do not have obvious "efficiency" interpretations. Institutional sources of variation in hiring practices not examined here include U.S. state laws, which vary appreciably in the freedom they grant to employers and the protections they provide for potential employees (Herman 1994).

Additional research is required to better understand several occupationally related differences in staffing methods reported here. In particular, differences involving occupational prestige and gender composition merit further attention. The extent to which these are products of occupational features such as authority, routinization, or expected attachment to the employer represent important questions to be addressed by future studies of the hiring process.

This chapter has examined the human resource practices that bridge the boundary between the establishment and the external labor market. Succeeding chapters use the NOS data to investigate variations in training practices and both wage and nonwage compensation for those employees who successfully pass through the screens of recruitment and selection.

## Notes

1. The questions were not repeated if the core and GSS occupations were identical, or if the managerial or administrative occupation matched either the core or GSS occupations. In case of redundancy between the core and GSS occupations, a response is said to refer to the core occupation; likewise, a response is counted as the core or GSS occupation when either overlaps with the managerial occupation.

2. A small number of informants responded to the question on interview length in "days." We have assumed 8-hour days in converting these responses into minutes.

3. These studies do not distinguish between different types of tests, as the NOS data do. In addition, they do not allow for within-establishment variation in the use of selection methods for different occupations. Cohen and Pfeffer's (1986) data include measures of test use for different occupations, but they combined these measures into a single establishment-level "use of tests" scale.

4. Because the NOS did not record specific occupational titles for managerial or administrative occupations, it was not possible to assign occupational prestige scores to them. To permit use of data on managerial occupations in the multilevel analyses reported here, these records were assigned a mean prestige score (47), and a dummy variable distinguishing managerial from GSS and core occupation records was entered into the analysis.

5. The responses to these indicators are scored from 1 ("never") to 3 ("frequently").

6. Marsden and Campbell (1990) also reported a tendency for workers in larger establishments to have located their jobs via direct applications. They assigned a structural interpretation to this finding: Direct applications rate a greater chance of success at establishments where many potential vacancies exist.

7. The establishment-level commonalities are probably not attributable to the order in which survey questions were administered to NOS informants. In the NOS interview schedule, several unrelated items intervened between repetitions of the question sequences on recruiting for different occupations.

8. Because the occupational-level variance differs from observation to observation in the logistic model, one cannot partition the unexplained variance into establishment-level and occupational-level components as readily as we do in Tables 7.4 and 7.6.

9. To reduce skew, the natural logarithms of the measures of extensiveness and intensity in Table 7.3 are taken as dependent variables in Table 7.6.

# 8

# Job Training in U.S. Organizations

DAVID KNOKE

ARNE L. KALLEBERG

The job training practices of U.S. employers affect employees from the executive suite to the loading dock, enhancing skills from basic literacy to interpersonal sensitivity. Job training is often endorsed as part of a policy solution to the United States' labor force problems (U.S. Department of Labor 1989). Training is a central component in programs and policies to eliminate illiteracy, reduce poverty, retool displaced workers, improve technical proficiency, and impart social skills to corporate managers.

Three decades ago, Jacob Mincer (1962), one of the founders of the human capital approach, concluded that (at least for males) on-the-job training is as important as formal schooling when measured in dollar costs.

Today, postschool training by U.S. corporations is even more pervasive (Useem 1993b). Nearly 18 million workers, comprising 16% of the labor force, identify formal company programs as their main source for improving job skills in their current jobs, more than those citing informal on-the-job training (15%), schools (13%), or other methods (7%) (U.S. Department of Labor 1992; see also Brown 1990). Private-sector organizations spent $50 billion on formal programs, according to a 1994 survey by *Training* magazine (see Knoke 1996).

A new training ideology is rapidly eclipsing the traditional segmented pattern in which universities educated the professionals and technicians, companies primed the executives, unions apprenticed workers in the skilled trades, and government prepared the disadvantaged. Facing competitive world economic pressures that have eroded America's market positions, employers are now using job training as one means of coping with changes fostered by technological innovation, market competition, organizational restructuring, and demographic shifts.

Although training is an integral part of the employer-employee relationship, direct evidence about company training practices based on representative samples of diverse employing organizations has only recently become available (U.S. Bureau of Labor Statistics 1994). Despite a thriving applied commerce in training programs (Carnevale, Gainer, and Villet 1990), research projects have seldom investigated employer training programs and practices using diverse organizational samples (one exception is Bishop 1994). Most evidence on employer training programs and practices comes from case studies, self-reported labor force surveys, or highly restricted samples of organizations (typically skewed toward very large firms). In this chapter and the following, we examine several research hypotheses about employer-provided job training programs and practices, using the 1991 NOS.

## Theories About Firm Training

Which firms provide their employees with job training? There are four major theoretical approaches that attempt to answer the questions of the prevalence, causes, and consequences of employer job training: the human capital, credential screening, social structural, and institutional accounts.

## Human Capital Theory

Human capital explanations of employers' efforts to train their workers emphasize the firm's rational decision to invest in upgrading employees' skills with expectations of generating productivity, quality, and competitiveness gains for the organization. The early human capital theorists stressed the supply of worker characteristics while largely deemphasizing the employer's demand for labor (Schultz 1963; Becker 1964; Mincer 1974; Blaug 1976). As its core proposition, the theory proposed that workers rationally invest in developing their personal productive capacities to maximize their lifetime expected earnings (more generally, their status attainments). Those activities that increase productive skills—formal education, job searching, work experience, training, health—are rewarded with higher income. The importance of preemployment formal schooling lies in its presumed enhancement of a potential worker's productivity, which is preferred by employers. Such general human capital skills as literacy, numeracy, and punctuality can be readily transferred between many jobs. The role of postemployment training, however, is a "question . . . that continues to haunt the human-capital research program" (Blaug 1976, p. 840).

Investments in human capital after leaving formal schooling take two basic forms: (a) informal work experiences, such as learning-by-doing on the job, coaching by coworkers, and monitoring by supervisors; and (b) formal training programs, conducted both on-site and off-site, in which explicit instructions are given apart from productive tasks. An economically rational firm can be expected to provide job training only when it anticipates that it can capture sufficiently increased worker productivity to offset its training costs.

*General training,* for example, in such easily portable skills as reading and arithmetic, does not allow an employer to reap the benefits of improved employee productivity because a trained worker's wage will rise in a competitive labor market by exactly the amount of the increased marginal product. Because the generally trained worker's enhanced productivity enables her to quit to take a higher-paying job elsewhere, the firm would lose its investment in that worker. A major conclusion of human capital theory is that firms would provide general job training to an employee "only if they [employers] did not have to pay any of the costs" (Becker 1964, p. 12). Therefore, a trainee must bear the entire costs of her general training, by accepting lower wages during the training period. The inducement to accept this training wage cut is the worker's expectation of subsequently earning much higher wages through her greatly enhanced productivity (Farkas, England, and Barton 1988). Apprenticeship programs similarly involve lower wages during training, with later compensation in the form of higher wage rates. In effect, firms "sell" general training to workers by inducing them to accept initially lower wages than available elsewhere, but later paying them increased wages to reward their improved performance. This hypothesis is consistent with survey data on earnings profiles that show employee wages rising sharply with years of work experience until middle age, at which point they level off then decline shortly before retirement (Murphy and Welch 1990). (This pattern presumes that most training occurs early in an employee's career.)

In contrast to general training, *specific training* increases the productivity of workers only within the firm that provides it (Becker 1964). Because firm-specific skills and knowledge (for example, operating a unique machine or serving a special clientele) are useless elsewhere, a specifically trained worker has little opportunity to take these skills to another employer, but also no reason to pay for the costs of her training. Firms are willing to pay for specific training, discounted for long-run equilibrium, because larger profits will result from their specially trained workers' increased productivity. To keep employees from quitting and taking their training investments with them, employers also should be willing to pay somewhat higher posttraining wages, in effect providing employees with some return on their training investments. Human capital theory hypothesizes that wages increase and job quits decrease with an employee's length of time in the firm, assuming that the amount of specific training is proportional to tenure with an employer (Farkas, England, and Barton 1988). If workers receive a mix of both general and specific training, "the fraction of costs paid by firms would be inversely related to the importance of the general component, or positively related to the specificity of the training" (Becker 1964, p. 23).

Whether companies can reap productivity gains by providing general training to their employees depends in part on supply and demand features of labor markets that enable trained employees to more easily obtain work with other employers. Obtaining distinct measures of firm-specific and general skills has been elusive. Similarly, accurate measurement of both the employer's and the employee's decisions in the job matching and job training process is also very difficult. Consequently, an empirical assessment of the hypothesis that company training tends predominantly to be firm-specific has proven to be intractable. As a result, the human capital approach has not been of much use for predicting actual company job training decisions.

### Credential-Screening Approaches

Credential and screening principles emphasize the demand-side characteristics of employers' recruitment practices (Berg 1970; Spence 1974; Stiglitz 1975; Collins 1979). Firms face pools of applicants with uncertain abilities, from which they must make new hires. They select new workers based on assessments of available information about probable employee qualities and their likelihood of remaining with the employer long enough to repay any company investments in informal work experience and formal job training. Because directly monitoring an applicant to determine her actual abilities and performance is costly, firms fall back on using the applicant's formal schooling credentials and other visible attributes as signs of general skills, such as cognitive learning, social competence, and motivation to persist on task. In the strong version of screening theory (Blaug 1976), firms interpret formal school certificates as indicators of the job applicant's preexisting abilities, regardless of whether the candidate's educational experiences did anything to enhance his or her productive capacity. Some sociological analysts argue that schools actually make individuals more skillful and employable, by developing both their human and cultural capital (DiMaggio 1982). Other theorists view schools mainly as labelers of existing competencies, in effect serving as efficient sorters of students by identifying and certifying those aptitudes and abilities most desired by employers. Thus, the well-known positive relationship between education and earnings results from firms sending clear signals to the labor market that applicants who present higher educational qualifications will receive the better-paid jobs.

In weaker versions of the screening hypothesis, employers treat educational credentials as indicators of applicants' potential for filling company jobs that require further specialized training. Rather than certifying that the recipient has acquired job relevant abilities, a diploma signifies only the holder's latent aptitudes for obtaining such skills under the employer's tutelage. For example, Thurow's (1975) job competition model consists of a labor queue in which job applicants are lined up by the firm according to their perceived trainability potential. Formal education credentials serve as indirect evidence of "absorptive capacity" (p. 88), even if no relevant cognitive skills were learned in school. The farther a student has persisted with formal schooling, the more likely she is to be compliant at order taking, punctuality, test taking, and stick-to-itiveness. The firm will place such candidates higher in its hiring queue as preferred low-training-cost applicants. Evidence that workers with higher education credentials receive more company training than those with less education supports this weak screening hypothesis. The screening principle generalizes to other visible attributes used in making judgments about applicant productivity. Thus, some employers seem to believe that the race and gender of job candidates offer clues about their potential trainability and labor force persistence. For example, young women may be perceived as more likely than young men to quit the labor force to raise their children. "Statistical discrimination" results whenever an employer acts to reduce the perceived risks of hiring an unstable or untrainable employee by using the person's gender, race, age, or other attributes as a screening device, thereby attributing to that worker the alleged average traits of a group (Thurow 1975).

Credentialism seems most pertinent to the hiring decision, where limited information is available about the productivity and trainability of prospective workers. Bills (1988) argued that credentials are used mainly to get a foot in the company door, after which other evidence becomes more relevant to training, promotions, and wage increases. Subsequent to hiring, firms use a probationary period during which they directly observe a new recruit's performance (Barron, Black, and Lowenstein 1987). This close monitoring allows for more precise assessments of how well the new worker fits the entry-level job. Supervisors make posthire appraisals about the recruit's technical and social skills and learning capacity, evaluating her potential for enhanced productivity through various employer training programs. Only workers who are judged to possess higher ability will be retained in the firm's workforce beyond the probationary period. In the credentialist view, general education obtained in school prior to employment has limited relevance for both firms and workers in the allocation of labor between work positions. It serves less as an index of acquired skills than as a crude, low-cost proxy for potential performance qualities desired by employers. As firms become more familiar with their employees' actual abilities, the relevance of formal education for career trajectories fades (Bills 1988; but see Lillard and Tan 1992 for differences across age and gender groups). Consequently, credentials may only weakly explain which persons are most likely to be trained by their employers.

## Structural Explanations

The structure of work settings may facilitate or constrain individual job training opportunities. The costs of monitoring, evaluating, training, and placing qualified employees varies substantially across the range of firms in the economy. The *new structuralism* in the sociology of work emphasizes the role of work structures and economic institutions (organizations, industries, markets, and classes) in generating inequalities within society as a whole (Baron and Bielby 1980; Kalleberg and Berg 1987; Hachen 1990). These elements include such "normative and coercive factors" (Bridges and Villemez 1991, p. 748) as union power, establishment size, internal labor markets and other occupational systems, the extent of government employment, and gender and race discrimination. In the structural perspective, the primary factors determining which individuals will receive company-provided training lie not so much in personal resources as in workers' access to bureaucratic employment systems, to specialized internal labor markets, and to social networks linking organizations, industries, and occupational communities (Baron and Bielby 1984; Granovetter 1985; Lorence 1987a). Such complex work contexts constitute explicit or implicit rules and regulations that shape the training opportunities and rewards that employers make available to their employees. These organizational structures may directly affect training decisions, apart from the importance of individual human capital and credentials. For example, computer manufacturing companies require system analysts with very advanced and highly specialized software and hardware skills. When external labor markets, comprising mixes of recent school graduates and experienced workers willing to leave their current employers, persistently fail to furnish the demanded skills, computer manufacturers are compelled to create such employees for themselves. Thus, Apple constructed an enormous Silicon Valley "campus" to educate its future generations of employees in the latest technical developments.

The particular job training structures and processes that firms create for matching workers to jobs do not operate uniformly across a highly differentiated economy, but are localized in various niches. Certain industries are more likely than others to develop formal training programs, elaborate internal labor markets, and compensation packages to attract and retain a highly skilled workforce (the Polaroid strategy), wheras others seek mainly to replenish a rapidly turned-over workforce with unskilled raw recruits (the McDonald's solution). Similarly, some firms collaborate with their employee unions to design more extensive training procedures, whereas others resist union incursions onto the shop floor (Ferman, Hoyman, Cutcher-Gershenfeld, and Savoie 1991). Structural analysts grapple with basic explanations of where, when, and how training policies and practices arise to slot workers into internal organizational positions.

To retain and induce quality performances from their best employees, firms design training programs and practices (as well as wage and benefit packages) to encourage their most competent workers to acquire the additional skills necessary for advancement to positions of higher status and pay, better working conditions, and broader responsibilities. The congruence increases between specific jobs and a worker's experience-acquired and training-acquired competencies as an employee advances along a promotion trajectory within a firm internal labor market. Earnings, fringe benefits, and pensions likewise increase with employee promotions into higher grades, both because of improved worker productivity from training and experience and because the firm is compelled to make above-market inducements to prevent other firms from raiding its skilled work-force.

**Institutionalization**

Firms' training decisions are driven in part by prevailing conventions regarding appropriate behaviors in the society at large and among peer organizations. Various institutional theories are enjoying revivals among sociologists (Powell and DiMaggio 1991) and economists (Furubotn and Richter 1991). Although disagreements exist, many institutionalists emphasize that organizational forms and actions emerge and persist not only through conscious rational-choice designs but also through cognitive and cultural conventions that assume a rulelike status in social thought and action. A common institutional theme is the importance for explaining organizational behaviors of such elements as "symbolic systems, cognitive scripts, and normative codes" (Scott 1992, p. 3). Organizations and their employees are mutually shaped by the larger cultural environments within which they are embedded. These environmental conditions induce substantial uniformity among organizational practices, including job training programs and policies, by conferring greater legitimacy on organizations that adopt conventional structures. As a result of these external normative constraints, most organizations operating in a common field come increasingly to resemble one another over time.

The concept of organizational citizenship is of particular importance for understanding company job training. This idea points to the institutional emergence of norms about employee job rights and benefits. After World War II, personnel practices in the largest firms encouraged strong organizational ties to employees, inducing their commitment by offering education and training, job security, comprehensive benefits, and career opportunities (Baron, Dobbin, and Jennings 1986). Employers' job training practices inevitably came to reflect a pervasive elaboration of employee job rights. A variety of forces—technological task performance demands, professional association standards, union grievance procedures, legislation and judicial mandates for equal employment opportunities—converged to transform the workplace into a legalized institution whose employees increasingly came to expect a sense of participatory citizenship in their work roles (Sutton et al. 1994). Historically, company educational opportunities became legitimated and diffused across many employment contexts as part of the generally expanding norms of organizational citizenship (Monahan, Meyer, and Scott 1992; Chapter 12, this volume). Scott and Meyer (1991) generated a series of hypotheses about the likelihood that modern organizations will offer formal training of one type or another. They argued that employers tend to copy generally valued models of employee instruction that are only ambiguously linked to firm-specific tasks and purposes but that were similar to the ways that traditional educational systems operated. For example, several major corporations operate company colleges replete with curricula, examinations, and degrees. Societal pressures to develop participants' skills became so pervasive that many company training forms and processes were extended to all sorts of organizational contexts. Where such institutionalization is most strongly entrenched, a firm's conformity to external training norms should be strongest.

In summary, the four theoretical perspectives reviewed above each point to distinct answers to the question of which firms provide job training to their employees. The human capital approach asserts that rational firms will invest only in those firm-specific training skills whose costs they can expect to recapture through improved worker productivity; employees must pay for their own general skills training. The credential-screening principles emphasize that training is one component in an elaborate recruitment, hiring, and promotion process. Firms use formal school certifications as proxies for other worker characteristics to select and place new workers perceived as most receptive to skill enhancement. Organizational structuralists point to the constraints and opportunities that formal work settings impose on training, particularly the impact of firm size, bureaucracy, unionization, and internal labor markets. And the institutionalist perspective underscores the normative and cultural influences from the external environment that shape an organization's decisions about appropriate training activities. These themes recur as we next review empirical research and state testable hypotheses about the sources of company training programs.

## Research Hypotheses

A comprehensive theory of job training in U.S. organizations does not exist, and we do not propose to develop and test one here. Previous research and theory about job training, conducted primarily by labor economists and organization researchers, however, has identified several sets of important explanatory variables whose influences we review. One variable, of course, is organizational size. Other explanations for why large organizations provide more training are that large organizations have formalized job structures, have internal labor markets, are more unionized, and operate in environments that encourage investment in training. We discuss these alternative explanations to the hypothesis that a net effect of company size on training results from the higher employee monitoring costs borne by large firms.

### Organizational Size

Available evidence indicates a positive relation between organizational size and job training at both the establishment and firm levels (Cohen and Pfeffer 1986). Some research suggests a curvilinear relation, with the smallest and largest employers providing the most training (Brown, Hamilton, and Medoff 1990). Barron, Black, and Lowenstein (1987, 1989) found that five training activities (e.g., hours of instruction given to new employees by managers, supervisors, and coworkers) increased nonlinearly with the number of employees (logged) and the existence of subsidiaries outside the local area.

Several theoretical explanations for the organizational-size-training relationship exist. Using principal-agent theory, labor economists have hypothesized that the costs of gathering information about an employee's job performance at each step of the search, hiring, retention, and compensation processes are much greater for large than for small establishments (Lazear 1981; Oi 1983a). Referring explicitly to wage differentials, Stigler (1962) argued that organizational size serves as a proxy for the costs to employers of gathering information about employees. He suggested that small employers can directly observe the performance of new workers, so the lower wage rates in small plants reflect in part the lower costs to the small-scale employer of judging quality. The higher monitoring costs among large establishments lead to the development of production methods that increase workforce size proportionately less than their expanding output would demand (Barron et al. 1987). Thus, large establishments substitute capital stocks, search and screen applicants more carefully, and train their employees more extensively. Economies of scale mean that large organizations also incur lower marginal costs of training additional employees than do small organizations (Brown, Hamilton and Medoff 1990).

> *H 8.1:* **Large establishments are more likely to provide formal job training programs than are small establishments.**

### Labor Unions

The relationship between labor unions and job training by employers is less clear than for organizational size because of contradictory implications about unions' representation of worker interests. Utility-maximizing theories of pure and bilateral monopoly posit that unions seek to raise their members' wages, even at the expense of nonunion employees and company efficiency (Oswald 1985). But, a union monopoly over labor supply is complicated by its organizational interests: As collective bargaining boosts workers' compensation, companies tend to replace workers with capital. Hence, to avoid their members' loss of employment, unions also have a stake in assisting employers to increase union workers' productivity. Freeman and Medoff (1984) argued that by reducing employee quit rates unions lower a firm's hiring and training costs. Because the risk of a worker quitting is lower in unionized workplaces, unionization can increase an employer's "incentives for investment in skills specific to an enterprise, which also raises productivity" (p. 14). Ironically, although the union principle that internal promotions should be made according to seniority discourages workers' resistance to job training, it often places less qualified workers in more desirable jobs, reducing productivity. "Which of these effects dominates is an empirical question" (Freeman and Medoff 1984,

p. 15). Most empirical evidence, however, reveals a negative relationship between unionization and training, which suggests that employers believe the latter effect dominates. Duncan and Stafford (1980) found that blue-collar union members received substantially less on-the-job training compared to nonunionized employees. From lower wage returns to age and experience among union members, Mincer (1983) concluded that the total training is less in union firms, as confirmed by employee self-reports. Lillard and Tan (1992) found that union membership reduced the probability of company training for older men, but had no effect among women or younger men.

> *H 8.2:* **Establishments with unionized employees provide less training than nonunionized establishments.**

### Workforce Composition

In making training investment decisions for employees who are expected to boost firm productivity, employers use many attributes of workers, including gender and race. Statistical discrimination results when employers try to reduce their risks of hiring unstable or untrainable employees by basing decisions on such visible worker attributes as gender and race (Thurow 1975). Several studies found that women and minorities receive less formal and informal training than do men (Duncan and Hoffman 1979; Boston 1990; Lynch 1991; Lillard and Tan 1992). Many employers seem to act as though training investments in women and minorities are less likely to be recaptured through future productivity because these employees allegedly have weaker labor force attachments. For example, women's periodic exits for child rearing are alleged to lead to a higher rate of job turnover for women than for men, although the empirical evidence is equivocal (England 1992).

> *H 8.3:* **Establishments with workforces that are predominantly male and white provide more formal training than establishments with predominantly female and minority workers.**

### Internal Structures

Baron and Bielby (1980), drawing attention to an emergent new structuralism paradigm of stratification, argued that explanations of worker and firm outcomes must take account of technological, administrative, and political arrangements in the enterprise within which workers are embedded. To explain company job training, the most relevant structures are the workplace social organization and, especially, the division of labor (those rules regulating tasks performed by employee positions). These structures are crucial for solving the primary problem in organizational sociology identified by Granovetter (1981): explaining how workers' attributes and interests are matched with employers' decisions and job requirements to create norms for the hiring, training, promotion, layoff, reward, and control of labor. Workplace structures, consisting of norms and behaviors connecting job positions and their incumbents in common patterns of interaction, vary along two important dimensions: (a) formalization and (b) the presence of firm internal labor markets.

Formalization is the codification of tasks and classification of jobs, ranging from simple to elaborate categorizations defining job holders' explicit rights and duties. In stipulating job skill requirements, employers may generate obligations to assist new and current employees in attaining greater job proficiency through formal training programs.

Firm internal labor markets (FILMs), the promotion trajectories that link jobs within an organization, seek to improve the match between specific jobs and workers' experience-acquired and training-acquired competencies (Althauser 1989; Chapter 5, this volume). As with external labor markets, the primary function of a FILM is to allocate the available workers (including applicants) into a set of open firm positions (jobs). This sorting process eventually results in a maximally efficient match between workers' skills and the firm's production requirements (Granovetter 1981). An internal labor market restricts the numbers and types of workers who are eligible to enter the vacancies, generally giving priority to employees previously hired at or promoted from lower hierarchical levels. Employers may tie a worker's progress within a FILM to formal training experiences intended to impart the skills they deem necessary for advancement. By directly tying investments in human capital to job ladders, employers generate strong incentives for their trained workers that prevent competitors from luring them away (Ryan 1984).

*H 8.4:* **Establishments with formalized internal structures and FILMs are more likely to provide formal training than are those with few differentiated internal structures.**

**Environments**

All organizations operate within environmental contexts composed of other organizations and the broader social, cultural, and legal conditions to which they must adapt. Aldrich (1979) conceptualized two major environmental dimensions: resource flows and information exchanges across organizational boundaries. Organizations compete for scarce resources, especially favorable financial terms—the most successful competitors are able to avoid dependence on others and achieve autonomy in dealing with critical contingencies (Pfeffer and Salancik 1978). The information-flow dimension consists of cognitions and beliefs about external uncertainties as filtered through key organizational decision-makers' perceptions, and it forms the basis for maintaining or modifying organizational routines. Technological innovations in procedures for making goods or delivering services constitute a powerful information environment that shapes organizational behavior (Bamber and Lansbury 1989). Institutionalized values and norms, as legitimated by competitors, customers, governmental regulators, and professional associations, comprise another formative environment, especially where technologies are ambiguous and market forces are unpredictable (Meyer and Scott 1983).

Although little theory or research exists on environmental influences on job training, companies are likely to provide more employee training when skilled workers are harder to hire and where resource dependencies permit the diversion of resources from production. Thus, resource-rich organizations confronting rapid technological advances, intense domestic and international competition, and high demands for skilled labor may invest in improving their current employees' skills (as well as in pirating from other organizations' trained workers holding comparable positions). The institutional view of job training emphasizes that employers tend to adopt prevalent models of employee instruction that may be only loosely coupled to their organization's tasks and purposes (Scott and Meyer 1991).

> *H 8.5:* **Establishments in resource-rich, complex, competitive, and institutionalized environments provide more job training than those operating in other conditions.**

The five hypotheses on job training above represent varying theoretical and empirical positions and reflect the orientations among the labor economists who have devoted the greatest attention to the issue. Although stated as bivariate propositions, these hypotheses must be examined by multivariate analysis to ascertain whether any other relationships might account for our observations. For example, are unionized workplaces more likely to provide training simply because they are unionized or because they tend to be large organizations operating in institutionalized environments?

## The Scope of Company Training

Several aspects of formal training efforts vary greatly across establishments, including the existence of programs, the number of participants, and training costs. In all analyses reported in this chapter, we present only results based on unweighted data. Recall from Chapter 2 that the NOS multiplicity design sampled establishments proportional to their number of employees, giving larger organizations a higher probability of selection. Thus, such descriptive statistics as percentages and means refer to the average work settings experienced by the U.S. labor force, not to the (unweighted) proportion of organizations exhibiting specific attributes. Although we often refer to the relative frequency of establishment characteristics, readers should interpret those statistics as reflecting the exposure rates of typical workers. The 1991 NOS informants were first asked, "Apart from on-the-job training, in the past *two years* did [Org Name] provide *any* employees with formal job training, either on or off the premises?" *Any training* is a dichotomous dependent variable, coded 1 for the presence of any formal training and 0 for no training program. More than two thirds of the U.S. labor force works in establishments that offered some kind of formal training (72%).

If training occurred, informants were asked, "In total, including staff time and all other costs, about how much money has [Org Name] spent on training *in the past 2 years?*" *Training budget* is the natural logarithm of the dollar amount; organizations having no training are coded 0. Of those establishments with training programs, the median training expenditure was $15,000 during the previous 2 years (mean = $344,885, indicating a substantial positive skew).

To measure the number of training participants, informants were asked, "Within the last 2 years, how many employees participated in formal training?" *Employees trained* is the percentage of employees trained; organizations without training are coded 0. The median establishment trained 55.6% of its workforce (mean = 63.8%). Two logged expenditure measures are (a) *Employee costs,* the training budget divided by the number of employees (for all organizations); and (b) *trainee costs,* the training budget divided by the number of persons trained (for organizations with training programs). The medians were $56 and $365, respectively (means = $392 and $1,206).

The NOS collected detailed information about establishment training programs, but we confine ourselves here to only brief descriptions of these measures (see Knoke 1996 for more detailed analyses). Among organizations with training programs, 77% use their own staffs to conduct training on-site, whereas 61% also pay outside agencies, consultants, or schools to conduct on-site training, and 90% send at least some employees to off-site training. Among subsidiaries and branches of larger organizations (which are about half the sample), 71% either bring in trainers from the parent organization or send their employees off-premises to be trained. For courses conducted off-site, most organizations (71%) pay their employees' participation costs through a combination of tuition benefits or reimbursements (91%) and paid release time from work (69%). State, local, and federal governments pay for some training in only a minority of establishments (18%); the federal Job Training Partnership Act is involved in less than 3% of all programs. A majority of informants (51%) feel that the amount of resources their organization devoted to training remained roughly constant over the past 2 years. But, 43% report that training expenditures increased during that interval. A majority (53%) say that their organizations devote more resources to training than other places of roughly the same size.

Informants in establishments with training programs report that the purpose of training to a "great extent" or to "some extent" is to (a) "provide or improve managerial skills" (88%); (b) "train employees in the use of computers and other new equipment" (80%); (c) "train them on the safe use of equipment or tools" (73%); and (d) to "teach remedial skills in literacy or arithmetic" (16%). Emulation of competitors ("to keep up with the training practices of other organizations that do work like yours") is a major reason for providing training (78%), followed by legal requirements (57%) and union contracts (15%). A majority of informants (57%) agree that formal job training is an "essential" or "very important" factor in their employees' promotion chances.

All but a handful of organizations formally evaluate their training programs. NOS asked about four methods of program assessment by: (a) formal testing of trainees (49%); (b) trainee opinions (51%); (c) supervisor evaluations of employee performance (56%); and (d) program director assessments (41%). The median number of evaluation techniques used is 2.00 (mean = 1.95). Informants rate the overall effectiveness of their training efforts as "highly effective" (60%) or "somewhat effective" (37%), with less than 1% saying they are "not at all effective."

## Results

Table 8.1 reports the estimated coefficients from logistic regression analyses of the presence or absence of any formal job training program (our first dependent variable) for all 688 establishments studied. The sets of independent variables correspond to Hypotheses 8.1 through 8.5. A baseline equation that includes only the constant produced a log-likelihood of −410.2 for one degree of freedom. Predicting the modal category, "training program present," for all establishments would be correct, by chance, for 72% of them.

The equation in column 1 includes the two logged size measures (for both the establishment and its parent firm, if present), the parent organization dummy variable, as well as logged establishment age. It is a significant improvement over the constant-only model ($G^2 = 259.4$, $df = 4$). Correct placements occur in 83% of the cases (91% of the organizations with training, 41% of those without training). Only the coefficients for logged establishment size and the parent dummy variable, however, are significant at $p < .05$ or better. Hence, Hypothesis 8.1—that large organizations provide more training than small ones—is supported, although the size effect seems to be concentrated at the establishment level, presumably because the formal job training measure applies only to programs at that level. The significant parent dummy shows that subsidiaries and branches of organizations are more likely than freestanding organizations to have formal training programs. Figure 8.1 demonstrates how the percentage of establishments with any formal training increases strongly with size, from less than 20% for establishments with fewer than 5 employees to more than 90% for those with more than 500 employees.

Contrary to Hypothesis 8.2—that unionized organizations provide less training than nonunionized organizations—both coefficients in column 2 of Table 8.1 are positive and significant. Establishments in which union negotiations have important impacts on the earnings of core production workers are more likely to have formal training programs. Similarly, the

**Table 8.1** Logistic Regression Coefficients Predicting Job Training Program: 688 Establishments From the National Organizations Study, 1991

| Independent Variables | 1 | 2 | 3 | 4 | 5 | 6 | 7 |
|---|---|---|---|---|---|---|---|
| Constant | -2.02*** | 0.38** | 1.25*** | -.96*** | -2.23*** | -3.15** | -3.14*** |
| Organization size and age | | | | | | | |
|   Establishment size (ln) | .71*** | | | | | .34*** | .29*** |
|   Parent size (ln) | .04 | | | | | -.10 | |
|   Parent dummy | 1.50* | | | | | .89 | |
|   Establishment age (ln) | .04 | | | | | -.07 | |
| Unionization | | | | | | | |
|   Core worker union | | 1.39*** | | | | .41 | |
|   Industry unionization | | .02** | | | | .00 | |
| Workforce composition | | | | | | | |
|   White workforce (percentage) | | | -.01* | | | .01 | |
|   Women workforce (percentage) | | | .01* | | | .01 | |
| Internal structure | | | | | | | |
|   Formalization | | | | 3.16*** | | 2.52*** | 2.53*** |
|   Internal labor markets | | | | .94*** | | .61** | .57** |
| External environment | | | | | | | |
|   Industry profit rate | | | | | 24.40* | -.93 | |
|   Industry compensation level | | | | | -.00 | .00 | |
|   Industry assets | | | | | .27 | -1.97* | |
|   Industry unemployment rate | | | | | -.22** | -.15 | |
|   Complexity | | | | | 1.76*** | 1.05* | 1.03* |
|   Uncertainty | | | | | -.18 | -.00 | |
|   Market competition | | | | | .36** | .30* | .29* |
|   Foreign competition | | | | | .16 | .05 | |
|   Institutionalization | | | | | .45*** | .03 | |
| Organization type | | | | | | | |
|   Public | | | | | 1.38** | -1.64* | |
|   Nonprofit | | | | | 2.22*** | -.75 | |
|   Profit-making | | | | | — | — | |
| Log-likelihood | -281.5 | -380.7 | -405.4 | -260.4 | -329.5 | -239.0 | -248.6 |
| Degrees of freedom | 5 | 3 | 3 | 3 | 12 | 22 | 6 |
| Correctly placed (percentage) | 83.1 | 71.7 | 71.7 | 84.3 | 77.5 | 85.6 | 84.9 |

* $p < .05$; ** $p < .01$; *** $p < .001$ (two-tailed tests).

more unionized an industry, the more likely an establishment in that industry is to offer training. The workforce composition hypothesis, Hypothesis 8.3, is not supported either (column 3 of Table 8.1): Both the

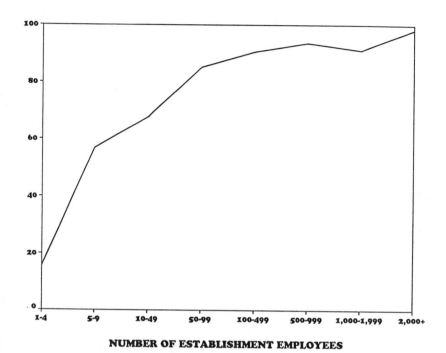

**Figure 8.1.** Any Company Training, by Size

negative coefficient for percentage of whites and the positive effect of the percentage of women are contrary to our expectations.

Hypothesis 8.4 asserts that establishments with formalized job and internal labor market structures are more likely to provide training than are establishments with simple structures. Both measures in column 4 of Table 8.1 are positive and statistically significant. Moreover, the improvement in fit is substantial, with correct placements rising to 84.3%. Figure 8.2 shows how the percentage of establishments with any training increases strongly from 22% for establishments at the lowest FILM quintile to 92% for those at the highest quintile.

In column 5, the positive coefficient for industry profit rate indicates that organizations operating in richer environments do more training, whereas the negative unemployment coefficient implies that more training is done where labor supplies are tight. Three other significant coefficients also support Hypothesis 8.5: Training is more prevalent in establishments operating in complex environments, in the presence of strong product and

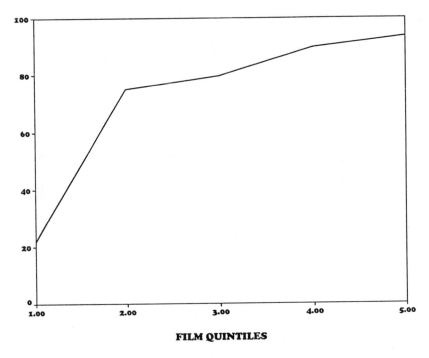

**Figure 8.2.** Any Company Training, by FILM Quintiles

service market competition, and in the presence of higher levels of institutionalization. Finally, dummy variables reveal that public and nonprofit
organizations are more likely than profit-making firms to provide formal
training.

The equation reported in column 6 in Table 8.1 includes all predictors;
only the significant predictors are retained in column 7. The unionization
and workforce composition variables are not significant after controlling
for other factors. But establishment size, formalization, internal labor
markets, environmental complexity, and market competition remain significant factors influencing job training programs. The coefficient for
logged establishment size, however, is reduced to less than half its original
magnitude. The internal structure measures, formalization and internal
labor markets, remain especially robust, whereas two environmental indicators, complexity and market competition, are barely significant. Equation 7 correctly places 85% of establishments in the sample (93% of those
with training programs and 64% of those without them).

**Table 8.2** Tobit Regression Coefficients Predicting Percentage of Employees Trained and Job Training Expenditures: Establishments From the National Organizations Study, 1991

| Independent Variables | Training Budget (ln) 1 | Employees Trained (percentage) 2 | Employee Costs (ln) 3 | Trainee Costs (ln) 4 |
|---|---|---|---|---|
| Constant | −4.05*** | −85.61*** | −2.23* | −3.70** |
| Establishment size (ln) | 1.06*** | .06 | .07 | .14 |
| White workforce | .02* | — | — | — |
| Women workforce | — | .23* | | |
| Formalization | 7.10*** | 95.35*** | 4.99*** | 5.63*** |
| Internal labor markets | 1.35*** | 17.11*** | .92*** | .94*** |
| Complex environment | 2.50** | — | 1.64** | 1.63** |
| Market competition | .66** | 9.32* | .48** | .47* |
| Industry unemployment rate | −.36** | — | −.27** | −.25* |
| Industry compensation level | — | — | — | .001* |
| σ | 4.44*** | 66.94*** | 2.94*** | 3.30*** |
| Log-likelihood | −1,241.8 | −2,670.2 | −1,083.3 | −1,102.1 |
| Degrees of freedom | 9 | 7 | 18 | 9 |
| Constant model log-likelihood | −1,493.9 | −2,773.5 | −1,250.4 | −1,271.7 |
| (Number of establishments) | 581 | 650 | 581 | 571 |

* $p < .05$; ** $p < .01$; *** $p < .001$ (two-tailed tests).

To conserve space, Table 8.2 displays only the final results for the other four dependent variables associated with job training: training budget, employees trained, employee costs, and trainee costs. Because these four measures are highly intercorrelated, they should yield substantively similar results. To take advantage of information about organizations providing no training, we analyze limited dependent (censored) variables by the tobit method: Establishments with no training are coded 0, whereas those reporting the percentage of employees trained and training dollars (logged) are coded on continuous scales. Evidence supporting the size hypothesis (H 8.1) is almost nonexistent: Logged establishment size is associated only with increases in the total training budget. Neither unionization variable is significant in any equation, rejecting Hypothesis 8.2. Scant support emerges for the workforce composition hypothesis (H 8.3), in that the percentage of whites is associated with increases in the total training budget, whereas the percentage of women is associated only with increases in the percentage of employees trained. But, consistent with Hypothesis 8.4, the greater an establishment's formalization and internal labor market, the greater is its training activity. Similarly, both market competition and environmental complexity are related to increases in job training in all but one instance, supporting Hypothesis 8.5. A high industry unemployment rate is associated with decreases in training expenditures, whereas higher industry compensation levels call forth higher spending per trainee, lending additional support to Hypothesis 8.5, which addresses the importance of environmental resources for company job training programs.

## Conclusion

Formal job training programs are widely diffused among U.S. work organizations. Our analyses of diverse organizations from the 1991 National Organizations Survey examined five hypotheses about job training programs that had previously been examined using only employee surveys or samples of employers that were limited in their diversity. A major result is a clarification of the effect of organizational size that has long been noted by labor economists. Consistent with the monitoring-costs hypothesis drawn from principal-agent theory, formal job training programs are more likely to be provided by large establishments than by small ones. However, when training effort (as measured by the percentage of workers trained and the amounts of money spent per employee or per trainee) is examined in conjunction with other explanatory factors, the net impact of organizational size is reduced to nothing. That is, differences associated with organizational size are largely due to other substantive explanatory variables. Similarly, scant evidence exists for the hypotheses that unionization and workforce composition are related to employers' decisions to invest in their employees' human capital formation through job training programs.

The main variables influencing establishment-level job training programs involve the internal structures and the external environments of these organizations. High levels of formalization and extensive internal labor markets are especially associated with greater job training efforts. Where establishments spell out employees' jobs in great detail—documenting their rights and duties as organizational participants—and where they create extensive job ladders and promotion procedures, they also provide more comprehensive and generous job training. Company managers presumably view formal training as an integral component of a larger human resources program that defines employees' positions in the organization. Both employees and organizations may develop explicit understandings about appropriate mechanisms for continually upgrading workers' skills and enhancing the organization's productivity. Unions may play a crucial role in fostering training where internal labor markets are least developed (see Chapter 9). Another striking result is the consistent impact of certain environmental conditions on job training practices. Increased environmental complexity and market competition, both of which tap informants' perceptions of organizational relationships with other organizations, are consistently related to higher training expenditures and larger numbers of workers trained. By developing a workforce at the frontier of skill development, an organization can better adapt to diverse and rapidly changing market conditions.

We conceptualized and empirically examined employer-provided training programs and practices as outcomes of organizational characteristics and contexts. Additional analyses, combining the NOS establishment training data with the individual GSS workers' data, confirm that neither individual-level nor job-level measures are as important for explaining formal training as the organizational factors we examined (Jacobs, Lukens, and Useem 1994). Job training itself may influence organizational behavior by mediating the effect of the production methods and marketing strategies into which an organization seeks to integrate its workforce. For example, particular production technologies may compel employers to hire only those candidates they perceive to be most committed to the labor market and least costly to train or replace. Thus, the training needs of an organization, circumscribed by specific production requirements, can shape the organization's workforce composition. Similarly, where workers are trained in organization-specific production procedures, employers may develop internal labor markets to secure their workers' commitment to the organization and to prevent the subsequent loss of their training investments. And, where senior workers are used to train other employees, the former need some assurance from the employer that they are not training their own replacements. Disentangling the detailed causal order among internal organizational structures, external environments, production technologies, worker attributes, and training activities requires a complex, multilevel longitudinal research design for organizational data collection. None is currently available. The substantive results of our analyses of a cross-sectional survey of a diverse sample of employers should serve, however, as a first step toward that ambitious project.

# 9

# Training, Unions, and Internal Labor Markets

DAVID KNOKE

YOSHITO ISHIO

We continue our examination of organizations' job training programs and practices by focusing on several of the diverse institutional structures in which many firms embed their training activities. These structures offer workers strong incentives to participate in specific types of occupational training, strengthening their interests in remaining with the company. One particularly important set of inducements is that of job ladders and internal labor markets graded by pay, status, and promotion. Another important source of company training is labor unions' demands that employers provide their members with formal training opportunities to enhance job security and competitive employment advantages. Labor unions and internal labor markets, therefore, represent two distinct mechanisms for fostering close-knit relations between firms and workers, which may function independently but may also interact.

This chapter uses the NOS data to examine how unions and internal labor markets jointly affect formal training for core production employees. In particular, we uncover a conditional relationship: For both white-collar and blue-collar core occupations, company-provided job training increases with internal labor market development in nonunionized establishments. But in unionized workplaces, core occupation training is high across all internal labor market levels, suggesting that unions foster training opportunities for their members where internal labor markets are absent or poorly developed.

## Occupational Training

Both the skill requirements and the amount of job training provided by employers differ greatly according to their employees' occupations. Some jobs require extensive vocational knowledge in addition to practical work experience, whereas other tasks can be picked up through brief orientations and informal practice sessions. The job skills and knowledge of professional and craft employees generally involve significant periods of formal schooling prior to employment. Both professional associations and craft unions seek control over the entry of new workers into these occupations by specifying the types and amounts of training required and using qualifying examinations (Weiss 1987). For example, lawyers, accountants, and nurses encounter stiff certification programs and comprehensive testing en route to obtaining licenses to practice. Similarly, machinists, electricians, and plumbers must typically acquire their skills from vocational-technical schools and apprenticeships. In contrast, such office workers as receptionists, data entry clerks, and file clerks face much lower learning requirements because their tasks often can be quickly learned through "osmosis," while performing their jobs without losing productivity (Doeringer and Piore 1971, p. 18). Much unskilled and semiskilled work also requires only strength (digging ditches) or vaguely defined interpersonal skills (taking orders at a fast-food restaurant). The general transferability of low-skill workers makes organizational training programs for these occupations especially difficult for firms to justify, according to conventional economic cost-benefit criteria.

Employer investments in additional worker training parallel the skill content of jobs. Where frequent technological innovations require that workers continually obtain new skills, employer subsidization of their learning may be the only practical way for employees to stay up to date. The demands for skill upgrading may originate because a firm has reorganized its production processes or because external scientific and technical developments have expanded the knowledge base necessary for successful job performance. These conditions are more likely for upper white-collar (managerial and professional) and upper blue-collar (skilled crafts) occupations than for lower white-collar and blue-collar jobs in which technical innovations occur less frequently and may be accommodated more easily within the firm through an increased fine-grained subdivision of labor (Ryan 1984).

Using mainly employee surveys, several analysts have discovered substantial differences in training across occupational categories. Using the 1976 National Longitudinal Survey (NLS) of young men, Rumberger (1984) found that training was most prevalent in professional and technical occupations (41%), followed by skilled manual workers (30%), with the least amounts in managerial (14%) and clerical and sales occupations (5%). In an analysis of the 1983 Current Population Survey (CPS) of employees, Boston (1990) calculated the percentages of occupations needing "specific skills or training to obtain your current (last) job." White-collar occupations (professional and managerial specialties, sales and clerical) and precision product crafts (mechanics and construction) had much higher skill and training requirements (74.3%) than most blue-collar occupations (service, operative, transport, and farming—25.1%). From similar findings about training in employee surveys, Brown (1990) concluded that the biggest difference was between different occupational groups, with professional, technical, and managerial workers obtaining roughly twice as much training as service workers; other white-collar and blue-collar workers fell in between these two occupational groups.

Evidence on firm-provided occupational training is less extensive. The 1991 CPS found that 12% of all workers "qualified for their job skills in formal company (employer) training programs," whereas 16% cited such programs as their main source for skill improvement training (U.S. Department of Labor 1992, pp. 8, 46). The occupations receiving the most skill improvement training were technicians and related support (26%); executive, administrative, and managerial (25%); and professional specialties (20%). The least company training went to handlers, equipment cleaners, and laborers (5%); workers in farming, forestry, and fishing (3%); and private household occupations (0%) (U.S. Department of Labor 1992, p. 46). The Organization of Work in American Business survey of 875 large establishments (with 50 or more employees in nonagricultural industries) revealed that 51% of professional and technical workers, but only 27% of core blue-collar workers, received formal training away from their work stations, a difference that remained significant after controlling for a variety of organizational characteristics (Osterman 1993).

## Firm Internal Labor Markets

Theorists disagree about the origins and consequences of firm internal labor markets (FILMs) for workers and companies. Marxist scholars depict the linking of jobs into elaborate promotion chains as a bureaucratic control strategy created by capitalists to fragment the workforce, thwart labor union organizing drives, and foster worker compliance with management directives to extract surplus labor value for the corporation (Burawoy 1979; Edwards 1979; see also Chapter 5, this volume). By enticing employees to seek highly stratified job placements that are differentially graded in pay and status, the company induces individual striving for upward mobility at the expense of working-class solidarity.

Both neoclassical and neoinstitutional microeconomists depict FILMs as optimally efficient solutions to workers' and firms' common interests in exchange relationships having stable continuity. Gary Becker's (1964) human capital analysis distinguished between general and firm-specific job training according to whether a worker's skills readily transfer to other employers. Rapid turnover of employees who gain firm-specific skills would constitute a costly loss of an organization's human capital investments, because any replacement hires would also have to be trained. From the worker's side, the nontransferability of his or her firm-specific skills means that no wage premium can be gained by leaving to work for another company. Consequently, those companies most heavily dependent on firm-specific skills will design their internal labor markets as hierarchical reward mechanisms to encourage their most valued employees to maintain a long tenure at the organization.

Transaction cost analysts, noting the difficulties in negotiating and enforcing explicit long-term contracts, concur that FILMs emerge from mutual interests in creating long-term cooperative relationships: "Skills acquired in a learning-by-doing fashion and imperfectly transferable across employers need to be embedded in a protective governance structure, lest productive values be sacrificed if the employment relation is unwittingly severed" (Williamson 1981, p. 563). Principal-agent theories (Oi 1983a; Pratt and Zeckhauser 1991) imply that inherent difficulties in monitoring employee job performance, especially in technologically complex and interdependent bureaucratic production systems, encourage internal labor market solutions. Where the costs of gathering and evaluating information during the recruitment, hiring, retention, promotion, and compensation processes are greatest, employers tend to substitute capital stocks for labor, to search and screen applicants more carefully, and to train their employees more extensively. Hence, FILMs are rational adaptations to uncertain labor conditions, enabling an enterprise to fill job vacancies with committed and motivated workers who are attracted by the opportunities for promotions, status, and skill upgrading.

Very little empirical research exists on the relationship of FILMs to organizational training programs and practices. Pfeffer and Cohen (1984), in an analysis of 309 San Francisco area establishments with more than 100 employees, found positive correlations between internal labor markets and measures of on-the-job training, out-of-service training (away from the workplace), and vestibule training (given before the worker assumes full duties). The net relationships between these training variables and FILM arrangements were much stronger among nonmanufacturing than among manufacturing organizations. Knoke and Kalleberg's (see Chapter 8, this volume) analysis of the NOS data found a very strong relationship between FILMs and five company training measures (any formal training program, percentage of workers trained, size of training budget, per-employee and per-trainee expenses), after controlling for organization size, unionization, workforce composition, formalization, and external environments. They did not, however, disaggregate these relationships by types of occupation, as we do in the following analyses.

## Labor Unions

Utility-maximizing theories of pure and bilateral monopoly posit that labor unions seek to raise member wages at the expense of nonunion labor and firm efficiency (Oswald 1985). Despite extensive confirmation that union power boosts employees' wages and improves their working conditions (Lewis 1986), the effect of unions on company occupational training is unclear. Relatively few formal bargaining contracts contain job training provisions, although this situation may be changing. Training programs that are jointly conceived, implemented, monitored, and evaluated by unions and management are a recent innovation in industrial relations, often growing out of apprenticeship and employee-involvement programs (Ferman et al. 1991). Any union impact on company training is most likely indirect, operating by altering the incentive structures facing management and influencing their personnel practices.

Freeman and Medoff's (1984) *two faces* model of union functions suggests alternative ways that unions influence employers to increase their training investments (see also Freeman 1980). The *monopoly face* enables unions to raise wages above competitive labor market levels. Because higher wages in unionized firms attract a larger hiring queue (that is, the supply of labor for union jobs exceeds the demand), employers can afford to be more selective in hiring higher-quality workers—that is, by accepting only those applicants with better initial job skills or those who are perceived to be more trainable. To offset the cost advantages enjoyed by nonunionized competitors paying lower wages, unionized employers invest in additional employee training to boost productivity. Because collective bargains boost employee compensation, firms tend to replace workers with capital (with the magnitude depending on the price elasticity of the downward sloping labor demand curve). Consequently, to avoid their members' loss of employment, unions also develop a stake in assisting employers to increase union workers' productivity.

The *collective voice/response face* of unionism refers to a group's power to resolve disputes about workplace conditions through negotiations with employers and to provide discontented workers with a voice alternative to quitting (Freeman and Medoff 1984). Because unionization reduces employee turnover and increases job tenure, unionized firms face lowered hiring and training costs. With the risk of losing human capital investments now much reduced, unionized employers have strong incentives "for investment in skills specific to an enterprise, which also raises productivity" (Freeman and Medoff 1984, p. 14).

A parallel political perspective on unions recognizes that all organizations include interest groups whose conflicting preferences are resolved through negotiation and compromise (Pfeffer 1981, pp. 27-29). Union ideology favors applying the seniority principle in staffing, promotion, and other personnel decisions, leading to a more homogeneous workforce.

Union contract clauses typically stipulate that senior employees must fill the higher level vacancies, whereas outside hires are restricted to entry-level jobs. On the one hand, unions tend to resist company training programs that advantage some categories of labor more than others. On the other hand, because the seniority principle distributes rewards according to tenure and not individual effort and performance, older union workers are usually willing to provide informal training and assistance to younger employees, knowing that they are not jeopardizing their own jobs. Thus, seniority may enhance firm productivity by reducing worker resistance to some forms of training. Ironically, the greater reliance on length of tenure in allocating jobs can lower productivity in that persons may be placed in jobs for which they are less qualified than other workers. "Which of these effects dominates is an empirical question" (Freeman and Medoff 1984, p. 15).

Most of the empirical evidence on unions and training, based on samples of individuals, reveals a negative relationship. Using the 1975-1976 Time Use Survey, Duncan and Stafford (1980, p. 366) found that blue-collar union respondents received substantially fewer hours of weekly training as part of regular work (3.8 hours) than did nonmembers (4.6 hours). Similarly, the amount of training taken separately from usual work but during the work period was also lower for union than nonunion employees (0.4 hours vs. 1.5 hours per week). Based on the lower wage returns to age and experience of union members in the pooled 1968-1978 Panel Study of Income Dynamics (PSID), Mincer (1983, pp. 238-241) concluded that total training is less in union firms. Using the 1969-1971 National Longitudinal Surveys, he also found that old nonunion stayers had significantly more training than union stayers and union joiners (Mincer 1983, p. 240).

Using the 1983 CPS and the 1966-1981 NLS young men, young women, and older men cohorts, Lillard and Tan (1992) analyzed "who gets training, how much, and why, and the effects of training on earnings and employment" (p. 45). They demonstrated that many kinds of training occur, serving a variety of purposes. In particular, their data show that union membership (a) increased the probability of receiving company training for getting a job for CPS men, (b) decreased the probability of receiving company training for improving job skills for CPS men, (c) had no impact on receiving either type of company training for CPS women, (d) decreased the probability of receiving company training for mature NLS men, but (e) had no effect on receiving company training for young NLS men and women. The analysis of unionization and company training in the 1991 NOS reported in Chapter 8 found a greater likelihood of formal training if a union represented an establishment's core production workers and a higher percentage of industry workers were unionized. But neither union variable remained statistically significant after controlling for size, formal structure, and environmental factors. The following sections further analyze the training programs directed specifically at the NOS organizations' core production and service workers.

## Core Occupation Training

To identify each NOS establishments' core production occupation, the informants were first asked, "What is the product produced or service provided here?" They were then asked, "What is the job title for the employees who are most directly involved with [the product or service described]?" These core employee occupations were classified by the three-digit titles used in the 1980 Census and by the two-digit 1989 National Opinion Research Center occupational prestige scores (see Davis and Smith 1991, pp. 827-35). We concentrate here on four major occupational groupings: upper white-collar (professional, technical, and managerial); lower white-collar (sales and clerical); upper blue-collar (craftsmen, foremen, and transportation); lower blue-collar (operatives, laborer, service, and farm workers).

In all analyses reported in this chapter, we present only results based on unweighted data. As we discussed in the last chapter, readers should interpret those statistics as reflecting the exposure rates of typical workers. For example, slightly more than half the labor force is employed by establishments whose core employees hold white-collar occupations (35% upper and 19% lower), with the remainder working in blue-collar occupations (26% upper and 20% lower). As Figure 9.1 shows, however, the four types of core occupations are not evenly distributed across 10 major industrial categories. In only two industries—business services and public administration—do the majority of core production occupations fail to fall within one of the four categories. Lower blue-collar core positions are the core occupation in more than 80% of the agriculture and mining establishments; most of these occupations are engaged in farming. Similarly, large majorities of the workforces in construction, manufacturing, and transportation are in establishments in which upper blue-collar employees are the core occupation. Lower white-collar occupations (sales and cleri-

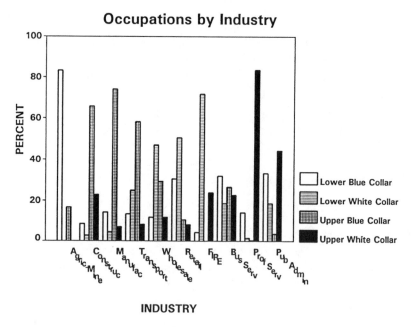

**Figure 9.1.** Core Production Employee Occupations, by Industry

cal) make up the core production workers in approximately half the establishments in the wholesale and retail trade industries, and in more than two thirds of those in the finance, insurance, real estate (FIRE) sector. Professional occupations are "core" in the vast majority (more than 80%) of the establishments in the professional services industry. Although no single occupational group includes a majority of core occupations for establishments in the public administration sector, its proportion of lower blue-collar core occupations is higher than any other industry, whereas its proportion with core occupations in the upper white-collar category is second only to the professional services industry.

The majority of formal training programs provided by companies targets both core production workers and managers. Among those NOS organizations offering some formal training program (establishments covering 72% of the U.S. labor force), more than 90% report training some core employees during the preceding 2 years. Similarly, 90% also report training managers and administrators in this period. Fewer than 1% of establishments train some other occupation without providing training to either managers or core workers. Figure 9.2 shows that nearly identical

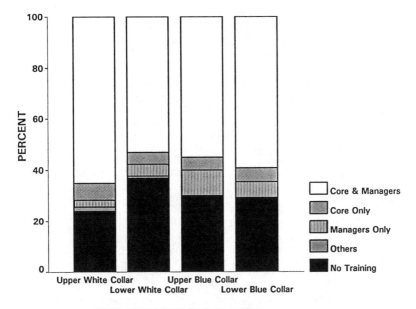

**Figure 9.2.** Types of Training, by Core Occupation

occupational training patterns occur within each of the four broad core production employee categories. (These percentages also include the 28% of the NOS labor force working in establishments that do not offer formal training programs, as indicated in Figure 9.2 by solid black bar segments.) Training is classified here as provided to (a) both core occupations and managers, (b) only core workers, (c) only managers, (d) exclusively some other occupation, or (e) no employees. Few differences are noteworthy. Establishments that employ lower white-collar employees in the core occupation are slightly more likely to offer no formal training programs, whereas those with upper white-collar core positions are slightly more likely to provide training. The two blue-collar categories exhibit intermediate levels of training, casting strong doubt on previous researchers' claims that company job training is heavily targeted toward nonmanual employees. Instead, formal training programs for core workers and their managers have apparently diffused widely across the entire occupational spectrum.

**Table 9.1**  Purposes of Job Training for Four Core Occupational Groups (percentages of labor force in establishments with programs)

|  | Purpose of Training Programs | | | |
|---|---|---|---|---|
| Core Production Worker Occupation | Basic Skills | Equipment Safety | Computer Skills | Managerial Skills |
| Upper white-collar | 15.3 | 62.0 | 87.7 | 91.1 |
| Lower white-collar | 7.2 | 54.8 | 82.1 | 81.9 |
| Upper blue-collar | 26.8 | 89.8 | 81.1 | 88.2 |
| Lower blue-collar[a] | 13.8 | 88.3 | 63.8 | 87.2 |
| All establishments | 16.6** | 73.1*** | 80.2*** | 88.2 |
| N | 481 | 484 | 484 | 484 |

a. Includes farming occupations.
*$p < .05$; **$p < .01$; ***$p < .001$.

Some evidence in support of the differential distribution of occupational training emerges on examining the specific purposes of training programs. Table 9.1 displays the prevalence of four types of training programs in the four occupational groups, with three distributions showing significant differences between groups. (These data exclude establishments without training programs.) Given the way the informant interview was structured, we cannot be certain that core workers always participated in each type of program, but because core employees were shown above to be the targets of most company programs, such an inference seems warranted. Basic skills instruction is the least common purpose of company training, accessible to just one sixth of the labor force. These remedial skills are most frequently taught in establishments employing upper blue-collar core workers (27%) and are least prevalent in organizations with lower white-collar workers (7%). Training in the safe use of equipment and machinery is clearly concentrated among manual workers, with nearly 90% of upper and lower blue-collar establishments having this type of program, whereas both white-collar groups receive much less safety instruction. Training in computer skills follows the opposite pattern: Nearly 90% of establishments with upper white-collar core occupations provide such instruction, whereas less than two thirds of companies with lower blue-collar workers offer computer training. The only training purpose showing no significant differences between occupational groups is managerial skills. About 9 of 10 establishments have such formal programs, suggesting that almost every organization considers improving its managerial employees' skills to be an indispensable activity.

## Unions and FILMs

We identified the unionization of an establishment's core production workers from responses to a battery of nine items asking about factors "determining the earnings of [Core Occupation] here." If an informant reported that union negotiations were "very important," we considered the core employees to be unionized. The percentage of establishments in which core workers are unionized, according to this measure, is 19%, which is roughly the level of union membership in the national labor force (Freeman and Medoff 1984, p. 27; Goldfield 1987). Three industries account for the majority of unionized core employees: manufacturing (26% unionized), transportation (26%), and professional services (25%). Fewer than 10% of establishments' labor forces in the agriculture-mining, retail trade, and FIRE industries have unionized core workers. Of our four broad occupational categories, the lower white-collar group is the least unionized (10%), but the other three categories have comparable levels (upper white-collar, 23%; upper blue-collar 23%; lower blue-collar 18%).

We analyze two measures of internal labor market structures in the NOS establishments. The first focuses narrowly on the hiring pattern for core production employees, whereas the second measure is the broader indicator of firm job ladders used in many preceding chapters. The core hiring measure was created from dichotomous responses to, "Do you sometimes fill [*Core Occupation*] vacancies with people already employed at [*Organization*]?" An affirmative response implies that opportunities to move into the core production jobs are available to currently employed workers. A negative response suggests that recruitment is not restricted and that new production workers may be hired from outside the organization's current workforce.

A majority of employees (58%) work in establishments where current employees sometimes fill core occupation vacancies. The broader internal labor market scale was constructed from information on three establishment occupations (core workers, the GSS respondent's job, and managers or administrators), as described in Chapter 5. These two internal labor market measures are very strongly correlated ($r = +.67$), in large part because the core occupation is involved in both variables.

Figures 9.3 and 9.4 display establishment job training programs broken down by core employee occupations (white-collar or blue-collar), hiring procedures (internal or external), and unionization (present or absent). In

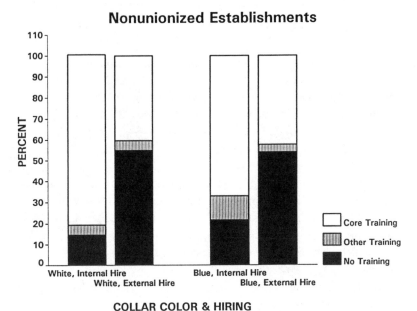

**Figure 9.3.** Training by Core Hiring by Collar, Nonunionized Establishments

the nonunionized establishments shown in Figure 9.3, core occupation training programs depend on whether the core employees are hired from current personnel or from outside the establishment. Core training programs are far more prevalent when hiring occurs internally than for external hires in both the white-collar (81% vs. 40%) and blue-collar (67% vs. 42%) organizations. These training-hiring relationships are statistically significant for both core occupation groups ($\chi^2 = 52.1$, $df = 2$, $p < .0001$ for white-collar cores; $\chi^2 = 25.3$ $df = 2$, $p < .0001$ for blue-collar cores), but log-linear models fitted to the combined data indicate that the magnitude of covariation is identical for both classes of occupations. In contrast, as shown in Figure 9.4, no relationship exists between core training and hiring procedures for the workforces of the unionized establishments. Of establishments with white-collar core workers, training programs are only slightly more prevalent for those companies hiring core workers internally (88%) than for organizations hiring externally (71%). In the unionized blue-collar core work force, the difference almost completely disappears (81% versus 78%). These relationships are not statistically significant for either job classification ($\chi^2 = 3.2$, $df = 2$, $p = .19$ for white-collar; $\chi^2 = 0.1$, $df = 2$, $p = .93$ for blue-collar).

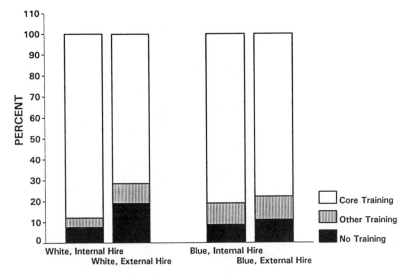

**Figure 9.4.** Training by Core Hiring by Collar, Unionized Establishments

Unionized establishments are more likely to offer training programs to their core workforces (83%) than are nonunionized ones (61%). The unionization impact is especially pronounced where workers are hired into the core occupations from outside the company. That is, unions appear to boost access to company training for persons not currently part of an internal labor pool, whereas core employees who enter a nonunionized workshop from outside are much less likely to receive formal training. The union's importance for training may arise in part because training requirements are explicitly written into collective bargaining contracts, as is the case for 31% of the employees of establishments with core worker unions. But an informal role is also likely. Unions that represent core workers presumably have a strong say in how those core employees are selected, and thus they can more easily compel an employer to treat all workers identically, regardless of the route by which they enter the core occupation. In contrast, nonunionized workplaces may screen out less-trained core job applicants. By creaming the better candidates, these companies would need to provide far less formal training to the core workers hired through the external labor pool.

**BLUE COLLAR CORE EMPLOYEES**

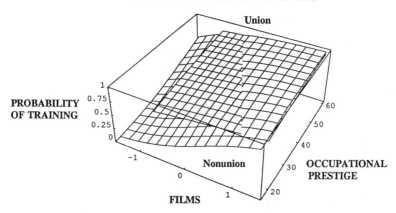

**WHITE COLLAR CORE EMPLOYEES**

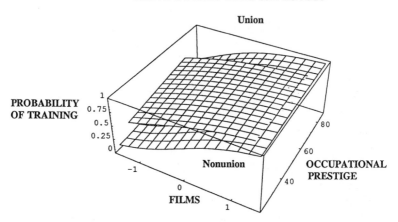

**Figure 9.5.** Probability of Core Training, by FILMs and Occupational Prestige in Union and Nonunion Establishments for Blue-Collar and White-Collar Core Employees

The two diagrams in Figure 9.5, whose perspectives are presented from above looking down, describe the complex relationships between company-provided training, core occupational prestige, unionization, and internal labor markets. The curved surfaces were derived from the logistic regression equations shown in Table 9.2, a separate equation for the four occupation and union status combinations. The top diagram in Figure 9.5 displays the relationships for the establishments with blue-collar core

**Table 9.2** Logistic Regressions of Core Occupation Training on Firm Internal Labor Markets and Occupational Prestige for Establishment Core Workers and Unionization Status

| Independent Variables | Core Worker Collar and Unionization | | | |
| --- | --- | --- | --- | --- |
| | White-Collar, No Union | White-Collar, Union | Blue-Collar, No Union | Blue-Collar, Union |
| Constant | −0.31 | 0.25 | −1.70* | 0.02 |
| FILM score | 1.46*** | 0.07* | 1.48*** | 0.48 |
| Occupational prestige | 0.02* | 0.02 | 0.07* | 0.04 |
| −2LL | 287.2 | 70.1 | 230.9 | 92.6 |
| Model chi-square | 85.3*** | 6.6* | 68.3*** | 2.5 |
| *df* | 2 | 2 | 2 | 2 |
| *N* | 280 | 87 | 217 | 95 |

*$p < .05$; ***$p < .001$.

employees, whereas the lower diagram graphs the same relationships for the white-collar establishments.[1] Each diagram contains two curved surfaces: The upper surface represents the labor forces of unionized establishments and the lower surface represents those for nonunionized workplaces. The vertical axis indicates the estimated proportion of workers whose employers provide company training, ranging from 0 to 1.00.

For nonunionized workplaces, in both diagrams, the probability of a formal core training program increases sharply as internal labor markets become more developed (a standardized variate along the horizontal axis to the left). Similarly, training program probability increases with higher core employee occupational prestige (along the horizontal axis to the right). But for workers in unionized establishments, no significant occupational prestige effect occurs, whereas the probability of a training program increases significantly with FILMs only for the white-collar cores. In both diagrams in Figure 9.5, the regression surfaces for the unionized organizations lie above the nonunionized surfaces when FILMs are least developed (at the far left), and converge to the same probabilities when FILMs are most elaborated (to the right). In other words, core worker unions appear to compensate their members for an underdeveloped internal labor market, thereby enabling both blue-collar and white-collar core workers in such work settings to gain greater access to company training than their counterparts in nonunionized establishments. As with the hiring practices examined above, nonunionized core employees experience relative disadvantage in their opportunities for company job training where internal labor markets are undeveloped.

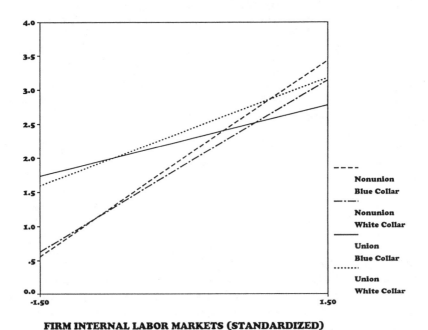

FIRM INTERNAL LABOR MARKETS (STANDARDIZED)

**Figure 9.6.** Importance of Training for Promotion by FILMs, for White-Collar and Blue-Collar Union and Nonunion Establishments

Finally, we analyzed the NOS informants' response to the question, "Apart from formal education, how important is formal training as a factor in employees' promotion chances?" Establishments without formal training programs were coded 0, whereas responses ranging from "not at all" "important" to "essential" were coded from 1 to 4. This dependent variable was regressed on the core occupational-prestige variable and the FILM variable within each of four occupation and unionization categories.[2] As shown in Figure 9.6, the greatest contrasts occur between union and nonunion workplaces, whereas the white-collar and blue-collar differences are relatively small. Although training grows increasingly important for all four types of core employees' promotion chances as internal labor markets develop, the strength of these relationships varies by unionization. Both union groups' regression lines lie above both nonunion lines when establishments have minimal internal labor markets (at the left on the horizontal axis). The regression slopes for the two unionized groups, however, are much gentler than the two nonunion slopes. Consequently the two pairs of regression lines converge for all establishments at the most highly developed FILMs (at the right on the horizontal axis). Far from being irrelevant to employees' promotion opportunities, unions seem to compensate for weak internal labor markets; that is, unions apparently foster company training as a promotion factor in the absence of formal internal mechanisms that link training to job ladders. Once such structures become fully elaborated, however, any benefit to core workers from their unions in tying promotions to training disappears.

## Conclusion

Formal job training is widespread within U.S. work organizations, available to a large majority of the employees in the 1991 National Organizations Survey establishments. Much of this activity concentrates on the core employees—those workers who produce the company's main product or service—and their managers. Contrary to the impression from previous research, organizations in which the core workers are in blue-collar occupations are as likely to provide access to formal training as often as companies composed of white-collar core workers. Some content differences are evident in training programs, with upper blue-collar core workers more likely to be exposed to basic skills and equipment training and upper white-collar core workers more often provided with computer training programs. Management training is uniformly spread across the occupational spectrum, presumably because employers recognize the relevance of supervisory skills for coordinating the performances of all types of employees.

Firm internal labor markets and labor unions are important for employee careers, each affecting organizationally provided training programs. These relationships are almost identical in establishments employing white-collar and blue-collar core workers. The more extensively an organization develops its job ladders, the more likely it is to use formal training programs as mechanisms for enabling workers to advance to positions of higher prestige, pay, and responsibility. The presence of a labor union representing core workers not only is associated with greater firm-provided training efforts but also seems to offset the adverse effects of an absent or poorly developed internal labor market for all types of workers.

Unionized establishments are more likely than nonunionized ones to provide training to core workers recruited from outside the organization. Unionized employers lacking fully developed internal labor markets are more likely to offer core employee training than are similar nonunionized employers. The perceived importance of job training for employee promotion chances is much greater in unionized than in nonunionized establishments where internal markets are lacking. Thus, contrary to previous findings based on employee surveys, the NOS establishment data clearly identify an important positive relationship between training and unions, which operates at all occupational levels.

The preceding analyses are necessarily static comparisons of the training activities by employers with different occupational and structural characteristics. Subsequent research should investigate the dynamic evolution of employer training programs and practices, with particular attention to the role of labor unions. Can firm-specific skills training be measured? Can protection of such skills from competitor enticement be demonstrated to be a central concern of employers? How do unions representing core production employees affect the creation of internal labor markets? Does union support for worker training stimulate the subsequent development of internal job ladders, or is it an outcome of employer efforts to insulate the skilled workforce from external temptations? Do unions affect company training programs primarily by shaping the incentive structures facing employers or more formally through negotiating collective bargains stipulating employee training? How do unions handle the inherent conflicts between senior workers interested in protecting their positions and younger employees desiring skill training to improve their chances for career advancement? In what ways do formal training programs interact with informal on-the-job skills transfers? As worldwide competitive forces reshape the business environment, are increasingly collaborative training arrangements between labor and management blurring the traditional lines of workplace authority? These questions imply some form of longitudinal analysis to track the differentiation and growth of organizational training activities over time. Adaptation of the NOS sampling framework to a panel design would go a long way toward providing some answers.

# Notes

1. The four equation surfaces are graphed only over the ranges of the two independent variables for the four unionization-collar color combinations. Although a logistic regression equation is linear in the logarithms, it is nonlinear when transformed into probabilities (in that $p = e^z/(1 + e^z)$); consequently, the expected probabilities graphed in Figure 9.5 are curved surfaces rather than flat planes.

2. These four linear regression equations are as follows:

White-collar, no union: $Y = 1.47^{***} + .008 X_1 + 0.84 X_2^{***}$

White-collar, union: $Y = 2.89^{***} - .009 X_1 + 0.53 X_2^{**}$

Blue-collar, no union: $Y = 0.99^{**} + .029 X_1^* + 0.96 X_2^{***}$

Blue-collar, union: $Y = 1.66^{***} + .017 X_1 + 0.35 X_2$

Where $X_1$ is the core occupation's prestige; $X_2$ is the establishment's standardized FILM score; $^{**}p < .01$; and $^{***}p < .001$. In plotting Figure 9.6, we used the mean occupational prestige for each union-collar color group: 52.1 for nonunion white-collar, 55.9 for union white-collar, 34.7 for nonunion blue-collar, and 35.1 for union blue-collar.

# 10

# Organizational
# Differences in Earnings

ARNE L. KALLEBERG

MARK E. VAN BUREN

Work organizations are central to stratification systems and processes in the United States and other industrial societies. The economic life chances of the majority of people in such nations are largely determined by their organizational positions and memberships. Organizational structures define the boundaries of internal labor markets and are key contexts for examining labor market outcomes such as earnings differentials (Sørensen 1983). As such, organizations generate inequality by influencing how jobs are created and rewarded and how people are matched to these jobs. Stratification processes are also highly salient for understanding many aspects of the workings of organizations: Economic rewards influence employees' commitment, productivity, and other aspects of the employ-ment relation (Baron and Pfeffer 1994).

Despite the importance of organizations for stratification, studies of organizations usually neglect distributional questions such as, "Who gets what and why?" Moreover, research on stratification—at least until recently—generally ignores organizations. Instead, most studies of earnings differences focus either on (a) differences between individuals (e.g., as in the status attainment tradition in sociology or the human capital framework in econom-ics) or (b) differences between societies or large geographic units. These kinds of studies can provide only a partial picture of inequality in that they ignore the organizational structures that link phenomena at micro and macro levels of analysis. Earnings differences are generated at multiple levels: at the organizational level; within organizations due to characteristics of occupa-tions, jobs, and individuals; and between organizations due to industrial differences, patterns of unionization, and other contextual variations.

Organizational structures generate earnings differences in two main ways. First, workers who work in particular kinds of organizations—such as large establishments or those with firm internal labor markets—earn more, on average, than workers with equivalent levels of education and other human capital and individual attributes. Second, some attributes of organizations create more or less dispersion, or earnings inequality, be-tween workers in different positions within these organizations. We will examine the first issue—how organizational characteristics affect the *levels* of employees' earnings—in this chapter. We focus on the degree of earnings *inequality* within organizations in Chapter 11.

## Organizational Differences in Earnings

An organization's size has been called "the most important correlate of diversity in organizational structure" (Aldrich and Marsden 1988, p. 373; see also Blau and Schoenherr 1971; Child 1973; Kimberly 1976). Size is also the most frequently used organizational variable in studies of stratifi-cation and in explanations of why employees in some organizations earn more than those in others. Size is generally used as a proxy for other theoretically relevant variables that are often poorly specified (cf. our discussion of size differences in training in Chapter 8). Kimberly's (1976) descriptions of size as a "theoretical wasteland" and as the sociologist's "black box" are unfortunately still too accurate.

One close correlate of size is an organization's complexity and differentiation. Larger organizations are more complex and exhibit greater horizontal and vertical differentiation (Blau and Schoenherr 1971; Child 1973; see Chapter 4, this volume). Larger organizations also often have highly formalized relations with their employees (e.g., Child 1973). The effects of complexity and formalization on earnings, however, are hard to anticipate. For example, although some writers have suggested that formalization may enhance earnings (e.g., Stolzenberg 1978; Garen 1985; Villemez and Bridges 1988), formalization may instead be associated with lower earnings if it leads to job simplification. These offsetting expectations underscore the need to control for the skill level of occupations within the establishment. The organization's occupational mix may well account for any effect of formalization on earnings.

Larger organizations are also more likely to have firm internal labor markets (FILMs—see Chapter 5, this volume; Villemez and Bridges 1988; Brown and Medoff 1989; Van Buren 1992). The relationship between FILMs and earnings is also ambiguous. On the one hand, there are reasons to expect a negative relationship between FILMs and earnings. If membership in a FILM is associated with greater fringe benefits and promotion opportunities (see Kalleberg and Van Buren 1996), then FILM members should be more willing to work for lower wages than workers who are not, and employers should have less need to pay "efficiency wages" by raising the earnings of FILM members beyond the market rate. On the other hand, there are also reasons to expect a positive relation between FILMs and earnings. FILMs provide opportunities for training, particularly in firm-specific skills, which presumably raise productivity and thereby enhance earnings. Another plausible explanation for a positive association between FILMs and high wages is an institutional one: High wages (as with internal promotions) might reflect an effort on the part of firms to establish a favorable position and image in the labor market. Finally, a positive relationship between FILMs and earnings may be spurious: For example, organizations with FILMs may be those that have less competition in product markets, or for some other reason are better able to secure higher profits, and on this basis are able to pay higher wages.

## Explaining Organizational Differences in Earnings

Sociologists and economists have identified at least six clusters of variables that may help explain why employees of various kinds of organizations differ in their levels of earnings. These sets of concepts include (a) product market characteristics, (b) labor market characteristics, (c) relations between organizations and their institutional environments, (d) job characteristics, (e) unionization, and (f) labor force quality.

**Product Market Characteristics**

Large organizations are usually assumed to operate in more concentrated product markets, to have greater market power, and consequently, to have more "excess" profits to share with employees in the form of wages. Such organizations are also likely to be more capital intensive. In that profitability and capital intensity are correlated with concentration, these industry characteristics may help to explain why organizations in more concentrated product markets tend to pay their employees higher wages (Weiss 1966; Averitt 1968; Mellow 1982; DiPrete 1990).

Sociologists in the dual economy/economic segmentation tradition echo this argument, and often use employment size (and other measures of size, such as assets and capital intensity) as a criterion for dividing the economy into core and peripheral economic sectors. Dual economy research has not, however, convincingly explained why large organizations are persuaded to share their higher profits with their workers (see Sørensen 1983).

**Labor Market Characteristics**

Some organizations must pay higher earnings to elicit a sufficient number of applicants for job openings (Mellow 1982; Weiss and Landau 1984). Obtaining the needed number of employees may be more difficult for bigger employers (local labor market conditions being equal) in that they have a larger number of vacancies to fill (Brown and Medoff 1989). An indirect test of this hypothesis might assume that large organizations are especially likely to experience a shortage of labor if they are located in areas with low unemployment rates. A labor shortage would encourage employers to pay higher wages (Sengenberger 1981).

Another explanation related to labor markets rests on the assumption that smaller establishments are more likely than larger establishments to be located in smaller communities (Lester 1967). On this basis, employees of smaller establishments could have fewer opportunities for alternative employment than those employed by larger organizations located in larger, higher paying labor market areas. Size-of-organization earnings differentials could thus reflect size-of-place differences. Brown and Medoff (1989), however, found little evidence to support the argument that the size-earnings relation varies between metropolitan and nonmetropolitan areas (see also Bailey and Schwenk 1980).

### Institutional Forces

Larger, more complex and formalized organizations are more likely to be concerned with legitimating their personnel practices and compensation policies by conforming to accepted principles of human resource management. Institutional forces may thus induce larger organizations (at least in the United States) to pay their employees higher earnings. Such human resources practices are rooted in the history of this country's labor relations. For example, size-earnings differentials in the United States have been documented as far back as 1890 (Brown, Hamilton, and Medoff 1990).

### Unionization

Larger organizations and those with firm internal labor markets are more likely to be unionized (e.g., Lester 1967; Villemez and Bridges 1988). Unionized organizations often pay their employees higher earnings and provide them with better fringe benefits. Union "threat effects" may also motivate nonunionized, large organizations to provide their employees with higher economic rewards to avoid unionization in the future. Neither the union-wage nor union-avoidance hypotheses was supported by Brown and Medoff's (1989) evidence, which indicated that the size-earnings differential held for both unionized and nonunionized workers, as well as for industries that were both likely and unlikely to be unionized (see also Bailey and Schwenk 1980). These findings do not necessarily undercut the unionization explanations if one considers that internal equity pressures created by unions (or the threat of unionization) could help to increase wages for nonunion workers.

### Job Characteristics

Bigger, more complex organizations and those with firm internal labor markets are more likely to have jobs that require higher skill levels in that they invest more in firm-specific training. The reasons given for this range from a desire by *firms* to reduce monitoring costs by having more qualified workers (Oi 1983b) to larger *establishments* having more capital-intensive production processes and more specialized divisions of labor that require higher skills (Hamermesh 1980; Mellow 1982). Higher skill levels should, in turn, be associated with greater earnings.

The extent to which output and productivity can be easily measured is another job characteristic that may be related to organizational structures such as size, complexity, formalization or firm internal labor markets. Oi's (1983b) explanation of the size-earnings differential, for example, assumed that large employers sought to minimize their higher monitoring costs by hiring better qualified workers. A related argument also starts with the assumption that monitoring costs are higher in larger organizations. This view, however, suggests that instead of hiring more qualified workers, large employers pay more for workers of the same quality because they are less able to judge accurately their productivity. The earnings premiums paid by large employers thus result from imperfect information (Mellow 1982; Garen 1985). Brown and Medoff (1989) questioned the validity of this argument by showing that the size-earnings differential held even among piece-rate workers, a group for which large employers evidently do not have monitoring disadvantages.

Authority or supervisory status is a characteristic of a person's job position whose associations with organization size, complexity, and firm internal labor markets have not been well established in past research. There is some evidence that these relationships are complex. Villemez and Bridges (1988), for example, found a curvilinear association between size and supervisory status. In any event, we expect that supervisors should obtain higher levels of earnings than persons who do not supervise other employees.

### Labor Quality

Larger, more differentiated organizations tend to have higher-quality labor forces. By this reasoning, employees of bigger organizations earn more money because they are "better" workers than persons employed by smaller organizations. Alternatively, larger organizations or those with firm internal labor markets may attract higher-quality workers because they pay higher wages. Sorting and selection mechanisms help to channel higher-quality workers to larger organizations (e.g., Evans and Leighton

1988). Larger organizations or those with firm internal labor markets are likely to encourage longer-term employment relations, thereby enhancing labor quality through training, socialization, and experience.

Brown and Medoff (1989) obtained considerable support for the labor quality explanation of the size-earnings differential: Labor force quality accounted for about half of the size-earnings difference in several data sets. Evans and Leighton (1988) found that larger firms had more highly educated workers, but did not find support for the argument that pay premiums in larger organizations were a reward for employees' greater productivity. In both studies, size-earnings differentials persisted even after labor quality was controlled.

## Variables

The data sets used to study the relation between organizational characteristics and earnings in the United States have been generally based on surveys of employees, and have not supplemented individual-level data with detailed information on organizations (for exceptions, see Kalleberg and Lincoln's 1988 analysis of manufacturing plants in the United States and Japan; see also the 1994 analysis by le Grand, Szulkin, and Tåhlin of Sweden and that by Kalleberg and Marsden, 1995, of Norway). Those that have included data on both employees and their employers—such as Hodson's (1984) or Bridges and Villemez's (1994)—did not measure many of the organizational variables identified above. The National Organizations Study data set overcomes this limitation in that it includes rich structural information on a heterogeneous sample of organizations and is linked to individual-level data on employees of these organizations from the 1991 General Social Survey (GSS).

### Measures of Earnings

Our measure of earnings is the natural logarithm of the GSS respondent's reported annual income last year from his or her main job. The mean level of earnings of GSS respondents was $24,101, with a standard deviation of $17,376. This earnings measure is an attribute of individuals, not an estimate of what the establishment as a whole does in the way of compensation. Robust estimates of organizational properties can hardly be obtained from a single individual. Our analysis examines how earnings are related to the organizational and individual explanatory variables. Most organizational-level explanatory variables are discussed in Chapter 3. Appendix 10.1 provides details on variables that we have not discussed elsewhere: These include individual-level measures drawn from the 1991 GSS, industry-level measures of product-market characteristics, and areal measures of labor market characteristics.

## Results

### Correlations

Table 10.1 presents correlations between employees' (log) earnings and the organizational and other explanatory variables. These correlations indicate that employees earn more if they work in larger establishments and firms, but earnings are not necessarily higher in multiestablishment firms. Earnings are higher in establishments that are more differentiated, formalized, and have firm internal labor markets.

People who work in concentrated industries earn more. Employees of government agencies earn more than those who work in profit-making or nonprofit organizations. Unemployment lowers earnings: The 1986 civilian labor force unemployment rate in the GSS respondent's "primary sampling area"—usually an SMSA—is negatively correlated with earnings.

Education and seniority with an employer are both positively correlated with earnings. Women earn appreciably less than men. And supervisors and union members earn more than nonsupervisors and nonunion members, respectively. There appear to be no earnings differences between whites and nonwhites in this sample.

The GSS respondents' occupational-specific vocational preparation and occupational prestige are positively related to earnings. Finally, earnings are higher when it is more difficult to measure one's job performance.

### Regressions

Table 10.2 presents OLS estimates (unstandardized coefficients) obtained from regressions of (logged) employees' earnings on the explanatory variables. The results of several equations are reported. Column 1 presents coefficients from regressions of earnings on establishment and firm size alone. Column 2's equation adds employee characteristics, as well

**Table 10.1**  Correlations Between Employees' Earnings and Explanatory Variables

| Variables | Earnings |
|---|---|
| Establishment size | .17*** |
| Firm size[a] | .29*** |
| Multiestablishment | .05 |
| Exogenous variables | |
|   Education | .33*** |
|   White | .02 |
|   Female | −.33*** |
|   Mean establishment size | .11* |
|   Size of place | .07 |
|   Unemployment rate | −.14** |
|   Industry concentration | .16*** |
|   Institutional influence | .05 |
|   Profit-making | −.06 |
|   Nonprofit | −.07 |
|   Government | .17*** |
| Endogenous variables | |
|   Differentiation | .22*** |
|   Formalization | .11* |
|   Firm ILMs | .18*** |
|   Union membership | .12* |
|   Proportion white | −.03 |
|   Full-time | .47*** |
|   Tenure | .29*** |
|   Tenure$^2$ | .20*** |
|   Training time | .41*** |
|   Supervisor | .26*** |
|   Measurability | .17*** |
|   Occupational prestige | .39*** |
| Controls | |
|   Hours | .38*** |
|   Self-employed | −.01* |

a. Measured for multiestablishment organizations only.
*$p \le .05$; **$p \le .01$; ***$p \le .001$ (2-tailed tests).

as controls for hours worked and self-employment status. Column 3 includes the exogenous variables associated with the organization's environment (product markets, labor markets, and institutional forces). Column 4 adds the organizational variables that are assumed to mediate in part the relationship between size and earnings (complexity, employment relations, and union membership). Finally, column 5 adds the remaining, individual-level intervening variables (job characteristics, employer tenure, and full-time status).[1] We excluded from the analysis cases that had missing data

**Table 10.2** Determinants of Employees' Earnings (Logged) ($N = 414$)

| | Models | | | | |
|---|---|---|---|---|---|
| Variables | *1*[a] | *2* | *3* | *4* | *5* |
| Establishment size | .261(.117)* | .311(.112)** | .237(.116)* | .068(.140) | .075(.135) |
| Establishment size × multi. | –.100(.188) | –.111(.156) | –.094(.156) | –.048(.172) | –.077(.151) |
| Multiestablishment | –.813(.446) | –.765(.397) | –.760(.393) | –.901(.440)* | –.565(.402) |
| Firm size | .089(.029)** | .087(.023)*** | .081(.023)*** | .075(.024)** | .054(.023)* |
| Establishment size$^2$ | –.029(.013)* | –.034(.011)** | –.022(.012) | .012(.013) | –.010(.013) |
| Establishment size$^2$ × multi. | .021(.019) | .019(.015) | .015(.015) | .012(.016) | .002(.014) |
| Mean establishment size | | | .010(.063) | .013(.062) | –.040(.058) |
| Size of place | | | –.050(.024)* | –.055(.023)* | –.046(.020)* |
| Unemployment | | | –.021(.013) | –.015(.042) | –.016(.012) |
| Concentration | | | .129(.193) | .068(.194) | .232(.183) |
| Institutional influence | | | .008(.036) | .006(.038) | –.014(.035) |
| Nonprofit | | | –.122(.126) | –.105(.124) | –.125(.114) |
| Government | | | .266(.086)** | .218(.089)* | .103(.088) |
| Differentiation | | | | .121(.056)* | .085(.051) |
| Formalization | | | | –.069(.186) | –.123(.168) |
| Firm ILMs | | | | .183(.064)** | .191(.058)** |
| Union membership | | | | .072(.098) | .073(.096) |
| Tenure | | | | | .052(.010)*** |
| Tenure$^2$ | | | | | –.001(.0003)*** |
| Training time | | | | | .072(.033)* |
| Supervisor | | | | | .152(.076)* |
| Measurability | | | | | .008(.035) |
| Occupational prestige | | | | | .008(.004)* |
| Education | | .096(.012)*** | .099(.014)*** | .099(.014)*** | .061(.014)*** |
| White | | –.012(.084) | –.050(.086) | –.060(.086) | –.119(.083) |
| Female | | –.467(.078)*** | –.421(.081)*** | –.414(.080)*** | –.365(.074)*** |
| Self-employed | | .115(.157) | .136(.156) | .178(.152) | .042(.136) |
| Hours | | .471(.120)*** | .449(.117)*** | .451(.113)*** | .342(.104)*** |
| $R^2$(adj.) | .057 | .310 | .320 | .336 | .443 |

a Unstandardized coefficients with standard errors in parentheses.
*$p \le .05$; **$p \le .01$; ***$p \le .001$ (2-tailed tests).

on either size or earnings; we substituted means for missing data on the other variables.[2]

Larger establishments pay slightly more than smaller ones, but the effects of establishment size do not differ for single versus multiestablishment firms. The effects of establishment size on earnings are not significant once we control for the organizational (column 4) and individual-level (column 5) explanatory variables.[3] In multiestablishment firms, there is an additional earnings differential across firms of various sizes. Only about a third of this differential is accounted for by our explanatory variables (compare column 5 with columns 1 and 2). Our inability to account for *firm size*-job reward differentials no doubt largely reflects the limited information collected by the NOS on the larger firm.

After statistical adjustments for the influences of other explanatory variables, neither industrial concentration nor the unemployment rate has an independent effect on earnings.[4] Surprisingly, however, the size of the place or community has a negative effect on earnings. This unexpected result may be due in part to our imperfect measures of labor markets. Our areal measures refer to the sampling units in which GSS respondents reside, and such areas do not necessarily overlap perfectly with the labor markets in which these respondents participate.

Our measures of institutional forces (the institutionalization scale from Chapter 3 and the dummy variables for auspices) are unrelated to earnings, with the possible exception that government employees may enjoy a small earnings advantage over those working for profit-seeking organizations (see columns 3 and 4).

We tested for the possibility of interactions between the size measures and occupational category (i.e., blue-collar vs. white-collar) in our data. These results (not shown) indicated that there were no significant differences in the effects of either establishment or firm size for white-collar as opposed to blue-collar occupation for earnings. This contrasts with Villemez and Bridges' (1988) findings: They report that firm size was important for white-collar workers, whereas establishment size was salient for blue-collar workers (which, they argued, results because blue-collar workers are more place-bound).

FILM membership is the organizational characteristic (other than size) that is most strongly related to earnings (columns 4 and 5). Our interpretation of this positive effect of FILMs is not unambiguous, however, in that our data indicate the extent that FILMs are developed within an establishment, not whether a given person belongs to a FILM. Thus, we have not shown that individuals in FILMs have greater earnings, but rather that organizations with FILMs tend to pay higher wages than those less apt to have FILMs.

As expected, we find that women earn less than men. In addition, in accord with findings of past individual-level studies, the GSS respondent's earnings are positively related to (a) his or her education, (b) supervisory status (weakly), (c) amount of vocational preparation, and (d) occupational prestige. Employer tenure is positively related to earnings, but this differential declines at higher levels of tenure.

## Conclusion

The maxim Bigger Is Better is true in the sense that employees of larger organizations obtain higher levels of earnings. These size-earnings differentials reflect organizational, industrial, geographical, and individual characteristics.

Our analysis of earnings in this chapter was limited because we had only one respondent in most organizations. We were unable, therefore, to separate organizational and individual effects on earnings—that is, we could not distinguish between-organization differences from the effects of individual variables within organizations. Moreover, a single estimate of earnings for most establishments provides an incomplete picture of how size and other organizational variables affect earnings: We are able to examine organizational differences in mean levels, but not the earnings dispersion within organizations. A comprehensive explanation of the impact of organization size on earnings (and other stratification outcomes) should take into account the likely possibility that size and other explanatory variables affect the *dispersion* of job rewards within organizations as well as their average levels. We do this for earnings in Chapter 11.

## Notes

1. We sought to minimize the impact of possible heteroscedasticity by correcting our standard errors using White's (1980) consistent covariance matrix of estimators.

2. We also tried to reestimate our earnings models using weighted least squares (WLS), using information on the distribution of earnings within organizations. Plant managers in the NOS were asked to indicate the lowest, highest, and modal annual earnings for up to three occupations within the organization (the occupation of the GSS respondent, managers, and the *core* occupation, defined as the one most directly involved with producing the organization's main good or service; see Chapter 11). These earnings data enabled us to estimate roughly the variance in earnings within the organization. Using this information, we weighted each observation by the inverse of the estimated standard deviation of earnings within the organization. This procedure gives less weight to larger establishments in that there is greater variation in earnings within larger organizations. The pattern of results produced by the WLS analyses (not shown) did not differ substantially from the results reported in Table 10.2.

3. We replicated the analyses reported in Table 10.2 using two alternative earnings measures obtained from the NOS survey: (a) the modal annual earnings of persons in the organization who had the same occupation as the GSS respondent and (b) the mean modal earnings in the organization (computed as the average of the modal earnings in three occupations: the GSS respondent's occupation, the core occupation, and managers). The results using these measures were similar to those presented in Table 10.2, though the effects of establishment size on earnings remained significant in all equations.

4. Firm size was more strongly related to earnings ($p < .05$) in manufacturing industries than in service industries, but establishment size had similar effects on earnings in manufacturing and service industries.

# APPENDIX 10.1

## Description of Explanatory Variables

### Product Market Characteristics

*Concentration*: Percentage of assets held by firms with $100 million or more assets in the two-digit SIC industry in which the GSS respondent's organization is classified (mean = .53; *SD* = .22).

### Labor Market Characteristics

*Size of place*: Population of GSS respondent's county of residence (in millions) (mean = .77; *SD* = 2.76).

*Unemployment*: Civilian Labor Force Unemployment Rate (1986) in the primary sampling unit where the GSS respondent resides (mean = 7.10; *SD* = 2.75).

### Employee Characteristics

*Education*: Highest year of education that the GSS respondent completed (mean = 13.60; *SD* = 2.75).

*Female*: Dichotomous variable indicating whether (1) or not (0) the GSS respondent is a woman (mean = .49; *SD* = .50).

*White*: Dichotomous variable indicating whether (1) or not (0) the GSS respondent is white (mean = .87; *SD* = .34).

## Job Characteristics

*Training time*: Specific Vocational Preparation score for the GSS respondent's occupation (an indicator of the amount of training time required to perform the GSS respondent's occupation), taken from the *Dictionary of Occupational Titles* measures for the 1980 census. Values for this measure of training time range from *Short demonstration only* (1) to *Over 10 years* (10) (mean = 5.46; $SD$ = 1.48).

*Measurability*: Average of two items that assess GSS respondent's perception of the difficulty of measuring the quality and quantity of his or her work. Values on each item range from *Very easy* (1) to *Very hard* (4). Cases with missing values on both items were assigned the mean value of this variable (mean = 1.75; $SD$ = 0.75).

*Supervisor*: Dichotomous variable identifying whether (1) or not (0) the GSS respondent supervises the work of others (mean = 0.37; $SD$ = 0.48).

*Occupational prestige*: NORC/GSS Occupational Prestige scores for the 1980 Census Occupational Classification (mean = 44.45; $SD$ = 13.64).

## Employer Tenure

*Tenure*: Number of years the GSS respondent has worked for his or her present employer (mean = 8.23; $SD$ = 8.97).

## Controls

*Hours*: Natural logarithm of the number of hours worked weekly by the GSS respondent (mean = 3.61; $SD$ = .49).

*Full-time*: Dichotomous variable indicating whether (1) or not (0) the GSS respondent works full-time (mean = .82; $SD$ = .38).

*Self-Employed*: Dichotomous variable indicating whether (1) or not (0) the GSS respondent is self-employed (mean = .14; $SD$ = .35).

# 11

# The Structure of
# Organizational
# Earnings Inequality

ARNE L. KALLEBERG

MARK E. VAN BUREN

Individual-level analyses of earnings, such as those presented in Chapter 10, cannot tell us the circumstances under which we observe more or less dispersed distributions of earnings. A positive effect of size on wages, for example, does not say anything about the distribution of earnings within organizations. It is possible that large organizations generally pay more than small ones, but that organizations of different sizes have similar wage distributions (as measured, for instance, by inequality indexes such as the coefficient of variation). Moreover, "meritocratic" organizations that reward employees according to their performance may have more earnings dispersion than organizations whose reward systems are based on egalitarian principles. Inequality is a significant property of social organizations that is generated—at least in part—at the organizational level of analysis (see Baron 1984; Tolbert 1986; Hedström 1991).

Studies of how organizations differ in the degree and nature of inequality are relatively rare (notable exceptions are the work of Pfeffer and Langton 1988; Baron, Kalleberg, Lincoln, Pfeffer, and Pommerenke 1989; Hedström 1991; and Baron and Pfeffer 1994). Moreover, previous studies of this topic have yielded contrary results: Pfeffer and Langton's (1988) analysis of academic departments suggests there is more earnings inequality in larger organizations, whereas Sakamoto and Chen (1993) report that earnings inequality declines with firm size in both the United States and Japan. This literature has not produced a sustained inquiry that has resulted in cumulative findings, and reviews have consistently pointed to the need for more studies of inequalities within organizations (e.g., Baron 1984; Scott 1992).

In this chapter, we examine the extent of, and some reasons for, earnings dispersion using data from the National Organizations Study. We disaggregate earnings inequality within organizations into two distinct components: within-occupation and between-occupation dispersion. We begin by identifying some central correlates of organizational inequality that have been suggested by previous theory and research on organizational wage structures. We then introduce measures of both earnings inequality within organizations and our explanatory variables and analyze the patterns of association among them.

## Hypotheses of Organizational Sources of Earnings Inequality

We classify our hypotheses about the determinants of organizational earnings inequality into three main sets. These are related to (a) an organization's context, (b) the organization's structure, and (c) the composition of the organization's labor force.

### Organization Context

Previous research suggests that an organization's size is positively related to its average level of earnings (see Kalleberg and Van Buren 1992,

1996; Chapter 10, this volume). Also, most studies indicate that larger organizations are more likely to have a greater dispersion in wages than smaller organizations (but see Sakamoto and Chen 1993). Pfeffer and Langton (1988), for example, found that larger academic departments had greater earnings inequality. Larger organizations exhibit more vertical differentiation, having more ranks or levels that may be associated with earnings differences. Larger organizations also tend to have greater horizontal differentiation and to have more firm internal labor markets. Thus, our arguments for why these organizational structures are related to dispersion (see below) may also explain in part why inequality should increase with size. In addition, the sheer size of large organizations is likely to hinder social comparison processes that tend to reduce earnings inequality (Baron and Pfeffer 1994). Our first hypothesis is as follows:

> *H 11.1.* **Larger establishments have greater earnings inequality than smaller establishments.**

It is well known that unions attempt to reduce wage inequality in general, often by increasing the earnings of the lowest paid workers (see Freeman and Medoff 1984). Unions also help to generate equality within organizations, due in part to decentralized collective bargaining processes that take place at the firm level. We hypothesize the following:

> *H 11.2.* **Unionized organizations (or establishments in highly unionized industries) have less earnings inequality than organizations in less unionized industries.**

There is less previous research on how our two other dimensions of an organization's context are related to earnings inequality, and so our hypotheses about them are necessarily more speculative. We hypothesize that the level of unemployment in the organization's geographic area is likely to affect wage levels. We suggest that highly valued employees are less able to command higher-than-average wages when unemployment is high in that there is then a larger pool of possible replacements for them. This would tend to narrow their earnings advantage over their less productive coworkers, thereby compressing the earnings distribution within organizations. We speculate further that unemployment should primarily affect within-occupation inequality, as opposed to between-occupation inequality. This is because labor markets tend to be segmented by occupation:

Members of the same occupation compete with each other for jobs and earnings, and the supply and demand mechanisms that influence earnings differentials operate within occupations. We do not necessarily expect areal unemployment rates to affect earnings inequality between occupations in that people in different occupations are less likely to compete with each other. We hypothesize the following:

> *H 11.3.* **Higher unemployment rates are associated with less earnings inequality within occupations, but not necessarily between occupations.**

Finally, we expect nonprofit organizations to have less earnings inequality than profit-seeking and government organizations. Nonprofit organizations may be less subject to the pressures and exigencies of profit maximization and efficiency. Moreover, nonprofit organizations may be especially influenced by ideological pressures toward more equal wage structures. We hypothesize the following:

> *H 11.4.* **Nonprofit organizations have less earnings dispersion than other types of organizations.**

### Organization Structure

Modern organizations are dominated by the use of bureaucratic systems of control (Edwards 1979; Lincoln and Kalleberg 1990; see also Chapter 4, this volume). These organizational structures tend to be characterized by high levels of vertical and horizontal differentiation and by firm internal labor markets.

Vertical differentiation refers to the number of levels in the organization, from the plant manager to the lowest position. A considerable amount of empirical research has shown that vertical differentiation (i.e., rank) and pay are closely linked in most organizations (Rosenbaum 1980; Spilerman 1986; Hedström 1991). We expect, however, the correspondence between rank and earnings to be specific to occupations that are part of the authority hierarchy of organizations, which refers mainly to managers. That is, our measures of vertical differentiation should be sensitive primarily to the amount of earnings inequality between managers.

We also expect an organization's degree of horizontal differentiation (i.e., specialization of functions) to be positively related to earnings inequality primarily between managers. Less clear is the expected relationship between horizontal differentiation and earnings inequality in nonmanagerial occupations. On the one hand, the unequal skill demands associated with specialization produce the need to compensate people differently and thereby increase inequality, especially between occupations. On the other hand, specialization might lower skills throughout the organization's nonmanagerial workforce, resulting in relatively low earnings differentials. We hypothesize the following:

> *H 11.5.* **Organizations with more vertical and horizontal differentiation have greater inequality among managers. Vertical differentiation should be unrelated to inequality both within and between nonmanagerial occupations.**

FILMs (see Chapter 5, this volume) help to create and legitimate inequality within occupations or job clusters by stratifying individuals vertically via a hierarchy of positions with increasing levels of pay. This suggests that FILMs will be positively related to inequality *within* both managerial and nonmanagerial occupations. At the same time, it might also be argued that FILMs help to reduce wage differentials across occupations. As part of a bureaucratic control strategy, FILMs tend to promote meritocracy, possibly by standardizing wage structures within job grades and across different job clusters. Consequently, employees at the same level in different occupations are perhaps more likely to receive similar wages when FILMs are present. We hypothesize the following:

> *H 11.6.* **Organizations with more FILMs have higher degrees of inequality within occupations, but less dispersion between occupations.**

### Labor Force Composition

Individual-level studies of wage determination have found that wages are related to tenure and education, that men earn more than women (e.g., Pfeffer and Ross 1990), and that whites earn more than blacks (in Chapter 10 we found support for all of these relationships except race). This is true even for people holding the same job, regardless of performance. At the organizational level, there are at least two possible effects of such demo-graphic composition on inequality. The first is simply an extension of the individual-level effect on wages: If income is determined in part by the characteristics of individuals, then, ceteris paribus, the more heterogeneous persons are within an organization along these dimensions, the more unequal should be the earnings within the organization. Pfeffer and Langton (1988), for example, have shown that organizations (academic departments) with greater gender heterogeneity have more earnings inequality.

A second, more subtle, effect is due to social psychological processes of social comparison, equity, or relative deprivation, all of which tend to reduce inequality (Frank 1984; Baron and Pfeffer 1994). There is more attraction and communication among similar others (Berscheid and Walster 1969), for example, which facilitates social comparison and tends to heighten pressures to reduce income dispersion. Hence, we would predict that the more demographically heterogeneous the organization, the higher the degree of earnings inequality. Both of these lines of reasoning suggest the following hypothesis:

> *H 11.7.* **Organizations with greater heterogeneity (with regard to gender and race) should have more dispersion in earnings than organizations with more homogeneous gender and race compositions.**

## Measuring Organizational Earnings Inequality

Our primary measures of earnings inequality are based on information obtained from managers about the annual earnings of (a maximum of three) occupations within each organization (see the discussion in Chapter 3).[1] For each occupation, the NOS survey asked three questions about earnings levels: (a) the *lowest* annual earnings of a person in that occupation within the organization, (b) the *highest* annual earnings in the occupation, and (c) what *most* persons in that occupation earned annually in this organization (the mode). Table 11.1 presents descriptive statistics on the nine variables collected in this fashion (three data points for each of three occupations). Annual earnings range from a low of $1,000 a year (for a "guide") to $1,000,000 a year (for a top manager and for a "financial services" salesperson). Our measures of earnings inequality are derived from these

**Table 11.1** National Organizations Study (NOS) Earnings Inequality Items

| NOS Question Number | Description | Mean | Median | Standard Deviation | Minimum | Maximum | N |
|---|---|---|---|---|---|---|---|
| V205 | Lowest annual earnings of managers ($) | 28,977 | 26,000 | 12,294 | 3,000 | 80,000 | 463 |
| V206 | Highest annual earnings of managers ($) | 73,394 | 60,000 | 73,150 | 4,000 | 1,000,000 | 457 |
| V207 | Annual earnings of most managers ($) | 37,941 | 37,500 | 16,795 | 1,500 | 100,000 | 565 |
| V217 | Lowest annual earnings of CORE employees ($) | 19,665 | 18,573 | 10,058 | 1,500 | 89,444 | 534 |
| V218 | Highest annual earnings of CORE employees ($) | 36,472 | 30,000 | 49,565 | 2,215 | 1,000,000 | 528 |
| V219 | Annual earnings of most CORE employees ($) | 25,245 | 23,000 | 16,227 | 1,500 | 163,000 | 594 |
| V230 | Lowest annual earnings of General Social Survey (GSS) employees ($) | 19,446 | 18,000 | 10,151 | 1,000 | 61,000 | 468 |
| V231 | Highest annual earnings of GSS employees ($) | 35,203 | 27,144 | 60,817 | 3,150 | 1,000,000 | 465 |
| V232 | Annual earnings of most GSS employees ($) | 24,832 | 22,500 | 15,707 | 1,500 | 150,000 | 564 |
| V243 | SUBJINEQ: Subjective measure of variability of earnings among organizational positions (1 = very small, 5 = very great) | 3.385 | 3 | 1.029 | 1 | 5 | 636 |

variables (see Table 11.2, which presents descriptive statistics on our various measures of earnings dispersion and the formulas we used to compute them).

We also asked NOS respondents for their perceptions about whether the variability of earnings among all positions in their establishment was (a) very small, (b) small, (c) moderate, (d) great, or (e) very great. We include this as a subjective measure of inequality within the organization.

As we have discussed, we conceptualize earnings inequality within organizations as consisting of two components: (a) differences in earnings *between different occupations* and (b) differences in earnings of individuals *within the same occupation.* This distinction follows from our assumption that earnings inequality is generated both at the organizational level and within organizations. Consistent with this view, we have suggested some ways in which these two components of earnings inequality are related in different ways to specific explanatory variables; for example, Hypothesis 11.3 predicts that unemployment rates should reduce inequality within occupations, but not necessarily between occupations. Figure 11.1 diagrams the relationship between these two types of inequality.

BETWNOCC, our measure of the degree of inequality *between* occupations, is based on the standard deviation of the three occupations' modal earnings.[2] For each occupation, we constructed measures of inequality *within* each occupation (WITHNMGR, WITHNCOR, and WITHNGSS) by taking the standard deviation of the occupation's lowest, modal, and highest annual earnings. Managerial occupations have the highest average earnings (Table 11.1), as well as the greatest dispersion in earnings (Table 11.2). GSS occupations—which constitute a representative sample of U.S. occupations—have the least earnings dispersion (Table 11.2) and the lowest earnings levels (Table 11.1). The earnings level and dispersion in the core occupation of the establishments are on average, slightly above those in the GSS occupations. We also constructed an organizational-level measure of within-occupation earnings inequality (AVGWITHN) by averaging the within-occupation measures over the number of distinct occupations for which we had data. Finally, we combined the between-occupation and within-occupation measures to produce an overall measure of earnings inequality for the entire establishment (TOTLINEQ).

Table 11.3 presents correlations between the six objective measures of earnings inequality previously described and the subjective indicator. For comparison purposes, we also present correlations of these inequality variables with measures of the modal earnings in the three kinds of

**Table 11.2** Construction of Earnings Inequality Measures

| Measure | Mean | Standard Deviation | Minimum | Maximum | N |
|---|---|---|---|---|---|
| Total Inequality: TOTLINEQ = SQRT (AVGWITHN$^2$ + BETWNOCC$^2$) | .567 | .235 | .093 | 1.65 | 378 |
| Inequality Within Managers: WITHNMGR = STD (LOG (Lowest Manager), LOG (Manager Mode), LOG (Highest Manager)) | .424 | .274 | 0 | 1.60 | 461 |
| Inequality Within CORE Occupation: WITHNCOR = STD (LOG (Lowest CORE), LOG (CORE Mode), LOG (Highest CORE)) | .280 | .222 | 0 | 1.68 | 531 |
| Inequality Within GSS Occupation: WITHNGSS = STD (LOG (Lowest GSS), LOG (GSS Mode), LOG (Highest GSS)) | .248 | .213 | 0 | 1.68 | 467 |
| Average Inequality Within Occupations: AVGWITHN = average of within inequality measures across distinct occupations in the organization | .333 | .168 | 0 | 1.13 | 403 |
| Inequality Between Occupations: BETWNOCC = STD (LOG (Manager Mode), LOG (CORE Mode), LOG(GSS Mode)) | .409 | .291 | 0 | 2.12 | 522 |

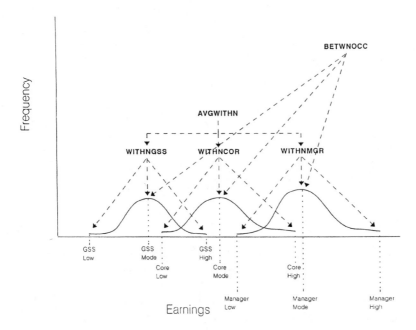

**Figure 11.1.** Relationships Between Earnings Inequality Variables

occupations (MGRMODE, COREMODE, and GSSMODE) and in the organization as a whole (GRANMODE). The NOS respondent's perception of degree of earnings inequality within the organization is most strongly related to inequality between managers. This correlation might result in that most NOS informants *are* managers; perhaps they are most aware of and sensitive to differences within this group. The average within-occupation inequality appears to be unrelated to the amount of between-occupation inequality, reinforcing our assumption that these measures tap distinct aspects of inequality. The total inequality measure is most strongly related to our indicator of between-occupation inequality, though it is also moderately correlated with each of our within-occupation dispersion measures.

## Measures of Explanatory Variables

Most of the explanatory variables we use in our analysis are described in Chapter 3. We use four variables to represent dimensions of the organi-

**Table 11.3** Correlations Between Inequality Measures

| Measure | SUBJINEQ | BETWNOCC | WITHNMGR | WITHNCOR | WITHNGSS | AVGWITHN |
|---|---|---|---|---|---|---|
| BETWNOCC | .028 | | | | | |
| WITHNMGR | .155*** | .035 | | | | |
| WITHNCOR | .124** | .127** | .083 | | | |
| WITHNGSS | .007 | .035 | .062 | .606*** | | |
| AVGWITHN | .126* | .074 | .714*** | .685*** | .637*** | |
| TOTLINEQ | .105* | .857*** | .366*** | .395*** | .344*** | .543*** |
| MGRMODE | .233*** | .001 | .129** | .192*** | .125** | .145** |
| COREMODE | .258*** | −.342*** | .098* | .143** | .059 | .136** |
| GSSMODE | .144*** | −.399*** | .073 | .143** | .121** | .136** |
| GRANMODE | .278*** | −.098* | .127** | .208*** | .109* | .187*** |

*$p \le .05$; **$p \le .01$; ***$p \le .001$.

zation's context: establishment size, the degree of unionization in the establishment's industry, and nonprofit status (see Chapter 3). In addition, we use an indicator of the total unemployment rate in the organization's industry. We measure an organization's structure by three variables: firm internal labor markets (FILMs—see Chapter 5) and horizontal and vertical differentiation (see Chapter 3).

Finally, we use several variables to describe the organization's work force: heterogeneity by gender and by race.[3, 4]

First, we measure the overall degree of gender heterogeneity (HET-SEX) as follows:

$.5 - |$ *Proportion female in the establishment* $- .5 |$ (mean = .23; $SD = .16$).

We measure occupation-specific gender heterogeneity (Managers: .18, .19; Core: .14, .16; GSS: .11, .16) as follows:

$.5 - |$ *Proportion female in the occupation .5 |.*

Our measure of the overall degree of racial heterogeneity (HETRACE) is as follows:

$.5 - |$ *Proportion whites in the establishment* $- .5 |$ (mean = .14; $SD = .15$).

We also include a measure of the percentage of the establishment's employees who are employed part-time (PCTPT) (mean = .16; $SD = .23$)

as a control; earnings presumably vary more when there are larger fractions of part-time workers receiving earnings that vary by time worked as well as wage rates.

## Correlations of Earnings Inequality Measures With Explanatory Variables

Table 11.4 presents correlations between the explanatory variables and each of our measures of earnings inequality (and, for comparison, overall modal earnings). These correlations provide initial tests of our hypotheses.

### Organization Context

As expected, larger establishments are associated with greater overall inequality (as well as higher average earnings). The link between size and inequality, however, appears to be due entirely to the correlation of size and inequality within managerial occupations; size is unrelated to between-occupation inequality and to inequality within either core or GSS occupations. Hypothesis 11.2 is strongly supported: Establishments in highly unionized industries have less overall inequality, and they have lower levels of earnings inequality between as well as within occupations. Unionization is correlated with inequality only in the core and GSS occupations: Inequality among managers—who are generally not unionized and thus not directly affected by collective bargaining—is unrelated to the degree of unionization within the industry.

Hypothesis 11.3 receives some support: The unemployment rate is negatively related to earnings dispersion within each of the three occupations, though this correlation is significant only for core occupations. As predicted, the unemployment rate is unrelated to inequality between occupations.

Hypothesis 11.4 receives modest initial support: Nonprofit establishments have less inequality between occupations—but not within occupations—than profit-seeking or government organizations. Despite the lower inequality between occupations in nonprofit organizations, their managers were still more likely than their counterparts in other types of organizations to perceive that there is a great deal of inequality in their organizations. This suggests the possibility that managers in nonprofit organizations are particularly sensitive to relatively small amounts of inequality.

**Table 11.4** Correlations of Earnings Inequality Measures With Explanatory Variables

| Variables | SUBJINEQ | BETWNOCC | WITHNMGR | WITHNCOR | WITHNGSS | AVGWITHN | TOTLINEQ | GRANMODE |
|---|---|---|---|---|---|---|---|---|
| LESTSIZE | .391*** | -.040 | .427*** | .077 | -.048 | .250*** | .132** | .408*** |
| PCTUNION | .033 | -.137** | -.064 | -.114** | -.108* | -.143*** | -.226*** | .305*** |
| TOTUNEM | -.147*** | .025 | -.067 | -.094* | -.095 | -.142** | -.034 | -.158*** |
| NPROFIT | .119** | -.100** | -.025 | .046 | -.044 | -.039 | -.114* | .218*** |
| FILMS | .363*** | -.165*** | .277*** | .089* | .045 | .220*** | -.076 | .359*** |
| HORZDIFF | .332*** | -.053 | .450*** | .035 | -.067 | .269*** | .120* | .359*** |
| VERTDIFF | .361*** | -.015 | .333*** | .050 | -.043 | .175*** | .080 | .369*** |
| HETSEX | .138*** | .088* | .177***[a] | .156***[a] | .196***[a] | .186*** | .153*** | .270*** |
| HETRACE | .229*** | -.013 | .159*** | -.021 | -.054 | .049 | .017 | .180*** |
| PCTPT | -.071 | .250*** | -.037 | .028 | .107* | .045 | .206*** | -.231*** |

a. Correlation with occupation-specific measure of gender heterogeneity.
*$p \leq .05$; **$p \leq .01$; ***$p \leq .001$.

**Organization Structure**

Inequality among managers appears to be influenced more by internal organizational structures than are inequalities between GSS or core occupations. This contrasts with our previous finding for external market variables (especially unionization and unemployment), which indicated that external labor market dynamics were less strongly related to inequality between managers than between the GSS and, especially, the core occupations.

The correlations between our measures of differentiation and earnings inequality provide initial support for Hypothesis 11.5. Both horizontal and vertical differentiation are positively associated with inequality within managerial occupations, but not within either the core or GSS occupations, or between occupations.

Consistent with Hypothesis 11.6, FILMs are positively correlated with inequality within core and, especially, managerial occupations, but they are negatively associated with inequality between occupations. These contrasting effects cancel each other, producing a negligible, non-significant relationship between FILMs and total organizational inequality.

The NOS respondent's perception of the degree of organizational inequality is positively correlated with all three measures of organization structure. This likely reflects the strong positive correlations of the structural measures with the degree of objective inequality within managerial occupations.

**Organizations' Labor Force Composition**

The results for gender heterogeneity provide initial support for Hypothesis 11.7: Gender heterogeneity is positively associated with both between-occupation inequality and each of our measures of within-occupation inequality. By contrast, racial heterogeneity is correlated (positively) only with inequality between managers. Gender, as well as racial heterogeneity, is positively correlated with perceived earnings inequality.

# Regressions of Earnings Inequality
# Measures on Explanatory Variables

Table 11.5 presents the results of ordinary least squares (OLS) regressions of our measures of earnings inequality and modal earnings on the

**Table 11.5** Earnings Inequality Regressions[a]

| Variables | SUBJINEQ | BETWNOCC | WITHNMGR | WITHNCOR | WITHNGSS | AVGWITHN | TOTLINEQ | GRANMODE |
|---|---|---|---|---|---|---|---|---|
| LESTSIZE | .080(.036)* | .018(.012) | .040(.011)** | .010(.010) | -.001(.010) | .013(.008)+ | .029(.012)* | .027(.021) |
| PCTUNION | -.006(.003)* | -.001(.001) | -.002(.001)* | -.002(.001)** | -.002(.001)* | -.002(.001)** | -.003(.001)** | .006(.002)** |
| TOTUNEM | -.036(.023) | -.003(.008) | -.003(.007) | -.010(.007) | -.015(.007)* | -.013(.005)* | -.014(.008)+ | -.014(.012) |
| NPROFIT | .149(.107) | -.077(.034)* | -.067(.031)* | -.011(.029) | -.032(.028) | -.030(.022) | -.074(.030)* | .140(.060)* |
| FILMS | .083(.021)** | -.023(.007)** | .007(.006) | .006(.006) | .010(.006)+ | .006(.005) | -.017(.007)** | .007(.012) |
| HORZDIFF | .064(.103) | -.014(.034) | .103(.031)** | -.014(.028) | -.019(.029) | .041(.022)+ | .021(.031) | .064(.059) |
| VERTDIFF | .212(.071)** | .025(.023) | .051(.021)** | .012(.020) | -.011(.019) | .011(.014) | .016(.064) | .113(.038)** |
| HETSEX | .194(.281) | .223(.096)* | .097(.074)b | .196(.073)**b | .282(.070)**b | .122(.067)+ | .263(.095)** | .725(.160)** |
| HETRACE | .866(.290)** | .019(.096) | -.034(.087) | -.101(.079) | .055(.079) | -.031(.062) | -.024(.087) | -.053(.165) |
| PCTPT | -.039(.190) | .315(.064)** | .038(.063) | -.010(.055) | .032(.053) | .035(.046) | .211(.064)** | -.429(.107)** |
| F | 17.29** | 5.59** | 14.30** | 2.35** | 3.43** | 5.96** | 6.38** | 20.03** |
| $R^2$-Adj. | .252 | .102 | .277 | .033 | .066 | .139 | .157 | .287 |
| N | 485 | 404 | 349 | 397 | 347 | 306 | 291 | 473 |

a. Unstandardized coefficients with standard errors are in parentheses.

b. Coefficient from occupation-specific measure of gender heterogeneity.

$+p \leq .10$; $*p \leq .05$; $**p \leq .01$.

explanatory variables.[5] We include part-time employment in each equation, to control for the average amount of labor supplied by employees in the organization.

### Organization Context

The multivariate results for size parallel the correlations in Table 11.4. There are size differentials in earnings dispersion only within managerial occupations. Managers in large establishments perceive greater earnings inequality than those in smaller workplaces.

Support for Hypothesis 11.2 is provided by the negative effects of unionization on wage dispersion within occupations and on total inequality; unionization appears to have some spillover effects in that it reduces inequality within managerial occupations as well as within GSS and core occupations. The effect of unionization on between-occupation inequality is also negative but not statistically significant.

Consistent with Hypothesis 11.3, higher unemployment rates are negatively related to earnings dispersion, but only within occupations, not between them. This effect, however, is significant only for the GSS occupation. As suggested above, we speculate that the effect of unemployment may reflect the segmentation of supply and demand mechanisms along occupational lines.

Nonprofit establishments have less total inequality than other types of organizations, supporting Hypothesis 11.4. This relationship appears to be due mainly to differences between nonprofit and other organizations in the degree of between-occupation inequality and in dispersion within managerial occupations.

### Organization Structure

Consistent with Hypothesis 11.5, both horizontal and vertical differentiation have strong net effects on inequality within managerial occupations. Horizontal differentiation has a small positive effect on within-occupation inequality, but vertical differentiation does not. Neither dimension of differentiation is related to between-occupation inequality, and only vertical differentiation is associated with our measure of subjective inequality.

Hypothesis 11.6 also receives some support: FILMs have the predicted positive effect on within-occupation inequality, though this is significant only for the GSS occupation, and FILMs are negatively related to between-occupation dispersion. Here, too, the perception that FILMs increase inequality is not supported by the actual earnings data. Although there is less total earnings inequality in organizations that are more likely to have FILMs, managers in such organizations perceive that there is *greater* inequality than do their counterparts in organizations with few or no FILMs.

### Labor Force Composition

As expected, gender heterogeneity is positively related to between-occupation and within-occupation inequality, particularly for nonmanagerial occupations. This positive effect of heterogeneity on inequality could be due either to the relative lack of social comparison processes in heterogeneous organizations or to statistical discrimination and other disadvantages that women experience relative to men in organizations. By contrast, racial heterogeneity does not appear to be related to any of our objective inequality measures,[6] though NOS respondents perceived that it raised inequality in their organizations (see SUBJINEQ).

## Conclusion

Analyzing patterns of organizational earnings dispersion is important because these inequalities have pervasive consequences for both individuals and organizations. Earnings differences between permanent and contingent organizational members (see Chapter 13, this volume) have been linked to the growing dualism between the incomes of the "haves" and the "have nots" in the United States in recent years (see Harrison 1994). Complaints about the large gaps between very well-paid CEOs and poorly paid rank-and-file workers in American corporations have led to public outcries about unfairness and have on occasion prompted legislative action to restrict executives' compensation. The degree of inequality within organizations also leads to social comparison processes that in turn have important influences on job satisfaction, turnover, and other workers' reactions (see Baron and Pfeffer 1994).

We have decomposed wage dispersion within organizations into two parts: within-occupational inequality and dispersion between occupations. Our results show that using an overall measure of organizational earnings inequality would have obscured the differential impact of some correlates of inequality on these two dimensions. For example, we found that larger and more differentiated organizations were associated with greater inequality, but only within managerial occupations. Unemployment rates were (negatively) associated with inequality only within nonmanagerial (especially GSS) occupations. Organizations with firm internal labor markets had less inequality between occupations. And, greater gender heterogeneity was associated with more inequality both between and within occupations. Moreover, managers' perceptions of greater inequality were linked to some characteristics—such as FILMs and racial composition—that objectively had opposite effects, or no effect at all, on total dispersion.

Admittedly, our data are less than ideal. We would have liked to have had a more systematic accounting of the earnings associated with jobs and occupations within organizations. In particular, having multilevel data on samples of individuals within each organization would allow us to separate the effects of organizational-level and individual-level variables on earnings. Nevertheless, our analyses provide tentative support for a number of hypotheses about the determinants of earnings inequality within organizations.

## Notes

1. The core, GSS, and manager occupations were distinct in 321 organizations. In 288 organizations, there were only two distinct occupations (i.e., either the core and GSS, the GSS and manager, or the core and manager occupations were the same). The three occupations were identical in 77 organizations. The correlations among earnings dispersion measures within these occupations (e.g., those presented in Table 11.3) are thus inflated to the extent that there is overlap among them.

2. BETWNOCC was set to "missing" for organizations with data on less than two distinct occupations (see Footnote 1).

3. The correlation between our measure of gender heterogeneity and percentage of female is .046, whereas the correlation between racial heterogeneity and percentage of whites is −.59.

4. The NOS did not contain information on the educational composition of organizations or on organizational averages of experience or other human capital variables.

5. We used tolerance and variance inflation indexes to test for high collinearity between variables that were strongly correlated (especially establishment size and the measures of organization structure). We found no evidence of excessive collinearity between these measures.

6. We estimated models that added measures of percent female and percent white to those reported in Table 11.5 (results not shown). Percent female was unrelated to all inequality measures; percent white was negatively related to between-occupation and total inequality. Adding these measures did not alter the effects of any of the other explanatory variables except racial heterogeneity, which was negatively related to between-occupation ($p < .10$) and total ($p < .10$) inequality. We also estimated models in which we substituted percent female and percent white for the heterogeneity measures. Only percent white was (negatively) related to (between-occupation) inequality ($p < .01$). The effects of the other explanatory variables were the same as those reported in Table 11.5.

# 12

# Cui Bono?

## *Employee Benefit Packages*

DAVID KNOKE

The problems in obtaining quality child care that scuttled two Clinton administration nominees for attorney general in 1992 underscore persistent shortcomings in employee benefits available to the U.S. labor force. Fringe benefits, in various forms of nonwage labor compensation and paid non-work activity, emerged as major components in the labor contract after World War II. (The War Labor Board controlled wages to fight inflation, but allowed increases in noncash benefits on the assumption they were on the fringe of wages and could not affect immediate purchasing power and consumer demand; Yoder and Staudohar 1982.) Employer programs expanded substantially following the Supreme Court's 1949 *Inland Steel* decision that made pensions a mandatory collective bargaining issue. Private sector practices diversified in parallel to such mandatory federal programs as unemployment compensation and old age income protection

(Social Security Act of 1935), health insurance (Medicare Act 1965), and private pension regulation (ERISA 1974). Federal tax code changes encouraged employers to offer tax-exempt or tax-deferred benefits (Employee Benefits Research Institute [EBRI] 1990).

Demographic trends, especially an aging baby boom population and increased female labor force participation, contribute to emerging demands for new programs, including dependent care (child and elderly), long-term care, unmarried domestic partner coverage, and flexible benefit (cafeteria) packages (EBRI 1990; Hayghe 1988; Johnston 1989). After expanding rapidly for 3 decades, however, private pension coverage fell sharply in the 1980s, apparently as a consequence of the declining economic position of less skilled male workers in an international economy (Bloom and Freeman 1992).

Employer-provided benefits currently make up approximately 30% of total labor compensation costs (Grossman 1992), but the range of actual coverage varies greatly. U.S. Department of Labor surveys for 1989 to 1990 reveal that medical care plans covered about 83% of full-time workers (part-time employees, accounting for some 20 million workers, were not included). Life insurance (81%), paid holidays and vacations (88%), and retirement plans (68%), paid sick leave (64%), and dental care (52%) also ranked high. But only a minority of all employees were covered by sickness and accident insurance (32%), long-term disability insurance (31%), unpaid maternity leave (31%), savings and thrift plans (17%), and stock options or profit sharing (1%). White-collar workers tended to fare better than blue-collar workers, and government workers typically enjoyed better coverage than those in the private sector (Grossman 1992; U.S. Department of Labor 1990). This chapter seeks to account for variation between patterns of employer benefit provisions in the National Organizations Study.

## Theoretical Perspectives and Hypotheses

Theoretical explanations of nonwage benefits, drawn from economic and sociological perspectives, are summarized in the following along with hypotheses to be tested at the organizational level of analysis.

### Human Capital Investments

Human capital interpretations emphasize that firms seek to protect themselves against future loss of their investments in increasing employee productivity (Oi 1962). For example, Becker (1964) hypothesized that firms will pay for the specific training of employees (e.g., learning to operate a unique machine) only when it increases their productivity within the firm, thus discouraging them from quitting to take jobs with other employers. Trainees therefore contribute to their training costs by accepting initially lower wages during the training period, with expectations of earning subsequently much higher wages through their greatly enhanced productivity (Farkas, England, and Barton 1988). Deferred fringe benefits serve as a similar line of defense against job quits, because vested workers would lose their future compensation. Both parties to a labor contract seek to minimize their uncertainties about investment returns by agreeing to deferred benefits in long-term bargains (Hashimoto 1981). Empirical evidence, however, suggests that labor turnover is inversely related to firm-specific human capital investments, whereas actual productivity may be unrelated to employee seniority (Hart 1984; Medoff and Abraham 1980; Parsons 1972). These findings, as well as the difficulty of separating firm and worker investments in human capital, cast doubt on the usefulness of human capital assumptions in explaining variation in benefit provisions. In any event, testable implications are not derived.

### Organizational Capacity

Another perspective on why some firms offer more diverse and generous benefits emphasizes organizational capacity, especially the ability to achieve economies of scale. Organizational size is strongly correlated with many firm and worker behaviors, including job searches, investments, training, job satisfaction, turnover, unionization, wages, and fringe benefits (Brown, Hamilton, and Medoff 1990; Burke and Morton 1990; Knoke and Kalleberg 1994; Osterman 1994b). Although bigger may not always be better (Villemez and Bridges 1988), larger firms often possess sufficient slack resources (retained earnings or credit lines) to afford more comprehensive worker compensation programs that small employers cannot sustain. For example, a larger employee pool typically allows a firm to acquire insurance discounts and to reduce its administrative overhead costs for program management. Firms enjoying favorable profit positions can more easily invest some of their earnings back into enhancing the quality of worker life than can firms that perform at or below the margin of profitability (Kotlikoff and Smith 1983).

*Hypothesis 12.1.* **The greater the organizational capacity, the more comprehensive an organization's employee benefit programs.**

**Worker Demands**

Employers intermittently react to their workers' needs, whether from organized pressures and threats or from anticipating problems in worker application and effort. Employers who deal with relatively powerless labor populations—minority, female, and younger workforces—are less responsive to their needs than employers who face primarily older white male workers (O'Rand 1986). Labor unions are a major vehicle for pressuring employers to offer their members higher wages (Lewis 1986) and better fringe benefits (Freeman 1981; O'Rand and MacLean 1986; Woodbury 1983) than those provided to nonunion workers. Unions often have or hire expertise essential to evaluate alternative compensation packages and to monitor their performance. Professional and technical workers value such nonwage rewards as flexible hours, career and professional advancement opportunities, and stock options (Von Glinow 1988).

*Hypothesis 12.2.* **The greater the employee demand for benefits, the more comprehensive an organization's employee benefits.**

**Environmental Conditions**

Firms that operate in demanding external environments—facing complex and unpredictable processes in tight labor markets and highly competitive product markets (Aldrich and Marsden 1988)—seek to acquire dependable and reliable workforces by offering their employees more comprehensive nonwage compensation packages. Generous benefits secure a loyal and stable workforce that is committed to the organization to which their fate is bound. Contemporary organizational practices also reflect the institutional dimensions of their environments (Powell and DiMaggio 1991; Zucker 1987). To the extent that employee benefits represent legitimated practices that have differentially diffused across economic sectors, some employers face stronger external pressures to conform to their industry's norms. For example, personnel practices and job training may reflect less a rational choice of the most effective organizational structures and more a cultural selection of normatively sanctioned forms that have little demonstrable relationship to actual performances (Scott and Meyer 1991). In the same respect, extensive employee benefit packages may have diffused and become legitimated among those employment contexts where good *organizational citizenship* is highly valued (Monahan, Meyer, and Scott 1992). Consistent with the institutional perspective, Osterman (1994b) found that U.S. establishments deployed work and family programs (such as day care, parental leaves, and flexible working hours) if they had a human resources department and were publicly traded on the stock market.

> *Hypothesis 12.3.* **The more unpredictable, competitive, and institutionalized an organization's environments, the more comprehensive its employee benefit package.**

Finally, to assess whether differences in benefit programs occur across broad economic sectors, a distinction among profit-making, nonprofit, and public employers is made. The research hypotheses appear above in bivariate form, but their test requires indicators of each concept and multivariate analysis procedures for assessing the net explanatory contributions of each factor, as subsequently described.

## Measuring Benefits

Toward the middle of the NOS interview, the following question was posed to informants, "Now I'd like to ask you about the kinds of benefits (Organization) provides to its employees. For each benefit, please tell me whether or not (Organization) offers it to any of its employees." The list contained 12 items (see Table 12.1):

1. Medical care
2. Dental care
3. Life insurance
4. Sick leave
5. Maternity leave
6. Elderly care
7. Flexible hours

**Table 12.1**  Benefit Programs of U.S. Establishments

| *Benefit Program* | *Percentage* |
|---|---|
| Medical or hospital insurance | 86.6 |
| Life insurance | 78.9 |
| Maternity or paternity leave with full re-employment rights | 77.2 |
| Sick leave with full pay | 75.9 |
| Pension or retirement programs | 71.7 |
| Formal job training program | 71.7 |
| Dental care benefits | 66.7 |
| Long-term disability insurance | 63.1 |
| Flexible hours or flextime scheduling | 60.2 |
| Drug or alcohol abuse programs | 55.1 |
| Cash or stock bonuses for performance or merit | 42.7 |
| Profit sharing or stock option programs | 27.8 |
| Assistance in caring for elderly family members | 17.3 |
| Day care for children, on-site or elsewhere, or help to employees to cover day care costs | 15.8 |
| *N* | 688 |

8. Cash or stock bonuses
9. Pensions
10. Profit-sharing
11. Drug and alcohol abuse programs
12. Disability insurance

Two additional benefits were the focus of detailed questions elsewhere in the interview: formal job training programs and child care. Thus a total of 14 dichotomous indicators of establishment benefit provisions are available. Measures of the explanatory concepts used in testing the research hypotheses are described in Appendix 12.1 (See Chapter 3 for more details on these measures.)

## Distributions of Employee Benefits

Table 12.1 displays the distributions of the 14 benefit programs. Each percentage is based on the unweighted NOS data set. It reflects the proportion of the U.S. labor force in which each type of benefit is available. The most prevalent programs, provided to more than three fourths of employees, are medical and hospital insurance, life insurance, maternal and paternal leave (unpaid), and sick leave (paid). More than half the workers are employed in establishments that offer pensions, formal job training, dental care, disability insurance, flextime, and alcohol and drug abuse treatment programs. The lowest coverage rates occur for cash bonus plans, profit-sharing plans, elderly care, and child care, with the latter two options available to only about one employee in six.

The basic dimensions underlying the organizational benefits programs were revealed by confirmatory factor analyses (CFA) of the 14 indicators. Because each benefit program was measured as a dichotomy (present or absent), the appropriate statistic for measuring their covariation is the tetrachoric correlation (Muthén 1981; O'Brien and Homer 1987). The PRELIS program (Jöreskog and Sörbom 1986) calculated the tetrachoric values shown in Table 12.2. These values were then entered into the LISREL 7 program (Jöreskog and Sörbom 1989) and a series of CFA models were estimated. The standardized item loadings from the best-fitting model are displayed in Table 12.3.[1]

To set the metric scale for each factor, a factor loading for one indicator of each factor is fixed in the original, unstandardized version of this CFA model. This is done for pensions for the first factor, child care for the second, and profit sharing for the third. These indicators were chosen because each item loads significantly on only one factor. The three factors are very highly correlated (.95 for factors 1 and 2; .53 for 1 and 3; .46 for 2 and 3). But the patterns of item loadings are quite dissimilar. Six benefits are primarily or exclusively associated with the first factor: medical, dental, life, and disability insurance; pensions; and drug and alcohol abuse treatment programs. Five programs load significantly only on the second factor: formal job training, sick leave, maternity leave, child care, and elder care. The third factor is dominated by the profit-sharing and cash bonus indicators, although the medical and life insurance measures have small yet statistically significant loadings on it.

Based on these results, three scales were constructed from the highest-loading indicators in each dimension. The personal benefits package of medical, dental, and life insurance, pensions, and drug and alcohol abuse has an internal consistency reliability of .87 (Cronbach's $\alpha$). The familial benefits package of maternity leave, child care, elder care, sick leave, and job training has an $\alpha$ of .65, while the two-item participant benefits scale of cash bonuses and profit sharing has an $\alpha$ of only .49. Table 12.4 displays the univariate distributions of these three scales, which are simply counts

**Table 12.2** Tetrachoric Correlations Between Dichotomous Benefit Measures

| Program | 1 | 2 | 3 | 4 | 5 | 6 | 7 | 8 | 9 | 10 | 11 | 12 | 13 | 14 |
|---|---|---|---|---|---|---|---|---|---|---|---|---|---|---|
| 1. Medical | 1.00 | | | | | | | | | | | | | |
| 2. Dental | .91 | 1.00 | | | | | | | | | | | | |
| 3. Life | .95 | .81 | 1.00 | | | | | | | | | | | |
| 4. Sick leave | .82 | .77 | .74 | 1.00 | | | | | | | | | | |
| 5. Maternal leave | .79 | .74 | .72 | .80 | 1.00 | | | | | | | | | |
| 6. Elder care | .40 | .53 | .50 | .37 | .46 | 1.00 | | | | | | | | |
| 7. Flextime | .24 | .20 | .09 | .29 | .12 | .22 | 1.00 | | | | | | | |
| 8. Cash bonus | .42 | .29 | .31 | .31 | .21 | .19 | .24 | 1.00 | | | | | | |
| 9. Pensions | .84 | .82 | .80 | .73 | .72 | .44 | .02 | .16 | 1.00 | | | | | |
| 10. Profit sharing | .59 | .39 | .53 | .40 | .35 | .10 | .11 | .51 | .47 | 1.00 | | | | |
| 11. Drug abuse | .88 | .73 | .75 | .69 | .68 | .45 | .06 | .28 | .83 | .39 | 1.00 | | | |
| 12. Disability | .84 | .75 | .80 | .69 | .71 | .49 | .16 | .20 | .81 | .51 | .74 | 1.00 | | |
| 13. Job training | .66 | .61 | .72 | .65 | .68 | .41 | .18 | .26 | .67 | .35 | .73 | .69 | 1.00 | |
| 14. Child care | .38 | .47 | .37 | .52 | .34 | .22 | .25 | .11 | .54 | .10 | .49 | .44 | .54 | 1.00 |

**Table 12.3** Confirmatory Factor Analysis: Factor Loadings for 13 Benefits, Completely Standardized Solution

| Benefit Program | Factor 1 | Factor 2 | Factor 3 |
|---|---|---|---|
| Medical or hospital insurance | .83*** | | .30** |
| Life insurance | .81*** | | .20* |
| Dental care benefits | .90*** | | |
| Pension or retirement programs | .90[a] | | |
| Drug or alcohol abuse programs | .87*** | | |
| Long-term disability insurance | .87*** | | |
| Sick leave with full pay | | .88*** | |
| Maternity or paternity leave | | .86*** | |
| Formal job training program | | .80*** | |
| Assistance in caring for elderly family members | | .53*** | |
| Day care for children | | .53[a] | |
| Profit-sharing or stock option programs | | | .89[a] |
| Cash or stock bonuses for performance or merit | | | .56*** |

a. The coefficient variance is fixed to 1.0 to set factor metric in nonstandardized solution for the model.
*$p < .05$; **$p < .01$; ***$p < .001$.

**Table 12.4.** Percentage Distributions of Numbers of Personal, Familial, and Participant Benefits

| Number of Benefits | Personal Benefits | Familial Benefits | Participant Benefits |
|---|---|---|---|
| None | 10.8 | 11.9 | 48.5 |
| 1 | 4.4 | 7.8 | 32.4 |
| 2 | 8.4 | 18.9 | 19.0 |
| 3 | 6.7 | 36.9 | — |
| 4 | 9.2 | 20.6 | — |
| 5 | 19.5 | 3.8 | — |
| 6 | 41.1 | — | — |
| Total | 100.0 | 100.0 | 100.0 |
| N | 688 | 688 | 688 |

of the number of benefit programs of each type that employers provide. Personal benefits are by far the most prevalent type, with more than 60% of workers employed by establishments that offer at least five of the six programs. In contrast, less than 25% of employees are covered by four of the five familial benefits, and almost half have neither of the participant programs.

**Table 12.5.** Unstandardized Poisson Regression Analyses of Three Benefit Count
Scales

| Independent Variables | Personal Benefits | Familial Benefits | Participant Benefits |
|---|---|---|---|
| Constant | .12 | −.55** | −1.47*** |
| Establishment size | .09*** | .10*** | .09*** |
| Parent size | −.02 | −.02 | .08** |
| Parent dummy | .34** | .41** | −.37 |
| Establishment age | .06** | .05** | −.05 |
| Women in workforce | −.02*** | -.0003 | -.004* |
| Market competition | .07** | .05 | .13* |
| Institutionalization | .07*** | .07** | .07 |
| Benchmarking | .05 | .10* | .16*** |
| Public sector | .15* | .14 | −1.55*** |
| Nonprofit sector | .05 | .10 | −.77*** |
| Log-likelihood | −1,336.5 | −1,087.9 | −658.9 |
| Degrees of freedom | 11 | 11 | 11 |
| Log-likelihood for constant-only model | −1,548.4 | −1,214.6 | −745.4 |
| N | 688 | 688 | 688 |

$*p < .05; **p < .01; ***p < .001.$

## Multivariate Analyses of Benefits

Poisson regression is an appropriate method of multivariate analysis
whenever the dependent variable is a discrete count (Greene 1990, pp. 707-
9). Table 12.5 displays the coefficients from three Poisson regression
equations in which the personal, familial, and participant benefits frequen-
cies are the respective dependent variables. (These analyses were performed by the LIMDEP program; Greene 1989.) Only those predictors that
were significant in at least one equation were retained. Each equation was
a significant improvement in fit over a baseline, constant-only model, as
shown by the goodness-of-fit statistics (log-likelihoods) at the bottom of
the table.[2] Because the Poisson regression coefficients are unstandardized,
comparisons of effects within equations are not feasible, given the differing
metric scales of the independent variables. To save space, standard errors
are not shown, but the significance levels of coefficients are indicated with
asterisks.

Several independent variables are significantly related to the numbers
of benefits of each type provided by establishments. Hypothesis 12.1, that
greater organizational capacity produces more comprehensive benefits, is

supported by the positive coefficients for logged establishment size in all three equations, by the coefficient of the parent organization dummy variable in the personal benefits and familial benefits equations, and by the logged size of the parent organization in the participant benefits equation. The positive coefficient for the log of establishment age in the personal and familial benefits equations indicates that older organizations are more likely to offer these inducements, but establishment age is unrelated to participant benefits. Other measures of organizational capacity—industry concentration levels, profit rates, and average and net compensation levels—failed to reach statistical significance in any equation.

Hypothesis 12.2, that employee demands affect the provision of benefits, receives support only from coefficients for the percentage of women in the establishment's workforce, which are significantly negative in both the personal and participant benefits equations; that is, the higher the proportion of women, the less likely is an employer to offer such benefits. Other employee demand indicators—racial composition of the workforce, unionization, and part-time employment—failed to achieve statistical significance in any equation, however. Thus employee demand does not appear to be a very potent factor behind employer provision of benefits.

Hypothesis 12.3, that unpredictable, competitive, and institutionalized environments stimulate more comprehensive benefits, is supported by coefficients for three indicators, each of which is significant in two of the three equations. The greater the market competition, institutionalization, and the better an organization stands according to benchmarking criteria, the larger the number of benefits available from an employer. Several other environmental indicators failed to reach significance in any equation— measures of complexity, uncertainty, foreign competition, perceived future problems, and unemployment in the establishment's industry.

Finally, the two dummy variables for broad economic sectors show that, relative to the profit-making sector, public-sector establishments are more likely to provide personal benefits, whereas both the public and nonprofit sectors are less likely to offer participant benefits (clearly, profit-sharing and stock-ownership plans make no sense in those contexts). Familial benefits are not provided differentially across the three sectors.

The preceding analyses examined how predictor variables relate to the provision of each type of benefit. But benefit programs are not mutually exclusive. By dichotomizing and cross-tabulating the personal benefits scale (at five or more of the six programs) and familial benefits scale (at three or more of the five programs), a new classification yields four

**Table 12.6.** Unstandardized Multiple Logistic Regression Analyses of Benefit Combinations (omitted category is low benefits of both types)

| Independent Variables | High Personal, Low Familial | Low Personal, High Familial | High Personal, High Familial |
|---|---|---|---|
| Constant | −10.31*** | −6.89*** | −10.56*** |
| Establishment size | .65*** | .39** | .96*** |
| Parent size | .19 | −.23 | .28* |
| Parent dummy | .68 | 2.75** | .29 |
| Establishment age | .09 | .33* | .14 |
| Part-time employees | .003 | .001 | −.01* |
| Whites in workforce | .002 | .004 | .02*** |
| Environmental complexity | −.09 | .03 | .32* |
| Market competition | .59* | .10 | .46* |
| Institutionalization | .24 | .50** | .38** |
| Future problems | .80* | .48 | .09 |
| Net compensation | .004*** | .0001 | .0003** |
| Public sector | .72 | .21 | 1.04 |
| Nonprofit sector | .98 | .79 | 1.43** |
| Log-likelihood | | −486.8 | |
| Degrees of freedom | | 14 | |
| Log-likelihood for constant-only model | | −785.3 | |
| N | | 688 | |

*$p < .05$; **$p < .01$; ***$p < .001$.

packages. Establishments may offer (a) fewer benefit programs of both types (29.8% of the sample); (b) many personal benefits but few familial benefits (8.9%); (c) many familial but fewer personal benefits (9.6%); or (d) many benefits of both types (51.7%). Table 12.6 presents a multiple-category logistic regression analysis (again conducted using LIMDEP) in which the first category (fewer benefits of both kinds) is the reference group; that is, the regression coefficient appearing in a row indicates how that independent variable affects the logged odds that an establishment provides the benefit combination in a given column, rather than fewer benefits of either type (i.e., the reference category). As before, only independent variables that had at least one significant coefficient were retained in the final equation.

The log-likelihood values at the bottom of Table 12.6 show that this logistic regression substantially improves the fit over a constant-only equation. Although the equation correctly places 75.8% of all observations (compared to 51.7% correct for placements on the basis of the modal category—both types—in the constant-only model), it performs well only in those establishments offering fewer benefits of both kinds (87.3% correctly placed) and those providing higher amounts of both kinds (93.8%). Its ability to identify correctly the cases in the two mixed types is weak (4.9% and 9.1% correct for the high-personal/low-familial and low-personal/high-familial combinations, respectively).

Consistent with Hypothesis 12.1, larger establishments (logged values) are more likely to provide all three benefit combinations, relative to establishments that provide fewer benefits of either type. But the parent organization dummy is significant only for the high-familial/low-personal package, whereas parent size (logged) is significant only for the both-high category. The log of establishment age is significant only for the high-familial/low-personal package, meaning that older organizations tend to specialize in that combination. Net compensation (the annual difference between industry mean total compensation and wages) is positive for the high-personal/low-familial and the both-high categories, meaning that firms in industries with higher nonwage benefits are likely to offer more comprehensive packages. In support of Hypothesis 12.2, two indicators of employee demand have significant effects: The larger the percentage of part-time employees and the higher the proportion of nonwhite workers, the less likely an establishment is to provide many benefits of both types. Consistent with Hypothesis 12.3, four environmental indicators have significant positive coefficients for one or more of the packages: environmental complexity, market competition, institutionalization, and anticipated future problems. Finally, the contrasts among the three broad economic sectors are generally not significant, with only the nonprofit sector more likely than the others to offer high numbers of both kinds of benefits.

## Conclusion

United States employers offer their employees a great diversity of nonwage compensation, ranging from the widespread provision of health insurance to rare child care assistance. These benefit programs are packaged into three distinct bundles. The conventional employee-centered benefits (medical-dental-life-disability insurance and substance abuse assistance) are the most widely available policies. Benefits that enhance family welfare (parental leave, dependent care, plus sick leave and job training) are more recent additions to the labor contract and not so pervasive in employing organizations. The least prevalent options give workers a stake in their firms' performance through cash-stock-profit participation.

Tests of three broad hypotheses about the sources of interorganizational variation in benefit provision revealed that employee demand, as measured by workforce composition and unionization, is a surprisingly ineffective predictor. Instead, the major prerequisites to more comprehensive employee benefits appear to be larger internal capacity (establishment size and total nonwage compensation) and rivalry with other organizations (greater market competition, institutionalization, and high standing in benchmarking performance criteria).

This snapshot of U.S. organizations' benefit packages in the 1990s gives a tantalizing glimpse of the arrays of nonwage compensation offered to employees. Cross-sectional data about which types of organizations currently offer what kinds of benefits fail to capture the dynamic processes involved in the creation and change of benefit programs and their substantive implications. Missing from the portrait is a longitudinal dimension that would animate this static picture and provide greater detail about the scope of worker coverage within organizations. We know that corporations have greatly expanded the variety and breadth of benefits since World War II, but that pattern may already have begun to reverse itself. The business press is filled with reports of business resistance to mandated employer financing of medical coverage that thwarted President Clinton's health care reform proposals in the mid-1990s (e.g., Bowers 1994). Pensions, child care, and the financing of job training also will loom increasingly large in future company efforts to trim their labor costs. At the heart of this contention over company benefits lies a historic struggle over the expansion of citizenship rights into the economic realm.

In his magisterial essay on the development of a universal citizenship status, T. H. Marshall (1973) argued that three basic rights and their embodying institutions emerged in temporal succession. Civil rights preceded political rights, which in turn antedated social rights: "From the right to a modicum of economic welfare and security to the right to share in the full social heritage and to live the life of a civilized being" (Marshall 1973, p. 72). Marshall emphasized the historical role of public schools and social service agencies as the institutional manifestations of these social rights. He could not foresee that, by the end of the 20th century, many would turn to the labor contract as a basis for providing many economic rights. Clinton administration proposals to mandate company provision of job training and medical care clearly envisioned enlarging the scope of employer-provided benefits for workers. Management resisted these proposals as perceived encroachments on company prerogatives, and the thwarting of any significant change in national health policy indicated that the time for expansion had not yet arrived. Regardless of how these scenarios eventually unfold within the shadow of enormous budget deficits and a parlous world economy, immense opportunities lie ahead for researchers to study benefits as one of the changing human resources practices of work organizations.

## Notes

1. Initial analyses revealed that the flextime variable did not load highly with any other measures (see the small correlations in Table 12.1), so it was not considered further. A CFA model that allowed the 13 remaining indicators all to load on only one factor yielded a poor fit according to the chi-square criterion ($\chi^2 = 129.6$, $df = 65$, $p < .001$), although both the adjusted goodness-of-fit (AGOF) index and the root mean square residual (RMSR) indexes had very good values (AGOF = .991, RMSR = .067). A two-factor CFA model improved the fit markedly ($\chi^2 = 58.7$, $df = 53$, $p = .28$; AGOF = .995, RMSR = .045). But an inspection of the factor loadings suggested that the cash bonus and profit-sharing measures probably constituted a distinct dimension from the other indicators. A three-factor CFA model yielded an excellent fit ($\chi^2 = 43.5$, $df = 43$, $p = .45$; AGOF = .996, RMSR = .039). A final three-factor CFA model, which fixed to zero all item loadings that were not significant at $\alpha = .05$ in the preceding model, produced a very acceptable fit ($\chi^2 = 59.8$, $df = 60$, $p = .48$; AGOF = .996, RMSR = .048).

2. A test of the null hypothesis that independent variables have no effect is $G^2 = (-2LL_0)$ $-(2\ LL_1)$, where $LL_0$ is the log likelihood of the constant-only equation and $LL_1$ is the log likelihood of the equation including the predictors. If the null hypothesis is true, $G^2$ is distributed as a chi-square variable with degrees of freedom equal to the number of independent variables.

## APPENDIX 12.1

### Measures of Explanatory Concepts

#### Organizational Capacity

*Establishment size:* The natural log of the establishment's number of employees (full-time plus part-time).

*Parent organization:* A dichotomous (dummy) variable coded 0 if the establishment is an independent organization, 1 if it is a branch or subsidiary of a larger organization.

*Parent size:* Natural log of the establishment's parent's number of employees (0 if no parent).[1]

*Average compensation level:* Industry average annual total compensation per employee (wages and fringes, in dollars).

*Net compensation level:* Industry average annual nonwage compensation per employee (average compensation minus wages, in dollars).

*Profit rate:* Industry annual profits (percentage of assets).

*Concentration level:* Industry assets held by firms with more than $250 million in assets (percentage of assets).

*Age:* Natural log of number of years since the establishment was created.

## Worker Demand

*Female workforce:* Percentage of establishment workforce (full-time and part-time) that is female.

*White workforce:* Percentage of establishment workforce (full-time and part-time) that is white.

*Part-time employment:* Percentage of establishment workforce that is employed part-time.

*Unionization:* Percentage of industry workers in 1988 belonging to unions (from Curme, Hirsch, and MacPherson 1990).

## Environmental Conditions

*Environmental complexity:* Average agreement with four items ("The techniques, skills, and information needed by [Organization] are changing very rapidly"; "To achieve our goals, it is essential to work cooperatively with many other organizations"; "Our relations with other organizations are sometimes marked by conflict"; "[Organization] concentrates on doing what it does well and takes few risks").

*Environmental uncertainty:* Average agreement with two items ("[Organization] reacts mostly to outside pressures"; "Making long-range plans for this organization is hindered by the difficulty of predicting future events").[2]

*Market competition:* Amount of competition in the organization's main market or service area, on a 4-point scale from "none" (1) to "a great deal" (4).

*Foreign competition:* Amount of competition in the main market or service area from foreign organizations, on the same scale.

*Future problems:* Average extent problems expected over the next 3 years, on a 3-point scale from "not a problem at all" (1) to "a major problem" (3), across the following areas: hiring qualified workers; retaining qualified workers; improving employee compensation and benefits; relations with unions; government regulations; improving quality of products, services, or programs; developing new products, services, or programs; increasing productivity (see Chapter 3, Table 3.2).

*Benchmarking:* Informants were asked to use 4-point response scales (from "much better" (4) to "worse" (1) to compare their organization's performance over past 3 years to "other organizations that do the same kind of work" with regard to quality of products, services, or programs; development of new products, services, or programs; ability to attract essential employees; ability to retain essential employees; satisfaction of customers or clients; relations between management and other employees; relations between employees in general (see also Chapter 6).[3]

*Institutionalization:* Number of positive responses to four items ("Does [Organization] belong to an association of organizations like it?"; "Is [Organization] subject to a periodic review by an outside accreditation or licensing organization?"; "In evaluating [Organization's] performance, to what extent do you pay attention to practices of other organizations like [Organization]?"; "How much are [Organization's] operations regulated by government agencies?").[4]

*Unemployment rate:* Industry annual unemployment rate (percentage of workforce).

*Economic sectors:* Three dummy variables identifying (a) public organizations, (b) private nonprofit organizations, and (c) profit-making organizations.[5]

To preserve cases for analysis, missing values of all variables were replaced by either the mean or the mode (as appropriate) of the observations with nonmissing values.

## Notes

1. Because the parent size measure is not meaningful for establishments that are not branches or subsidiaries, both the parent size variable and the parent dummy must be entered into an equation to estimate correctly the effect of size on a dependent variable. Both measures have zero values for the independent establishments; hence only the intercept contributes to those establishments' dependent variable score (net of other predictors' effects). But the effect for subsidiary and branch establishments is composed of the sum of three terms: the intercept, the parent dummy coefficient, and the product of the coefficient for the parent size variable times the logged parental size.

2. The six environmental turbulence items plus a seventh ("The political climate right now is very favorable to our goals") were subjected to a principal components factor analysis with varimax rotation. The four complexity items loaded highly on the first factor (eigenvalue = 1.65, percentage of variance explained = 23.6), and the two uncertainty items loaded highly on the second factor (eigenvalue = 1.16, percentage of variance explained = 16.6). The political climate item did not load highly on either factor. Scale reliabilities are .433 for complexity and .337 for uncertainty.

3. Principal components factor analysis showed the seven items loading highly on one factor (eigenvalue = 3.20, percentage of variance = 53.4, scale reliability = .848).

4. A principal components factor analysis showed all four items loading highly on a single factor (eigenvalue = 1.68, percentage of variance explained = 42.0, scale reliability = .538).

5. Because these three dummy variables are linearly dependent, only two can be entered as predictors in multivariate equations. The public and nonprofit dummies were included, and thus profit-making organizations serve as a reference category. Because public and nonprofit organizations do not have meaningful scores on either the profit-level or the concentration-level variables, the two dummies are always used when either of those two predictors is specified.

# Organizations and the Changing Workforce

# 13

## Contingent Employment in Organizations

*Part-Time, Temporary, and Subcontracting Relations*

ARNE L. KALLEBERG

KATHRYN SCHMIDT

Employment relations in the United States are changing (see, e.g., Kochan, Katz, and McKersie 1986; Belous 1989). During the past 15 years, U.S. work organizations have moved away from the traditional model of employment in which most male employees were connected to their employers on a full-time, relatively permanent basis. Employees were expected to be loyal and committed to their employers, who reciprocated by granting them job security and long-term employment. This postwar period of long-term, steady employment in the United States is ending, as employment relations are becoming less permanent and secure. Organizations are changing from structures built around jobs to shifting kinds of work that need to be done (Bridges 1994). This transformation in employment relations is replacing the "old covenant" (characterized by an exchange of job security for performance and loyalty) with a "new covenant" in which employers train workers and help them to become employable in a variety of companies (Waterman, Waterman, and Collard 1994) but make no promises of continued employment (O'Reilly 1994).

These less permanent forms of employment are often described as *contingent work*. Originally coined by Conference Board economist Audrey Freeman in the mid-1980s to refer to conditional employment relations, this term has been expanded to include workers who are employed in jobs that do not fit the traditional description of a full-time, permanent job with benefits (Callaghan and Hartmann 1991; Parker 1994). Polivka and Nardone (1989) define *contingent work* as

> any job in which an individual does not have an explicit or implicit contract for long-term employment and one in which the minimum hours worked can vary in a non-systematic manner. (p. 11)

In contingent jobs, it is understood from the outset that employment security is limited (Appelbaum 1992). The notion of contingent employment refers to the nature of the *relationship* between an employer and employee, not solely to the type of task performed or the individual worker. From the employer's viewpoint, contingent employment represents a variable (rather than fixed) labor cost, and provides the basis for achieving greater flexibility and lower costs (Pfeffer 1994). From the employee's point of view, the basic difference between *regular* and *contingent* employment is captured by the dictionary definition of contingent as "uncertain of occurrence" (Olmsted and Smith 1989, p. 373).

Contingent work takes various forms (Polivka and Nardone 1989). The most commonly studied types of contingent employment are *part-time, temporary,* and *contract* employment. We focus on these three relations in this chapter. They illustrate two types of externalized work activities identified by Pfeffer and Baron (1988): (a) Temporary and (often) part-time employment are relations of limited duration; (b) subcontracting (and often temporaries) entails the shifting of tasks from a firm's own employees to persons who are employed by someone else.[1]

Persons having contingent employment relations now constitute a sizeable portion of the U.S. labor force. A frequently cited estimate is that in

1988 between 25% and 30% of all employees in the U.S. civilian labor force
(29.9 million to 36.6 million workers) were either part-time workers, temporary workers, contract employees, or independent consultants (Belous
1989).2 Moreover, the rate of growth in the use of temporary and part-time
workers exceeded the growth rate of the entire labor force in the United
States during the 1980s (see Belous 1989; Pollack and Bernstein 1986). A
reflection of these trends is that Manpower Inc. became the nation's largest
private employer in 1992, employing twice as many people (560,000) as
General Motors (once the biggest employer) (Swoboda 1993).

In this chapter, we first discuss some conceptual and theoretical issues
related to the organization of contingent employment relations. We then
use the NOS data to examine the extent to which these three major types
of contingent work—singly and in various combinations—are used by U.S.
work organizations. We then consider how the types of contingent work
are related to selected characteristics of organizations.

## Explaining the Growth of Contingent
## Employment Relations in the United States

Part-time and temporary work arrangements are not new; employers
have used them in the past to adjust for supply-demand imbalances. But
the dramatic increase in contingent employment relations is striking, as is
that they are often replacing more permanent relationships. Several "demand side" reasons are given for this growth in contingent workers. First,
rapid social and economic changes beginning in the mid-1970s transformed the relatively certain and standardized manufacturing markets of
the period from 1945 to 1973 (see Staber and Aldrich 1988) into increasingly uncertain, volatile, and turbulent markets. Intensified international
competition and technological changes led employers, especially in manufacturing, to seek greater flexibility in their production processes and in
their relations with their employees (Piore and Sabel 1984).

Accompanying the growth in international competition in the 1980s were
domestic economic changes such as privatization, deregulation, and mergers
and acquisitions. These conditions increased employer concerns with short-
term, narrow indicators of economic performance and motivated them to seek
to reduce their labor costs by lowering wages and, especially, reducing fringe
benefits. Many corporate executives saw dismissing workers or externalizing
production as the fastest way to reduce labor costs (Parker 1994). This

cost-saving explanation is somewhat independent of that based on employers' needs for flexibility in adapting to the pressures of competing in a global market. The latter does not necessarily imply a lowering of wages and reduction of fringe benefits, two consequences that are currently associated with contingent work (see Callaghan and Hartmann 1991).

The growth of contingent work also partly reflects industrial shifts in the U.S. economy. Part-time and temporary jobs are more common in service industries (see Table 13.1 following), and the growth of this economic sector has increased the use of contingent workers. This is due in part to the relatively small size of such organizations (Appelbaum 1992).

Finally, social and demographic changes—such as the increase in the employment of women and in the number of older people—within the United States have been important in creating a supply of workers for contingent work arrangements. These labor force trends have also helped to create employee demand for more flexible schedules than are possible with full-time employment. The breakdown of traditional barriers between the workplace and other aspects of workers' lives—family, education, and community and leisure activities—have increased desires for work schedules that are more adaptable to other commitments (Olmsted and Smith 1989). The argument, however, that employers created contingent work schedules in response to employee demand should not be overstated in that the increase in contingent employment consists mainly of workers who would choose full-time employment if it were available (e.g., Callaghan and Hartmann 1991).

## Overview of the Three Types of Contingent Employment Relations

### Part-Time Work

Part-time work is generally defined as any job that regularly employs a person less than 35 hours per week (U.S. Department of Labor 1988). According to the Bureau of Labor Statistics (BLS), 19.6 million workers worked fewer than 35 hours in 1990, representing 18% of the total U.S. civilian workforce of 108.7 million (Callaghan and Hartmann 1991). Part-time work is the most common of the three types of contingent work, constituting more than half of the contingent workforce. The percentage of part-timers has grown steadily since 1957, when 12.1% of the civilian labor force worked part-time. This growth in the proportion of part-time workers has exceeded the increase in overall employment in the United States: Belous (1989) estimates that between 1980 and 1988 the civilian labor force grew by 14%, whereas part-time workers increased by 21%. The U.S. trends parallel the increase in part-time work in most advanced industrial nations, though the rate of this increase has varied considerably among countries (de Neubourg 1985).

Women are more likely than men to work part-time. By 1988, about two thirds of the part-time labor force was made up of women; about 11% of male workers and about 27% of female workers had a part-time job (Tilly 1990, table 1). Younger workers—who often combine schooling with work—and older workers (55 and older) are also overrepresented among part-time workers.

The quality of part-time jobs differs. Tilly (1990) distinguishes among *short-time, secondary,* and *retention* part-time jobs. In short-time jobs (which make up less than 10% of all part-time employment), employers temporarily reduce employees' hours rather than lay them off. Secondary part-time jobs (which constitute the bulk of part-time work) are characterized by relatively low skill, low pay, low fringe benefits, low productivity, and high turnover. Retention part-time jobs are generally offered by employers to valued and usually highly-skilled employees whose life circumstances prevent them from working full-time (e.g., women with young children).

Part-timers also differ in their reasons for working less than full-time. Many people work part-time involuntarily, because they cannot find full-time work. In 1990, about a quarter of those working part-time did so involuntarily: 4.5% of all labor force members worked part-time involuntarily, compared with 13.6% of all labor force members who did so voluntarily. Involuntary part-time work accounted for about two thirds of the growth of part-time work between 1969 and 1988 (Tilly 1990). Moreover, there is no evidence that the proportion of women who work part-time voluntarily increased during the 1980s. The relatively rapid growth of involuntary part-time employment underscores the importance of focusing on the demand-side of the labor market to account for the expansion of part-time work (Ehrenberg, Rosenberg, and Li 1988; Tilly 1990).

**Temporary Work**

Temporary workers are those hired for a limited duration, which is usually measured in days, weeks, or months, rather than years (Callaghan and Hartmann 1991). Hiring occurs either through a temporary ("temp" agency or directly by the employer. Almost all of what we know about temporary workers, however, comes from the Bureau of Labor Statistics

data for two industry categories: (Temporary Help Supply—THS—SIC
7362 and Help Supply Services—HSS—SIC 7363). (Estimates based on
these industry categories tend to underestimate the use of temporaries in
that they do not count in-house temporary employees.)

Temporary employment is the fastest-growing form of contingent
work: It increased 225% between 1980 (400,000) and 1991 (1.3 million)
(Belous 1989; see also Carey and Hazelbaker 1986; Hartmann and Lapidus
1989). A 1986 Bureau of National Affairs survey indicates that the use of
temporary employees that year was 400% higher than in 1970 (Olmsted
and Smith 1989). The five major industry sectors within the temporary help
industry (1992 percentage of total industry payroll) were clerical (46.6),
industrial (27.7), technical (10.2), medical (8.8), and professional (5.3).
Medical-related temporary help providers are the fastest growing part of
the industry (U.S. Department of Labor 1988; Parker 1994).

The recessionary period of the early 1980s led to an increasing use of
temporary workers. This allowed employers to increase productivity and
provide extra staffing as demand rose without making permanent commitments to employees (Bureau of National Affairs 1986). The growth in
demand for temporary employment was accompanied by a surge in temporary help agencies that offered employers a supply of trained employees
for a lower and more flexible wage and benefit bill. The growth of the
temporary help industry also resulted from the actions of national and state
temp associations, which successfully raised employers' consciousness
about ways to take advantage of temporary employment relations (Parker
1994). Although the trend has been most pronounced in the last few years,
the use of temporary workers may be in part cyclical: A survey by a market
research firm estimated that temporary jobs represented only 9.6% of the
new jobs added to the U.S. economy in 1994, compared with 26.5% and
15.6% in 1992 and 1993, respectively. On the other hand, economist
Audrey Freedman maintains that a significant number of workers will
continue to be hired on an as-needed basis (Lawlor 1994).

As with part-timers, a substantial portion of temporaries do this kind
of work involuntarily. Parker (1994) concludes, on the basis of his interviews with temps, that although some workers choose temporary schedules, most temporary workers would prefer full-time, permanent employment. This is consistent with Golden and Appelbaum's (1992) analysis,
which found that the increase in temporaries during the 1980s was almost
totally driven by demand-side factors such as the volatility in labor demand, intensified price competition, employers' desire to cut payroll costs,

and labor's declining bargaining power. As with part-time work, temporary work is a form of underemployment, and temps earn relatively lower wages and receive fewer fringe benefits than full-time workers.

### Subcontracting

Subcontracting refers to a variety of often diverse arrangements in which an employing organization pays a non-employee or another organization for a needed product or service. Subcontracting relations take many forms, including independent contractors, third party producers, consultants, and those leased or hired on a special project basis. For example, employee leasing firms contract to provide a specified number and type of worker to the client employer for a specified time period, handling all hiring, firing, payroll, and personnel issues for the client.

Extant data do not permit reliable estimates of how many workers in the U.S. labor force are involved in various types of subcontracting relationships. A Bureau of Labor Statistics survey of selected manufacturing companies between 1979 and 1986 (cited in Parker 1994, p. 60) showed that a majority used some sort of subcontracting arrangement. A study of 442 firms by the Bureau of National Affairs found that 13% increased their use of temporary workers and outside contractors for administrative and business support contracts and production subcontracting (Abraham 1988). There are also indications that the number of subcontracting arrangements may be rising. For example, employment in the business service sector increased 87.3% from 1980 to 1991 (from 3.3 million workers to 6.18 million) (Parker 1994). Another indicator is the growth of self-employed persons (from 8.5 million in 1980 to 10.3 million in 1991, a 21.2% increase—see Belous 1989), especially the increase in independent contractors.

# U.S. Work Organizations' Use of Contingent Employment Relations

## What We Can Learn About Contingent Employment From Surveys of Organizations

Most of what we know about contingent work comes from surveys of *individual* labor force members. Surveys of individuals ask them about their part-time, temporary, and contractual employment experiences. This information makes it possible to examine important issues such as what kinds of people (e.g., men as opposed to women, young as opposed to old, black vs. white, low education vs. high education) experience these kinds of contingent work arrangements and in what occupations and industries they work. A particularly valuable and useful survey of individuals is the February 1995 Current Population Survey, which included a supplement on contingent work. This survey provides the best information to date on the distribution of types of contingent work in the U.S. labor force.

Official statistics about part-time work based on surveys of individuals may be misleading in that they count part-time workers, not jobs. There were more part-time jobs than part-timers in the early 1990s, as a record number of people held multiple part-time jobs.

Another limitation of surveys of individuals is that they do not enable us to understand the kinds of *organizations* in which contingent employment occurs. Data on diverse organizations are needed to address many important questions related to contingent employment. For example, to what extent are U.S. companies increasingly hiring temporary, fixed-term, task-specific, or part-time labor to perform jobs once held by regular, full-time, career-ladder employees? Is contingent work replacing the "traditional" model or do contingent and noncontingent work coexist in the same workplace? These questions cannot be settled using labor force surveys of individuals in that they require (ideally, longitudinal) information on workplace organization structures.

Unfortunately, there is little extant information on how contingent workers are used by different types of organizations. An exception is the national Conference Board survey of contingent labor in 521 of the largest U.S. corporations (see Christensen 1989). This study, however, focused on large organizations, ignoring the small and medium-sized organizations that constitute the bulk of workplaces in the United States. Most organization studies of contingent work, such as those of subcontracting in the U.S., have generally been based on single corporations or industries, making it difficult to generalize to the economy as a whole (see Aldrich and Staber 1988).

The National Organizations Study contains data that allow us to examine, in a limited way, the use of contingent employment by U.S. work organizations. We first discuss the extent to which each type of contingent employment is used, singly and in various combinations, by the NOS organizations. We then suggest some elements of a theory of the organization of contingent employment and present descriptive data on how the use

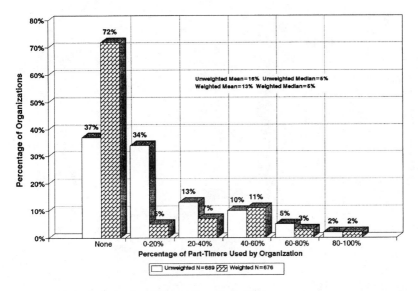

**Figure 13.1.** Organizations' Use of Part-Time Workers

of part-time and temporary employment or subcontracting covaries with key organizational characteristics.

**Part-Time Work**

Figure 13.1 shows how the use of part-time workers is distributed across the NOS organizations. The NOS data do not enable us to distinguish between different types of part-time jobs or between persons who work part-time voluntarily and those who do so involuntarily. Almost two thirds of the NOS organizations use part-time workers,[3] as compared with 90% of the large organizations in the Conference Board study who used part-timers (Christensen 1991). The mean percentage of the NOS organizations' workforces that works part-time is 16% (unweighted; 13% weighted) and the median is 5% (both weighted and unweighted).

**Temporary Work**

Figure 13.2 indicates that about 15% of the organizations in the NOS sample use temporary workers for either the core occupation, the GSS occupation, or for managers. (The weighted percentage of organizations

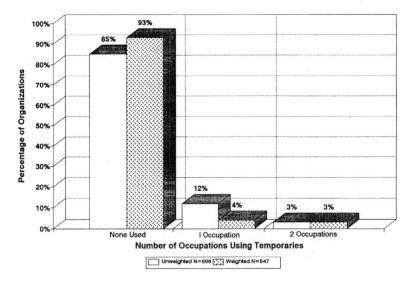

**Figure 13.2.** Organizations' Use of Temporary Workers

using temporaries is 7% since larger establishments are more likely to use temporaries—see Table 13.1). The tendency for larger organizations to use temporaries is suggested by the results of the Conference Board study of large companies, which found that 97% used temporary agency hires; another 49% used internal temporary pools (Christensen 1991). Of the organizations that use temporaries, 80% do so for one occupation, whereas the remaining 20% use them for two or more occupations.

The occupations in which temporaries were most often employed were nursing aides, orderlies, and attendants (in 8 organizations); registered nurses (in 7 organizations); elementary school teachers (in 7 organizations); and bus drivers, cashiers, data entry keyers, and secondary school teachers (3 organizations each).

**Subcontracting**

The NOS data tell us whether an organization subcontracts out the activity(ies) associated with the GSS and core occupations. The measure of subcontracting is based on the following question:

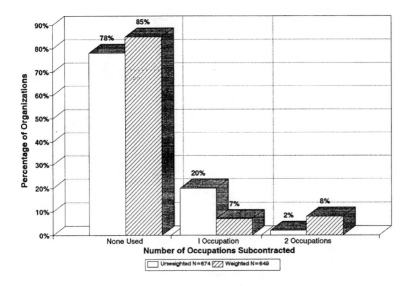

**Figure 13.3.** Organizations' Use of Subcontractors

> Is any of the work of (GSS occupation or core occupation) done by subcontracting, that is, performed by people not regularly on the organization's payroll? (Yes, No)

These data do not allow us to distinguish among types of subcontracting relations or to assess the total amount of subcontracting with which the organization is involved. Figure 13.3 indicates that 22% of the NOS organizations (unweighted; 15%, weighted) subcontract either the work of the core occupation, the GSS occupation, or both. This figure is considerably lower than that reported by the Conference Board study of large companies, which found that 78% of the organizations responding used independent contractors, defined as individuals working under limited-term contracts (Christensen 1991). Almost all of these organizations (20% unweighted) subcontract out only one occupation, not two. The pattern of occupational variation in subcontracting within organizations is similar to that for temporaries: Almost all (91%) of the organizations that subcontracted out the work of either the GSS or the core occupation did so for one of them, but not both.

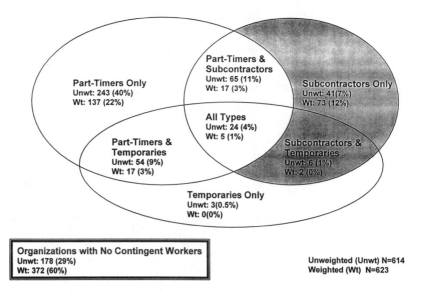

**Figure 13.4.** Organizations' Use of Contingent Workers

The occupational activities most often subcontracted were registered nurses, secretaries, and managers, n.e.c. (9 organizations each); elementary school teachers (8 organizations); social workers and nursing aides, orderlies, and attendants (5 organizations each); and secondary school teachers (4 organizations).

**Relations Among Types of Contingent Work**

The NOS data also allow us to assess the extent to which organizations use various combinations of these employment relations. This begins to address the question of whether there are contingent work "systems" or clusters in organizations in their human resource management practices. One can only estimate this with organizational data such as the NOS: Surveys of individuals can only (at best) tell us if a person is a contingency worker, not the patterns of contingent work present in his or her organization.

An overview of the overlap between types of contingent work is presented in Figure 13.4. Of the 614 organizations in the NOS for which we had complete data on all three types, 178 (29%) do not use any type of contingent work.[4] About 40% of the NOS organizations use part-timers alone (weighted, 22%), 7% (weighted, 12%) use subcontracting alone, but less than 1% (only three organizations) use temporaries alone as the sole contingent work strategy (percentages in Figure 13.4 do not add to 100% due to rounding).

The most common patterns of use of multiple contingent employment relations are to combine part-time and subcontracting (11% unweighted; 3% weighted), and part-time and temporary workers (9% unweighted; 3% weighted). Twenty-four organizations (4% of the NOS organizations, unweighted; 1%, weighted) use all three types of contingent work.[5]

## Organizational and Occupational Correlates of Contingent Employment Relations

The NOS data also permit us to examine how the three kinds of contingent employment relations are associated with particular organizational structures and social processes. Four theoretically important sets of correlates of contingent work are (a) an organization's context, (b) the organization's structure, (c) its gender composition, and (d) its occupational structure. (See Chapter 3 for a discussion of these measures.)

Table 13.1 shows how these explanatory variables are associated with each of the three types of contingent work. In the columns of this table, we present, respectively, (a) the number of NOS organizations in a particular category of an explanatory variable, (b) the percentage using contingent work of any kind, (c) the percentage using any part-time workers, (d) the percentage of part-timers in the organization's workforce, (e) the percentage using any temporary workers, (f) the percentage of the organization's workforce that is temporary, and (g) the percentage using any subcontractors.

### Organization Context

By the *context* of organizations, we refer to structures external to organizations that constitute part of their institutional and political-economic environments. These include product market (e.g., differences by manufacturing vs. service or whether the organization is unionized) and labor market (e.g., supply and demand of various occupations) characteristics. Also included are the organization's size and auspices (whether it is a profit-oriented, nonprofit, or government organization).

**Table 13.1** Correlates of Contingent Employment Relations

| Correlate | Number of Establish- ments | Percentage Using Contingent Work | Part-Time % Using Any | Part-Time Mean % of PT Employees | Temporary % Using Any | Temporary Mean % of Temp Employees | Subcontract % Using Any |
|---|---|---|---|---|---|---|---|
| Goods versus service | | | | | | | |
| Product | 99 | 56 | 38 | 3 | 7 | .5 | 21 |
| Service | 524 | 76 | 67 | 18 | 16 | 2.4 | 22 |
| Both | 65 | 85 | 76 | 24 | 7 | .6 | 26 |
| Organizational auspices | | | | | | | |
| Profit | 452 | 69 | 57 | 17 | 9 | 1.8 | 20 |
| Government | 91 | 74 | 64 | 9 | 10 | 1.6 | 17 |
| Nonprofit | 145 | 90 | 83 | 18 | 31 | 2.8 | 33 |
| Union pressure | | | | | | | |
| Low | 425 | 73 | 62 | 19 | 12 | 2.0 | 21 |
| High | 263 | 76 | 66 | 13 | 18 | 1.9 | 26 |
| Number of full-time employees | | | | | | | |
| ≤ 10 | 196 | 66 | 51 | 25 | 7 | 3.1 | 17 |
| 11-50 | 153 | 73 | 64 | 18 | 12 | 1.5 | 21 |
| 51-250 | 163 | 79 | 69 | 13 | 16 | 1.9 | 22 |
| ≥ 251 | 176 | 80 | 72 | 10 | 21 | 1.2 | 30 |
| Labor shortage | | | | | | | |
| No problem | 272 | 71 | 57 | 17 | 10 | 1.5 | 19 |
| Minor problem | 272 | 79 | 71 | 16 | 16 | 2.4 | 26 |
| Major problem | 110 | 81 | 75 | 20 | 23 | 2.7 | 29 |
| Departmentalization | | | | | | | |
| Low | 290 | 64 | 52 | 20 | 9 | 2.2 | 16 |
| High | 389 | 81 | 72 | 14 | 18 | 1.8 | 27 |
| Occupation prestige | | | | | | | |
| ≤ 32 | 178 | 76 | — | — | 9 | 1.4 | 17 |
| 33-43 | 179 | 67 | — | — | 15 | 2.7 | 17 |
| 44-58 | 152 | 63 | — | — | 8 | 1.1 | 20 |
| ≥ 59 | 166 | 89 | — | — | 24 | 2.5 | 35 |
| Percentage female | | | | | | | |
| ≤ 25 | 201 | 64 | 48 | 13 | 9 | 1.6 | 21 |
| 26-50 | 157 | 76 | 68 | 17 | 13 | 1.4 | 23 |
| 51-75 | 140 | 79 | 73 | 16 | 17 | 1.9 | 21 |
| ≥ 76 | 165 | 78 | 69 | 21 | 21 | 3.4 | 24 |

## Goods Versus Services

The service sector has a relatively high proportion of part-time and temporary jobs. Belous (1989, p. 22) estimates that service industries employ 40.5% of all part-time workers (retail trades employ an additional 27.5%). Mangum, Mayall, and Nelson (1985) found that the use of temporaries in the United States was more common in firms that were exposed to fluctuating product demand. The timing of service provision varies, often considerably, and it is necessary to fill peak hours. Moreover, the shift from manufacturing to services in the United States has been accompanied by a rise in the number of contingent work positions (Olmsted and Smith 1989). Parker (1994, p. 6) reports that the percentage of part-time workers within the service sector increased from 17.8% in 1979 to 31.1% in the mid-1980s. The shift within service industries to low-wage, low-skill jobs has also led to the increased use of part-time workers (Tilly 1990). Indeed, the growth of part-time employment during the 1980s was due primarily to the expansion of those industries (services and retail trade) that tend to employ part-timers; by contrast, the increase in part-time employment between the 1950s and 1970s was due largely to employers substituting part-time for full-time workers (Appelbaum 1992). Moreover, the growth of the service sector—especially the expansion of the business services industry—has also stimulated the growth of subcontracting (Parker 1994).

Table 13.1 shows how NOS organizations' use of contingent workers differs among industries that produce goods, provide services, or do both. Goods-producing industries are less likely to use part-time workers than those that either provide services or provide both products and services (the workforces of the latter group have the highest percentage of part-timers). Service-providers are also more likely to use temporaries than goods-producers. There appears to be no difference between service-providers and goods-producers in the extent to which they subcontract out work.

*Organizational Auspices*

Profit-oriented companies, government agencies, and nonprofit concerns are likely to be subjected to different kinds of institutional and other environmental pressures, and so they might be expected to use contingent workers differently. Public sector organizations have traditionally used subcontractors, in part due to the belief that subcontractors facing a profit motive will be more efficient than government employees (Donovan and Orr 1982). Parker (1994) relates how Donald Levine, director of the Office of Personnel Management, issued a directive in 1985 that gave federal agencies broad new authority to hire and retain temporary workers without going through the competitive selection process required for permanent civil service appointments. Not surprisingly, temporary workers are being used in large numbers in the public sector. The federal government employs about 300,000 temporary workers, usually working under 3-month to 6-month contracts that are automatically renewed if not canceled.

Table 13.1, however, provides no support for the hypothesis that government organizations are more likely to use contingent employment. In this sample, nonprofits are generally the type of organizations that appear to be most likely to use contingent workers, whereas profit-oriented organizations are least likely to do so. Nonprofits are most likely—and profit-oriented organizations the least likely—to use part-time workers, though government agencies have the smallest proportion of part-timers in their workforces. Nonprofit organizations are by far the most likely to use temporaries (and to have the highest proportion of temporaries in their workforces) and to subcontract out work.

*Unions*

Unions are generally assumed to be opposed to part-time and temporary work, as well as to subcontracting, because these forms of externalization help employers reduce their reliance on union workers and otherwise divide the labor force. Unions have begun, however, to realize that it is a mistake to leave part-time and other contingent workers outside the scope of collective bargaining, and they have begun to organize them and to fight for their pay and working conditions. Appelbaum and Gregory (1988) report that unions with high proportions of women and those based in public and private sector service industries (e.g., the UFCW—United Food and Commercial Workers; SEIU—Service Employees International Union) have had some success in organizing part-time and temporary workers and giving them some say over their conditions of work. Nevertheless, it is difficult for unions to organize such workers in view of their limited attachment to particular employers. This is one reason why employers may use more contingent workers in the presence of unionization. Unions have sought to limit subcontracting by bargaining for the reporting of subcontracting relations and the specification of activities that can be contracted.

Research has shown that part-time workers in the United States are about one third as likely as full-timers to belong to labor unions (Tilly 1990). Moreover, Callaghan and Hartmann (1991) report that few part-time workers and virtually no temporary or contract employees are represented by labor unions. Concern over the replacement of union workers with less costly nonunion workers hired through subcontracts has led to repeated legal action regarding what types of work may and may not be contracted out. The resulting rulings suggest that employers who seek to subcontract work already done by union employees must show that they have consulted with the union about the decision and that the subcontracting decision is an economic one not designed to weaken the union (Bureau of National Affairs 1986). The political and economic weaknesses of unions in the United States have made it difficult for them to exert much influence on employers' abilities to externalize work, however; this tempers our confidence in hypotheses about unions and contingent work.

We divided our measure of union pressure (see Chapter 3) at the median (i.e., 1) to form a dichotomous measure of the likelihood that the organization is (= 1) or is not (= 0) unionized. Table 13.1 indicates that there is virtually no difference between organizations subject to different amounts of union pressure in the use of contingent workers. Organizations facing greater union pressure are slightly more likely to use part-time workers, but their workforces consist of slightly fewer part-timers. More highly unionized organizations are also more likely to use temporaries and to subcontract out work. These results are not consistent with expectations that unionized organizations are less likely to use contingent work. At the same time, they do suggest that expanded use of contingent workers is part of an employer strategy to avoid constraints posed by organized labor.

## Establishment Size

Mangum, Mayall, and Nelson (1985) found that large firms relied more heavily on temporary workers than small and medium-sized firms. One reason for this might be that larger organizations have a harder time firing people and adjusting their hiring practices to changing conditions.

Our measure of organization size in Table 13.1 is based on the number of full-time persons employed by the establishment.[6] After dividing the sample into four size categories (1-10, 11-50, 51-250, and 251+), we found that two thirds of the smallest establishments use some kind of contingent work, compared to about 80% of establishments in the two largest categories. The largest organizations (those with 251 or more full-time employees) are most likely to use part-timers, temporaries, and to subcontract out work, whereas the smallest establishments (those with ten or less full-time employees) are least likely to use each of these three kinds of contingent work. The smallest establishments, however, had the highest *proportion* of part-time and temporary workers. The relationships between size and the use of each type of contingent work are generally monotonic.

*Labor Market Supply and Demand*

We might expect organizations that anticipate having difficulty obtaining qualified workers would rely more often on contingent workers—especially subcontracting relations—as a means of buffering themselves against uncertainty. Our measure of labor market conditions is the manager's response to the following question:

> Over the next 3 years, how big a problem will hiring enough qualified workers be for your organization? (Responses are coded 1 = "Not a problem at all," 2 = "A minor problem," and 3 = "A major problem.")

Table 13.1 shows that about 70% of the NOS organizations that do not anticipate having difficulty finding qualified workers in the future report using some kind of contingent work; slightly more (80%) of those who perceive a labor shortage in the future do so. This pattern holds for each type of contingent work, and the relationships between perceptions of different degrees of labor shortage and contingent work are monotonic: The greater the perceived labor shortage problem, the more likely the organization is to use part-timers, temporaries, and to subcontract out work.

**Organization Structure**

*Specialization*

Highly specialized organizations are more likely to use contingent employment relations. Greater specialization may enable an organization to define certain types of work as something to be done by outsiders or by those with marginal attachments. By contrast, organizations with little specialization are less apt to use contingent workers, ceteris paribus.[7]

Our measure of organizational specialization is based on the "departmentalization" scale, which indicates the number of distinct departments the organization has (see Chapter 3). We divided this measure at roughly the median (i.e., the lowest 290 organizations vs. the highest 389).

Table 13.1 indicates that more specialized establishments are indeed more likely to use contingent work. More specialized establishments are more likely to use part-timers and temporaries, though less specialized organizations have higher proportions of these contingent workers in their workforces (which reflects, in part, that less specialized organizations are smaller). Over a quarter (27%) of highly specialized organizations subcontract out work, compared to 16% of organizations that are not very specialized.

## Sex Composition of the Organization's Labor Force

Demographic changes such as the growth in the labor force participation of women—especially working mothers—have made employees more apt to prefer contingent work and have provided a pool of contingency workers from which employers can draw. As we have previously suggested, a reason often given for the widespread use of part-time and temporary workers is that women workers have sought more flexible work schedules. As we also discussed, however, this explanation is probably less important than employer demand for contingent workers (see Tilly 1990, for part-time work; and Golden and Appelbaum 1992, for temporaries). Thus, although there exists a pool of (especially female) contingent workers to be drawn from, there is no evidence that there has been an increase in the pool of part-timers as a share of the labor force. Rather, the number of part-timers has increased because the labor force is now larger.

Our measure of an organization's sex composition is the percentage of full-time women employed in the establishment. We divided this into four groups. Table 13.1 shows that establishments with less than 25% women employees are least likely to use contingent workers (64% of them do) but that there is not much difference between the other three groups (76% to 79% of them do). Less than half of the organizations with less than 25% full-time women employees use part-time workers at all, compared to about 70% of the organizations in the other three categories. Organizations with the lowest proportion of full-time women are also least likely to use temporaries, whereas organizations with the highest proportion of full-time women workers are most likely to do so. There is not much difference in the use of subcontractors in organizations with differing proportions of full-time women (21% to 24%).

**Occupational Structure**

Organizations may use contingent workers for different kinds of occupations. We can examine the links between occupational differences and the use of temporaries and subcontractors (but not part-timers) in that our measures of the former two kinds of contingent work are occupation-specific. We use the occupational prestige score of the respondent's occupation, a commonly used indicator of an occupation's overall "goodness," as our measure of occupational differentiation. This measure is highly correlated with other indicators of occupational structure such as skill, status, income, education, and so on. We divided the occupational prestige scale into four roughly equal parts.

Table 13.1 indicates that the relationship between occupational prestige and use of contingent workers is nonlinear: Occupations with the lowest and (especially) highest prestige are most likely to be used on a contingent basis by employers. Occupations with highest prestige are by far the most likely to be temporaries. This is somewhat at odds with Parker's (1994) argument that temporary occupations are more often unskilled, but it is consistent with our earlier examples of occupations in the NOS sample that were most often used as temporaries, such as registered nurses and teachers. High prestige occupations are also most likely to be subcontracted because these occupations have highly portable skills that can be transferred from one employer to another. This is consistent with Christensen's (1991) finding that large companies typically hired independent contractors for special skills that were not available in the firm. Occupations in the two lowest categories of prestige are least likely to be subcontracted.

## Conclusion

Contingent employment relations are becoming more pervasive in the United States. This chapter has examined NOS organizations' use of three major types of contingent employment relations: part-time employment, temporary work, and subcontracting of occupational activities. We found that over 70% of the organizations in the NOS sample use some form of contingent work. Part-time work is the most common type of contingent employment relation, used by over 60% of the NOS organizations, followed by subcontracting (nearly a quarter) and then temporaries (about

15%). Part-time workers tended to be used together with subcontractors or temporaries. Temporaries were rarely used alone.

The NOS data also allowed us to analyze how these three types of contingent work were associated with important explanatory variables. Establishments that produce a product (as opposed to a service) were less likely to use part-timers, as were profit-oriented companies; smaller, less specialized establishments; organizations that did not anticipate having difficulty hiring qualified workers; and organizations with fewer full-time women. Nonprofit organizations were most likely to use temporaries, as were unionized establishments and those that were relatively specialized. Nonprofit organizations were also most likely to subcontract out work, as were larger, more specialized establishments and those that anticipated future labor shortages.

The growth of contingent employment relations raises important and far-ranging questions about both organizations' management of human resources and their employees' experience of work. From an employer's point of view, contingent work provides some important advantages, such as greater flexibility and lower payroll costs, especially with regard to fringe benefits. Employers may also find it easier to control their work-forces by using contingent workers because they are less likely to unionize and their employment can be easily terminated. Dissatisfaction among permanent workers can also be forestalled by assigning boring and routine jobs to contingency workers.

On the other hand, contingent work brings with it certain disadvantages for employers: Contingency workers have little basis for loyalty to the organization and few reasons to work hard and perform well. The lack of loyalty may translate into sloppy work, making contingent workers very time-intensive to supervise. Getting temporaries or part-timers to show up for work may also require a big time investment for highly paid managers. As a consequence, the use of contingent workers may lower payroll costs, but it may reduce productivity at the same time; the combination of lower payroll and productivity may actually increase per unit labor costs. Thus employers taking the "low road" to cost cutting (by reducing payroll through the use of contingent workers) may not fare as well as those taking the "high road" by increasing productivity by relying on more permanent workers (see Appelbaum and Batt 1994). Employers choosing to rely on contingent workers must cope with the challenge of obtaining loyalty and performance from workers without offering them employment security.

To understand better the organization of contingent employment will require more refined analyses. What is the relation, for example, between the use of contingent workers and more traditional employment relations? Are firms able to use contingent work in tandem with more permanent employment relations by combining an internalized core of permanent, loyal workers, on the one hand, and an externalized periphery of contingent workers, on the other? Some writers have identified such "flexible firms" as archetypes of the modern era (Harrison 1994; Pfeffer 1994), but we know very little empirically about them (Hakim 1990). We also need to examine whether the growth in contingent work is a structural feature of the changing contexts of employment relations or a cyclical response to recessionary business conditions. It is too early to tell in that employers may be reluctant to hire full-time, year-round, permanent workers simply because they still remember the recession of the early 1990s, as well as other contractions (Parker 1994). It remains to be seen whether employers will overcome their reticence and begin again to seek more permanent employees.

From the point of view of individuals in the labor force, contingent work arrangements raise another set of questions. Workers generally do not enter contingent employment relations voluntarily, in that they must cope with employment uncertainty, relatively low wages, few (if any) fringe benefits, low chances for career advancement, low autonomy, and few opportunities to develop and use skills.[8] Harrison (1994) describes the growth in contingent work as the "dark side" of flexible production and claims that it has created a new form of industrial dualism. This has sharpened the division between permanent insiders and contingent outsiders, often within the same firm (see also Smith 1994). A reflection of this dualism is the growing polarization and inequality of earnings between working Americans.

The growth of contingent work also has important implications for the nation. Callaghan and Hartmann (1991) are disturbed by the growth and magnitude of contingent employment because of its negative impacts on the overall economy. Contingent jobs pay poorly, and low wages, therefore, make workers ineffective consumers. Moreover, inequities experienced by contingency workers—such as the lack of workplace protections—may place a burden on the welfare and health care systems. The use of contingent work may also signal problems with productivity and long-term competitiveness; these goals may well be served best by high-wage, low-turnover productivity strategies not the low-wage, high-turnover staffing strategy often associated with contingent work. Various types of contingent employment are almost certain to remain important components of employer-employee relations in the future.

## Notes

1. These three types of employment relations are not always "contingent." For example, some part-timers may have a relatively permanent, ongoing attachment to the employer. In addition, a temporary worker may be permanently employed by a temporary agency. And though some forms of subcontracting may involve contingent employment relations, such as outsourcing or outworking, other subcontracting relationships, such as network relations and alliances between organizations acting as independent contractors, may not. In short, the actual continuity in these types of employment is variable.

2. The size of the contingent labor force can only be approximated in that government statistics are not collected for contingent workers as a group (Appelbaum 1992; Callaghan and Hartmann 1991). The existence of overlap among categories also complicates the estimation of the number of contingent workers. For example, Callaghan and Hartmann (1991, p. 7) report a BLS estimate that 40% of temporary workers also work part-time. Subcontracting may also be a form of temporary employment in that leased employees usually have no expectation of permanent employment with the client (Callaghan and Hartmann 1991, p. 6).

3. A smaller percentage of the weighted sample uses part-timers, reflecting that larger organizations (which receive less emphasis when the sample is weighted) use small percentages of such workers (though they use *some* part-time workers more often; see Table 13.1).

4. The weighted percentage—60%—is higher in that smaller organizations are less likely than larger establishments to use contingent employment relations.

5. Of the organizations in which the GSS and core occupation were the same, 75% used neither temps nor subcontracting, 3% used both, and 22% used one but not the other. Of those organizations in which the GSS and core occupations differed, 64% used neither temps nor subcontracting; 6% used both temps and subcontracting in one of the occupations (only 1 organization used both temps and subcontracting for both occupations); and the remaining 30% used either temps or subcontracting, but not both.

6. In discussing size differences in contingent work, it is important to distinguish between firm and establishment size. In particular, service industries are characterized by large firms (K-mart, Wal-Mart, Sears, McDonalds) that have many comparatively small establishments. Large firms may make policies regarding contingent work that are applied to relatively small establishments.

7. Again, it is important to distinguish between firms and establishments. For example, large service firms such as McDonalds may be highly specialized, but have relatively unspecialized, small establishments.

8. Even "retention" part-time workers generally do not receive the same benefits as those granted full-time workers, though their work may include job security and other benefits not available to other part-time workers (Olmsted and Smith 1989, p. 63). Even with this most favorable form of part-time work, benefits are often not the same as those granted full-time workers. They may be prorated to the number of hours worked or to a percentage of the full-time benefits. Recent work legislation has deepened this disparity: The Family and Medical Leave Act excludes employees who work an average of less than 25 hours per week (Holmes et al. 1992, p. 53).

# 14

# Organizational Patterns of Gender Segregation

DONALD TOMASKOVIC-DEVEY
ARNE L. KALLEBERG
PETER V. MARSDEN

It is unusual for men and women to work in the same job in the same workplace. Most men work in jobs that are typically if not entirely filled by other men. Similarly, most women work in jobs with other women. This separation of men and women at work is referred to as gender job segregation. Until the 1970s, it was largely taken for granted that men and women would perform different jobs (Baron 1991; Goldin 1990).

Gender segregation is not a matter of separate but equal employment. Typically female jobs are characterized by low wages, short or absent career ladders, and little in the way of employer-provided training (Reskin

1993; Tomaskovic-Devey 1994). In the United States, women earn only about 70% of male hourly wages (Marini 1989). Recent studies estimate that the vast majority of this gender wage gap is associated with the gender composition of jobs (Petersen and Morgan 1995; Tomaskovic-Devey 1993a).

Gender segregation is becoming an important issue in many workplaces. Past research suggests that gender segregation is the result of both self-selection on the part of employees and sorting decisions made by employers and managers in workplaces (Jacobs 1989b; Reskin 1993; Tomaskovic-Devey 1993b). Because gender discrimination in employment is illegal, gender segregation in the workplace has become an issue of public policy. Employers who discriminate against women in hiring for traditionally male jobs face potential lawsuits from employees, job applicants, and (in extreme cases) from the U.S. Equal Employment Opportunity Commission. Firms that sell goods or services to the U.S. federal government must submit yearly equal employment opportunity plans and show progress toward meeting the goals in those plans, or risk the loss of federal contracts. Because women make up an increasing proportion of the labor force, including the highly skilled labor force, their limited presence in traditionally more attractive male jobs may artificially limit employers' access to talented workers, as well as women's access to better-paid employment.

## Gender Job Segregation in the NOS

Although there has been substantial previous research on U.S. gender segregation in employment, almost all previous studies have either ignored organizations by studying the gender composition of occupations measured across the entire society or examined a small, nonrepresentative set of organizations, as in case studies of sex segregation within individual firms. These studies have led to a series of strong conclusions about gender segregation. First, occupational gender segregation has been high across the century, although some declines have been evident since about 1970 (Jacobs 1989a; King 1992; Reskin 1993). Second, wages fall for both men and women in an occupation as the proportion of females rises; this has been established both in national studies of occupations and in studies of job titles within particular firms (Baron and Newman 1990; Bridges and Nelson 1989; England et al. 1988; Jacobs and Steinberg 1990; Parcel 1989).

Finally, comparisons of national-level and firm-based studies of occupations show that the degree of segregation and the consequences of segregation for earnings are both much higher when measures of segregation are based on samples of job titles within work organizations (Bielby and Baron 1986; Petersen and Morgan 1995; Tomaskovic-Devey 1993b). This is because most gender segregation in employment within organizations arises as a result of the assignment of men and women to different job titles. On the occupational level, it is clear that occupational titles such as secretaries and engineers are highly female and male, respectively. Sex segregation is obscured, however, in other occupations such as assembly line workers or office managers, who may be typically women in one plant or office, but predominantly men in another. Thus it is preferable to have measures of gender job composition within establishments for a general population sample. The NOS is unusual in that it contains establishment-level estimates of gender job composition for as many as three different occupations within each NOS establishment.

We are aware of only three previous studies that have assembled data on the sex composition of jobs within a variety of work establishments (Bielby and Baron 1986; Petersen and Morgan 1995; Tomaskovic-Devey 1993b). None of these was representative of the national population of jobs or organizations. Because the NOS establishments are representative of workplaces in the U.S. economy of 1991, by analyzing them, we are able to generalize with greater confidence than past studies permit.

In measuring gender job segregation, prior studies used *job* titles to identify positions within an organizational division of labor. Bielby and Baron (1986) point out that the use of job titles is particularly important in the study of large bureaucratic organizations, because in these, women's and men's work may be identical in all ways other than the job title (and, often, the wage). The NOS asked for information on the gender composition of up to three target occupations. The first was the detailed occupational title reported by the General Social Survey respondent who identified the establishment that later appeared in the NOS sample. We will refer to these positions as the "GSS job sample." The GSS recorded a sufficiently detailed *occupational* title at the establishment level that measures of segregation based on it are likely to be little different from those based on *job* titles. The GSS jobs are a representative national sample of work positions, drawn with probability proportional to size.

The second sample comprises the core jobs of the NOS establishments. As discussed in Chapter 3, the core job was defined as the "job title for the

**Table 14.1**  Proportion of Jobs in Gender Composition Categories for the Three
NOS Samples

| | *Percentage Female* | | | | | |
|---|---|---|---|---|---|---|
| | *All Male* | *Mostly Male* | *Gender Balanced* | *Mostly Female* | *All Female* | |
| | *0* | *1-29* | *30-70* | *71-99* | *100* | *N* |
| **All Jobs** | | | | | | |
| GSS sample | 30.2 | 13.5 | 19.0 | 14.3 | 23.0 | 636 |
| Core sample | 23.6 | 19.6 | 21.0 | 22.5 | 13.3 | 653 |
| Managerial sample | 26.2 | 23.4 | 30.6 | 5.7 | 14.2 | 650 |
| **Jobs With One Level Only Within Job Title** | | | | | | |
| GSS sample | 32.5 | 7.6 | 16.5 | 11.8 | 28.9 | 371 |
| Core sample | 31.3 | 12.3 | 16.3 | 18.7 | 19.0 | 318 |
| Managerial sample | 45.1 | 3.5 | 19.5 | 2.2 | 28.3 | 223 |
| **All Jobs—weighted[a]** | | | | | | |
| GSS sample | 50.1 | 1.4 | 8.3 | 1.5 | 38.6 | 636 |
| Core sample | 50.2 | 2.2 | 8.9 | 3.5 | 35.2 | 653 |
| Managerial sample | 52.1 | 2.2 | 10.6 | 0.4 | 34.8 | 650 |

a. Cases weighted to reflect the distribution of establishments rather than employment.

employees who are *most directly involved* . . . [with] the main product/service provided." The question eliciting core jobs specifically referred to job titles.

The final sample, which we call the managerial sample, is a bit more diffuse. The NOS question here asked about "managers and other administrators." The sex composition of the managerial sample probably combines that of a variety of more detailed job titles, many of which may be internally sex segregated, at least in large establishments. For this reason, our estimates of gender segregation in the managerial sample are likely to understate actual segregation, particularly in larger workplaces. GSS and core sample estimates of gender segregation should be quite accurate.

Table 14.1 reports the distribution of jobs across five gender composition categories (*all male, mostly male, gender balanced, mostly female* and *all female*) for the three NOS samples of jobs. Following Tomaskovic-Devey (1993b), a gender-balanced job is defined somewhat generously as one that has substantial, but not necessarily total, gender integration. To be counted as "gender balanced" in this chapter, a job must be between 30% and 70% male (or female).

The average job in the GSS sample is composed of 49% women and 51% men. Twenty-three percent of jobs are filled *only* by women and an additional 14% overwhelmingly (i.e., between 71% and 99%) by women. Thus about 37% of jobs are typically female jobs. The numbers are similar for male jobs; 30% of jobs in the GSS sample are all male, whereas an additional 13.5% are mostly (71% to 99%) male. Only 19% of all jobs are gender balanced, even according to the generous criterion used here. Thus, in 1991, most respondents worked in overwhelmingly gender-segregated jobs.

The general patterns for core jobs are similar, although somewhat higher proportions of these jobs are mostly male and mostly female, whereas the proportions in the all male and all female categories are correspondingly smaller. This would seem to imply that the core job in the average establishment is slightly more gender integrated than the average (i.e., GSS) job in the economy. This could, in part, reflect the larger average number of employees in core jobs (a median of 23.5 employees compared to only 8 in the GSS sample). As the total number of persons in a job grows, it becomes increasingly difficult for an employer to hire only men or only women for that job (Reskin and Roos 1990; Tomaskovic-Devey 1993b).

Half of managerial jobs are typically male, and more than a quarter are entirely male. It is also the case that almost a third of these managerial jobs are reported to be gender balanced. As we will see, this initially surprising level of integration primarily reflects the multiple job titles embedded in this managerial sample. Table 14.1 also displays a tendency for managerial work to be done by men in that the average managerial job in a NOS establishment is only 37% female.

The second panel of Table 14.1 looks only at those jobs that have a single level within the job title. These truncated samples cannot have multiple job titles and are more apt to be found in smaller establishments.[1] For all three job samples, estimated gender job segregation is higher when tabulated for single-level jobs. Those core and GSS jobs that have only one level within them are more likely to be all male or all female than the complete samples of core and GSS jobs, respectively. Managerial jobs with only one level are the most gender segregated in the table. Fully 73% of these managerial jobs are either all male (45%) or all female (28%). Very few are mixed (i.e., mostly male or mostly female), but about a fifth are gender balanced. Although we lack the data to tell exactly who occupies these gender-balanced managerial positions, it seems likely that they are in family owned firms managed by a couple or in other establishments in which males and females manage mostly women workers.

The final panel of Table 14.1 looks at the gender composition catego-ries when the data are weighted so that they represent a random sample of

**Table 14.2**   Index of Dissimilarity for GSS, Core, and Managerial Samples, as Well as for Three Comparison Samples

| | Sample Year(s) | General Population[a] | Core Jobs | Managerial Jobs |
|---|---|---|---|---|
| NOS all cases | 1991 | 77.5 | 72.5 | 60.3 |
| NOS single-level cases | 1991 | 80.0 | 78.5 | 81.5 |
| Bielby and Baron (1986)[b] | circa 1970 | 93.4 | Not Available | Not Available |
| Tomaskovic-Devey (1993b)[c] | 1989 | 76.8 | Not Available | 60.0 |
| Petersen and Morgan (1994)[d] | 1974-1983 | 82.0 | Not Available | Not Available |

a. For the NOS, this column reports results for the GSS job sample.
b. Nonrandom, but diverse, sample of California establishments.
c. Random sample of North Carolina jobs.
d. Sixteen industry wage surveys of nonexempt jobs.

organizations rather than the labor force context encountered by workers. The NOS sampled organizations proportional to employment size, and thus larger organizations were more likely to fall into the sample. The final panel treats each organization as equivalent, regardless of its number of employees. The level of gender segregation is much higher when measured across organizations (rather than across jobs). For example, our weighted estimates show that almost 89% of organizations have GSS jobs that are either all male or all female, and only 8.3% have GSS jobs that are gender integrated. The same extreme pattern is evident in the other two samples, with slightly more gender balance and fewer mostly female jobs in the managerial sample. Employment in organizations is overwhelmingly gender segregated. Larger organizations are more likely to include gender-integrated jobs, a theme we will return to shortly.

We have also computed indexes of dissimilarity of job distributions by sex for these samples. Table 14.2 presents these indexes.[2] The index of dissimilarity gives the proportion of women (or men) who would have to switch jobs (as well as, sometimes, employers) to achieve complete gender integration in employment within one of the three NOS job samples. A score of 100 implies complete gender segregation, whereas a score of 0 would mean that men and women are identically distributed across jobs.

The index of dissimilarity levels for the general population (i.e., the GSS job sample) from the NOS are quite similar to levels reported by Petersen and Morgan (1995) and Tomaskovic-Devey (1993b). All three segregation indexes are within a few points of each other. They suggest that about three quarters of women (or men) would have to be in different jobs to achieve complete gender integration. These are very high levels of segregation, although by comparison with the Bielby and Baron (1986) estimate for a diverse set of California firms around 1970, they suggest that there have been some real declines in levels of gender job segregation.

The indexes of dissimilarity for managerial jobs from the Tomaskovic-Devey (1993b) and NOS-All Cases studies are surprising in that although still high, they are substantially lower, at 60, than the segregation estimates for the general population (GSS job sample). This reflects, in part, the greater likelihood of women being excluded from *any* managerial job; this reduces the index of dissimilarity because the marginal distribution of men and women is taken as an equality baseline in computing the index. The index of dissimilarity for NOS managerial jobs with only a single level, however, is much higher; indeed, it is comparable to that for the GSS sample with only one level. This suggests that the lower index of dissimilarity for all managerial jobs reflects job title heterogeneity.

In summary, the data on gender segregation in the NOS suggest that gender segregation in employment within U.S. establishments was very high as recently as 1991. Its estimates of the level of gender segregation are very similar to other contemporary estimates for general populations. The NOS data yield estimates that are superior in many ways to those based on prior studies in that they are based on nationally representative samples of jobs, core jobs within establishments, and managerial employment. Previous estimates have been state-specific (California—Bielby and Baron 1986; North Carolina—Tomaskovic-Devey 1993a), from samples that were nonrandom (Baron and Bielby 1986), or of limited coverage (Petersen and Morgan 1995).

## Separate But Equal?

The existence of gender segregated employment per se would not be as problematic, if it were not so strongly associated with the quality of employment. Past research has made it clear that segregated employment almost always means unequal employment (Reskin 1988; Marini 1989; Reskin 1993; Tomaskovic-Devey 1993a; Petersen and Morgan 1995). Most equal employment opportunity activity is about reducing the inequality consequences of employment segregation. Affirmative action, for example, attempts to ensure that women have access to jobs that have traditionally been held by men (Leonard 1989). Comparable worth law-

**Table 14.3**  Yearly Earnings, Promotion Potential and Gender Composition of Jobs in the NOS

| | All Male | Mostly Male | Gender Balanced | Mostly Female | All Female | N |
|---|---|---|---|---|---|---|
| **Yearly Earnings (mean $)** | | | | | | |
| GSS sample | | | | | | |
| Lowest wage | 21,949 | 23,643 | 19,772 | 16,400 | 15,048 | 450 |
| Most common wage | 27,209 | 33,044 | 26,487 | 20,645 | 18,179 | 549 |
| Highest wage | 31,865 | 53,385 | 42,766 | 26,103 | 22,482 | 448 |
| Core sample | | | | | | |
| Lowest wage | 21,862 | 22,264 | 19,561 | 17,991 | 13,864 | 512 |
| Most common wage | 25,225 | 34,936 | 26,370 | 22,088 | 16,872 | 575 |
| Highest wage | 31,589 | 52,816 | 38,870 | 29,425 | 21,335 | 507 |
| Managerial sample | | | | | | |
| Lowest wage | 32,423 | 31,723 | 27,337 | 23,197 | 23,897 | 447 |
| Most common wage | 37,465 | 46,334 | 37,943 | 34,835 | 25,295 | 551 |
| Highest wage | 54,977 | 97,125 | 74,548 | 60,369 | 38,205 | 441 |
| **Promotion Potential** | | | | | | |
| GSS sample | | | | | | |
| Percentage multiple-level jobs | 34.4 | 66.3 | 47.9 | 50.5 | 24.7 | |
| N | 189 | 86 | 121 | 91 | 146 | |
| Promotion frequency (mean) | 0.69 | 1.43 | 1.07 | 1.31 | 0.75 | |
| N | 190 | 86 | 120 | 89 | 146 | |
| Core sample | | | | | | |
| Percentage multiple-level jobs | 32.5 | 68.8 | 61.3 | 58.5 | 24.9 | |
| N | 151 | 128 | 137 | 147 | 86 | |
| Promotion frequency (mean) | 0.72 | 1.39 | 1.18 | 1.34 | 0.66 | |
| N | 151 | 127 | 136 | 145 | 85 | |
| Managerial sample | | | | | | |
| Percentage multiple-level jobs | 38.9 | 94.7 | 77.9 | 86.5 | 30.4 | |
| N | 167 | 152 | 199 | 37 | 92 | |

NOTE: All relationships in this table are statistically significant below the .05 level.

suits, on the other hand, attempt to raise the lower wages typically female jobs pay when compared to typically male jobs (England 1992).

Table 14.3 displays the earnings differences associated with gender employment segregation. The NOS asked informants to report the highest and lowest wage as well as the most common wage for the GSS job title, for the core job title and for managers and other administrators. We have converted these reports into annual earnings estimates. Table 14.3 presents average high, low, and most common earnings for these three job samples, separately for the five gender composition categories. For all three samples, the general pattern is that people in typically male jobs are paid a great deal more than those in typically female jobs. The only exception to this generalization is that all male jobs receive average wages that are comparable to those for gender-balanced jobs. This reflects the organizational context of all male jobs. As we will see shortly, all male jobs are much more likely to be found in very small establishments. That low wages tend to be paid by smaller establishments is well-known in the literature (e.g., Villemez and Bridges 1988; Chapter 10, this volume).

To get a sense of the degree of wage inequality that arises from gender segregation, it is instructive to compare the average low earnings of mostly male and all female jobs. In the GSS job sample, the average low earnings for mostly male jobs is $23,643, $1,161 more than the average *high* salary for all female jobs. The numbers are similar for jobs in the core sample. Only in managerial jobs is the low value for mostly male jobs actually lower than the high value for all female jobs. For all comparisons—low, average, and high earnings for GSS, core and managerial samples— earnings rise as jobs become increasingly male. The male job earnings advantage is strongest in the highest wage categories in all cases. Male jobs tend to be paid more and are more likely to be very highly paid.

Another aspect of wage inequality is the degree of dispersion in earnings (see Chapter 11). Figure 14.1 pictures the earnings data from Table 14.3 for the GSS job sample. Not only are male jobs paid more, but the earnings for male jobs cover a much broader range. The truncation of the earnings distribution for female jobs means that there is very little room for earnings growth in typically female jobs.

The second panel of Table 14.3 focuses on access to internal career ladders (see also Chapter 5). Generally speaking, it is gender-integrated jobs that tend to have multiple levels, especially those with many men. In the managerial sample, 94.7% of mostly male jobs have multiple levels. Gender integration is more likely to occur in larger establishments, and jobs in larger establishments have longer job ladders. The chances of multiple levels are about half as great in all male or all female jobs, by comparison to gender-integrated jobs.

For GSS and core jobs, the NOS also asked about the frequency of promotions above the target job. The possible answers were (0) never, (1) not very often, (2) often, or (3) very often. Most jobs have very limited promotion opportunities. The average frequency (scored on this scale) for the GSS sample was only 0.96; for the core job sample it was 1.08. In general, for both core and GSS jobs, these generally low promotion

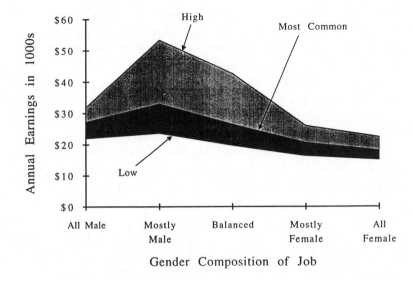

**Figure 14.1.** Average High, Low, and Most Common Earnings for Gender Composition Categories, GSS Jobs

opportunities are nonetheless higher in gender-integrated jobs than they are in all male or all female jobs. These patterns primarily reflect that gender-integrated jobs are found in larger workplaces and completely segregated jobs are found in very small ones (where promotions are rare for everybody). For the average job in the U.S. economy (i.e., that represented by the GSS sample), mostly male jobs have advantages in promotion potential (levels within the job), as well as promotion frequency.

Sex composition is strongly associated with earnings. Typically female jobs are paid less than typically male jobs and have much lower potential career growth in earnings attached to them. Career mobility opportunities are lowest in all male and all female jobs. The increased opportunity for promotion in integrated jobs is largely a reflection of the different types of organizations that tend to include those jobs. It is to this topic that we now turn.

## Organizational Variation in Gender Segregation

Although gender segregation is substantial, it is far from complete. In Table 14.1, we saw that about a fifth of jobs can be thought of as at least roughly gender balanced and that about half have at least some gender integration. This section examines how organizational differences are linked to the likelihood of finding men and women working together in the same job title in the same workplace.

A good place to begin this examination of organizational variation in gender employment segregation is to ask what factors lead to segregation in the first place. In the literature, there are three basic explanations. The first focuses on the labor supply behavior of job applicants. If, because of socialization, family responsibilities, or varying sources of information in personal networks, women and men apply for different jobs, gender segregation results (Polachek 1979; Becker 1981; Marini and Brinton 1984; Jacobs 1989b). The second set of explanations focuses on actions of employers. They may allocate men and women into sex-typical jobs because of traditional gender stereotypes (Milkman 1987; Reskin and Padavic 1988); as the consequence of a taste for discrimination (Becker 1971); because of suspicions that women will be less productive (Phelps 1972; Arrow 1973; Bielby and Baron 1986); or as an outcome of collusion with male workers (Hartmann 1976). They may also use recruitment methods that tend to attract applicants of one sex or the other. Actions by other employees are a third source of gender segregation: Male employees may attempt to maintain their advantages by monopolizing privileged positions in workplaces (Cohn 1985; Milkman 1987; Reskin 1988; Cockburn 1991; Tomaskovic-Devey 1993b).

There are, then, numerous social forces with the potential to produce gender-segregated employment in organizations. Some societal forces that may reduce gender segregation are equal employment opportunity laws and cultural changes in gender stereotypes that have accompanied the women's movement. The reduction in gender segregation between 1970 and 1990 reported in Table 14.2 reflects these global changes (see also Jacobs 1989a; King 1992).

We do not have direct evidence available in the NOS about the relative utility of these three general accounts of the creation of gender-segregated employment. In previous research, one of us has concluded that the preponderance of evidence in past research points toward employers, managers, and coworkers as the primary agents behind widespread gender segregation (Tomaskovic-Devey 1993b). We do have reason to suspect, however, that employers and coworkers can be constrained from discrimination and gender segregation by organizational structure.

There is considerable theoretical reason to believe that organizational processes may encourage or discourage the degree of gender segregation.

In this section, we examine how organizational structure, market sector and competition, and overall establishment employment patterns affect the degree of gender segregation in the NOS workplaces.

### Organizational Structure

Organizations vary tremendously in how they coordinate their work processes as observed in Chapter 4. All organizations must create a division of labor; a set of rights and responsibilities for participants; and a method of coordinating tasks and the flow of information, personnel, and materials. Small and young organizations often accomplish these tasks in incremental steps. As a problem arises, an owner figures out a solution. If organizations grow in size, they often must institutionalize more formal bureaucratic modes of organizing activities. The general process of bureaucratization typically involves both formalization and specialization. The predicted effects of these modes of coordination on gender segregation, however, are quite different.

The first structural aspect of bureaucratization—formalization—may produce less gender segregation. Because we know that there are many social forces operating through labor supply, gender stereotypes employers hold, and defense of privileged access to good jobs by male workers, it seems reasonable to expect that establishments lacking any formalization of work roles would tend to have very high gender segregation. Employment relations that rely on traditional assumptions and unmonitored interaction patterns may be more likely to permit discriminatory workplace practices. On the other hand, when formal rules make line managers accountable to both employees and upper management, exclusionary practices may become less common. When the employment relation is characterized by formal job descriptions (including explicit listings of required credentials and experience) where employees are seen as having rights as well as duties (often through an employee handbook or union contract), and when job openings are formally advertised or posted, exclusions on the basis of sex or race may occur less often. Sutton et al. (1994) suggest that one outcome of formalization may also be grievance procedures that ensure due process and enhance the legitimacy of decision making in the firm. Presumably this includes the tendency to allocate people to jobs based on competencies rather than gender. (See Bridges and Villemez, 1994, for a study of organizational and race and gender differences in bureaucratic employment institutions, as well as due-process practices.)

Szafran (1982), reviewing a literature that consists largely of case studies, concludes that job segregation declines with increases in the formalization of the employer-employee relationship. Both gender segregation and gender wage inequality decline as the degree of formalization of employment relations increases in workplaces (Anderson and Tomaskovic-Devey 1995; Tomaskovic-Devey 1993a). Similarly, Gottfried (1992) suggests that formalization of hiring rules might reduce gender-based job discrimination in the skilled trades by increasing the prospect that women may attain unionized jobs.

In an interesting study that supports these ideas, McIlwee and Robinson (1992) compared the career mobility of women engineers in two establishments. The first, an aerospace firm dependent on government contracts, had a high level of formalization in decision making. The second one, an innovative computer firm, was controlled by technically oriented engineers. Although the aerospace firm was populated by traditionally sexist older male engineers and the computer firm by younger, more gender-flexible, male engineers, women engineers had much better careers in the aerospace firm. McIlwee and Robinson concluded that the formal rules and procedures in the aerospace firm imposed due process, reduced gender discrimination, and led to a management-dominated work culture. The informal innovative computer firm was dominated by a very competitive engineering work culture. Formalization of the employment relationship protected the women engineers from their male coworkers and the masculine engineering culture in the aerospace firm.

Table 14.4 provides data on the relationship between the formalization of the employment relationship and gender segregation. In the NOS, a series of questions asked about the presence or absence of specific documents dealing with personnel matters (see Chapter 4). These included written job descriptions, performance records, personnel evaluation procedures, and so forth. The answers to seven items were combined into a scale that measures the overall employment formalization in the establishment. Low scores mean the establishment has few rules and regulations governing employment relationships (see Chapter 4). Immediately apparent from Table 14.4 is that the establishments in which completely gender-segregated jobs are situated have much lower formalization. This is true across all three samples of jobs. It is also the case (reported in Appendix Table 14.1) that establishments with more formalized employment relations employ a higher percentage of women workers overall. This is consistent with the findings reported by Bridges and Villemez (1994) for "bureaucratic control" indicators in a sample of jobs in the Chicago metropolitan area.

**Table 14.4** Organizational Structure and Gender Composition of Jobs in the NOS

| | All Male | Mostly Male | Gender Balanced | Mostly Female | All Female | N |
|---|---|---|---|---|---|---|
| Mean Formalization | | | | | | |
| GSS sample | .59 | .91 | .76 | .91 | .63 | 633 |
| Core sample | .53 | .87 | .78 | .88 | .51 | 653 |
| Managerial sample | .56 | .89 | .81 | .88 | .55 | 650 |
| Mean Departmentalization | | | | | | |
| GSS sample | .18 | .46 | .27 | .35 | .16 | 627 |
| Core sample | .12 | .42 | .26 | .35 | .11 | 647 |
| Managerial sample | .07 | .48 | .33 | .40 | .07 | 643 |
| Mean Establishment Employment Size | | | | | | |
| GSS sample | 474 | 1152 | 889 | 694 | 165 | 627 |
| Core sample | 67 | 1147 | 718 | 788 | 32 | 743 |
| Managerial sample | 40 | 1455 | 725 | 776 | 38 | 640 |
| Percentage Distribution Within Establishment Size Categories | | | | | | |
| General social survey sample | | | | | | 627 |
| Under 20 employees | 47.2 | 3.3 | 11.3 | 1.4 | 36.8 | 212 |
| 20 to 100 employees | 27.8 | 11.1 | 24.7 | 19.1 | 17.3 | 162 |
| Over 100 employees | 18.6 | 23.3 | 21.7 | 21.3 | 15.0 | 259 |
| Core sample | | | | | | 643 |
| Under 20 employees | 46.3 | 4.1 | 12.8 | 6.4 | 30.3 | 218 |
| 20 to 100 employees | 17.5 | 19.9 | 27.7 | 27.1 | 7.8 | 166 |
| Over 100 employees | 8.5 | 32.4 | 23.2 | 33.2 | 2.7 | 259 |
| Managerial sample | | | | | | 640 |
| Under 20 employees | 46.6 | 4.4 | 18.4 | .5 | 30.1 | 206 |
| 20 to 100 employees | 31.9 | 12.7 | 35.5 | 6.6 | 13.3 | 166 |
| Over 100 employees | 7.1 | 44.4 | 37.3 | 9.0 | 2.2 | 268 |

NOTE: All relationships in this table are statistically significant below the .05 level.

A second argument about the process of bureaucratization leads in the opposite direction. It holds that the specialization of tasks implied by bureaucratization leads to both the opportunity for segregation and an enhanced motive for strong exclusionary practices (Bielby and Baron 1984; Cockburn 1988). Opportunities for sex segregation increase with bureaucratization due to rank differentiation, skill specialization for relatively unique jobs, and deskilling and fragmentation of mass production jobs. Establishments that have increased departmentalization may be developing a division of labor that enhances the opportunity to proliferate job titles and facilitates gender segregation (Baron and Bielby 1986).

The second panel of Table 14.4 summarizes the relationship between a measure of departmentalization of the establishment and gender segregation.

The departmentalization scale measures the number of specific functional tasks (e.g., personnel, finance, marketing) in the establishment that are placed in formally distinct departments (see Chapter 4). Most establishments have no separate departments, but a few large ones have many. The pattern here is not so clear-cut. In completely gender-segregated jobs we find the lowest level of departmentalization, reflecting the tendency of the jobs to be in very small establishments. For gender-integrated jobs, the pattern conforms to expectations. That is, gender-balanced jobs tend to be found in establishments with lower levels of departmentalization than do mostly male and mostly female jobs. In the multivariate analysis reported later in this chapter, however, we find that departmentalization is not a statistically significant source of gender segregation, net of other predictors.

We have already suggested that small establishments would be highly gender segregated because of their exposure to general societal tendencies toward gender stereotyping and discrimination. Bielby and Baron (1984, 1985) found that smaller (10 to 20 employees) and larger (over 100 employees) establishments had higher levels of gender segregation than medium (21 to 99 employees) sized establishments. They later argued (1986) that as task differentiation increases, the degree of segregation increases as well, because it becomes easier to proliferate job titles and socially isolate women and men in different jobs. When small establishments begin to grow, they need to hire more people, some of whom will be women. Segregation will decline not only at the establishment level but also at the job level because there is still a low level of differentiation and bureaucratization. As firms continue to grow, they acquire the administrative capacity associated with new divisions of labor and bureaucratization, and this yields the capacity to link social distinctions to job titles. Bielby and Baron's (1985) argument is that bureaucratization enhances an organization's ability to re-create divisions of labor that conform to societal expectations, male employee preferences, or employer tastes for discrimination. Baron and Bielby, however, had no direct measures of these divisions of labor but based their argument on the findings about establishment size previously discussed.

There is also a simple structural explanation for the higher level of segregation in small firms. In small firms, the average job has fewer incumbents. All jobs with only a *single* incumbent must be, of course, totally segregated. Jobs with two incumbents could easily end up all female or all male, even if there were no deliberate gender segregation process. In general, as job size increases, the probability of segregation under a random baseline model of allocating persons to positions decreases (Mayhew and

Schollaert 1981). Thus we can expect segregation tendencies to be particularly high in the smallest firms as a result of job size alone.

The bottom two panels of Table 14.4 display the relationship between establishment size and gender segregation. The expectation that small establishments are more likely to include gender-segregated jobs is strongly supported. All male and all female jobs tend to be found in small establishments. Fully 84% of jobs in establishments with 20 or fewer employees are completely gender segregated in the GSS job sample. The comparable figures for the core and managerial job samples are both 77%. It is clearly the case that gender segregation tends to occur in smaller establishments. We cannot tell from the NOS if this is the result of rampant stereotyping or the structural constraint of small average job size. We suspect that both are operating.

What happens when establishments grow? Does increased size lead to lower gender segregation? Based on our cross-sectional data, we conjecture that the answer is yes, up to a point. Larger establishments are less likely to have completely gender-segregated jobs. This is true across all three samples, and is particularly striking for managerial jobs. Of course, the managerial sample includes all managers and administrators in the establishment, rather than a single job title. The largest establishments probably have a division of labor among managers that involves some gender segregation not apparent in Table 14.4.

Among gender-integrated jobs, the pattern is somewhat different. As Bielby and Baron (1984) predicted, gender balance is most likely to be found in establishments with more than 20, but fewer than 100 employees. This conclusion is clear for both the GSS and core samples. The managerial sample, on the other hand, shows a continued increase in the size of the gender-balanced category in the larger establishments. We suspect that this reflects the heterogeneity of the management job category in large establishments rather than genuinely higher gender balance at the job title level. For the managerial sample, as compared with the GSS and core samples, larger establishments have lower proportions of jobs that are mostly female and higher proportions that are mostly male. This suggests that the typical pattern of managerial gender integration in large establishments involves women moving into male jobs rather than men moving into female jobs.

### Competing Market Principles

According to neoclassical economic theory, there should be no gender segregation in a market economy, unless men and women prefer different kinds of work. Competition and profit goals should eliminate gender-based exclusion from good jobs as economically rational employers hire cheaper female labor. Over time, competitive market pressure should erode segregation and, eventually, gender-based inequality (Becker 1971). This leads to the conclusion that only establishments that are isolated from market pressure (i.e., those that operate in oligopolistic or otherwise protected markets) will have the resources to indulge their "tastes for discrimination" for very long (Tolbert 1986). This reasoning predicts that establishments with significant market competition should have lower gender segregation. It also predicts that gender segregation should be higher in the state and nonprofit sectors of the economy, which typically do not have to compete for customers in markets.

Although the market competition hypothesis has a strong theoretical basis in neoclassical economic reasoning, there is not much prior evidence to support it. Gender segregation and gender wage inequality have been found to be lower (Anderson and Tomaskovic-Devey 1995; Tomaskovic-Devey 1993a) in the state sector than in the private sector. Similarly, Pfeffer and Ross (1990), studying gender inequality between university administrators, found higher inequality in private universities than in public ones. Quite a few other studies have found that gender and racial inequality tends to be higher in the private sector than in the public sector (see the review in Pfeffer and Ross 1990). According to the interpretations offered by these researchers, these results contradict the market predictions from neoclassical economics.

The first panel of Table 14.5 presents evidence pertaining to these predictions about gender segregation and market pressures. Is gender segregation higher in the state and nonprofit sectors because of their insulation from market competition? For all three job samples, gender-balanced jobs are instead much more common in the nonprofit sector of the economy. The government and for-profit sectors have a roughly equal incidence of gender-balanced jobs. On the other extreme, for-profit establishments are more apt to have completely gender-segregated jobs (60% in the GSS and 44% in the managerial and core samples) than are either government or nonprofit establishments. Private sector establishments are more likely to be very small, and some of this higher segregation may reflect the structural constraints of small size. Interestingly, government establishments have the lowest proportions of mostly female and all female jobs in each sample; the highest proportion of mostly male jobs is found in the government sector.

**Table 14.5** Sector, Market Competition and Gender Composition of Jobs in the NOS

| | All Male | Mostly Male | Gender Balanced | Mostly Female | All Female | N |
|---|---|---|---|---|---|---|
| Percentage Distributions Within Sectors | | | | | | |
| GSS sample | | | | | | 636 |
| Profit | 36.2 | 13.8 | 16.2 | 10.0 | 23.8 | 420 |
| Government | 32.1 | 24.7 | 19.8 | 7.4 | 16.0 | 81 |
| Nonprofit | 10.4 | 5.9 | 27.4 | 31.9 | 24.4 | 135 |
| Core sample | | | | | | 653 |
| Profit | 29.3 | 19.8 | 18.1 | 17.7 | 15.1 | 430 |
| Government | 23.8 | 41.7 | 17.9 | 11.9 | 4.8 | 84 |
| Nonprofit | 5.8 | 5.8 | 31.7 | 43.9 | 12.9 | 138 |
| Managerial sample | | | | | | 650 |
| Profit | 28.4 | 25.1 | 28.2 | 3.1 | 15.3 | 426 |
| Government | 33.7 | 27.9 | 29.1 | 2.3 | 7.0 | 86 |
| Nonprofit | 14.5 | 15.2 | 39.1 | 15.9 | 15.2 | 138 |
| Market Competition (means) | | | | | | |
| GSS sample | 3.38 | 3.48 | 3.25 | 3.20 | 3.30 | 535 |
| Core sample | 3.36 | 3.46 | 3.23 | 3.31 | 3.22 | 551 |
| Managerial sample | 3.28 | 3.42 | 3.37 | 3.37 | 3.17 | 548 |

NOTE: The relationship between sector and gender composition is statistically significant for all three occupation or job categories. The relationship between market competition and gender composition is not statistically significant for any of the three job samples.

If we assume that before 1970 almost all jobs in all sectors were gender segregated, then contemporary comparisons across sectors may tell us something about the pattern of gender integration since 1970. In government jobs, gender integration seems to mean the entry of women into formerly male jobs rather than men's integration into typically female jobs. In the nonprofit sector, on the other hand, much of the gender integration appears to involve men entering into formerly female jobs.

The second panel of Table 14.5 presents data for an indicator of market competition. The NOS informants were asked how much competition their establishments face in their market and could respond (1) none, (2) very little, (3) a moderate amount, or (4) a great deal. The prediction from the economic model is that increased market competition forces establishments to minimize labor costs and eliminate discriminatory practices. This panel is striking in that market competition is unrelated to the gender composition of jobs for all three job samples. This is the only variable we will look at in this chapter that has no statistically significant relationship with the gender composition of jobs.

It is quite clear from Table 14.5 that the predictions from neoclassical economic theory about the efficiency and discrimination-ameliorating effect of market competition are not borne out for any of the three job samples in the NOS. These predictions have not been supported in other research either. This does not mean that capitalist markets are inefficient in other realms, but it seems that they have little consequence for gender segregation and gender inequality. The finding that the government and (especially) the nonprofit sectors have lower gender segregation than the for-profit private sector probably reflects higher penetration and enforcement of equal employment opportunity initiatives among government units and their contractors in the nonprofit sector.

To our knowledge, the very high degree of gender integration in the nonprofit sector has not been highlighted in previous research. We speculate that this result might be a product of progressive leadership in these organizations, which often have women in powerful decision-making roles. Baron (1991) reports that gender integration can happen more quickly in establishments that employ women in top management positions. It is also the case (reported in Appendix Table 14.1) that nonprofit establishments hire, on average, about 25% more women than do government or for-profit establishments.

**Organizational Demography**

It may also be the case that gender segregation at the job level simply reflects fundamental strategies employers use to minimize the cost of doing business. Some employers, perhaps because of market competition or desires to make high profits or (in the public sector) the wish to minimize tax costs to citizens, may develop labor recruitment strategies that minimize labor costs. Such employers may design divisions of labor that rely heavily on female or part-time workers, precisely because these workers are often paid comparatively low hourly wages. There is some evidence that the size of the female labor force increases in more labor-intensive industries (Bridges 1980, 1982; Wallace and Kalleberg 1981). In that women as a group are typically paid less and are more likely as individuals to choose to work part-time to complement family work activity, gender job segregation may be simply a derivative of the more general cost minimization strategies followed by some employers. Other employers, perhaps those that rely on technological investments to produce high value added for their firms or those dependent on male-dominated professions

**Table 14.6** Organizational Demography and Gender Composition of Jobs in the NOS

| | All Male | Mostly Male | Gender Balanced | Mostly Female | All Female | N |
|---|---|---|---|---|---|---|
| Percentage Female in Establishment (mean) | | | | | | |
| GSS sample | 27.4 | 30.4 | 53.5 | 74.5 | 74.1 | 612 |
| Core sample | 19.8 | 29.9 | 53.9 | 76.9 | 85.8 | 630 |
| Managerial sample | 31.1 | 34.4 | 59.5 | 79.1 | 82.2 | 622 |
| Percentage Part-Time in Establishment (mean) | | | | | | |
| GSS sample | 13.9 | 13.6 | 18.1 | 21.6 | 19.1 | 627 |
| Core sample | 12.9 | 10.3 | 17.2 | 22.4 | 21.5 | 643 |
| Managerial sample | 15.6 | 9.7 | 19.0 | 24.4 | 23.0 | 640 |

NOTE: All relationships in this table are statistically significant below the .05 level.

such as law, craft production, or engineering, may recruit more male and full-time labor forces.

Table 14.6 reports the relationship between the overall proportion of female employees in an establishment and the presence of gender-segregated work. As one would expect, establishments that employ more women have more female jobs and establishments that employ more men have more male jobs. Gender-balanced jobs are found in establishments that average about 54% female (60% for the managerial sample). There is a slight suggestion that gender balance in jobs is more likely to occur in establishments where a majority of all employees are women. This pattern is somewhat more pronounced for the managerial sample. Establishments having labor forces with higher proportions of part-time workers are more likely to hire women and to have more typically female jobs. Although the incidence of male and female jobs is linked to the gender composition of the whole establishment, and to a lesser extent to the proportion of part-time workers, this table does not provide evidence that the degree of gender segregation is strongly tied to either of these aspects of organizational demography.

## A Multivariate Model of Gender Segregation

Since the explanations that we have been examining are to some extent mutually contingent, we explore a multivariate model of the segregation process. The explanations are mutually contingent in that the organizational

**Table 14.7**  Regression Analysis of Job Segregation Index on Organizational Characteristics for the Three NOS Job Samples

| Independent Variables | GSS Job Sample | Core Job Sample | Managerial Job Sample |
|---|---|---|---|
| Levels within job sample | -2.33† | -3.91† | -7.27† |
| Formalization | -1.85 | -4.20† | -3.32* |
| Departmentalization | -1.70 | .18 | -8.68† |
| Establishment size (×1,000) | -.12† | -.10† | -.15 |
| Establishment size$^2$ (×1,000,000) | .03† | .02* | .09 |
| Profit | 3.99† | 4.18† | .63 |
| Government | 2.24 | 4.44† | .84 |
| Market competition | .30 | .22 | -.56 |
| Establishment employment | | | |
| Percentage female | -.01 | -.02 | -.09† |
| Percentage white | .00 | .02 | .01 |
| Percentage part-time | -.04 | -.03 | -.05† |
| Constant | 39.24† | 37.24† | 47.47† |
| $R^2$ | .054 | .070 | .143 |

$*p < .05;$ $†p < .10.$

characteristics we have been examining are in many instances likely to occur together. Large organizations are more likely to be departmentalized and to have higher formalization scores (Chapter 4). Part-time work is more likely to be found in the for-profit sector than in government establishments (Chapter 13). A multivariate analysis allows us to examine the effect of one characteristic (e.g., formalization) on the degree of gender segregation while statistically controlling for the influence of other characteristics.

The three columns of Table 14.7 refer to measures of gender job segregation for the three job samples in the NOS. A measure of job *segregation* is not the same as the gender *composition* measure that appears in the previous tables. Instead, we took the percentage of females in the job, which varies between 0 (all male) and 100 (all female), and subtracted 50. This leaves a measure that varies between −50 and +50, with 0 indicating complete gender balance. We then took the absolute value of that measure; hence negative values become positive whereas positive values are unchanged. A score of 50 thus means that a job is completely gender segregated—either all male or all female. A score of 30 means the job is relatively segregated, either 80% male or 80% female. A score of 10 suggests substantial integration, whereas 0 means complete gender balance. This measure of segregation refers to a single job, rather than a whole sample of jobs. It allows us to examine a single summary measure of segregation, rather than examining each composition category (all male, mostly male, gender balanced, mostly female, or all female) separately.

The rows in Table 14.7 list organizational characteristics that are thought to influence the degree of gender job segregation. The table presents three columns of regression coefficients. Negative coefficients mean that, controlling for the other row variables, a higher score on a variable is associated with less job segregation. A positive coefficient means the variable leads to higher job segregation.

Table 14.7 includes two variables that were not discussed in depth in the previous sections. The first is an indicator variable telling whether (1) or not (0) the target job had more than one level. This variable is used as a control to take into account cases where multiple job titles might have been reported as a single job category in the NOS. As we noted earlier (Table 14.1), this is most likely to apply to the managerial sample. The other new variable is the proportion of minority employees in the establishment. It is also included as a control variable, in case gender segregation and race segregation are alternative strategies that employers use to organize their labor process or minimize labor costs (see the discussion in Cohn 1985).

Table 14.7 presents the estimates of the amount of gender job segregation associated with each of these organizational characteristics, statistically controlling for the other characteristics. As expected, measured segregation is lower when there are multiple job levels. This coefficient is especially large in the managerial sample, where we expect that the problem of measurement error in the segregation index is highest. Using the levels variable as a control limits the extent to which this measurement error contaminates our estimates of other organizational effects on job segregation.

As predicted, formalization is associated with less gender segregation in all three samples. This relationship is statistically significant (at the .05 level) for core jobs and for managerial jobs (.10 level). Because they make up the most central part of the production process for establishments, it is precisely core jobs at which most formalized procedures are targeted.

Departmentalization, unexpectedly, is significantly associated with *lower* segregation among managers. Following Bielby and Baron (1986), we expected that the division of labor associated with departmentalization might increase the capacity of the firm to proliferate job titles and segregate tasks. In that this effect is confined to the managerial sample, it suggests that there is something about departmentalization that creates additional

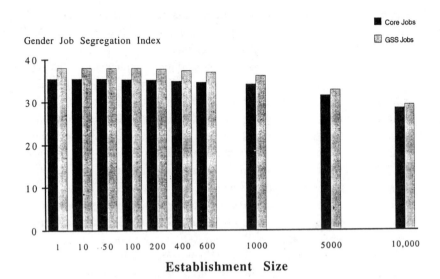

Figure 14.2. Establishment Size and Predicted Gender Job Segregation

opportunities for women to enter managerial jobs. It may be that this represents the creation of specialized office functions such as personnel or marketing that are less gender stereotyped.[3]

The meaning of the effect of size must take into account that we have already controlled for formalization and departmentalization. Because increased size leads to both increased formalization and departmentaliza-tion, the interpretation of any remaining size effects has to do with some aspect of size other than the proliferation of departments or formal employ-ment practices. Size has no effect on managerial segregation over and above its association with departmentalization. For both the GSS and core samples, establishment size has a curvilinear relationship with gender segregation. Figure 14.2 displays that relationship, net of the other vari-ables in Table 14.7, for both the GSS and core samples. Very large establishments have lower gender segregation. Tomaskovic-Devey (1993b) also found that gender segregation declines with larger establishment size. Although there is a general trend for gender segregation to decline as establishments grow, it does not amount to even 1% decline until estab-lishments reach about 1000 employees. This suggests that after we have controlled for the correlates of size in Table 14.7, it is only extremely large establishments that show further declines in gender segregation. Only 14% of establishments in the NOS sample have more than 1,000 employees. Because this sample is weighted proportionate to establishment size, a much smaller percentage of all establishments are this large (see Chapter 3). This large size effect may reflect the visibility of these organizations to both the Equal Employment Opportunity Commission and the Office of Federal Contract Compliance. A complementary explanation might be that these establishments have more developed and professional equal opportunity staffs.

Returning to Table 14.7, we see that for both the GSS and core samples, profit-making establishments have more job segregation than nonprofit establishments. Government establishments are not significantly different from nonprofit workplaces in their degree of gender segregation for the GSS or managerial job samples, but have significantly more gender segregation in their core jobs than do nonprofit concerns. In fact, in core jobs, the degree of gender segregation is slightly higher among governmental employers than it is in the private sector. This suggests that efforts to reduce gender segregation among government employers have been weakest in core production and service activities and stronger in administrative support functions.

Again, we find that reported market competition is unrelated to the degree of job segregation. There is no support for the market competition hypothesis, but substantial suggestion that gender balance is most common in the nonprofit sector for all types of work and in some jobs in government establishments. It may be the case that there is wide variation in the degree of segregation in government jobs, depending on whether they are found in federal, state, or local government establishments.

The gender, race, and part-time employment composition of establishments are unrelated to the degree of gender job segregation in the average (GSS) job. This is also true for the core production jobs in these establishments. Managerial jobs are more likely to be gender integrated when establishments have high proportions of women or part-time employment. Neither of these findings is an unambiguous sign of progress. Women share the managerial stage with men when women and part-time workers constitute the bulk of the work force. Because wages are typically lower for women and part-time workers, these integrated managerial positions may be largely overseeing low-wage, low-benefit jobs. Although this is clearly better than excluding women from all managerial jobs, it seems to represent integration into managerial work in the least desirable form of managerial employment (see Bird 1990; Reskin and Padavic 1994, chap. 5).

The race composition of the establishment is unrelated to the degree of gender job segregation, suggesting that race and gender segregation are not alternative strategies for minimizing labor costs. In fact, the percentage whites is negatively related to percentage of females for the core and managerial job samples (see Appendix Table 14.1). If anything, employers are more likely to hire women and minorities simultaneously rather than as substitutes for one another.

## Conclusion

Gender job segregation in the United States is very high. We have produced the first nationally based estimates of the frequency of gender balanced jobs. Only 19% of jobs can be called gender balanced by our criterion of 30% to 70% male or female. In that establishments in the NOS sample were drawn proportional to employment size (see Chapter 2), the samples of jobs studied here are weighted toward those in larger U.S. establishments. Thus we estimate that 19% of the labor force works in gender-balanced jobs. Most men work in typically male jobs. Most women work in typically female jobs.

As jobs become increasingly female in their composition they afford their incumbents progressively lower earnings and career prospects. Gender segregation is not a case of "separate but equal." Rather, as in U.S. racial segregation, separate is never equal but becomes the basis for the creation of inequality and hierarchy (Reskin 1988).

Gender segregation is not, however, inevitable. Our analyses suggest that personnel policies matter. Establishments with formalized employment practices and those under equal employment enforcement scrutiny have lower gender segregation. Moreover, pressure toward equal employment need not come only from outside regulators. Organizational leadership—the degree of commitment to equal opportunity by top officials—can be an important source of pressure to reduce gender inequality in workplaces (Baron 1991; Cockburn 1991; Tomaskovic-Devey 1993b).

Additional analyses of the organizational production of gender segregation should focus on the roles of employee job search processes and of employer hiring decisions in allocating people to gender-stereotyped jobs.

Future research on the inequality consequences of gender segregation also might fruitfully explore gendered patterns of job training and promotion within organizations. Such research would complement the findings presented here about organizational structures and levels of gender job segregation in the establishments surveyed by the NOS.

## Notes

1. In the unweighted NOS sample, the correlations between establishment size (log) and presence of multiple levels range between .32 (GSS jobs) and .60 (managerial jobs).
2. These indexes compare the distributions of men and women across core, GSS, and managerial jobs in different establishments. The indexes of dissimilarity reported in Tables 2.4 to 2.6 compare distributions of NOS, CPS, and GSS cases across size, occupational, and industrial categories.
3. There is some indication that managerial occupations in areas such as personnel and labor relations or public relations are again becoming sex-typed, but now with predominantly female incumbents (Reskin and Roos 1990; Donato 1990).

## APPENDIX 14.1

**Table 14A.1** Regression Analysis of Percentage Female on Organizational Characteristics for the Three NOS Job Samples (regression coefficients)

|  | GSS Percentage Female | | Core Percentage Female | | Managerial Percentage Female | |
|---|---|---|---|---|---|---|
| Levels within jobs | −6.77* | −4.01† | −2.39† | −.47 | −6.12* | −4.38* |
| Formalization | 9.00* | 3.50 | 6.54† | −.09 | 1.82 | −3.89 |
| Departments | −7.98 | −10.30* | −2.80 | −4.16 | −3.10 | −3.47 |
| Establishment size | −.09 | .02 | .03 | 1.60* | −.70 | .00 |
| Establishment size$^2$ | .01 | −.07 | −.02 | −.03† | .08 | −.00 |
| Profit | −22.61* | −6.20† | −23.89* | −4.28† | −16.89* | −3.88 |
| Government | −28.60* | −4.23 | −38.45* | −8.51* | −23.47* | −3.01 |
| Market competition | −1.26 | −.14 | −1.97 | −.47 | −.33 | .80 |
| Establishment employment |  |  |  |  |  |  |
|   Percentage female |  | .84* |  | 1.00* |  | .66* |
|   Percentage white |  | −.05 |  | −.10* |  | −.07* |
|   Percentage part-time |  | −.03 |  | .07† |  | .10* |
| Constant | 68.70* | 16.80* | 70.75* | 9.11 | 56.61* | 15.07* |
| $R^2$ | .079 | .431 | .106 | .660 | .056 | .373 |

*$p < .05$; †$p < .10$.

# 15

# Gender Differences and Organizational Commitment
## Influences of Work Positions and Family Roles

PETER V. MARSDEN
ARNE L. KALLEBERG
CYNTHIA R. COOK

Organizational commitment (OC) is a key construct for examining the match between individuals and organizations. People who are highly committed to their work organizations are willing to devote more effort to the organization, identify more with the values of the employer, and seek to maintain their affiliation with the organization (Steers 1977). Managers want committed employees because such workers are assumed to have higher levels of effort and performance and lower rates of turnover and absenteeism, with attendant reductions in costs of replacement and training (see Mowday, Porter, and Steers 1982). From a societal point of view, committed workers may contribute to economic growth and high levels of productivity. High commitment may also be desirable from an individual standpoint to the extent that committed workers are better compensated or have better career prospects. There may, however, be negative side effects of high organizational commitment for the individual, such as stress, career stagnation, and family strains (Mowday et al. 1982; Mathieu and Zajac 1990).[1]

The continuing rise in the rate of labor force participation of women (Oppenheimer 1992) has led to concerns that the more extensive family involvements of women might reduce their levels of organizational commitment. Other recent observers (e.g., Koretz 1992; *The Economist* 1992) suggest that economic productivity suffers due to a failure to make full use of the potential of committed women. The questions of whether there are differences between men and women in their levels of organizational commitment—and, if such differences are present, why—thus emerge as important research issues for studies of work and family in the 1990s. We will address these issues in this chapter. Our results demonstrate that overall, there is a weak tendency for men to display higher levels of organizational commitment. This is primarily attributable to the tendency of women to hold jobs with fewer commitment-enhancing features. Differences between men and women in family ties have relatively little to do with gender differences in OC. Indeed, once we statistically adjust for job, family, and career factors, our data indicate, if anything, that there is a tendency for women to display slightly higher organizational commitment.

### Sources of Gender Differences in Commitment

There is no shortage of ideas about why men and women might differ in levels of organizational commitment; Giele (1988), Marini (1988), and Bielby (1992) review major lines of argument. The various arguments, however, do not always lead in the same direction. Our discussion of potential sources of gender differences in OC distinguishes between *job* and *gender* perspectives (others drawing such contrasts include Feldberg and Glenn 1979; Lorence 1987b; Loscocco 1990; de Vaus and McAllister 1991). Job models treat the work people do and the settings they do it in as the principal explanatory factors structuring employment outcomes, whereas gender models emphasize personal characteristics, sex role socialization, and linkages to family situations—especially in explaining employment outcomes for women.

A job perspective would explain gender differences in OC on the basis of the different kinds of jobs that men and women tend to hold. Such a view is appealing because occupational sex segregation is so pervasive, especially at the level of detailed occupations (Bielby and Baron 1986; Reskin and Padavic 1994; Chapter 14, this volume). To the extent that features of jobs and work situations affect OC, such segregation could lead to gender differences in OC.

Much prior theorizing about OC has emphasized job-related and organization-related factors. Lincoln and Kalleberg (1990, pp. 13-16) argue that organizational structures foster commitment or loyalty and attachment in four ways. By facilitating *participation* through, for example, work re-design or sociotechnical systems, employers can provide workers with a sense of control and partnership. Increased feelings of community and pride are encouraged by structures facilitating *integration,* including cultural symbols and rituals or programs that help to nurture collegial social relations. Structures that facilitate *individual mobility and career development,* such as promotion ladders, build commitment by encouraging employees to have a long-term orientation to an organization,[2] whereas those that create *legitimacy* do so by conferring a sense of citizenship on workers. Lincoln and Kalleberg's (1990) empirical analyses of U.S. and Japanese workers support the claim that these features of jobs and organizations are associated with OC, as do results of many other studies (e.g., Mowday et al. 1982; Mathieu and Zajac 1990).

In addition to the design of jobs and work settings, OC may be affected by individual differences in rewards received from work. High earnings and fringe benefits indicate that an employer places high value on an employee, and may be reciprocated by higher commitment levels. Nontransferable fringe benefits such as retirement plans can become "side bets" (Becker 1960) that keep employees from seeking work elsewhere, whereas promotion experiences may encourage them to think of a career within an organization. Gerson (1985) argues that a woman's choice to commit herself to a career in a workplace, rather than to take a domestic pathway, is strongly affected by experiencing either expanding or blocked workplace opportunity in her early years of employment.

There are well-documented gender differences in most of these aspects of jobs that have been found to be associated with OC. Although male and female jobs differ little in occupational prestige, they differ substantially in income and promotion prospects (Giele 1988, p. 301; Reskin and Padavic 1994; Chapter 14, this volume). The jobs held by women tend to have fewer of the commitment-enhancing features mentioned above: Women are less likely to be in supervisory positions, for example (Wolf and Fligstein 1979), and when they are, tend to have a narrower scope of authority than do men (Reskin and Ross 1992). Men are more frequently found in jobs that offer high autonomy, that is, self-direction and freedom from close supervision (e.g., Lincoln and Kalleberg 1990, p. 90). Hence, a job perspective would lead us to expect a zero-order gender difference in OC (with men displaying higher levels) that is explained by adjustments for gender differences in job and career variables.

In discussing gender models, we consider both those arguments that would lead to general differences between men and women in *levels* of OC and those that imply gender-specific differences in the strength with which factors are associated with OC. Gender models are based on a heterogeneous set of factors said to differ between men and women. Among these are family roles and socialization, as well as varying labor market opportunities.

Family affiliations arguably affect commitment in both general and gender-specific ways. It is intuitive to posit that attachments to one collectivity compete with those to another—and, therefore, that persons who have extensive ties to groups other than their employers may have lower levels of OC. This notion is sometimes used to motivate examination of possible conflict between professional and organizational commitments (e.g., Mueller et al. 1992). In this chapter, we treat employers and families as competitors for an individual's loyalty. From this standpoint, extensive family ties—marriage, children—should lower OC for both men and women. To the extent that women are more likely to have such ties, for example, because they are more often single parents, the "competing affiliations" strand of the family ties argument would imply lower commitment levels for women.

The traditional breadwinner-homemaker division of family roles also leads to an expectation that men will exhibit higher commitment levels. This could be either the result of gender socialization practices[3] or of human capital investment decisions by husbands and wives that seek to maximize returns to the family unit (see discussion in Huber 1986). Either way, this leads to the presumption that women are less committed to their organizations than are men and (among other things) that they can be expected to leave their jobs at higher rates than men. Indeed, the practice of "statistical discrimination" is predicated on such gender stereotypes (Bielby and Baron 1986; see also Berger, Rosenholtz, and Zelditch 1980). If this line of reasoning is accurate, any overall gender differences in OC will not vanish after adjustments for male-female differences in features of jobs.

Arguments based on a traditional household division of labor also suggest that family ties may have *different,* gender-specific effects on the commitment of men and women. For example, marriage and children may heighten organizational commitment for men while lowering it for women, if sex roles dictate that men should provide for the family whereas women should maintain and nurture it.

Some gender arguments revolve around claims that men and women have different psychological traits that predispose them toward different levels of commitment. For example, it has been argued that women have more extensive social and affiliative interests than men do (see Giele 1988, p. 311), perhaps as a result of different gender socialization practices. The evidence for such gender differences is, however, at most equivocal (Maccoby and Jacklin 1974; Block 1976).[4] Such differences might lead to higher commitment on the part of women. We are unable to measure psychological traits directly in our study. If such differences exist and are associated with commitment, they are pooled with other unmeasured differences between men and women in the empirical results subsequently presented.

A different consideration suggesting that women will display higher levels of OC focuses on the more limited choices that women face within the labor market. Sources of such limitations include structural barriers to entry into male-dominated occupations and family ties that prevent women from searching for jobs beyond the geographic area in which they reside. In light of these limited alternatives, it is argued that dissonance-reduction processes lead women to place greater value on the positions they hold than would men in comparable circumstances. Kalleberg and Griffin (1978) and de Vaus and McAllister (1991) suggest that employees place less importance on rewards when they view those rewards as unattainable. Thus Lincoln and Kalleberg (1990, p. 154) reason that employed women display higher commitment levels than comparable men. Similarly, Hodson (1989) accounts for higher-than-anticipated levels of job satisfaction among women by positing that men and women use different comparison groups in evaluating their jobs. (See also Bielby and Bielby 1988, pp. 1034-5, on work effort.)

A final line of reasoning has to do with selectivity. Several analysts suggest that women may have more choice than men as to whether to be employed;[5] if so, it is not implausible to argue that decisions by women to seek employment might reflect a predisposition toward commitment to work and employers. Hakim (1991) argues that there are two latent types of working women, one oriented toward a "homemaker career" and the other "committed to work as a central life goal" (p. 101), which suggests that the low-commitment group may move into and out of the workforce as circumstances demand. Fiorentine (1988, p. 247) argues that homemaking and family activities constitute a "normative alternative" to occupational success for women, but not for men: "Women have fewer disincentives to change or lower their career goals when faced with doubts about their ability or when the career pursuit becomes personally unsatisfying" (p. 247). Gerson (1985) more specifically distinguishes between *domestic* and *nondomestic* pathways for women, documenting the way in which choices between these are patterned by life-course contingencies. Following from such observations, one would expect that those women in the labor force are more likely to display high commitment levels than otherwise comparable male labor force participants.

The considerable body of theorizing about how job and gender factors may affect OC does not provide us with any one clear expectation about how men and women differ in OC. We next turn to a review of the available empirical evidence.

**Prior Research**

The literature on organizational commitment is vast, with many studies considering numerous explanatory factors, including gender. We focus here on those studies that have explicitly examined gender differences in OC. The literature review in Mowday et al. (1982) cites several studies in support of the claim that "women as a group were found to be more committed than men" (p. 31). Among these are Grusky's (1966) study of managers in a large public utility, which found that women displayed higher levels of commitment than men; Grusky relates this to the higher barriers that women must overcome, a variant on the dissonance argument previously discussed. Hrebiniak and Alutto (1972) studied teachers and nurses, finding women less likely to leave their employers. Finally, Angle and Perry (1981) found that female bus drivers were more committed than male ones.

Two recent meta-analyses of the literature seek to summarize systematically the results of correlational studies on the link between gender and OC.[6] Mathieu and Zajac (1990) located 14 samples that had examined the gender-OC relationship. These found, on average, that women displayed slightly higher commitment: Across the studies, the mean correlation between a dummy variable identifying men and OC was −0.145. There was substantial variation around this, however; Mathieu and Zajac report a standard deviation of 0.165, and conclude that "there appears to be no consistent relationship between sex and levels of OC" (p. 177). Similar conclusions follow from Cohen and Lowenberg's (1990) examination of 10 samples in which the gender-OC correlation was studied. They report (p. 1022) a mean correlation of 0.035 and a 95% confidence interval ranging from –0.174 to 0.245; on this basis Cohen and Lowenberg decide that they cannot draw any conclusion about a significant relationship between gender and OC.

Most extant studies are based on highly clustered samples. For example, Aryee and Heng (1990) report a correlation of 0.44 between sex and OC among supervisors in a Singapore manufacturing company; the relationship, however, was not significant among shopfloor workers. Chelte and Tausky (1986) examined the gender-OC link separately for three occupational groups in a university, finding no consistent pattern. In a study of employees in one plant of a *Fortune* 100 firm, Gaertner and Nollen (1989) found no relationship between gender and OC once indicators of the firm's employment practices and employee career experiences were controlled.

Some studies do use evidence obtained from employees of several organizations. For example, Mottaz (1988) found a zero-order gender difference in OC in a sample of employees from six moderate-size organizations in a single community, but this difference disappeared when measures of work rewards were controlled. In broader samples of workers from manufacturing plants in the United States and Japan, however, Lincoln and Kalleberg (1990, p. 134) found that women displayed higher OC levels, after adjustments for a variety of position, task, reward, and value indicators.

In sum, prior research reveals inconsistent conclusions. The broad majority of the studies available have been conducted using samples drawn from single work organizations. None, to our knowledge, is based on a nationally representative sample of the labor force. Given that there are wide organizational variations in gender composition and employment practices, it seems quite hazardous to generalize from any given study—a caution that is accentuated by the conclusions of the two meta-analyses previously cited. Moreover, many prior studies examine bivariate correlations only—they do not control measures of job attributes or family roles when estimating gender differences in OC. In the research reported in the following, we study the relationship between gender and commitment in a nationally representative sample, with ample control variables. This is responsive to Mathieu and Zajac's (1990, p. 191) call for more cross-organizational studies.

**Studying Organizational Commitment**
**Using the 1991 General Social Survey Data**

Our analysis in this chapter relies on individual-level data gathered in the General Social Survey, which was used to draw the sample of work establishments surveyed by the NOS. That the GSS is conducted with a representative national sample is notable. Because so much research on organizational commitment has used samples clustered within work organizations, it is difficult to know how far a set of results based on a given organization might be generalized beyond that setting. Of course, we are unable to study within-organization variations, in that GSS respondents work for different employers. The GSS sample, however, allows us to generalize our findings to the U.S. labor force with much more confidence than the employer samples used in other research.

Our analysis focuses on the 912 respondents who were employed in full-time or part-time jobs at the time of the GSS interview or who had jobs but were not at work because of illness, vacation, or strike (see Chapter 2). Of those respondents in the labor force who were interviewed, 120 (14%) are self-employed. Because most research on OC is concerned with predicting employee behaviors such as absenteeism and tardiness, it is not clear that self-employed persons should be included in our analyses. Moreover, questions about loyalty to an employer may well mean something different when the respondent *is* the employer. Still, inclusion of the self-employed is of interest because, by design, they have been excluded from prior studies of OC; including them makes the sample representative of people in the U.S. labor force. As a result of these conflicting considerations, we present many results separately for the entire sample and for the employee and self-employed subsamples.

**Measuring Organizational Commitment**

The dependent variable in our analyses is an organizational commitment scale based on six questions included in the Work Organization module in the GSS (see Chapter 2). The interview items used in constructing the OC scale we analyze appear in Table 15.1. The wording of these items corresponds to that used in the Indianapolis/Tokyo Work Commitment Study (Lincoln and Kalleberg 1990, p. 75).[7] Items 1 through 5 bear a close resemblance to Items 1, 3, 4, 5, and 6 (respectively) of the 15-item Organizational Commitment Questionnaire (OCQ) of Mowday et al. (1982,

**Table 15.1** Items Included in the Organizational Commitment (OC) Scale

Please tell me how much you agree or disagree with the following statements. Would you say that you *strongly agree, agree, disagree, or strongly disagree?*

1. I am willing to work harder than I have to in order to help this organization succeed.
2. I feel very little loyalty to this organization [reverse-coded].
3. I would take almost any job to keep working for this organization.
4. I find that my values and the organization's values are very similar.
5. I am proud to be working for this organization.
6. I would turn down another job for more pay in order to stay with this organization.

SOURCE: Davis and Smith (1991, pp. 468-469).
NOTE: Responses (except for the one reverse-coded item) were scored as follows: *strongly agree* (4), *agree* (3), *disagree* (2), *strongly disagree* (1). For all respondents in the labor force, the organizational commitment (OC) scale averaging the six items has a mean of 2.87 and a standard deviation of 0.54. Its estimated reliability (Cronbach's $\alpha$) is 0.78. For the employee subsample, the scale has a mean of 2.79, a standard deviation of 0.49, and a reliability of 0.74.

p. 221). The items here capture the major aspects of commitment measured by the OCQ (see Mowday et al. 1982, p. 27); Item 1 reflects willingness to exert effort on behalf of the organization; Items 2, 4, and 5 concern belief in and acceptance of the organization's goals and values; whereas Items 3 and 6 measure the desire to maintain membership in the organization.

Respondents were assigned the mean of their scores on the six items as their score on the commitment scale.[8] For all respondents in the labor force, the scale has an internal consistency ($\alpha$) reliability of 0.78;[9] in the employee subsample, it has a lower but still acceptable reliability of 0.74.

## Zero-Order Gender Differences

Table 15.2 displays the mean levels of commitment for men and women found in the 1991 GSS data. Among all working respondents—both employees and self-employed persons—men score significantly higher (about .10 units, or .19 standard deviations) on the commitment scale than do women. The zero-order correlation between a dummy variable identifying men and the organizational commitment scale is 0.092, a result well within the bounds found in the meta-analyses mentioned above.

When the 120 self-employed persons interviewed by the GSS are omitted from the analysis, the gender difference in OC falls to .03 (.06 standard deviations) and becomes statistically insignificant. As shown by contrasting the second and third columns of Table 15.2, self-employed

**Table 15.2** Zero-Order Gender Differences in Organizational Commitment

| | Mean Commitment Scores | | |
|---|---|---|---|
| Gender | All Employed Respondents | Employees Only | Self-Employed Respondents |
| Female | 2.82 (443) | 2.77 (407) | 3.35 (35) |
| Male | 2.92 (450) | 2.80 (365) | 3.40 (85) |
| Total | 2.87 (893) | 2.79 (772) | 3.38 (120) |
| *t*-statistic | 2.77 | 0.86 | 0.47 |

NOTE: One female respondent did not answer the question that asked whether she was an employee or a self-employed person.

people have substantially higher OC scores than employees; the gender difference in the first column is in large part a result of the fact that men are more often self-employed than are women (see correlation in Table 15.3 below).

## Further Exploring Gender Differences

The findings displayed in Table 15.2 do not demonstrate how levels of OC differ between men and women holding comparable jobs or with comparable family affiliations. We developed measures for many of the commitment-related features discussed earlier—including, in particular, job-career factors and family roles—in an effort to better understand the gender difference. We discuss these sets of indicators briefly in the following paragraphs. Appendix 15.1 includes a more complete discussion of the measures, with their means and standard deviations.[10]

### Job Attributes and Career Experiences

We used several variables in our attempt to capture gender differences in work roles and career patterns. Several of our indicators of work positions are individual-level measures of the commitment-enhancing structures identified by Lincoln and Kalleberg (1990). Autonomy is our most direct indicator of participation, but this concept is also partially captured by our measure of the respondent's position in an authority structure. Integration is tapped by a variable assessing the quality of workplace relations, whereas opportunities for mobility and careers are measured by an indicator of the presence of regular promotion procedures. An employee's perception of the degree to which nonmerit criteria are used in awarding pay raises and promotions serves to measure one aspect of legitimacy. A final indicator of work position, organization size (natural log), does not correspond directly with any of these features, but it is arguably associated with several of them (career opportunities and formal rules, for example, are more often present in larger organizations). In analyses that use the entire sample, we also include a dummy variable distinguishing self-employed persons from employees.

To measure compensation, we included a measure of (logged) annual earnings and a measure of the availability of fringe benefits. We also included two indicators of career experiences: (a) the length of the employee's tenure with the employer and (b) the respondent's assessment of his or her past rate of advancement in the organization.

In the upper panels of Table 15.3, we show the simple correlations between these explanatory measures and gender and OC, computed for the entire employed GSS sample. Six variables describing work positions are associated with commitment in the manner expected; the correlations for autonomy and the quality of workplace relations are largest among these. In that there are also significant gender differences for five of the work position variables, the prospect that controlling them will affect the gender difference in OC is good. To a lesser degree, this is also true of the career and compensation variables, notably the pace of advancement and earnings.

**Family Roles**

We examined family roles using four indicators. Current family status was measured by marital status and the number of children 12 or younger in the household.[11] A scale reflecting acceptance of nontraditional roles for women was included to measure sex role orientation, which arguably should enhance organizational commitment, especially among women. Finally, we included an assessment of the perceived frequency of conflict between responsibilities at home and on the job.

We see in Table 15.3 that the correlations of these indicators with gender and OC are modest. Male respondents are slightly more likely to be currently married, and married people are a little more likely to be high on OC. People living in households with many children tend to display somewhat lower commitment. Respondents who say that job and home often are in conflict display significantly lower levels of organizational commitment, as expected;

**Table 15.3**  Zero-Order Correlations of Gender and Organizational Commitment With Variables Measuring Work Positions and Other Affiliations (all employed respondents)

| Variables | Correlation With Gender (male) | Correlation With Organizational Commitment |
|---|---|---|
| Gender (male) | — | .092** |
| Work Position | | |
| Position in authority hierarchy | .205** | .342** |
| Autonomy | .132** | .427** |
| Perceived quality workplace relations | .011 | .415** |
| Promotion procedures (dummy) | .081** | .012 |
| Nonmerit reward criteria | −.153** | −.228** |
| Workplace size (log) | −.027 | −.175** |
| Self-employment (dummy) | .145** | .380** |
| Career experiences | | |
| Years with employer | .091** | .161** |
| Advances with this employer | .152** | .146** |
| Hours worked last week (or typical) | .259** | .126** |
| Full time worker (dummy) | .186** | .079** |
| Compensation | | |
| Annual earnings (log) | .313** | .131** |
| Number of fringe benefits | .048+ | .029 |
| Family affiliations | | |
| Currently married (dummy) | .087** | .074* |
| Number of persons aged 12 or less in household | −.032 | −.104** |
| Frequency of job-home conflict | −.064* | −.124** |
| Sex role nontraditionalism | −.206** | −.033 |
| Sociodemographic controls | | |
| White (dummy) | .068* | .030 |
| Years education | .018 | .010 |

+$p < .10$; *$p < .05$; **$p < .01$.

such conflicts are slightly more common among women. Finally, though women have a tendency to hold more nontraditional sex-role conceptions, those holding such views do not differ appreciably from those holding more traditional conceptions in their levels of OC.[12]

**Selective Inclusion in the Labor Force**

As noted, virtually all studies of OC have been conducted using employee samples clustered within a relatively small number of work organizations. Likewise, the GSS commitment items were asked only of currently employed persons. To the degree that decisions about entry into the labor force are related to predispositions toward OC, this raises the possibility of sample selection bias in correlations and regression coefficients (Berk 1983).

The criterion for selection into our sample is based on employment status or labor supplied. Two indicators reflecting this are available in the GSS: (a) whether the respondent described his or her employment status as full-time or part-time and (b) the number of hours worked per week. We see in Table 15.3 that men tend to supply somewhat more labor—that is, they tend to be full-time employees and tend to work more hours than employed women. Those supplying more labor, in turn, tend to be somewhat more committed to their employers. Because the associations involving hours worked are somewhat stronger than those that use the full-time/part-time distinction, we use the hours worked measure as our control for potential selectivity in subsequent analyses.[13]

**Multivariate Analysis**

To examine the ways in which the independent variables identified above affect the gender difference in OC, we conducted several multiple regression analyses using subsets of the independent variables. The results of our most comprehensive analyses, in which gender differences are estimated after controlling a set of 17 explanatory variables, are summarized in Table 15.4.[14] We present these results separately for the employee and self-employed subsamples (columns 2 and 3) as well as for all respondents in the labor force (column 1).[15] Of special interest are the partial regression coefficients for gender in the first line of this table.

The results of these analyses are straightforward: Gender differences in OC are shaped most by differences in the kinds of jobs that men and women have. This conclusion holds for all employed respondents, for the employee subsample, and even for the small self-employed subsample. In Table 15.4, we see that variables that measure attributes of work positions are the major features that have net effects on OC. We know from Table 15.3 that there are significant gender differences for most of the positional variables.

Gender differences in family roles do little to shape male-female differences in OC. When only the three family affiliation variables were included as predictors (results not shown), we found that higher OC was

**Table 15.4**  Multiple Regressions of Organizational Commitment on Gender and
Variables Measuring Features of Work Positions and Other Affiliations

| Explanatory Variables | Regression Coefficients | | |
|---|---|---|---|
| | All Employed Respondents | Employees Only | Self-Employed Respondents |
| Gender (male) | −.057 | −.060+ | −.053 |
| Work position | | | |
| Position in authority hierarchy | .049** | .029 | .193** |
| Autonomy | .149** | .140** | .388* |
| Perceived quality workplace relations | .168** | .179** | .144 |
| Promotion procedures (dummy) | .061+ | .074* | −.094 |
| Nonmerit reward criteria | −.067** | −.064** | −.014 |
| Workplace size (log) | −.002 | −.004 | .086+ |
| Self-employment (dummy) | .318** | — | — |
| Career experiences | | | |
| Years with employer | .009 | .004 | .039 |
| Advances with this employer | .042+ | .033 | .074 |
| Hours worked last week (or typical) | .001 | .002 | .000 |
| Compensation | | | |
| Annual earnings (log) | .003 | .009 | −.056 |
| Number of fringe benefits | .018* | .016* | −.019 |
| Family affiliations | | | |
| Currently married (dummy) | .045 | .037 | .040 |
| Number of persons aged 12 or less in household | −.011 | −.008 | −.029 |
| Frequency of job-home conflict | −.029 | −.022 | −.041 |
| Sociodemographic controls | | | |
| White (dummy) | −.042 | −.020 | −.307 |
| Years education | −.004 | −.003 | .005 |
| Constant | 1.567** | 1.504** | .887 |
| $R^2$ | .345 | .269 | .416 |
| N | 735 | 656 | 79 |

+$p < .10$; *$p < .05$; **$p < .01$.

associated with marriage and the absence of young children but that the
male-female difference in OC from Table 15.2 remained largely intact. In
Table 15.4, we see that family roles have no net influence on OC, once we
adjust for differences in work positions and compensation.

Once all of the explanatory variables are controlled, we observe that
the partial coefficient for gender becomes negative; indeed, it is statistically
significant at the .10 level for the employee subsample. This suggests that
levels of OC are, if anything, higher for women than for comparable men.
As previously discussed, there are several possible explanations for this

difference, which is net of job-career variables and family affiliations; unfortunately, we do not have sufficient data to decide between these.

We focus in this chapter on gender differences, but we will comment briefly on some of the other results presented in Table 15.4. The coefficients for many of the explanatory variables are consistent with those reported in the prior literature on OC; job-related features are the strongest correlates of commitment among those studied. Commitment is especially heightened by autonomy and positive workplace relationships, but dampened when an employee perceives that nonmerit criteria influence the allocation of raises or promotions. The findings suggest that generous fringe benefits are more important than high wages in shaping commitment to an employer, and, as shown in Table 15.2, that the OC scores of self-employed people are substantially larger than those of employees. Overall, we account for more than a third of the variance in the OC measure for the entire sample and more than a quarter of it within the employee subsample.

In that no prior studies examine OC for self-employed people, we make some passing observations about the results in the third column of Table 15.4. Though the number of self-employed people is small and the results are therefore only suggestive, it appears that the scope of authority is a major factor in shaping OC for the self-employed. This is shown by the significant coefficients for authority, autonomy, and workplace size. The gender difference among the self-employed is estimated to be nearly the same as that among employees.

## Are Correlates of Commitment Gender-Specific?

The final analyses that we report here examine the possibility that there may be gender differences in the processes leading to organizational commitment. If family roles compete more strongly with work roles for women than for men, for example, then we should expect some interactions of such variables with gender in their effects on commitment. There are reasons to expect other coefficients to differ by gender as well. Loscocco (1989, p. 387), for example, finds that the relationship between authority and the related attitude of work commitment is positive for men but negative for women. She argues that this reflects differences in the nature of the authority attached to male and female supervisory positions (see also Reskin and Padavic 1994). Lorence (1987b) finds that the way in which

**Table 15.5** Gender-Specific Regressions for Organizational Commitment (all employed respondents)

| | *Regression coefficients* | | |
|---|---|---|---|
| *Explanatory Variables* | *Women* | | *Men* |
| Work position | | | |
| Position in authority hierarchy | .015 | | .075** |
| Autonomy | .159** | | .135** |
| Perceived quality workplace relations | .191** | | .142** |
| Promotion procedures (dummy) | .072 | | .035 |
| Non–merit reward criteria | −.010 | *** | −.135** |
| Workplace size (log) | .002 | | −.012 |
| Self-employed (dummy) | .314** | | .273** |
| Career experiences | | | |
| Years with employer | .018 | | .012 |
| Advances wth this employer | .042 | | .053 |
| Hours worked last week (or typical) | .001 | | .000 |
| Compensation | | | |
| Annual earnings (log) | .023 | | −.040 |
| Number of fringe benefits | .011 | | .026* |
| Family affiliations | | | |
| Currently married (dummy) | −.011 | *** | .145** |
| Number of persons aged 12 or less | | | |
| in household | .027 | *** | −.050$^+$ |
| Frequency of job–home conflict | −.056* | | −.009 |
| Sociodemographic controls | | | |
| White (dummy) | .044 | | −.120$^+$ |
| Years education | −.009 | | .004 |
| Constant | 1.450** | | 1.704** |
| $R^2$ | .355 | | .365 |
| N | 369 | | 366 |

NOTE: The gender-specific equations presented here are derived from an equation that includes interaction terms between gender and all other variables; $R^2$ for that equation is 0.364. The $F$-statistic for test of the hypothesis that there are no gender differences between equations is 1.218 on 17 and 699 *df*, $p > .10$. $+p < .10$; $* p < .05$; $** p < .01$; ***$t$ statistic for gender difference in coefficients exceeds 2.0.

age, autonomy, and occupational status are associated with job involvement differs between men and women.

We estimated a model including interaction terms between gender and each of the 17 independent variables included in the analyses reported in Table 15.4. The results appear in Table 15.5; we present gender-specific regression coefficients for ease of interpretation.[16] Table 15.5 gives results for the entire sample; findings based on the employee subsample are quite similar.

Overall, Table 15.5 provides, at most, weak evidence of differences between men and women in the factors associated with OC; the sets of coefficients in the male and female equations do not differ significantly.[17] Three tests for gender differences in specific coefficients, however, are significant at the nominal level of .05.[18] Thus, the correlates of OC appear to be largely similar among males and females.

With these caveats in mind, we briefly discuss the gender differences that are suggested by Table 15.5. Two family affiliations have coefficients that differ by gender. Being married appears to raise commitment among men, but not among women. This finding is broadly consistent with a gender model placing emphasis on a man's responsibility as a provider. The homemaker counterpart of such a model is not supported, though, in that married and unmarried women do not differ in OC. The presence of younger children in the household has a more negative coefficient among men than among women, a finding inconsistent with the claim that there is stronger competition of family and work roles for women.[19]

We do not have a ready interpretation for the other difference suggested by Table 15.5. We find that for men, perceptions that nonmerit criteria are used in allocating rewards appear to reduce OC; this does not hold for women. We stress, however, that all three of the gender differences in regression coefficients identified in Table 15.5 are of borderline significance (see note 18).

## Conclusion

We can summarize our results concisely: Men tend to have slightly higher overall levels of organizational commitment than women, a difference primarily attributable to gender differences in commitment-related job and career attributes. Women, however, may be slightly more committed to their employers than are men in comparable positions. We find little evidence to suggest that gender differences in OC are a product of differences between men and women in family roles, or that the relationships of such roles to organizational commitment differ appreciably by gender. In that it has been shown that OC is related to turnover (e.g., Mowday et al. 1982; Randall 1990), it is notable that these findings are quite consistent with those from studies of gender differences in quit rates (Viscusi 1980; Blau and Kahn 1981). Likewise, they are compatible with Bielby and Bielby's (1988) results for male-female differences in work effort.

We are left with the impression that gender differences in this area are quite modest. This is consistent with Marini's (1988) observation that, in general, gender differences are believed to be larger than they in fact are. As we have noted, there exist rationales for presuming that both men and women will display greater organizational commitment, but the results of our analyses lead us to the conclusion that the difference in OC between men and women is far smaller than within-gender variation. Moreover, the principal factors enhancing or reducing this form of attachment to an organization have far less to do with characteristics of persons than with attributes of positions.

That OC is enhanced most by job-related variables suggests that employers seeking to increase the level of OC among female employees should be attentive to the same features that increase it for male employees: working conditions and opportunities (see Bielby 1992, p. 290). Our analysis finds that a positive interpersonal climate and the opportunity to work autonomously are of special relevance to OC.[20] Other pertinent organizational factors include the availability of regular promotion procedures and the perception that nonmerit criteria do not play a part in the allocation of rewards. Employers would do well, then, to foster an atmosphere of legitimacy within the workplace.

There is no suggestion in the data we have examined that policies aimed at alleviating work-family conflict would have a greater effect on OC among women than among men. The availability of child care assistance and benefits, for instance, is as strongly associated with OC for male as it is for female employees.[21]

Further studies of the interplay of work and family in shaping organizational commitment could include more detailed measures of household variables. It is possible that inclusion of more specific measures of the division of labor in the household or of amounts of time devoted to household management tasks would reveal stronger associations with OC than those isolated with the measures available to us. Such associations would not, however, be inconsistent with this chapter's finding that overall, gender differences in OC are limited. Instead, they would further explain why some women and men are more committed than others to their employers.

## Notes

1. We recognize and acknowledge the differences between organizational commitment (OC) and related, but conceptually and empirically distinct, attitudes such as work, career, or occupational commitment (Mueller, Wallace, and Price 1992).

2. See, for example, Gaertner and Nollen's (1989) argument that an employee's commitment is affected by employment practices that involve investments by employers in workers, such as promotion from within or company-provided training.

3. In this regard, Bielby and Bielby (1984) report for a sample of college women that "insulation from traditional role expectations, positive socialization experiences, and academic success all lead to greater work commitment" (p. 242).

4. Moreover, even if such differences did exist at one time (it is notable that studies cited by Block 1976, p. 285, in support of such differences date from the 1950s and 1960s), they may be changing as socialization patterns change. See Coser's (1986) discussion of gender differences in visual-spatial and mathematical abilities.

5. This is not to deny that most women, as with men, work out of economic necessity.

6. An additional meta-analysis presented by Randall (1990) deals only with the consequences of OC (performance, attendance, turnover, and tardiness).

7. Lincoln and Kalleberg, however, used a 5-point response scale (including a middle-position alternative of *neither agree nor disagree*) rather than the 4-point scale used in the GSS.

8. If a respondent gave substantive responses to 4 or 5 of the 6 items, values for nonsubstantive (*don't know, no answer*) responses to other items were regression-imputed (Little and Rubin 1987). That is, missing responses were predicted via linear regression of one item on the others (using coefficients estimated from cases with data on all items). No score on the scale was assigned to those respondents who answered three or fewer of the questions. Only 19 respondents were excluded from the analysis because of missing values for OC.

9. Though one can draw conceptual distinctions between *affective* and *continuance* aspects of OC, or between willingness to exert effort, belief in organizational values and goals, and intent to stay (see, for example, Mueller et al. 1992), the use of a unidimensional scale is appropriate to our purposes in this chapter. Moreover, a factor analysis of the six items reveals only one factor with an eigenvalue in excess of 1.0. This is also true of the longer OCQ: see Mowday et al. (1982, pp. 223-24).

10. Correlations between these measures and our focal variables (gender and OC) are displayed in Table 15.3 for the entire sample.

11. The GSS data file does not include information on the ages of the respondent's own children, though it does measure the number of children ever born. Our measure, though, refers to children in the household, regardless of whether they are the respondent's own children.

12. Because sex-role nontraditionalism is uncorrelated with OC and because its inclusion results in a substantial increase in missing data (the items in the nontraditionalism scale are asked of a random two thirds of GSS respondents; see Davis and Smith 1992), this variable is not included in the multivariate analyses we report subsequently.

13. Potential sample selection bias arises when observations are chosen on the basis of a dependent variable. In this study, *explicit* selection would involve sampling employees on the basis of their OC scores; the GSS does not do that. The potential selectivity problem here is instead one of *implicit* selection: By studying only labor force participants, we may indirectly select people with high levels of commitment—to the extent that entry into the labor force is sensitive to potential OC. A number of sophisticated statistical methods of adjusting for potential selection bias have been proposed (Winship and Mare 1992). If, however, the threshold for inclusion in a sample is based on one of the independent variables in an analysis, no selectivity problem is present (Berk 1983, p. 389). In that the criterion used in selecting our study sample from the entire GSS sample is based explicitly on current employment status or (equivalently) labor supplied (see interviewer instructions in Davis and Smith 1991, p. 449), controlling measures of these selection criteria serves to adjust for potential selectivity.

14. Regression coefficients presented in Table 15.4 were estimated for the 735 respondents providing data on all 19 variables. The principal source of missing data was refusal to answer the question on earnings.

15. Differences between the equations for employees and self-employed persons are not significant ($F = 1.40$ on 17 and 699 degrees of freedom, $p > .10$). We report the results separately because most prior interest in OC has been confined to employees. Note that the

small number of self-employed people in the GSS means that our ability to detect differences between employees and the self-employed is limited.

16. The results were estimated in an overall equation that added 17 cross-product terms (one for the product of gender with each of the other independent variables) to the regression reported in the first column of Table 15.4. This permits easy tests of hypotheses about gender differences in regression coefficients (see results reported between the columns of coefficients in Table 15.5). The coefficients of cross-product terms are not always easy to interpret, however, so we have presented the equivalent sets of gender-specific regression coefficients in Table 15.5.

17. The null hypothesis that the 17 independent variables have identical coefficients for men and women cannot be rejected at even the .10 level.

18. None of these, however, remains significant at the more demanding .0029 level that takes into account the multiple tests conducted here. The level of .0029 is obtained via a Bonferroni procedure that controls the Type I error rate in situations involving post hoc multiple comparisons. It is obtained by dividing the nominal (.05) significance level by the number of tests made (17); see, e.g., Jaccard, Turrisi, and Wan (1990, p. 28).

19. Family affiliations may, however, affect entry into the labor force quite differently for men and women. We examined a log-linear model for the cross-classification of employment status, gender, and number of children in the household for those GSS respondents aged 65 and under. The three-way interaction in that model is significant at the .001 level; estimated parameters indicate a positive association of employment and number of children for men, but a negative association of roughly equal magnitude for women.

20. The two largest standardized regression coefficients corresponding to the results given in Table 15.4 are (for the complete sample) those for the quality of workplace relations ($\beta = 0.257$) and autonomy ($\beta = 0.225$).

21. In the employee subsample, correlations of availability of employer-provided child care information and OC are 0.074 (women) and 0.130 (men); the respective correlations between child care assistance and OC are .057 and .055.

# APPENDIX 15.1

## Measures of Independent Variables

### Gender

Dummy variable identifying men (mean = .50; $SD$ = .50).

### Work Position

*Position in Authority Hierarchy:* An indicator of a respondent's structural position in a network of supervisory relations. The measure was obtained by summing four dummy variables identifying respondents who (a) directly supervise others as part of their official job duties, (b) indirectly supervise others because their subordinates have supervisory authority, (c) are not indirectly supervised because their supervisor has no superior, and (d) are not directly supervised (mean = 0.98; $SD$ = 1.10).

*Autonomy:* A 4-item scale, the mean of items measuring the extent to which a respondent says that he or she can work independently, has a lot of say over what happens on the job, is allowed to take part in making decisions, and is not closely supervised. Reliability (Cronbach's α) is .834 (mean = 2.95; *SD* = .81).

*Perceived Quality of Workplace Relations:* Mean of two items asking respondents to "describe relations in your workplace between management and employees" and "between coworkers/colleagues"; responses range from *very bad* (1) to *very good* (5) (mean = 4.09; *SD* = .78).

*Promotion Procedures:* Dummy variable identifying jobs in which there are regular procedures for promoting people to a higher level. (mean = .45; *SD* = .50)

*Nonmerit Reward Criteria:* Sum of three dummy variables indicating whether respondent believes that he or she is disadvantaged because of his or her race or sex, and whether he or she believes that raises are given to those workers who "have some favored relationship with the boss" (mean = .51; *SD* = .72).

*Workplace Size:* Natural logarithm of respondent's estimate of the number of persons employed at the site where he or she works; calculated after assigning midpoints to response categories offered (mean = 4.13; *SD* = 2.08).

*Self-Employment:* Dummy variable identifying self-employed respondents (mean = 0.14; *SD* = 0.35).

## Career Experiences

*Years with Employer:* Natural logarithm of respondent's report of length of service with current employer (mean = 1.29; *SD* = 1.42).

*Advances with this Employer:* Respondent's assessment of pace at which he or she has advanced with the current employer, from *lost some ground* (coded 1) to *advanced rapidly* (coded 4) (mean = 2.51; *SD* = 0.70).

*Hours Worked Last Week:* Respondent's report of the number of hours worked in the week prior to the interview; a report of hours worked in a typical week was substituted if respondent is employed but was not at work in the prior week (mean = 40.21; *SD* = 14.93).

*Full-time Worker:* Dummy variable identifying those who are employed fulltime (mean = 0.80; *SD* = 0.40).

## Compensation

*Annual Earnings:* Natural logarithm of respondent's own income from employment in 1990, calculated after assigning midpoints (in thousands of dollars) to response categories offered (mean = 2.82; *SD* = 0.98).

*Number of Fringe Benefits:* Number of benefits, out of 10, for which a person in a job similar to the respondent's is eligible. Benefits include pensions, medical insurance, dental benefits, paid sick leave, life insurance, profit sharing or stock options, performance-based or merit-based bonuses, paid maternity and paternity benefits, assistance with child care, and flextime scheduling (mean = 4.67; *SD* = 2.76).

## Family Affiliations

*Currently Married:* Dummy variable identifying currently married respondents (mean = 0.55; *SD* = 0.50).

*Number of Persons Aged 12 or Less in Household:* Number of persons 12 years of age or less in respondent's household (mean = 0.57; *SD* = 0.91).

*Frequency of Job–Home Conflict:* Respondent's assessment of the frequency with which family and household responsibilities make it difficult to devote full attention to work, from *never* (scored 1) to *frequently* (scored 4) (mean = 1.82; *SD* = 0.88).

*Sex–Role Nontraditionalism:* An 8-item scale, the mean of items measuring respondent's acceptance of three statements favoring nontraditional roles for women (would vote for a qualified woman for President, approves of a married woman working, feels that a working mother can have as warm a relationship with her children as can a nonworking mother) and rejection of five statements favoring traditional roles (a woman should help her husband's career rather than having her own, preschool children suffer if mother works, men should achieve outside the home while women care for home and family, men are better suited than women for politics, women should take care of running their homes and leave the running of the country to men) Cronbach's $\alpha$ = .777 (mean = 3.03; *SD* = .46).

## Sociodemographic Controls

*White:* Dummy variable identifying white respondents (mean = .85; *SD* = .36).

*Education:* Highest year of education completed (mean = 13.58; *SD* = 2.74).

NOTE: Means and standard deviations given are for all respondents in the labor force.

# 16

# Conclusions
# and Prospects

ARNE L. KALLEBERG
DAVID KNOKE
PETER V. MARSDEN
JOE L. SPAETH

The 1991 National Organizations Study was conceived as a single, cross-sectional project to learn about the feasibility and costs of designing and executing a survey of a representative national sample of work organizations and to obtain useful information about their organizational properties, structures, and human resource practices. Our efforts were guided by the belief that it is desirable, in the long run, to have a national database on organizations—based on a probability sample, not a convenience sample—that provides information for the organizations research community. One plausible model for such a database combines a core of structural variables and social indicators that pertain to all organizations (and that would, in an extended project, be monitored continuously) with modules that address specific research interests, such as staffing, training, and compensation (presumably the modules of a continuing organizational database would change from time to time).

As the contents of this book demonstrate, these objectives were largely accomplished: Data collection for the NOS was quite successful by the standards of organizations research. We have shown that it is possible to collect valid and reliable information on a large sample of diverse organizations and their employees. The resulting data are quite useful for studying the interrelations among diverse organizational structures, as well as the linkages between organizations and broader economic and labor force dynamics. We have also learned a good deal about how to improve the research design and implementation of future organizational surveys.

The substantive chapters of this book reflect accurately the great diversity of workplaces in the United States at the start of the 1990s. Many new dynamics and structures have resulted from a confluence of external forces compelling higher performance standards, increased employee skill requirements, and continuous workplace reorganization. Firms are not equally subject to these socioeconomic forces, nor are these changes moving each organization in the same direction at the same rate. Moreover, the changes in organizational structures and employment relations that we discussed in our opening chapter continue apace. International competition, declining productivity, and technological advances continue to transform the environments of organizations. At the same time, a changing labor force needs to continually adapt to new employment opportunities.

These dynamics underscore the need for continuing research on organizational change and the evolution of employment relations. Monitoring and explaining the complex interrelationships among these joint trends are critical intellectual and practical policy tasks in the decade ahead. The NOS constitutes an important benchmark against which such organizational changes in the United States can be measured, and thus future replications and extensions of the NOS will contribute relevant knowledge about them.

In this concluding chapter, we take stock of what we learned, both methodologically and substantively, from collecting and analyzing the NOS, and we speculate about some significant directions toward which the organizational research community may profitably turn in the future.

## Major Results From the 1991 NOS

The NOS has provided a series of snapshots of U.S. organizational demographics in the early 1990s. Together, these images form a complex portrait of the population of the work sites employing the American labor force. The nearly 700 NOS observational units (establishments) were sampled proportional to the size (number of employees) of those units. Hence, the data accurately reflect the organizational practices to which the labor force was exposed. By not placing any restrictions on workplace size, the NOS obtained information about the entire range of establishments. Thus, one clear advantage of the NOS compared to more restricted organizational survey designs is its ability to examine how size is associated with organizational work settings. Although small establishments (those with 10 or fewer employees) are by far the most common workplaces (see Table 3.1), a majority of Americans spend their working hours at much larger sites (with 50 or more employees). This wide variation in organizational size within the NOS has allowed us to make sophisticated quantitative assessments of how the fundamental structural condition of size covaries with diverse organizational structural dimensions and measures of human resource activities.

The preceding substantive research chapters contain numerous analyses, and we do not attempt to summarize them in detail here. Instead, we highlight some of their central findings as a reminder of the diversity of concerns that our analyses of the NOS have addressed.

1. Larger establishments are more complex than smaller establishments. Larger establishments have, for example, more vertical and horizontal *differentiation,* more *decentralized* decision making, more elaborate *formal* job descriptions, and lower *administrative intensity* (see Chapter 4). These differences between large and small organizations persist even after we statistically control for effects of contextual features such as auspices, environmental complexity, the presence of unions, and branch or subsidiary status.

2. There are appreciable differences in formalization and decentralization among public-sector, nonprofit, and private for-profit establishments, net of size and complexity. Branch or subsidiary establishments display higher levels of formalization and centralization than do comparable independent workplaces (Chapter 4). These findings substantiate theories that emphasize external and institutional sources of structural forms.

3. *Firm internal labor markets* (FILMs) are most likely to be found in larger, more formalized establishments that are branches or subsidiaries of larger firms. FILMs are also more common in establishments that produce products rather than services and especially common within those that produce both products and services (Chapter 5).

4. Formal *dispute resolution structures* are generally found in the same kinds of establishments that tend to have FILMs. The presence of these due process structures is associated with environmental circumstances including public and nonprofit auspices, unionization, and affiliation with a larger organization (Chapter 5).

5. Indicators of *control and coordination structures* cluster together in theoretically meaningful ways (Chapter 5): Two clusters are variations on "simple structure" used mainly in small, independent firms; the other three are types of bureaucracy associated with large nonunionized, large unionized, and small branch establishments

6. Characteristics of *high performance work organizations* also tend to cluster together to form a "system" (Chapter 6). Human resource policies and practices often identified with high performance organizations—such as training, group incentive plans, decentralization, and firm internal labor markets—are, in fact, associated with higher organizational performance.

7. U.S. establishments use a variety of *recruitment and selection processes* (Chapter 7). Newspaper advertisements and informal referrals from employees are the most frequently used methods to publicizing the availability of job opportunities to potential workers. Letters of reference are the most widespread approach to screening and selecting workers, but substantial minorities of workplaces draw on physical examinations, skills and proficiency tests, and tests for drug and alcohol use. Large and small establishments recruit and select employees in different ways: Large workplaces expend more resources on hiring. Professional referrals and newspaper advertisements are most apt to be used for identifying high-prestige employees and managerial workers. Highly female jobs are filled with persons recruited via advertisements and unsolicited approaches; selection efforts are generally less intense for such positions.

8. The large majority of U.S. establishments provide some type of *formal job training* program (Chapter 8). Formal job training programs are more

likely to be provided by large establishments than by small ones, but this size difference arises mainly because large organizations are more formalized and more apt to have FILMs. Higher training expenditures and higher numbers of workers trained are also more common in organizations situated in more complex environments and competitive markets.

9. Most training is directed at core employees (who produce the company's main product or service) and their managers (Chapter 9). Contrary to previous research, we find that blue-collar core occupations receive as much company training as do white-collar core workers. The more extensive an organization's internal labor market, the more likely are its training programs to be means for worker advancement into positions of greater responsibility and reward. The presence of a labor union representing core workers in wage negotiations is associated with greater firm-provided training effort. Unions also appear to play compensatory roles, offsetting absent or poorly developed internal labor markets, in fostering the development of formal training opportunities for core production workers.

10. Employees of larger organizations obtain higher levels of *earnings* (Chapter 10). Employees working in establishments with FILMs also earn more, as do people with more education, longer tenure with the employer, jobs that require longer training times, and occupations that have higher levels of prestige. Women earn less than men, whereas supervisors earn more than nonsupervisory employees.

11. There is more *earnings inequality* in larger and more differentiated organizations, but only within managerial occupations (Chapter 11). Organizations with FILMs have less inequality between different kinds of occupations, whereas gender heterogeneity enhances inequality between, as well as within, occupations.

12. Organizations provide their employees with three main kinds of nonwage *fringe benefits* (Chapter 12): (a) personal benefits packages, consisting of such traditional programs as medical, dental, life, and disability insurance; (b) family oriented benefits, including parental leave, sick leave, child and elder care, and job training; and (c) participant benefits including cash bonuses and profit sharing programs. The combination of both personal and familial benefits is most likely to be provided by larger establishments that are also branches or subsidiaries of other firms and operate in complex, competitive, and institutionalized environments.

13. Seventy-one percent of the NOS organizations (in the unweighted sample) use one or more types of *contingent workers* (part-time workers, temporary workers, and subcontractors), whereas only 4% use all three types (Chapter 13). Establishments are more likely to use contingent workers if they provide services (or both services and goods) rather than only produce goods, are nonprofit organizations rather than government agencies or profit-seeking companies, have more full-time employees, have a high degree of specialization, or have a high proportion of females.

14. U.S. organizations exhibit considerable *gender segregation* (Chapter 14): Most men work in typically male jobs, whereas most women work in typically female jobs. Only 19% of jobs can be called gender balanced, even by a generous criterion for "gender balance" of 30% to 70% male or female. Very large organizations have lower gender segregation than small ones. More formalized organizations have less gender segregation.

15. Men are slightly *more committed to their organizations* than are women (Chapter 15). The primary explanation for this gender difference in commitment is that men are more likely than women to hold jobs with commitment-enhancing features. Gender differences in family ties do little to affect the male-female difference in organizational commitment. When job attributes, career variables, and family ties are simultaneously controlled, we find that if anything, women tend to exhibit slightly greater commitment. Contrary to implications of some "gender" models, the correlates of organizational commitment do not appear to be appreciably different for men and women.

## Additional Research Using the NOS

The analyses presented in this book do not exhaust, by any means, the possible uses of the NOS data. Many opportunities remain for analyzing topics such as recruitment and selection practices, training, organizational and occupational sex segregation, fringe benefits and compensation, and organizational performance. For example, information on patterns of employment growth and decline in NOS establishments could be used to examine the consequences of downsizing (e.g., Van Buren 1994).

Moreover, we have only suggested (e.g., in Chapters 10 and 15) some of the ways in which the linked NOS-GSS data set could be used. Other examples of analyses linking NOS organizations and GSS respondents include Kalleberg and Van Buren's (1996) examination of organizational differences in job rewards such as fringe benefits, autonomy, and promotion opportunities (in addition to earnings); Marsden's (1994) analysis of selection practices from the point of view of organizations and individuals; and Kalleberg and Reskin's (1995) assessment of organizational differences in promotion rates of men as opposed to women (which they compare to sex differences in promotion in Norway).

Additional studies could add information from auxiliary sources. For example, Moody (1994) merged data on state-level, business-related policies and expenditures (e.g., taxes, unemployment benefits, educational expenditures, and investments in transportation infrastructure such as highways and airports) onto the NOS, using the available geographical location information. He found that a state's policies have a limited, local impact on organizational performance. The industry and occupation codes on the NOS also provide opportunities to merge additional auxiliary data with the organizational data available from the NOS. For example, information on occupational characteristics from sources such as the *Dictionary of Occupational Titles* could be used to examine how properties of the core and GSS occupations in the NOS are linked to patterns of sex segregation, earnings differences, promotion opportunities, and recruitment and selection.

## Future Research:
## Possible NOS Replications and Extensions

There are important issues related to organizations and their human resources that *cannot* be studied using NOS survey, however, in that we did not collect the requisite data. This was due to constraints such as those imposed by the length of interviews, the fact that we sought data from only one informant per organization, the inclusion of such a diverse group of organizations, and the cross-sectional design of the study. Topics that are not well suited for study with the current NOS data, but that are likely to become increasingly important in the 1990s, include health and safety, drug use, cultural diversity of the organization's work force, combining work and family, comparable worth and equal employment opportunity, job analysis and performance evaluation methods, the changing employment environment, and federal regulation or legislation of employment (e.g., see Heisler, Jones, and Bentham 1988; Wagel 1990).

The NOS could be modified in several respects to allow researchers to study these and other prominent issues within the context of a diverse sample of organizations. Many of these modifications could, nonetheless, sample organizations as we did in the 1991 NOS: Drawing a sample of organizations based on the affiliations found in a random sample from a human population offers a wide variety of design options and decisions (see Chapter 2). The probability proportionate to size design used in the NOS is appropriate for creating an organizational database that represents all types, ages, and sizes of work organizations. Nevertheless, we recognize also that this sampling design is not always optimal or practical; different sampling schemes, drawing on such sources as Dun and Bradstreet's lists of organizations (Osterman 1994a), may be preferable in some cases. For example, the use of lists avoids the considerable costs associated with conducting screening interviews to identify the employers of employed persons in a population. In the following sections, we sketch several design extensions and mention some substantive questions that could be studied more readily using these modified designs.

**Obtaining Multiple Informants**

The NOS is not well suited for testing social psychological theories about organizational participants' motives, beliefs, and behaviors. This is because the NOS-GSS contains data on (usually) one employee in each sampled organization and the NOS information about the organization was obtained (usually) from only one informant (usually a personnel manager) in each establishment.

Since there is only one informant per organization, researchers seeking to study the generation of a negotiated order or group decision making among organizational participants (e.g., Strauss 1978; Weick 1979) will find little to satisfy their appetite for data on detailed microlevel interactions. The NOS is not particularly useful for examining the interactions of the multiple stakeholders in an organization, including shareholders, employees, customers, and the societies in which they are located (Kochan and Useem 1992). Nor will theorists interested in significant internal processes such as principal-agent relations, or the learning of organizational routines and aspects of corporate culture find appreciable data to analyze (e.g., Levitt and March 1988; Pratt and Zeckhauser 1991). The NOS is also not well suited to studying new work systems in that data collected from only one respondent do not permit analysis of how often and how well employees collaborate with those in other organizational units, as when small groups of workers from diverse functional areas engage in adaptive problem solving about production techniques, delivery and service quality, and workplace health and safety.

Perspectives emphasizing culture, norms, and related aspects of the social construction of organizational life, as well as small group processes generally, are probably best studied by research designs based on case analysis or natural language (Pfeffer 1982). The NOS design, however, could be modified to permit better testing of such theories by obtaining multiple respondents in each organization.

Multiple respondents could be added in two ways, each appropriate for addressing a particular set of theoretical questions. First, more than one employee could be interviewed in each organization. This would permit the analysis of within-organization variation in workers' attitudes, job rewards, job duties and responsibilities, along with other features of work that differ within, as well as between, organizations. Within-organization differences are intimately related to operation of social comparison processes, for example.

Interviewing multiple employees within a single organization may be costly in that it often requires a relatively high degree of cooperation from the organization: If researchers are to make inferences to the organization's workforce, they must obtain a list of employees from which to sample (see Lincoln and Kalleberg 1990). Alternatively, an employee (chosen, for example, by a multiplicity design such as the one we used in this study) might be asked to nominate others who work in the establishment. Because respondents are probably more apt to name persons with whom they work closely, however, this would lead to a clustering of respondents that would be undesirable for many purposes, though by no means all purposes (studies of networks or team behaviors are two examples where clustering would be useful).

A second way to add additional informants would be to collect information on the organization from more than one manager. Multiple sources are probably not necessary to obtain valid information on some kinds of organizational properties, such as age, number of employees, or objective structural characteristics such as the number of authority levels in the establishment. Multiple informants, however, are needed to study diversity in the organizational goals and interests of stakeholders and such organizational features as "culture," which may be perceived differently by managers in different parts of the organization. In addition, a single manager (especially in human resources) in relatively large organizations is unlikely to be able to provide valid information about financing, personnel, technology, marketing, and other facets of the organization and its environment. In the NOS, we questioned additional informants in the case of knowledge deficits (see Chapter 2), but did not obtain multiple managerial reports so that their consistency or variability could be studied.

### Studying Change

Because the NOS is based on a cross-sectional snapshot of a very diverse population, it is not very useful for testing theories involving large-scale historical changes, institutional development, or ecological dynamics (e.g., Hannan and Freeman 1989; Scott and Meyer 1992). The NOS's cross-sectional design means that we can study the implications of theories of organizational change only indirectly, by testing dynamic hypotheses using comparative statics.

Consider an issue that requires the use of longitudinal data: the question of structural transformations in the corporation and their implications for work and wealth in the 1990s. Studying this requires a longitudinal survey to track organizations both forward and backward in time. In Fligstein's (1990) periodization of U.S. corporate evolution, the dominant focus of business strategy in the post-World War II era was on the bottom line. The finance-oriented chief executives who took control of the largest companies were not committed to any given industry and did not identify their firms with particular markets. Investments, mergers, and governmental industrial policies were largely driven by conceptions of company growth stressing short-term asset growth and equity gain, at the cost of long-term capital accumulation and job creation (Hayes and Abernathy 1980). More recently, the conglomerate form of organization, a firm composed of many unrelated businesses, largely vanished during restructuring, whereas network conceptions of regularized "firmlike" exchanges—a nexus of contracts among separate entities—seem to be emerging as the newest fashion in corporate combinations (Davis, Diekmann, and Tinsley 1994). Downsizing as a solution to profit woes reached bottom in many companies, which discovered belatedly that they had cut too deeply into muscle in their attempts to trim fat (Rose 1994). Assessing hypotheses related to these kinds of transformations requires that special attention be paid to changes over time in financial arrangements, as well as to the political activism of large and small businesses as they seek to manipulate their environments.

Deciding on the best design for a longitudinal series of organizational surveys involves its own complexities. (We discussed a variety of possible longitudinal designs at the end of Chapter 2.) Should entirely new samples of organizations be drawn each time (i.e., a repeated cross-sectional design), or should previously studied organizations be reinterviewed while new ones are added to replace refusals and those that have vanished as a result of merger or disbanding (i.e., a rotating panel design)? How closely spaced must waves of a longitudinal study be to capture meaningful organizational changes? Can the dates of key organizational events, such as mergers and reorganizations, be obtained with sufficient ease and accuracy to allow reconstruction of full event histories for each organization?

Tracking organizational changes into the future also requires decisions about the kinds of information that should be collected. Which variables for workers and organizations should always be included in employer-employee surveys to ensure comparability and the capacity to observe changes over time? What organizational social indicators beyond, say, size and structural complexity, are of sufficiently wide interest to the organizational research community to be included in most or all studies?

**Mapping the Environments of Organizations**

The 1991 NOS approached the measurement of organizational environments by relying, primarily, on the perceptions of establishment informants. As we noted above, this approach suffers in that the individuals making the reports necessarily offer subjective interpretations and visions limited by their location within the organization. A few "hard" measures of industry or geographic characteristics were also obtained from governmental sources and attached to the organizational records, but these were at high levels of aggregation and sometimes involved considerable time lags. This kind of information does not begin to reflect the full range of potential external influences to which organizations may be subject and the multiple environments within which they are embedded.

An organization's structure and functioning results from the influences of many types of environments, markets, and institutions. A challenge for future organizational research projects will be to develop and implement more rigorous and precise measures of the key environmental dimensions appropriate to the full range of industrial, legal, and political surroundings. Such generic concepts as instability, complexity, uncertainty, munificence, scarcity, and institutionalization require explicit operationalization and quantification at the level of the individual establishment's immediate boundary relationships. Because a survey of diverse organizations embraces an enormous array of contexts and conditions, it offers an ideal laboratory in which to examine the appropriateness of various scales and indicators for measuring the significant forces impinging on the workplace.

On the other hand, surveys of diverse organizations such as the NOS necessarily contain summary measures of context in that they must obtain measures that are applicable to all kinds of organizations. For example, in developing measures of technology that apply to diverse organizations, it is necessary to devise comparable abstract dimensions that permit comparisons between heterogeneous technological clusters, including railroading, education, oil refining, health care, banking, semiconductors, and restaurants, among many others. Perhaps the most plausible approach is to forego specific measures of technology by concentrating on capturing such general technological dimensions as batch versus continuous processing or Thompson's (1967) pooled-sequential-reciprocal interdependencies. Detailed distinctions among organizations would thereby be sacrificed for the capacity to make broad comparisons of how differing technological regimes are related to organizational structures, behaviors, and human resource practices.

Some issues, however, are perhaps best studied with restricted samples that permit more precise measurement of variables. Technology is one such variable. Broadly conceived, organizational technologies encompass both mechanical and human systems for transforming raw inputs into fabricated outputs. At a highly detailed level of analysis, many production and service technologies are industry specific or even firm specific. Studying specific kinds of technologies permits the researcher to measure them very precisely, as well as to obtain objective measures of outcomes such as performance (see, e.g., Kelley 1994).

## Interorganizational Networks

A future study similar to the NOS could also collect information on the network of interorganizational relations between a focal establishment and its organization set: the subcontractors, suppliers, customers, governments, competitors, interlocking directors, and other relevant organizations with which it exchanges money, personnel, authority, legitimacy, and power on a regular basis. What we have in mind here is an organizational parallel to the study of "egocentric" networks at the individual level (Marsden 1987). In 1985, the General Social Survey developed a survey protocol for efficiently enumerating personal networks that could be modified for investigating such interorganizational processes as labor recruitment and training, technology transfer, institutionalization, regulation, and collaboration with suppliers or customers. By capturing the important organizational actors and exchanges that constitute a focal organization's environment, a diverse organizational sample could make a significant contribution to understanding this empirically neglected, but much theorized, phenomenon.

To take a substantive example, both conventional economic and sociological theories of organizational behavior tend to overlook the importance of interorganizational networks for understanding firms' labor-contracting and job-training practices. The hiring and allocation of labor, however, are increasingly neither wholly external to the organization nor entirely confined within isolated physical and organizational locations. Rather, the ongoing transformation of the U.S. employment relation is generating new forms of labor exchange between organizations, whose significance may be better explained by interorganizational concepts and principles than by the atomistic actor approaches embodied in conventional economic and sociological theories of the firm. A network perspective on organizational behavior is likely to prove most useful for tracking the evolving U.S. employment system as it produces complex structures of employer-employee relations that involve internal and external elements simultaneously.

These topics illustrate some of the many important issues facing organizations and organizational researchers in the future. Our identification of these topics as candidates for future unrestricted diverse surveys of organizations reflects our particular blend of theoretical, substantive, and methodological interests. Other researchers certainly have their own views of the cutting-edge issues to which substantial intellectual attention and creative energy should be devoted, some of which are, without question, best studied using other research vehicles. We hope we have demonstrated the promise of studies such as the NOS for contributing to an understanding of the nature of organizations and for monitoring changes in organizational forms as we enter the 21st century.

# Appendix
## *Obtaining the NOS for Secondary Analyses*

We hope that many readers of this book will become sufficiently intrigued by the potential opportunities in the 1991 National Organizations Study that they will conduct their own research with these data. We strongly encourage such secondary data analyses, as many variables and hypotheses remain to be explored. Because the NOS was supported financially by public funds, through the National Science Foundation and the U.S. Department of Labor, it has been promptly released to the general user community. For information on how to obtain a copy of the data set and technical documentation, which includes the questionnaire for the establishment informant interviews, contact the Inter-University Consortium for Political and Social Research, P.O. Box 1248, Ann Arbor, MI 48106-1248; Phone (313) 764-2570. If your college or university is an ICPSR member, distribution can be arranged through your campus representative.

The data file includes information from the interviews with establishment informants for the NOS, the 727 corresponding General Social Survey respondent interviews, as well as industry-level variables at the two-digit Standard Industrial Classification for each establishment. Wherever a NOS establishment was the employer of a GSS respondent's spouse, the individual-level data about the spouse were assigned to the relevant

GSS variables (for example, the number of years of education, EDUC, was given the value reported in SPEDUC). Because GSS respondents are asked for very little information about their spouses, substantial missing data are present for those cases. We especially acknowledge the contributions of Alisa Potter and Mark E. Van Buren in preparing the data set for public release.

Neither the original investigators, the National Science Foundation that funded the NOS, nor the distributor or collector of the data should be held responsible for the analyses, interpretations, and findings presented in print by secondary users. The following is a form of a disclaimer that we encourage all users of these data to employ:

> The data (and tabulations) used in this (publication) were made available (in part) by (ICPSR, or the other archive or agency that distributed the data). The data for the 1991 National Organizations Study were originally collected by the Survey Research Laboratory at the University of Illinois and the National Opinion Research Center at the University of Chicago. Neither the original investigators or collectors of the data nor the distributor of the data bear any responsibility for the analyses or interpretations presented herein.

An appropriate citation to the NOS includes the following:

> Kalleberg, Arne L., David Knoke, Peter V. Marsden, and Joe L. Spaeth. *The 1991 National Organization Study* [machine readable data file]. University of Minnesota [producer] 1992. Inter-university Consortium for Political and Social Research (ICPSR) [distributor] 1993.

Individuals receiving the NOS data are strongly urged to inform the distributor of any errors and discrepancies discovered in the data. Users are particularly urged to contact the archive about problems and difficulties that prevented effective and convenient access to the data. This information is necessary to improve the data and to facilitate more efficient and economic data processing. Users are also requested to provide information to the authors about significant subsets and special aggregations of data that are developed in using these data. Finally, to provide agencies with essential information about the use of archival sources and to facilitate the exchange of information about research activities, users are expected to send two copies of each completed manuscript or thesis abstract to the distributor.

# References

Abraham, Katharine G. 1988. "Flexible Staffing Arrangements and Employers' Short-Term Adjustment Strategies." National Bureau of Economic Research Working Paper No. 2617. Cambridge, MA: NBER.

———. 1990. "Restructuring the Employment Relationship: The Growth of Market-Mediated Work Arrangements." Pp. 85-119 in *New Developments in the Labor Market: Toward a New Institutional Paradigm,* edited by Katherine G. Abraham and Robert B. McKersie. Cambridge, MA: MIT Press.

Aldrich, Howard E. 1979. *Organizations and Environments.* Englewood Cliffs, NJ: Prentice Hall.

Aldrich, Howard E. and Peter V. Marsden. 1988. "Environments and Organizations." Pp. 361-92 in *Handbook of Sociology,* edited by Neil J. Smelser. Newbury Park, CA: Sage.

Aldrich, Howard E. and Udo Staber. 1988. "Large Employers Take Charge: Increasing Differentiation in the U.S. Industrial Relations System." Paper presented at the Conference on Industrial Relations in Times of Regulation, Bad Homburg, West Germany, September 29-October 1.

Althauser, Robert P. 1989. "Internal Labor Markets." *Annual Review of Sociology* 15:143-61.

Althauser, Robert P. and Arne L. Kalleberg. 1981. "Firms, Occupations and the Structure of Labor Markets: A Conceptual Analysis." Pp. 119-49 in *Sociological Perspectives on Labor Markets,* edited by Ivar Berg. New York: Academic Press.

Anderson, Cynthia D. and Donald Tomaskovic-Devey. 1995. "Patriarchal Pressures: An Exploration of Organizational Contexts that Exacerbate and Erode Gender Earnings Inequality." *Work and Occupations* 22:328-356.

Angle, Harold L. and James L. Perry. 1981. "An Empirical Assessment of Organizational Commitment and Organizational Effectiveness." *Administrative Science Quarterly* 26:1-14.

Appelbaum, Eileen. 1992. "Structural Change and the Growth of Part-Time and Temporary Employment." Pp. 1-14 in *New Policies for the Part-Time and Contingent Workforce.*

*Economic Policy Institute Series,* edited by Virginia duRivage. Armonk, NY: M.E. Sharpe.

Appelbaum, Eileen and Rosemary Batt. 1994. *The New American Workplace: Transforming Work Systems in the United States.* Ithaca, NY: ILR Press.

Appelbaum, Eileen and Judith Gregory. 1988. "Union Approaches to Contingent Work Arrangements." Discussion paper FS I 88-8. Wissenschaftszentrum Berlin fur Sozialforschung.

Arrow, Kenneth. 1973. "The Theory of Discrimination." Pp. 3-33 in *Discrimination in Labor Markets,* edited by O. Ashenfelter. Princeton, NJ: Princeton University Press.

Arthur, Jeffrey B. 1992. "The Link Between Business Strategy and Industrial Relations Systems in American Steel Minimills." *Industrial and Labor Relations Review* 45:488-506.

Aryee, Samuel and Lau Joo Heng. 1990. "A Note on the Applicability of an Organizational Commitment Model." *Work and Occupations* 17:229-39.

Averitt, Robert T. 1968. *The Dual Economy: The Dynamics of American Industry Structure.* New York: Norton.

Bailey, Thomas. 1992. "Discretionary Effort and the Organization of Work: Employee Participation and Work Reform Since Hawthorne." Unpublished paper, Columbia University Teachers College.

Bailey, William R. and Albert E. Schwenk. 1980. "Wage Rate Variation by Size of Establishment." *Industrial Relations* 19:192-98.

Bamber, Greg J. and Russell D. Lansbury, eds. 1989. *New Technology: International Perspectives on Human Resources and Industrial Relations.* London, England: Unwin Hyman.

Barker, James R. 1993. "Tightening the Iron Cage: Concertive Control in Self-Managing Teams." *Administrative Science Quarterly* 38:408-37.

Barley, Stephen R. 1990. "The Alignment of Technology and Structure Through Roles and Networks." *Administrative Science Quarterly* 35:61-103.

Barnett, William P. and Anne S. Miner. 1992. "Standing on the Shoulders of Others: Career Interdependence in Job Mobility." *Administrative Science Quarterly* 37:262-81.

Baron, James N. 1984. "Organizational Perspectives on Stratification." *Annual Review of Sociology* 10:37-69.

———. 1991 "Organizational Evidence of Ascription in Labor Markets." Pp. 113-44 in *New Approaches to Economic and Social Analyses of Discrimination,* edited by Richard R. Cornwall and Phanindra V. Wunnava. New York: Praeger.

Baron, James N. and William T. Bielby. 1980. "Bringing the Firms Back In: Stratification, Segmentation, and the Organization of Work." *American Sociological Review* 45:737-65.

———. 1984. "The Organization of Work in a Segmented Economy." *American Sociological Review* 49:454-73.

Baron, James N., Alison Davis-Blake, and William T. Bielby. 1986. "The Structure of Opportunity: How Promotion Ladders Vary Within and Among Organizations." *Administrative Science Quarterly* 31:248-73.

Baron, James N., Frank R. Dobbin, and P. Deveraux Jennings. 1986. "War and Peace: The Evolution of Modern Personnel Administration in U.S. Industry." *American Journal of Sociology* 92:350-83.

Baron, James N., P. Devereaux Jennings, and Frank R. Dobbin. 1988. "Mission Control? The Development of Personnel Systems in U.S. Industry." *American Sociological Review* 53:497-514.

Baron, James N., Arne L. Kalleberg, James R. Lincoln, Jeffrey Pfeffer, and Pamela L. Pommerenke. 1989. "Wage Structures in Organizations: Determinants of Wage Dispersion in U.S. and Japanese Manufacturing Firms." Paper presented at Annual Meetings of the American Sociological Association.

Baron, James N. and Andrew E. Newman. 1990. "For What It's Worth: Organizations, Occupations and the Value of Work Done by Women and Non-Whites." *American Sociological Review* 55:155-75.

Baron, James N. and Jeffrey Pfeffer. 1994. "The Social Psychology of Organizations and Inequality." *Social Psychology Quarterly* 57:190-209.

Barron, John M. and John Bishop. 1985. "Extensive Search, Intensive Search, and Hiring Costs: New Evidence on Employer Hiring Activity." *Economic Inquiry* 23:363-82.

Barron, John M., John Bishop, and William C. Dunkelberg. 1985. "Employer Search: The Interviewing and Hiring of New Employees." *Review of Economics and Statistics* 67:43-52.

Barron, John M., Dan A. Black, and Mark A. Lowenstein. 1987. "Employer Size: The Implications for Search, Training, Capital Investment, Starting Wages, and Wage Growth." *Journal of Labor Economics* 5:76-89.

————. 1989. "Job Matching and On-the-Job Training." *Journal of Labor Economics* 7:1-19.

Becker, Gary S. 1964. *Human Capital: A Theoretical and Empirical Analysis with Special Reference to Education.* New York: National Bureau of Economic Research.

————. 1971. *The Economics of Discrimination,* 2nd ed. Chicago: University of Chicago Press.

————. 1981. *A Treatise on the Family.* Cambridge: Harvard University Press.

Becker, Howard S. 1960. "Notes on the Concept of Commitment." *American Journal of Sociology* 66:32-40.

Belous, Richard S. 1989. *The Contingent Economy: The Growth of the Temporary, Part-time, and Subcontracted Workforce.* Washington, DC: National Planning Association.

Berg, Ivar. 1970. *Education and Jobs: The Great Training Robbery.* New York: Praeger.

Berg, Ivar, ed. 1981. *Sociological Perspectives on Labor Markets.* New York: Plenum.

Berger, Joseph, Susan Rosenholtz, and Morris Zelditch, Jr. 1980. "Status Organizing Processes." *Annual Review of Sociology* 6:479-508.

Berger, Suzanne, Michael L. Dertouzos, Richard K. Lester, Robert M. Solow, and Lester C. Thurow. 1989. "Toward a New Industrial America." *Scientific American* 260:39-47.

Berk, Richard A. 1983. "An Introduction to Sample Selection Bias in Sociological Data." *American Sociological Review* 48:386-98.

Berscheid, Ellen and Elaine Hatfield Walster. 1969. *Interpersonal Attraction.* Reading, MA: Addison-Wesley.

Best, Michael. 1990. *The New Competition: Institution of Industrial Restructuring.* Cambridge, MA: Harvard University Press.

Bielby, William T. and James N. Baron. 1984. "A Woman's Place Is With Other Women: Sex Segregation Within Organizations." Pp. 27-55 in *Sex Segregation in the Workplace: Trends, Explanations, Remedies,* edited by Barbara F. Reskin. Washington, DC: National Academy Press.

————. 1985. "Organizational Barriers to Gender Equality: Sex Segregation of Jobs and Opportunities." Pp. 233-51 in *Gender and the Life Course,* edited by Alice S. Rossi. Hawthorne, NY: Aldine deGruyter.

————. 1986. "Men and Women at Work: Sex Segregation and Statistical Discrimination." *American Journal of Sociology* 91:759-99.

Bielby, Denise Del Vento. 1992. "Commitment to Family and Work." *Annual Review of Sociology* 18:281-302.

Bielby, Denise Del Vento and William T. Bielby. 1984. "Work Commitment, Sex-Role Attitudes, and Women's Employment." *American Sociological Review* 49:234-47.

————. 1988. "She Works Hard for the Money: Household Responsibilities and the Allocation of Work Effort." *American Journal of Sociology* 93:1031-59.

Bills, David B. 1988. "Educational Credentials and Promotions: Does Schooling Do More Than Get You in the Door?" *Sociology of Education* 61:52-60.
Bird, Chloe E. 1990. "High Finance, Small Change: Women's Increased Representation in Bank Management." Pp. 145-66 in *Job Queues, Gender Queues: Explaining Women's Inroads into Male Occupations*, by Barbara F. Reskin and Patricia A. Roos. Philadelphia: Temple University Press.
Bishop, John H. 1994. "The Impact of Previous Training on Productivity and Wages." Pp. 161-99 in *Training and the Private Sector: International Comparisons*, edited by Lisa Lynch. Chicago: University of Chicago Press.
Blair, Margaret M., ed. 1993. *The Deal Decade: What Takeovers and Leveraged Buyouts Mean for Corporate Governance*. Washington, DC: Brookings Institution.
Blau, Francine D. and Lawrence M. Kahn. 1981. "Race and Sex Differences in Quits by Young Workers." *Industrial and Labor Relations Review* 34:563-77.
Blau, Peter M. 1970. "A Formal Theory of Differentiation in Organizations." *American Sociological Review* 35:201-18.
———. 1972. "Interdependence and Hierarchy in Organizations." *Social Science Research* 1:1-24.
Blau, Peter M. and Richard A. Schoenherr. 1971. *The Structure of Organizations*. New York: Basic Books.
Blaug, Mark. 1976. "Human Capital Theory: A Slightly Jaundiced Survey." *Journal of Economic Literature* 14:827-55.
Block, Jeanne H. 1976. "Issues, Problems, and Pitfalls in Assessing Sex Differences: A Critical Review of the Psychology of Sex Differences." *Merrill-Palmer Quarterly* 22:283-308.
Bloom, David E. and Richard B. Freeman. 1992. "The Fall in Private Pension Coverage in the United States." *American Economic Review* 82:539-45.
Bluestone, Barry and Bennett Harrison. 1982. *The Deindustrialization of America*. New York: Basic Books.
Bohrnstedt, George W. and David Knoke. 1988. *Statistics for Social Data Analysis*, 2nd ed. Itasca, IL: F.E. Peacock.
Bollen, Kenneth A. 1989. *Structural Equations With Latent Variables*. New York: Wiley.
Boston, Thomas D. 1990. "Segmented Labor Markets: New Evidence from a Study of Four Race-Gender Groups." *Industrial and Labor Relations Review* 44:99-115.
Bowers, Brent. 1994. "Small Business Gets Set to Flex Its Muscle at White House." *Wall Street Journal*, September 8, B2.
Bridges, William. 1994. "The End of the Job." *Fortune*, September 19, pp. 62-74.
Bridges, William P. 1980. "Industrial Marginality and Female Employment: A New Appraisal." *American Sociological Review* 45:58-75.
———. 1982. "The Sexual Segregation of Occupations: Theories of Labor Stratification in Industry." *American Journal of Sociology* 88:270-95.
Bridges, William P. and Robert L. Nelson. 1989. "Markets in Hierarchies: Organizational and Market Influences on Gender Inequality in a State Pay System." *American Journal of Sociology* 95:616-59.
Bridges, William P. and Wayne J. Villemez. 1991. "Employment Relations and the Labor Market: Integrating Institutional and Market Perspectives." *American Sociological Review* 56:748-64.
———. 1994. *The Employment Relationship: Causes and Consequences of Modern Personnel Administration*. New York: Plenum.
Brown, Charles. 1990. "Empirical Evidence on Private Training." *Research in Labor Economics* 11:97-113.

Brown, Charles and James Medoff. 1989. "The Employer Size-Wage Effect." *Journal of Political Economy* 97:1027-59.

Brown, Charles, James Hamilton, and James Medoff. 1990. *Employers Large and Small.* Cambridge, MA: Harvard University Press.

Bryk, Anthony S. and Stephen W. Raudenbush. 1992. *Hierarchical Linear Models.* Newbury Park, CA: Sage.

Burawoy, Michael. 1979. *Manufacturing Consent: Changes in the Labor Process Under Monopoly Capital.* Chicago: University of Chicago Press.

Bureau of National Affairs. 1986. *Changing Workplace: New Directions in Staffing and Scheduling.* Washington, DC: Bureau of National Affairs.

Burke, Thomas P. and John D. Morton. 1990. "How Firm Size and Industry Affect Employee Benefits." *Monthly Labor Review* 113:35-43.

Burns, Tom and G. M. Stalker. 1961. *The Management of Innovation.* London: Tavistock.

Burt, Ronald S. 1992. *Structural Holes.* Cambridge, MA: Harvard University Press.

Callaghan, Polly and Heidi Hartmann. 1991. "Contingent Work: A Chart Book on Part-Time and Temporary Employment." Washington, DC: Economic Policy Institute.

Campbell, Karen E. and Rachel A. Rosenfeld. 1985. "Job Search and Job Mobility: Sex and Race Differences." Pp. 147-74 in *Research in the Sociology of Work,* Vol. 3, edited by Ida Harper Simpson and Richard L. Simpson. Greenwich, CT: JAI.

Cappelli, Peter, ed. 1996. *Change at Work.* New York: Oxford University Press.

Carey, L. and Kim Hazelbaker. 1986. "Employment Growth in the Temporary Help Industry." *Monthly Labor Review* (April):37-44.

Carnevale, Anthony P., Leila J. Gainer, and Janice Villet. 1990. *Training in America: The Organization and Strategic Role of Training.* San Francisco: Jossey-Bass.

Chelte, Anthony F. and Curt Tausky. 1986. "A Note on Organizational Commitment: Antecedents and Consequences Among Managers, Professionals, and Blue-Collar Workers." *Work and Occupations* 13:553-61.

Child, John. 1972. "Organization Structure, Environment, and Performance: The Role of Strategic Choice." *Sociology* 6:1-22.

———. 1973. "Predicting and Understanding Organization Structure." *Administrative Science Quarterly* 38: 168-85.

Christensen, Kathleen. 1989. "Flexible Staffing and Scheduling in U.S. Corporations." Research Bulletin No. 240. New York: The Conference Board.

———. 1991. "The Two-Tiered Workforce in U.S. Corporations." Pp. 140-155 in *Turbulence in the American Workplace,* by Peter B. Doeringer et al. New York: Oxford University Press.

Cockburn, Cynthia. 1988. *Machinery of Dominance: Women, Men and Technical Know-How.* Boston: Northeastern University Press.

———. 1991. *In the Way of Woman: Men's Resistance to Sex Equality in Organizations.* Ithaca, NY: ILR Press.

Cohen, Aaron and Geula Lowenberg. 1990. "A Re-examination of the Side-Bet Theory as Applied to Organizational Commitment: A Meta-Analysis." *Human Relations* 43:1015-50.

Cohen, Yinon and Jeffrey Pfeffer. 1986. "Organizational Hiring Standards." *Administrative Science Quarterly* 31:1-24.

Cohn, Samuel. 1985. *The Process of Occupational Sex-Typing.* Philadelphia: Temple University Press.

Collins, Randall. 1979. *The Credential Society: An Historical Sociology of Education and Stratification.* New York: Academic Press.

Commission on the Skills of the American Workforce. 1990. *America's Choice: High Skills or Low Wages?* Rochester, NY: National Center on Education and the Economy.

Corcoran, M., L. Datcher, and Greg J. Duncan. 1980. "Information and Influence Networks in Labor Markets." Pp. 1-37 in *Five Thousand American Families,* Vol. 8, edited by Greg J. Duncan and James N. Morgan. Ann Arbor: University of Michigan, Institute for Social Research.

Coser, Rose Laub. 1986. "Cognitive Structure and the Use of Social Space." *Sociological Forum* 1:1-26.

Cotton, John L., David A. Vollrath, Kirk L. Froggatt, Mark L. Lengnick-Hall, and Kenneth R. Jennings. 1988. "Employee Participation: Diverse Forms and Different Outcomes." *Academy of Management Review* 13:8-22.

Curme, Michael A., Barry T. Hirsch, and David A. MacPherson. 1990. "Union Membership and Contract Coverage in the United States, 1983-1988." *Industrial and Labor Relations Review* 44:5-29.

Cutcher-Gershenfeld, Joel. 1991. "The Impact on Economic Performance of a Transformation in Workplace Relations." *Industrial and Labor Relations Review* 44:241-60.

Daft, Richard L. 1986. *Organization Theory and Design,* 2nd ed. New York: West.

Davis, Gerald F., Kristina A. Diekmann, and Catherine H. Tinsley. 1994. "The Decline and Fall of the Conglomerate Firm in the 1980s: The Deinstitutionalization of an Organizational Form." *American Sociological Review* 59:547-70.

Davis, Gerald F. and Suzanne K. Stout. 1992. "Organization Theory and the Market for Corporate Control: A Dynamic Analysis of the Characteristics of Large Takeover Targets, 1980-1990." *Administrative Science Quarterly* 37:605-33.

Davis, James A. and Tom W. Smith. 1991. *General Social Surveys, 1972-1991: Cumulative Codebook.* Storrs, CT: Roper Center for Public Opinion Research.

———. 1992. *The NORC General Social Survey: A User's Guide.* Newbury Park, CA: Sage.

———. 1994. *General Social Surveys, 1972-1994: Cumulative Codebook.* Storrs, CT: Roper Center for Public Opinion Research.

Deal, Terrence E. and Allan A. Kennedy. 1982. *Corporate Cultures.* Reading, MA: Addison-Wesley.

de Neubourg, Chris. 1985. "Part-Time Work: An International Quantitative Comparison." *International Labour Review* 124:559-76.

de Vaus, David and Ian McAllister. 1991. "Gender and Work Orientation: Values and Satisfaction in Western Europe." *Work and Occupations* 18:72-93.

Dertouzos, Michael L., Richard K. Lester, Robert M. Solow and the MIT Commission on Industrial Productivity. 1989. *Made in America: Regaining the Productive Edge.* Cambridge, MA: MIT Press.

DiMaggio, Paul. 1982. "Cultural Capital and School Success: The Impact of Status-Culture Participation on the Grades of U.S. High School Students." *American Sociological Review* 47:189-201.

DiMaggio, Paul and Walter W. Powell. 1983. "The Iron Cage Revisited: Institutional Isomorphism and Collective Rationality in Organizational Fields." *American Sociological Review* 48:147-60.

DiPrete, Thomas A. 1990. "Is There a Nonspurious Link Between the Market Power and the Wage Structure of Firms?" *Research in Social Stratification and Mobility* 9:283-306.

Dill, William R. 1958. "Environment as an Influence on Managerial Autonomy." *Administrative Science Quarterly* 2:409-43.

Dobbin, Frank, L. Edelman, John W. Meyer, W. Richard Scott, and Ann Swidler. 1988. "The Expansion of Due Process in Organizations." Pp. 71-98 in *Institutional Patterns and Organizations: Culture and Environment,* edited by Lynne G. Zucker. Cambridge, MA: Ballinger.

Dobbin, Frank R., John R. Sutton, John W. Meyer, and W. Richard Scott. 1993. "Equal Opportunity Law and the Construction of Internal Labor Markets." *American Journal of Sociology* 99:396-427.

Doeringer, Peter B., Kathleen Christensen, Patricia M. Flynn, Douglas T. Hall, Harry C. Katz, Jeffrey H. Keefe, Christopher J. Ruhm, Andrew M. Sum, and Michael Useem. 1991. *Turbulence in the American Workplace.* New York: Oxford University Press.

Doeringer, Peter B. and Michael J. Piore. 1971. *Internal Labor Markets and Manpower Analysis.* Lexington, MA: D.C. Heath.

Donato, Katherine M. 1990. "Keepers of the Corporate Image: Women in Public Relations." Pp. 129-43 in *Job Queues, Gender Queues: Explaining Women's Inroads into Male Occupations,* by Barbara F. Reskin and Patricia A. Roos. Philadelphia: Temple University Press.

Donovan, Ronald and Marsha J. Orr. 1982. *Subcontracting in the Pubic Sector: The New York State Experience.* Ithaca, New York: Institute of Public Employment.

Dore, Ronald. 1973. *British Factory, Japanese Factory: The Origins of Diversity in Industrial Relations.* Berkeley: University of California Press.

Drabek, Thomas E., Rita Braito, Cynthia C. Cook, James R. Powell, and David Rogers. 1982. "Selecting Samples of Organizations: Central Issues and Emergent Trends." *Pacific Sociological Review* 25:377-400.

Dulworth, Michael R., Delmar L. Landen, and Brian L. Usilaner. 1990. "Employee Involvement Systems in U.S. Corporations: Right Objectives, Wrong Strategies." *National Productivity Review* 9:141-56.

Duncan, Greg J. and Saul Hoffman. 1979. "On-the-Job Training and Earnings Differences by Race and Sex." *Review of Economics and Statistics* 61:594-603.

Duncan, Greg J. and Frank P. Stafford. 1980. "Do Union Members Receive Compensating Wage Differentials?" *American Economic Review* 70:355-71.

Eaton, Adrienne E. and Paula B. Voos. 1992. "Union and Contemporary Innovations in Work Organization, Compensation, and Employee Participation." Pp. 173-215 in *Unions and Economic Competitiveness,* edited by Lawrence Mishel and Paula B. Voos. Armonk, NY: M.E. Sharpe.

Edelman, Lauren B. 1990. "Legal Environments and Organizational Governance: The Expansion of Due Process in the American Workplace." *American Journal of Sociology* 95:1401-40.

Edwards, Richard. 1979. *Contested Terrain: The Transformation of the Workplace in the Twentieth Century.* New York: Basic Books.

Ehrenberg, Ronald G., Pamela Rosenberg, and Jeanne Li. 1988. "Part-Time Employment in the United States." Pp. 256-87 in *Employment, Unemployment, and Labor Utilization,* edited by Robert A. Hart. Boston: Unwin Hyman.

Elbaum, Bernard. 1984. "The Making and Shaping of Job and Pay Structures in the Iron and Steel Industry." Pp. 71-107 in *Internal Labor Markets,* edited by Paul Osterman. Cambridge, MA: MIT Press.

Employee Benefits Research Institute. 1990. *Fundamentals of Employee Benefit Programs.* Washington, DC: Employee Benefits Research Institute.

England, Paula. 1992. *Comparable Worth: Theories and Evidence.* New York: Aldine de-Gruyter.

England, Paula, George Farkas, Barbara Stanek Kilbourne, and Thomas Dou. 1988. "Explaining Occupational Sex Segregation and Wages: Findings from a Model with Fixed Effects." *American Sociological Review* 53:544-58.

Evans, David S. and Linda S. Leighton. 1988. "Why Do Smaller Firms Pay Less?" *Journal of Human Resources* 24:299-318.

Farkas, George and Paula England, eds. 1988. *Industries, Firms, and Jobs: Sociological and Economic Approaches.* New York: Plenum.

Farkas, George, Paula England, and Margaret Barton. 1988. "Structural Effects on Wages: Sociological and Economic Views." Pp. 93-112 in *Industries, Firms, and Jobs: Sociological and Economic Approaches,* edited by George Farkas and Paula England. New York: Plenum.

Feldberg, Roslyn, and Evelyn Nakano Glenn. 1979. "Male and Female: Job Versus Gender Models in the Sociology of Work." *Social Problems* 26: 524-38.

Ferman, Louis A., Michele Hoyman, Joel Cutcher-Gershenfeld, and Ernst J. Savoie, eds. 1991. *Joint Training Programs: A Union-Management Approach to Preparing Workers for the Future.* Ithaca, New York: ILR Press.

Fiorentine, Robert. 1988. "Sex Differences in Success Expectancies and Causal Attribution: Is This Why Fewer Women Become Physicians?" *Social Psychology Quarterly* 51:236-49.

Flamholtz, Eric G., Yvonne Randle, and Sonja Sackmann. 1987. "The Tenor of Today." *Personnel Journal* 66:61-70.

Fligstein, Neil. 1990. *The Transformation of Corporate Control.* Cambridge, MA: Harvard University Press.

Frank, Robert H. 1984. "Are Workers Paid Their Marginal Product?" *American Economic Review* 74:549-71.

Freeman, John H. 1986. "Data Quality and the Development of Organizational Social Science: An Editorial Essay." *Administrative Science Quarterly* 31:298-303.

Freeman, Richard B. 1980. "The Exit-Voice Tradeoff in the Labor Market: Unionism, Job Tenure, Quits and Separation." *Quarterly Journal of Economics* 94:643-73.

Freeman, Richard B. and James L. Medoff. 1984. *What Do Unions Do?* New York: Basic Books.

Freeman, Robert B. 1981. "The Effect of Unionism on Fringe Benefits." *Industrial and Labor Relations Review* 34:489-509.

Freund, William C. and Eugene Epstein. 1984. *People and Productivity: The New York Stock Exchange Guide to Financial Incentives and the Quality of Work Life.* Homewood, IL: Dow-Jones-Irwin.

Furubotn, Eirik G. and Rudolf Richter, eds. 1991. *The New Institutional Economics.* College Station: Texas A&M University Press.

Gaertner, Karen N. and Stanley D. Nollen. 1989. "Career Experiences, Perceptions of Employment Practices, and Psychological Commitment to the Organization." *Human Relations* 43:975-91.

Gandz, Jeffrey. 1990. "The Employee Empowerment Era." *Business Quarterly* 55:74-79.

Garen, John E. 1985. "Worker Heterogeneity, Job Screening, and Firm Size." *Journal of Political Economy* 93:715-39.

Gerson, Kathleen. 1985. *Hard Choices: How Women Decide about Work, Career and Motherhood.* Berkeley: University of California Press.

Giele, Janet Z. 1988. "Gender and Sex Roles." Pp. 291-323 in *Handbook of Sociology,* edited by Neil J. Smelser. Newbury Park, CA: Sage.

Golden, Lonnie and Eileen Appelbaum. 1992. "What Was Driving the 1982-88 Boom in Temporary Employment?: Preference of Workers or Decisions and Power of Employers?" *American Journal of Economics and Sociology* 51:473-94.

Goldfield, Michael. 1987. *The Decline of Organized Labor in the United States.* Chicago: University of Chicago Press.

Goldin, Claudia, G. 1990. *Understanding the Gender Gap.* Oxford: Oxford University Press.

Goldthorpe, John N. and Keith Hope. 1974. *The Social Grading of Occupations: A New Approach and Scale.* Oxford: Clarendon Press.

Gordon, Margaret S. and Margaret Thal-Larsen. 1969. *Employer Policies in a Changing Labor Market.* Berkeley, CA: University of California, Institute of Labor Relations.

Gottfried, Heidi. 1992. "The Impact of Skill on Union Membership: Rethinking Gender Differences." *Sociological Quarterly* 33:99-114.

Granovetter, Mark. 1973. "The Strength of Weak Ties." *American Journal of Sociology* 78:1360-80.

―――. 1981. "Toward a Sociological Theory of Income Differences." Pp. 11-47 in *Sociological Perspectives on Labor Markets,* edited by Ivar Berg. New York: Academic Press.

―――. 1984. "Small Is Bountiful: Labor Markets and Establishment Size." *American Sociological Review* 49:323-34.

―――. 1985. "Economic Action and Social Structure: The Problem of Embeddedness." *American Journal of Sociology* 91:481-510.

Grayson, C. Jackson Jr. and Carla O'Dell. 1988. *American Business: A 2-Minute Warning.* New York: Free Press.

Greene, William H. 1989. *LIMDEP Version 5.1.* New York: Econometric Software.

―――. 1990. *Econometric Analysis.* New York: McGraw-Hill.

Grossman, Glenn M. 1992. "U.S. Workers Receive a Wide Range of Employee Benefits." *Monthly Labor Review* (September):36-39.

Grusky, Oscar. 1966. "Career Mobility and Organizational Commitment." *Administrative Science Quarterly* 10:488-503.

Hachen, David S., Jr. 1990. "Three Models of Job Mobility in Labor Markets." *Work and Occupations* 17:320-54.

Hakim, Catherine. 1990. "Core and Periphery in Employers' Workforce Strategies: Evidence from the 1987 E.L.U.S. Survey." *Work, Employment and Society* 4:157-88.

―――. 1991. "Grateful Slaves and Self-Made Women: Fact and Fantasy in Women's Work Orientations." *European Sociological Review* 7:101-21.

Hall, Richard H. 1963. "The Concept of Bureaucracy: An Empirical Assessment." *American Journal of Sociology* 69:32-40.

Hamermesh, Daniel S. 1980. "Commentary." Pp. 383-88 in *The Economics of Firm Size, Market Structure, and Social Performance,* edited by J. J. Siegfried. Washington, DC: Federal Trade Commission.

Hannan, Michael T. and John H. Freeman. 1989. *Organizational Ecology.* Cambridge: Harvard University Press.

Härdle, W. 1990. *Applied Nonparametric Regression.* New York: Cambridge University Press.

Harrison, Bennett. 1994. *Lean and Mean: The Changing Landscape of Corporate Power in the Age of Flexibility.* New York: Basic Books.

Hart, Robert A. 1984. *The Economics of Non-Wage Labour Costs.* London: Allen and Unwin.

Hartmann, Heidi. 1976. "Capitalism, Patriarchy and Job Segregation by Sex." Pp. 137-70 in *Women and the Workplace,* edited by M. Blaxall and B. Regan. Chicago: University of Chicago Press.

Hartmann, Heidi and June Lapidus. 1989. *Temporary Work.* Washington, DC: Institute for Women's Policy Research.

Hashimoto, M. 1981. "Firm-Specific Human Capital as a Shared Investment." *American Economic Review* 71:475-82.

Hayes, Robert H. and William J. Abernathy. 1980. "Managing Our Way to Economic Decline." *Harvard Business Review* (July-August):67-77.

Hayghe, Howard V. 1988. "Employers and Child Care: What Roles Do They Play?" *Monthly Labor Review* 113:38-44.

Heckscher, Charles. 1995. *White-Collar Blues: Management Loyalties in an Age of Corporate Restructuring.* New York: Basic Books.

Hedström, Peter. 1991. "Organizational Differentiation and Earnings Dispersion." *American Journal of Sociology* 97:96-113.

Heisler, William, W. David Jones, Philip O. Bentham, Jr. 1988. *Managing Human Resources Issues.* San Francisco: Jossey-Bass.

Herman, Susan J. 1994. *Hiring Right: A Practical Guide.* Thousand Oaks, CA: Sage.

Hickson, David J., C.R. Hinings, C.A. Lee, R.E. Schneck, and J.M. Pennings. 1971. "A Strategic Contingencies' Theory of Intraorganizational Power." *Administrative Science Quarterly* 16:216-29.

Hill, M. Anne and June E. O'Neill. 1992. "Intercohort Change in Women's Labor Market Status." *Research in Labor Economics* 13:215-86.

Hodson, Randy. 1984. "Companies, Industries, and the Measurement of Economic Segmentation." *American Sociological Review* 49:335-48.

———. 1989. "Gender Differences in Job Satisfaction: Why Aren't Women More Dissatisfied?" *Sociological Quarterly* 30:385-99.

Holmes, Deborah, Richard Belous, Joy Sheets, and Lisa Sementilli-Dann. 1992. *New Policies for the Part-Time and Contingent Workforce.* Armonk, NY: M.E. Sharpe.

Hrebiniak, Lawrence G. and Joseph A. Alutto. 1972. "Personal and Role-Related Factors in the Development of Organizational Commitment." *Administrative Science Quarterly* 17:555-72.

Huber, Joan. 1986. "Trends in Gender Stratification." *Sociological Forum* 1:476-95.

Ibarra, Herminia. 1992. "Homophily and Differential Returns: Sex Differences in Network Structure and Access in an Advertising Firm." *Administrative Science Quarterly* 37:422-47.

Ivancevich, J.M. and W. F. Glueck. 1983. *Foundations of Personnel/Human Resource Management,* rev. ed. Plano, TX: Business Publications.

Jaccard, James, Robert Turrisi, and Choi K. Wan. 1990. *Interaction Effects in Multiple Regression.* Newbury Park, CA: Sage.

Jacobs, David. 1981. "Toward a Theory of Mobility and Behavior in Organizations: An Inquiry into the Consequences of Some Relationships Between Individual Performance and Organizational Success." *American Journal of Sociology* 87:684-707.

Jacobs, Jerry. 1989a. "Long-Term Trends in Occupational Segregation by Sex." *American Journal of Sociology* 95:160-73.

———. 1989b.*Revolving Doors: Sex Segregation and Women's Careers.* Stanford, CA: Stanford University Press.

Jacobs, Jerry A., Marie Lukens, and Michael Useem. 1994. *Organizational, Job, and Individual Determinants of Workplace Training: Evidence from the National Organizations Survey.* Paper presented to Eastern Sociological Society annual meeting, Philadelphia.

Jacobs, Jerry and Ronnie Steinberg. 1990. "Compensating Differentials and the Male-Female Wage Gap: Evidence from the New York State Comparable Worth Study" *Social Forces* 69:439-68.

Jacoby, Sanford M. 1984. "The Development of Internal Labor Markets in American Manufacturing Firms." Pp. 23-69 in *Internal Labor Markets,* edited by Paul Osterman. Cambridge, MA: MIT Press.

———. 1985. *Employing Bureaucracy: Managers, Unions, and the Transformation of Work in American Industry, 1900-1945.* New York: Columbia University Press.

Johnston, William B. 1989. "Benefit Policies in a Turbulent Economy." Pp. 239-51 in *Business, Work, and Benefits: Adjusting to Change.* Washington, DC: Employee Benefits Research Institute.

Jörskog, Karl G. and Dag Sörbom. 1986.*PRELIS: A Program for Multivariate Data Screening and Data Summarization,* 1st ed. Mooresville, IN: Scientific Software.

———. 1989. *LISREL: A Guide to the Program and Applications,* 2nd ed. Chicago: SPSS Inc.

Kalleberg, Arne L. 1994. "The Flexible Firm: Patterns of Internalization and Externalization in U.S. Organizations." Unpublished paper, Department of Sociology, University of North Carolina at Chapel Hill.

Kalleberg, Arne L. and Ivar Berg. 1987. *Work and Industry: Structures, Markets and Processes.* New York: Plenum.

Kalleberg, Arne L. and Larry J. Griffin. 1978. "Positional Sources of Inequality in Job Satisfaction." *Sociology of Work and Occupations* 5:371-401.

Kalleberg, Arne L. and James R. Lincoln. 1988. "The Structure of Earnings Inequality in the United States and Japan." *American Journal of Sociology 94* (Supplement):S121-S153.

Kalleberg, Arne L., Peter V. Marsden, Howard E. Aldrich, and James W. Cassell. 1990. "Comparing Organizational Sampling Frames." *Administrative Science Quarterly* 35:658-88.

Kalleberg, Arne L. and Peter V. Marsden. 1994. "Organizational Commitment and Job Performance in the U.S. Labor Force." Pp. 235-57 in *Research in the Sociology of Work,* Vol. 5, edited by Ida Harper Simpson and Richard L. Simpson. Greenwich, CT: JAI.

———. 1995. "Organizations and Wage Determination in Norway: A Multi-Level Approach." *Comparative Social Research* 15:129-165.

Kalleberg, Arne L. and Arne Mastekaasa. 1994. "Firm Internal Labor Markets and Organizational Commitment in Norway and the United States." *Acta Sociologica* 37:269-86.

Kalleberg, Arne L. and Barbara F. Reskin. 1995. "Gender Differences in Promotion in the United States and Norway." *Research in Social Stratification and Mobility.* 14:237-264.

Kalleberg, Arne L. and Mark E. Van Buren. 1992. "Organizations and Economic Stratification: A Cross-National Analysis of the Size-Earnings Relations." *Research in Social Stratification and Mobility* 11:61-93.

———. 1996. "Is Bigger Better?: Explaining the Relationship between Organization Size and Job Rewards." *American Sociological Review* 61:47-66.

Kaufman, L. and P. J. Rousseeuw (1990). *Finding Groups in Data: An Introduction to Cluster Analysis.* New York: Wiley.

Kelley, Maryellen R. 1994. "Productivity and Information Technology: The Elusive Connection." *Management Science* 40:1406-25.

Kimberly, John R. 1976. "Organization Size and the Structuralist Perspective: A Review, Critique and Proposal." *Administrative Science Quarterly* 21:571-97.

King, Mary C. 1992. "Occupational Segregation by Race and Sex, 1940-1988." *Monthly Labor Review* 115:30-36.

Kish, Leslie. 1965. *Survey Sampling.* New York: Wiley.

———. 1966. "Sampling Organizations and Groups of Unequal Sizes." *American Sociological Review* 30:564-72.

Knoke, David. 1990. *Organizing for Collective Action: The Political Economies of Associations.* Hawthorne, NY: Aldine deGruyter.

———. 1996. "The Provision of Job Training." In *Change at Work,* edited by Peter Cappelli. New York: Oxford University Press.

Knoke, David and George W. Bohrnstedt. 1994. *Statistics for Social Data Analysis,* 3rd ed. Itasca, IL: F.E. Peacock.

Knoke, David and Arne L. Kalleberg. 1994. "Job Training in U.S. Organizations." *American Sociological Review* 59:537-46.

Kochan, Thomas A., Harry C. Katz, and Robert B. McKersie. 1986. *The Transformation of American Industrial Relations.* New York: Basic Books.

Kochan, Thomas A. and Robert B. McKersie. 1992. "Human Resources, Organizational Governance, and Public Policy: Lessons From a Decade of Experimentation." Pp. 169-86 in *Transforming Organizations,* edited by Thomas A. Kochan and Michael Useem. New York: Oxford University Press.

Kochan, Thomas A. and Michael Useem, eds. 1992. *Transforming Organizations.* New York: Oxford University Press.

Koretz, Gene. 1992. "America's Neglected Weapon: Its Educated Women." *Business Week,* January 27, p. 22.

Kotlikoff, Laurence J. and Daniel E. Smith. 1983. *Pensions in the American Economy.* Chicago: University of Chicago Press.

Lawler, Edward E. III. 1992. *The Ultimate Advantage: Creating the High-Involvement Organization.* San Francisco, CA: Jossey-Bass.

Lawler, Edward E. III, Gerald E. Ledford, Jr., and Susan Albers Mohrman. 1989. *Employee Involvement in America: A Study of Contemporary Practice.* Houston, TX: American Productivity and Quality Center.

Lawler, Edward E., III, Susan Albers Mohrman, and Gerald E. Ledford, Jr. 1992. *Employee Involvement and Total Quality Management: Practices and Results in* Fortune *500 Companies.* San Francisco: Jossey-Bass.

Lawlor, Julia. 1994. "Boom in Temp-Worker Hiring Eases." *USA Today,* February 28, p. 4B.

Lawrence, Paul R. and Jay W. Lorsch. 1967. *Organization and Environment: Managing Differentiation and Integration.* Homewood, IL: Irwin.

Lazear, Edward P. 1981. "Agency, Earnings Profiles, Productivity, and Hours Restrictions." *American Economic Review* 71:606-20.

le Grand, Carl, Ryszard Szulkin, and Michael Tåhlin. 1994. "Organizational Structures and Job Rewards in Sweden." *Acta Sociologica* 37:231-51.

Leonard, Jonathan S. 1989. "Women and Affirmative Action." *Journal of Economic Perspectives* 3:61-75.

Lester, Richard A. 1967. "Pay Differentials by Size of Establishment." *Industrial Relations* 7:57-67.

Levine, David I. 1990. "Participation, Productivity, and the Firm's Environment." *California Management Review* (Summer):86-100.

Levine, David I. and Laura D'Andrea Tyson. 1990. "Participation, Productivity, and the Firm's Environment." Pp. 183-243 in *Paying for Productivity,* edited by Alan Blinder. Washington, DC: Brookings Institution.

Levitt, Barbara and James G. March. 1988. "Organizational Learning." *Annual Review of Sociology* 14:319-40.

Levy, Frank. 1987. *Dollars and Dreams: The Changing American Income Distribution.* New York: Basic Books.

Lewis, H. Gregg. 1986. *Union Relative Wage Effects: A Survey.* Chicago: University of Chicago Press.

Lillard, Lee A. and Hong W. Tan. 1992. "Private Sector Training: Who Gets it and What Are Its Effects?" *Research in Labor Economics* 13:1-62.

Lin, Nan. 1990. "Social Resources and Social Mobility: A Structural Theory of Status Attainment." Pp. 247-71 in *Social Mobility and Social Structure,* edited by Ronald Breiger. New York: Cambridge University Press.

Lincoln, James R. and Arne L. Kalleberg. 1990. *Culture, Control, and Commitment: A Study of Work Organization and Work Attitudes in the United States and Japan.* New York: Cambridge University Press.

Little, R. J. A. and Donald B. Rubin. 1987. *Statistical Analysis with Missing Data.* New York: Wiley.

Longford, Nicholas T. 1993. *Random Coefficient Models.* Oxford, UK: Clarendon Press.

Lorence, Jon. 1987a. "Intraoccupational Earnings Inequality: Human Capital and Institutional Determinants." *Work and Occupations* 14:236-60.

———. 1987b. "A Test of 'Gender' and 'Job' Models of Sex Differences in Job Involvement." *Social Forces* 66:121-42.

Loscocco, Karyn A. 1989. "The Interplay of Personal and Job Characteristics in Determining Work Commitment." *Social Science Research* 18:370-94.

———. 1990. "Reactions to Blue-Collar Work: A Comparison of Women and Men." *Work and Occupations* 17:152-77.

Lynch, Lisa M. 1991. "The Role of Off-the-Job vs. On-the-Job Training for the Mobility of Women Workers." *American Economic Review* 81:151-56.

Maccoby, Eleanor Emmons and Carol Nagy Jacklin. 1͑ *The Psychology of Sex Differences.* Stanford, CA: Stanford University Press.

Mangum, Garth, Donald Mayall, and Kristin N͘ ͘ Temporary Help Industry: A Response to the Dual Internal Labor ͘ ͘ *Labor Relations Review* 38:599-611.

Mansfield, R. 1973. "Bureaucracy an͘ ͘f Organizational Structure." *Administrative Scie͘*

Marini, Margaret M. 1988. "Soci͘ of Sociology, edited by Edgar F. Borga͘ ͘ge.

———. 1989. "Sex Differe͘ ͘eview of Sociology 15:348-80.

Marini, Margaret M. and Mar͘ ͘upational Socialization." Pp. 192-232 in *Sex Segre͘* ͘s, Explanations, Remedies, edited by Barbara F. Reskin. ͘ ͘ Academy Press.

Marsden, Peter V. 1987. "Core Discuss͘ ͘ericans." *American Sociological Review* 52:122-31.

———. 1994. "Selection Methods in U.S. Est͘ ͘ents." *Acta Sociologica* 37:287-301.

Marsden, Peter V. and Karen E. Campbell. 1990. ͘ecruitment and Selection Processes: The Organizational Side of Job Searches." Pp. 59-79 in *Social Mobility and Social Structure,* edited by Ronald L. Breiger. New York: Cambridge University Press.

Marshall, Ray. 1986. "Working Smarter." Pp. 180-202 in *The Changing American Economy,* edited by David R. Obey and Paul Sarbanes. New York: Basil Blackwell.

Marshall, T. H. 1973. *Class, Citizenship, and Social Development.* Westport, CT: Greenwood.

Mathieu, John E. and Dennis M. Zajac. 1990. "A Review and Meta-Analysis of the Antecedents, Correlates, and Consequences of Organizational Commitment." *Psychological Bulletin* 108:171-94.

Mayhew, Bruce H. and Paul T. Schollaert. 1981. "A Structural Theory of Rank Differentiation." Pp. 287-323 in *Continuity in Structural Inquiry,* edited by Peter M. Blau and Robert K. Merton. Beverly Hills: Sage.

McIlwee, Judith and J. Greg Robinson. 1992. *Women in Engineering: Gender, Power and the Workplace.* Albany, NY: State University of New York Press.

McPherson, J. Miller. 1982. "Hypernetwork Sampling: Duality and Differentiation Among Voluntary Organizations." *Social Networks* 3:225-49.

———. 1983. "The Size of Voluntary Organizations." *Social Forces* 61:1044-64.

McPherson, J. Miller and Lynn Smith-Lovin. 1982. "Women and Weak Ties: Differences by Sex in the Size of Voluntary Associations." *American Journal of Sociology* 87:883-904.

Medoff, James L. and Katharine G. Abraham. 1980. "Experience, Performance, and Earnings." *Quarterly Journal of Economics* 95:703-36.

Mellow, Wesley. 1982. "Employer Size and Wages." *Review of Economics and Statistics* 64:495-501.

Meyer, John W. and Brian Rowan. 1977. "Institutionalized Organizations: Formal Structure as Myth and Ceremony." *American Journal of Sociology* 83:340-64.

Meyer, John W. and W. Richard Scott, eds. 1983. *Organizational Environments: Ritual and Rationality.* Beverly Hills, CA: Sage.

Meyer, Marshall W. 1972. "Size and the Structure of Organizations: A Causal Analysis." *American Sociological Review* 37:434-41.

Milkman, Ruth. 1987. *Gender at Work.* Urbana: University of Illinois Press.

Mincer, Jacob. 1962. "On-the-Job Training: Costs, Returns, and Some Implications." *Journal of Political Economy* 70(Supplement):50-79.

————. 1974. *Schooling, Experience, and Earnings.* New York: National Bureau of Economic Research.

————. 1983. "Union Effects: Wages, Turnover, and Job Training." *Research in Labor Economics* 2(Supplement):217-52.

Mintzberg, Henry. 1979. *The Structuring of Organizations.* Englewood Cliffs, NJ: Prentice Hall.

————. 1983. *Structure in Fives: Designing Effective Organizations.* Englewood Cliffs, NJ: Prentice Hall.

Mirvis, Philip, ed. 1993. *Building a Competitive Workforce: Investing in Human Capital for Corporate Success.* New York: Wiley.

Monahan, Sue, John W. Meyer, and W. Richard Scott. 1992. "Employee Training: The Expansion of Organizational Citizenship." Pp. 255-71 in *Institutional Environments and Organizations: Structural Complexity and Individualism,* edited by W. Richard Scott and John W. Meyer. Newbury Park, CA: Sage.

Moody, James W. 1994. *Do Politics Matter?: The Effect of State Characteristics on Organizational Performance.* Paper presented at Annual Meetings of the Southern Sociological Society, Raleigh, NC.

Mottaz, Clifford J. 1988. "Determinants of Organizational Commitment." *Human Relations* 41:467-82.

Mowday, Richard T., Lyman W. Porter, and Richard M. Steers. 1982. *Employee-Organization Linkages: The Psychology of Commitment, Absenteeism and Turnover.* New York: Academic Press.

Mueller, Charles W., Jean E. Wallace, and James L. Price. 1992. "Employee Commitment: Resolving Some Issues." *Work and Occupations* 19:211-36.

Murphy, Kevin M. and Finis Welch. 1990. "Empirical Age-Earnings Profiles." *Journal of Labor Economics* 8:202-29.

Muthén, Bengt. 1981. "Factor Analysis of Dichotomous Variables: American Attitudes Toward Abortion." Pp. 201-14 in *Factor Analysis and Measurement in Sociological Research,* edited by David Jackson and Edgar F. Borgatta. Beverly Hills, CA: Sage.

Nakao, Keiko and Judith Treas. 1994. "Updating Occupational Prestige and Socioeconomic Scores: How the New Measures Measure Up." Pp. 1-72 in *Sociological Methodology,* edited by Peter V. Marsden. Oxford, UK: Blackwell.

Narisetti, Raju. 1995. "Manufacturers Decry a Shortage of Workers While Rejecting Many." *Wall Street Journal,* September 9, p. A1.

O'Brien, Robert M. and Pamela Homer. 1987. "Corrections for Coarsely Categorized Measures: LISREL's Polyserial and Polychoric Correlations." *Quantity and Quality* 21:349-60.

O'Rand, Angela. 1986. "The Hidden Payroll: Employee Benefits and the Structure of Workplace Inequality." *Sociological Forum* 1:657-83.

O'Rand, Angela and Vicky M. MacLean. 1986. "Labor Market, Pension Rule Structure and Retirement Benefit Promise for Long-Term Employees." *Social Forces* 65:224-40.

O'Reilly, Brian. 1994. "The New Deal: What Companies and Employees Owe One Another." *Fortune,* 13(June):44-52.

Oi, Walter Y. 1962. "Labor as a Quasi-Fixed Factor." *Journal of Political Economy* 70:538-55.

———. 1983a. "Heterogeneous Firms and the Organization of Production." *Economic Inquiry* 21:147-71.

———. 1983b. "The Fixed Employment Costs of Specialized Labor." Pp. 63-116 in *The Measurement of Labor Cost,* edited by J. E. Triplett. Chicago: University of Chicago Press (for NBER).

Olian, J.D. and S. L. Rynes. 1984. "Organizational Staffing: Integrating Practice with Strategy." *Industrial Relations* 23:170-83.

Olmsted, Barney and Suzanne Smith. 1989. *Creating a Flexible Workplace: How to Select and Manage Alternative Work Options.* New York: AMACOM, American Management Association.

Oppenheimer, Valerie Kincade. 1992. "Labor Force." Pp. 1049-54 in *Encyclopedia of Sociology,* edited by Edgar F. Borgatta and Marie L. Borgatta. New York: Macmillan.

Osterman, Paul. 1988. *Employment Futures: Reorganization, Dislocation, and Public Policy.* New York: Oxford University Press.

———. 1993. "Skill, Training, and Work Organization in American Establishments." Cambridge: MIT Sloan School Mimeo.

———. 1994a. "How Common is Workplace Transformation and Who Adopts It?" *Industrial and Labor Relations Review* 47:173-88.

———. 1994b. *Explaining the Diffusion of Employer Based Benefits: The Case of Work/Family Programs,* Working paper. Cambridge, MA: MIT Sloan School.

Osterman, Paul, ed. 1984. *Internal Labor Markets.* Cambridge, MA: MIT Press.

Oswald, Andrew J. 1985. "The Economic Theory of Trade Unions: An Introductory Survey." *Scandinavian Journal of Economics* 87:160-93.

Parcel, Toby. 1989. "Comparable Worth, Occupational Labor Markets and Occupational Earnings: Results from the 1980 Census." Pp. 134-52 in *Pay Equity: Empirical Inquiries,* edited by Robert T. Michael, Heidi Hartmann, and Brigid O'Farrell. Washington DC: National Academy Press.

Parcel, Toby, Robert L. Kaufman, and Leeann Jolly. 1991. "Going Up the Ladder: Multiplicity Sampling to Create Macro-Micro Organizational Samples." Pp. 43-79 in *Sociological Methodology,* edited by Peter V. Marsden. Oxford, UK: Basil Blackwell.

Parker, Robert E. 1994. *Flesh Peddlers and Warm Bodies: The Temporary Help Industry and Its Workers.* New Brunswick, NJ: Rutgers University Press.

Parsons, Donald O. 1972. "Specific Human Capital: An Application to Quit Rates and Layoff Rates." *Journal of Political Economy* 80:1120-43.

———. 1990. "The Firm's Decision to Train." *Research in Labor Economics* 11:53-75.

Paterson, L. 1991. "Multilevel Logistic Regression." Pp. 5-18 in *Data Analysis with ML3,* edited by R. Prosser, J. Rasbash, and H. Goldstein. London, UK: University of London, Institute of Education.

Petersen, Trond and Laurie Morgan. 1995. "Separate and Unequal: Occupation-Establishment Segregation and the Gender Wage Gap." *American Journal of Sociology* 101:329-365.

Pfeffer, Jeffrey. 1981. *Power in Organizations.* Cambridge, MA: Ballinger.

———. 1982. *Organizations and Organizations Theory.* Cambridge, MA: Ballinger.

———. 1994. *Competitive Advantage Through People: Unleashing the Power of the Workforce.* Boston: Harvard University Press.

Pfeffer, Jeffrey and James N. Baron. 1988. "Taking the Workers Back Out: Recent Trends in the Structuring of Employment." Pp. 257-303 in *Research in Organizational Behavior,* Vol. 10, edited by Barry M. Staw and Larry L. Cummings. Greenwich, CT: JAI.

Pfeffer, Jeffrey and Yinon Cohen. 1984. "Determinants of Internal Labor Markets in Organizations." *Administrative Science Quarterly* 29:550-72.

Pfeffer, Jeffrey and Nancy Langton. 1988. "Wage Inequality and the Organization of Work: The Case of Academic Departments." *Administrative Science Quarterly* 33:588-606.

Pfeffer, Jeffrey and Jerry Ross. 1990. "Gender-Based Wage Differences: The Effects of Organizational Context." *Work and Occupations* 17:55-78.

Pfeffer, Jeffrey and Gerald R. Salancik. 1978. *The External Control of Organizations: A Resource Dependence Perspective*. New York: Harper and Row.

Phelps, Edmund S. 1972. "The Statistical Theory of Racism and Sexism." *American Economic Review* 62:659-66.

Piore, Michael and Charles F. Sabel. 1984. *The Second Industrial Divide*. New York: Basic Books.

Polachek, Solomon. 1979. "Occupational Self-Selection: A Human Capital Approach to Sex Differences in Occupational Structure." *Review of Economics and Statistics* 58:60-69.

Polivka, Anne E. and Thomas Nardone. 1989. "On the Definition of Contingent Work." *Monthly Labor Review* 112:9-17.

Pollack, M. A. and A. Bernstein. 1986. "The Disposable Employee Is Becoming a Fact of Life." *Business Week,* December 15, p. 52-56.

Powell, Walter W. and DiMaggio, Paul J., eds. 1991. *The New Institutionalism in Organizational Analysis*. Chicago: University of Chicago Press.

Pratt, John W. and Richard J. Zeckhauser, eds. 1991. *Principles and Agents: The Structure of Business*. Boston: Harvard Business School Press.

Prosser, R., Rasbash, J., and Goldstein, H. 1991. *ML3: Software for Multilevel Analysis Users Guide for V.2*. London, UK: University of London, Institute of Education.

Pugh, Derek S., David J. Hickson, and C. R. Hinings. 1969. "An Empirical Taxonomy of Structures of Work Organizations." *Administrative Science Quarterly* 14:115-26.

Pugh, Derek S., David J. Hickson, C. R. Hinings, and C. Turner. 1968. "Dimensions of Organization Structure." *Administrative Science Quarterly* 13:65-91.

Randall, Donna M. 1990. "The Consequences of Organizational Commitment: Methodological Investigation." *Journal of Organizational Behavior* 11:361-78.

Rees, A. 1966. "Information Networks in Labor Markets." *American Economic Review* 56:559-66.

Reich, Robert B. 1992. *The Work of Nations: Preparing Ourselves for 21st-Century Capitalism*. New York: Vintage.

Reskin, Barbara F. 1988. "Bringing the Men Back in: Sex Differentiation and the Devaluation of Women's Work." *Gender and Society* 2:58-81.

———. 1993. "Sex Segregation in the Workplace." *Annual Review of Sociology* 19:241-70.

Reskin, Barbara F. and Irene Padavic. 1988. "Supervisors as Gatekeepers: Male Supervisors' Response to Women's Integration in Plant Jobs." *Social Problems* 35:536-50.

———. 1994. *Women and Men at Work*. Thousand Oaks, CA: Pine Forge Press.

Reskin, Barbara F. and Patricia Roos. 1990. *Job Queues, Gender Queues: Explaining Women's Inroads into Male Occupations*. Philadelphia: Temple University Press.

Reskin, Barbara F. and Catherine E. Ross. 1992. "Jobs, Authority, and Earnings Among Managers: The Continuing Significance of Sex." *Work and Occupations* 19:342-65.

Reynolds, Paul D. 1994. *The Entrepreneurial Process: Preliminary Explorations in the United States*. Paper presented at the First Eurostat International Workshop on Techniques of Enterprise Panels, Luxembourg.

Roethlisberger, F. J. and William J. Dickson. 1939. *Management and the Worker*. Cambridge, MA: Harvard University Press.

Rose, Frederick. 1994. "Job-Cutting Medicine Fails to Remedy Productivity Ills at Many Companies." *Wall Street Journal,* June 7, p. A2.

Rosenbaum, James E. 1980. "Hierarchical and Individual Effects on Earnings." *Industrial Relations* 19:1-14.

Rumberger, Russell W. 1984. "The Incidence and Wage Effects of Occupational Training Among Young Men." *Social Science Quarterly* 65:775-88.

Ryan, Paul. 1984. "Job Training, Employment Practices, and the Large Enterprise: The Case of Costly Transferable Skills." Pp. 191-229 in *Internal Labor Markets*, edited by Paule Osterman. Cambridge, MA: MIT Press.

Sakamoto, Arthur and Meichu D. Chen. 1993. "Earnings Inequality and Segmentation by Firm Size in Japan and the United States." *Research in Social Stratification and Mobility* 12:185-211.

Salaman, G. 1980. "Classification of Organizations and Organization Structure: The Main Elements and Interrelationships." Pp. 56-84 in *Control and Ideology in Organizations*, edited by G. Salaman and K. Thompson. Cambridge, MA: MIT Press.

Schmidt, N., W. C. Borman, and Associates. 1993. *Personnel Selection in Organizations*. San Francisco: Jossey-Bass.

Schultz, Theodore W. 1963. *The Economic Value of Education*. New York: Columbia University Press.

Scott, W. Richard. 1983. "The Organization of Environments: Network, Cultural, and Historical Elements." Pp. 155-75 in *Organizational Environments: Ritual and Rationality*, edited by John W. Meyer and W. Richard Scott. Beverly Hills, CA: Sage.

———. 1992. *Organizations: Rational, Natural, and Open Systems*, 3rd ed. Englewood Cliffs, NJ: Prentice Hall.

Scott, W. Richard and John W. Meyer. 1991. "The Rise of Training Programs in Firms and Agencies: An Institutional Perspective." *Research in Organizational Behavior* 13:297-326.

———. 1992. *Institutional Environments and Organizations: Structural Complexity and Individualism*. Newbury Park, CA: Sage.

Sengenberger, Werner. 1981. "Labour Market Segmentation and the Business Cycle." Pp. 243-59 in *The Dynamics of Labour Market Segmentation*, edited by Frank Wilkinson. New York: Academic Press.

Shuster, Jay and Patricia Zingheim. 1992. *The New Pay: Linking Employee and Organizational Performance*. Toronto: Maxwell Macmillan Canada.

Smith, Vicki. 1990. *Managing in the Corporate Interest: Control and Resistance in an American Bank*. Berkeley, CA: University of California Press.

———. 1994. "Institutionalizing Flexibility in a Service Firm: Multiple Contingencies and Hidden Hierarchies." *Work and Occupations* 21:284-307.

Sørensen, Aage B. 1983. "Sociological Research on the Labor Market: Conceptual and Methodological Issues." *Work and Occupations* 10:261-87.

Spaeth, Joe. L. 1985. "Job Power and Earnings." *American Sociological Review* 50:603-17.

———. 1989. "Occupational Status, Resource Control, and Earnings." Pp. 203-19 in *Research in Social Stratification and Mobility*, Vol. 8, edited by Arne L. Kalleberg. Greenwich, CT: JAI.

Spence, Michael. 1974. *Market Signalling: Information Transfer in Hiring and Related Processes*. Cambridge, MA: Harvard University Press.

Spilerman, Seymour. 1986. "Organizational Rules and the Features of Work Careers." *Research in Social Stratification and Mobility* 5:41-102.

Staber, Udo and Howard Aldrich. 1988. "An Evolutionary View on Changes in Employment Relationships: The Evolution of Organizational Control in the U.S." Pp. 63-78 in *Management Under Different Labour Market and Employment Systems*, edited by Gunter Dlugos, Wolfgang Dorow, and Klaus Weiermair. New York: Walter deGruyter.

Staw, Barry M. and Eugene Szwajkowski. 1975. "The Scarcity/Munificence Component of Environments and the Commission of Illegal Acts." *Administrative Science Quarterly* 20:345-54.

Steers, Richard M. 1977. "Antecedents and Outcomes of Organizational Commitment." *Administrative Science Quarterly* 22:46-56.

Stigler, George J. 1962. "Information in the Labor Market." *Journal of Political Economy* 70:94-105.

Stiglitz, Joseph E. 1975. "The Theory of 'Screening,' Education, and the Distribution of Income." *American Economic Review* 65:283-300.

Stinchcombe, Arthur L. 1965. "Social Structure and Organizations." Pp. 142-93 in *Handbook of Organizations,* edited by James G. March. Chicago: Rand McNally.

Stolzenberg, Ross M. 1978. "Bringing the Boss Back in: Employer Size, Employee Schooling, and Socioeconomic Achievement." *American Sociological Review* 43:813-28.

Strauss, Anselm L. 1978. *Negotiations.* San Francisco: Jossey-Bass.

Sudman, Seymour. 1976. *Applied Sampling.* New York: Academic Press.

Sudman, Seymour, Monroe G. Sirken, and Charles D. Cowan. 1988. "Sampling Rare and Exclusive Populations." *Science* 240:991-96.

Sutton, John R., Frank Dobbin, John W. Meyer, W. Richard Scott. 1994. "The Legalization of the Workplace." *American Journal of Sociology* 99:944-71.

Swoboda, Frank. 1993. "Growing Ranks of Part-Time Workers Are Finding Fewer Benefits." *Raleigh News and Observer,* September 12, p. 5F. (Reprinted from the *Washington Post.*)

Szafran, Robert F. 1982. "What Kind of Firms Hire and Promote Women and Blacks: A Review of the Literature." *Sociological Quarterly* 23:171-90.

Thompson, James G. 1967. *Organizations In Action.* New York: McGraw-Hill.

Thurow, Lester C. 1975. *Generating Inequality: Mechanisms of Distribution in the U.S. Economy.* New York: Basic Books.

Tilly, Chris. 1990. "Short Hours, Short Shrift: Causes and Consequences of Part-time Work." Washington, DC: Economic Policy Institute.

Tolbert, Pamela S. 1986. "Organizations and Inequality: Sources of Earnings Differences Between Male and Female Faculty." *Sociology of Education* 59:227-36.

Tomaskovic-Devey, Donald. 1993a. "The Gender and Race Composition of Jobs and the Male/Female, White/Black Pay Gaps." *Social Forces* 72:45-76.

—————. 1993b. *Gender and Racial Inequality at Work: The Sources and Consequences of Job Segregation.* Ithaca, New York: ILR Press.

—————. 1994. "Race, Ethnic and Gender Earnings Inequality: The Sources and Consequences of Employment Segregation." *Report to the U.S. Department of Labor Glass Ceiling Commission.* Department of Sociology, North Carolina State University.

United States Bureau of Labor Statistics. 1994. *BLS Reports on Employer-Provided Training.* Washington, DC: U.S. Department of Labor press release 94-432.

United States Bureau of the Census. 1976. "Concepts and Methods Used in Labor Force Statistics Derived From the Current Population Survey." *Current Population Reports,* ser. P-23, no. 62. Washington, DC: Government Printing Office.

United States Department of Labor. 1988. *Flexible Workstyles: A Look at Contingent Labor.* Washington, DC: Government Printing Office.

—————. 1989. *Report of the Commission on Workforce Quality and Labor Market Efficiency.* Washington, DC: Government Printing Office.

—————. 1990. *Employee Benefits in Medium and Large Firms, 1989.* Bulletin 2363, Department of Labor and Bureau of Labor Statistics. Washington, DC: Government Printing Office.

—————. 1992. *How Workers Get their Training: A 1991 Update.* Washington, DC: Government Printing Office.

United States Departments of Labor and Commerce. 1993. "Conference on the Future of the American Workplace." Chicago, July 26.

Useem, Michael. 1993a. "Company Policies on Education and Training." Pp. 95-121 in *Building a Competitive Workforce: Investing in Human Capital for Corporate Success,* edited by Philip Mirvis. New York: Wiley.

Useem, Michael. 1993b. *Executive Defense: Shareholder Power and Corporate Reorganization.* Cambridge, MA: Harvard University Press.

Van Buren, Mark E. 1992. "Organizational Size and the Use of Firm Internal Labor Markets in High Growth Establishments." *Social Science Research* 21:311-27.

Van Buren, Mark E. 1994. *When Downsizers Become Rightsizers: Organizational Retrenchment During Periods of Strong Performance.* Paper presented at Annual Meetings of the Southern Sociological Society, Raleigh, NC.

Villemez, Wayne J. and William P. Bridges. 1988. "When Bigger is Better: Differences in the Individual-Level Effect of Firm and Establishment Size." *American Sociological Review* 53:237-55.

Viscusi, W. Kip. 1980. "Sex Differences in Worker Quitting." *Review of Economics and Statistics* 62:388-98.

Von Glinow, Mary Ann. 1988. *The New Professionals: Managing Today's High-Tech Employees.* Cambridge, MA: Ballinger.

Wagel, William H. 1990. "On the Horizon: HR in the 1990s." *Personnel* (January):11-16.

Wallace, Michael and Arne L. Kalleberg. 1981. "Economic Organization of Firms and Labor Market Consequences: Toward a Specification of Dual Economy Theory." Pp. 77-118 in *Sociological Perspectives on Labor Markets,* edited by Ivar Berg. NY: Academic Press.

Walton, Richard E. 1985. "From Control to Commitment in the Workplace." *Harvard Business Review* 63:76-84.

Waterman, Robert H., Jr., Judith A. Waterman, and Betsey A. Collard. 1994. "Toward a Career Resilient Workforce." *Harvard Business Review, July-August:87-95.*

Weick, Karl E. 1979. *The Social Psychology of Organizing,* 2nd ed. Reading, MA: Addison-Wesley.

Weiss, Andrew and Henry J. Landau. 1984. "Wages, Hiring Standards, and Firm Size." *Journal of Labor Economics* 2:477-99.

Weiss, Leonard. 1966. "Concentration and Labor Earnings." *American Economic Review* 56:96-117.

Weiss, Yoram. 1987. "The Effect of Labour Unions on Investment in Training: A Dynamic Model. Pp. 435-67 in *Economic Policy in Theory and Practice,* edited by Assaf Razin. New York: St. Martin's.

White, Halbert. 1980. "A Heteroskedasticity-Consistent Covariance Matrix Estimator and a Direct Test for Heteroskedasticity." *Econometrics* 48:817-38.

White, Robert W. and Robert P. Althauser. 1984. "Internal Labor Markets, Promotions, and Worker Skill: An Indirect Test of Skill ILMs." *Social Science Research* 13:373-92.

Williamson, Oliver E. 1981. "The Economics of Organization: The Transaction Cost Approach." *American Journal of Sociology* 87:548-77.

———. 1985. *The Economic Institutions of Capitalism.* New York: Free Press.

Winship, Christopher and Robert D. Mare. 1992. "Models for Sample Selection Bias." *Annual Review of Sociology* 18:327-50.

Winship, Christopher and L. Radbill. 1994. "Sampling Weights and Regression Analysis." *Sociological Methods and Research,* 23:230-57.

Wohlers, Eckhardt and Guenter Weinert. 1988. *Employment Trends in the United States, Japan, and the European Community: A Comparative Economic Study.* New Brunswick, NJ: Transaction Books.

Wolf, Wendy C. and Neil D. Fligstein. 1979. "Sex and Authority in the Workplace: The Causes of Sexual Inequality." *American Sociological Review* 44:235-52.

Womack, James P., Daniel T. Jones, and Daniel Roos. 1990. *The Machine That Changed the World.* New York: Rawson Associates.

"Women in Management: The Spare Sex." 1992. *The Economist,* March 28, pp. 17-19.

Woodbury, S. A. 1983. "Substitution Between Wages in the Presence of Fringe Benefits: An Expanded Model." *American Economic Review* 73:166-82.

Woodward, Joan. 1965. *Industrial Organization: Theory and Practice.* New York: Oxford University Press.

World Bank. 1990. *World Development Report 1990.* New York: Oxford University Press.

Wyatt Company. 1993. *Best Practices in Company Restructuring.* New York: Author.

Yoder, Dale and Paul D. Staudohar. 1982. *Personnel Management and Industrial Relations,* 7th ed. Englewood Cliffs, NJ: Prentice Hall.

Zucker, Lynne G. 1987. "Institutional Theories of Organization." *Annual Review of Sociology* 13:443-64.

————. 1981. "Guidebook to Organizational Data." Unpublished manuscript, Dapartment of Sociology, UCLA.

# Author Index

# Subject Index

365

# About the Authors

**Arne L. Kalleberg** is Kenan Professor of Sociology at the University of North Carolina at Chapel Hill, where he also serves as department chair. He is also an Adjunct Professor of Management at the Kenan-Flagler School of Business. His current research examines the impacts of human resource management practices on employees and the changing nature of employment relations in the United States and Norway.

**David Knoke** is Professor of Sociology at the University of Minnesota, where he specializes in the study of organizational behavior and social networks. His most recent book is *Comparing Policy Networks: Labor Politics in the U.S., Germany and Japan* (with Franz Urban Pappi, Jeffrey Broadbent, and Yutaka Tsujinaka).

**Peter V. Marsden** is Professor of Sociology at Harvard University, where he currently serves as department chair. He received a Ph.D. from the University of Chicago in 1979. His research interests lie in the areas of complex organizations, social networks, and quantitative methods. He was the editor of *Sociological Methodology* from 1991 until 1995.

**Joe L. Spaeth** is Professor Emeritus of Sociology and Research Professor Emeritus in the Survey Research Laboratory at the University of Illinois at Urbana-Champaign. He also holds a courtesy in the Department of Statistics at Oregon State University.

# About the Contributors

**Cynthia R. Cook** is a doctoral candidate in the Department of Sociology at Harvard University. She is writing her dissertation on the causes and consequences of close network ties between organizations and their customers, suppliers, and competitors.

**Yoshito Ishio** received his Ph.D. in sociology from the University of Minnesota in 1995. His dissertation analyzed interest group lobbying tactics in the U.S. labor policy domain. He is currently a research sociologist at the University of Tsukuba in Japan.

**James W. Moody** is a doctoral candidate in sociology at the University of North Carolina at Chapel Hill. His interests include classical social theory, quantitative methods, the relationship between politics and economics, and networks.

**Diane P. O'Rourke** is Coordinator of Research Programs at the Survey Research Laboratory at the University of Illinois, Urbana. Her research focuses on the cognitive aspects of responding to survey questions among culturally diverse respondents. She is currently a member of the Executive Council of the American Association for Public Opinion Research.

**Kathryn Schmidt** is a doctoral candidate in the Department of Sociology at the University of North Carolina at Chapel Hill. Her dissertation explores the extent of the use of contingent work arrangements among nurses and their effects of job content, job satisfaction, and work and family linkages. Her research interests are in the areas of gender, work, and theory.

**Donald Tomaskovic-Devey** is Professor of Sociology at North Carolina State University. He is currently exploring gender and racial segregation in organizations, organizational stratification more generally, and uneven economic development, particularly in the southern United States.

**Mark E. Van Buren** is a Senior Research Officer at the American Society for Training and Development. His present research includes the role of information technology in commercial banking and the relationship between human resource practices and performance from a systems perspective. He received his Ph.D. in sociology from the University of North Cardina at Chapel Hill in 1995.